PRACTICING CATHOLIC

PRACTICING CATHOLIC

Ritual, Body, and Contestation in Catholic Faith

Edited by

Bruce T. Morrill, Joanna E. Ziegler, and
Susan Rodgers

First published in 2006 by
PALGRAVE MACMILLAN™
175 Fifth Avenue, New York, N.Y. 10010 and
Houndmills, Basingstoke, Hampshire, England RG21 6XS
Companies and representatives throughout the world.

PALGRAVE MACMILLAN is the global academic imprint of the Palgrave Macmillan division of St. Martin's Press, LLC and of Palgrave Macmillan Ltd. Macmillan® is a registered trademark in the United States, United Kingdom and other countries. Palgrave is a registered trademark in the European Union and other countries.

ISBN 1–4039–7296–6

Library of Congress Cataloging-in-Publication Data

Practicing Catholic : ritual, body, and contestation in Catholic faith / Bruce T. Morrill, Joanna E. Ziegler, Susan Rodgers, editors.
p. cm.
Includes bibliographical references and index.
ISBN 1–4039–7296–6 (alk. paper)
1. Catholic Church—Customs and practices—Congresses. 2. Catholic Church—Liturgy—Congresses. I. Morrill, Bruce T. II. Ziegler, Joanna E. III. Rodgers, Susan.

BX1969. P73 2006
282—dc22   2005057420

A catalogue record for this book is available from the British Library.

Design by Newgen Imaging Systems (P) Ltd., Chennai, India.

First edition: April 2006

10 9 8 7 6 5 4 3 2 1

Printed in the United States of America.

CONTENTS

LIST OF FIGURES

PART I

Performance, Liturgy, and Ritual Practice

CHAPTER 1

Introduction

Bruce T. Morrill, S.J., Susan Rodgers, and
Joanna E. Ziegler

"The Catholic" is arguably any of a number of qualities of mind, theological insights, faith conditions, and institutional arrangements in the world. The distinctively Catholic might legitimately be taken, for instance, to be a stance of mercy toward the poor and disenfranchised—a generosity toward the socially vulnerable supported by New Testament records of Jesus' own life of service. Or the religion might be taken to have a defining devotional ethos that recurrently highlights the worship of Christ's many manifestations in the material and familial world. Such an understanding makes Catholicism a faith of lived experience, approachable through the world's bounty: via festive foods, ornate altars, and concrete life passage events embedded in kinship networks uniting actual persons, in history. Or "the Catholic" might also be seen to lie in the historical church's particular hierarchical power structure, with lines of authority extending "downward" from the Roman papacy through layers of male priestly officials and teaching offices. Or—no surprise for a messianic religion—Catholicism might also justifiably be seen as a religion of revolt, where faith-inspired critique takes on some of those same systems of male, ordained authority. Such a Catholicism would be made manifest through such means as popular faith traditions focused on the sort of holy mystics and women ecstatics who were so prominent in the European Middle Ages.

"The Catholic" is all these things and undeniably much more besides, but in this book Catholicism is explored as fundamentally a faith of ritual practice, that is to say, a religion whose core theology, individual believer's inner spiritual experiences, and a great variety of parochial and other social entities such as social, communal idenities come alive preeminently through participation in and a sense of ownership of rite. Catholicism's ritual heart is present for believers and observers most forthrightly via the Mass and through the priestly consecration and communal sharing of the Eucharist. Catholicism as a practiced, performative faith, nonetheless, also gains shape and sensibility through the religion's nearly endless panoply of ritual processions, sanctifications of statues, healing ceremonies, and devotional actions in the home, garden, grotto, school, and (again, not accidentally) the sports field and car. In other words, "the Catholic" has a ritual base that is exuberantly expansive, socially variegated, and creatively catholic, in both the senses of universal and traditional.

Practicing Catholic: Ritual, Body, and Contestation in Catholic Faith is the outgrowth of a conference by the same title held at the College of the Holy Cross in November of 2002. The subtitle adumbrates two features of the faith that have often flowed from Catholicism's ritual nature. First, conference participants posited the by-now familiar academic claim that Catholicism is a stunningly embodied religion. Catholicism valorizes the human body as a sanctified site molded by God, and as a place in the world for experiencing and representing the divine. The religion instills its ethos in generations of new Christians (young people, new converts) through an emotionally evocative language of sacrificial blood, bodily resurrection, sharing Christ's flesh, and tending to the suffering bodies of the afflicted. Catholic persons worldwide, joined into Catholic communities, are often seen from within the religion as the Body of Christ, a main locale of His presence in history following the Easter miracle. Beyond simply seeing Catholicism, however, as a religion that is unusually reliant on body symbolism, conference participants went further to examine the Catholic body-in-motion, as that was constituted within such performative ritual experiences as saints' processions, mystical chant, holy dance, sung death vigils, and tactile interactions with sacred statues (for instance, world Catholicism's recurrently rich practices of decorating and dressing stone or plaster Virgins, which are then moved through town or rural spaces in processions, as blessing events).

Beyond issues of embodiment, in our conference Catholic ritual was also explored as a site of contestation: a cultural locale where ideological disputes take place as part of lived, ceremonial experience. Ritual scenes such as a healing Mass in contemporary Massachusetts (where the clergy sex abuse scandal is, needless to point out, still raw) are often cultural scenes where theological meaning and interpretations of the official church's authority claims are much in dispute. This is our sense of contestation: a sort of raggedness of interpretation that occurs within faith communities during important rituals, often to creative and even transformative effect. Many Catholic rites, broadly construed, were examined in this light in the conference and, so, now in this book. From Joanne Pierce's analysis of new mother's churching rituals in twelfth century Europe to Daniel Goldstein's study of an annual saints' procession in a Bolivian shantytown, matters of hierarchy, identity, and power are in play.

Rite, embodiment, and contestation are conjoined elements of Catholic practice worldwide and across history that can spark lively debates among scholars from three particular scholarly disciplines: liturgical theologians, cultural anthropologists, and medievalist historians of art and of religion. These comprise the authors of this book, researchers who rarely gather in the same conference halls yet often focus on similar issues: the constitution of community through sacred speech, song, architecture, and festival (the European Middle Ages are replete with examples here, as are the village and peasant societies that anthropologists often study); the nature of ties between mythic narrative, performative ritual, and social community; rite and revelation; and the interrelations between faith and social hierarchy along multiple planes of gendered, governmental, and ecclesiastical power. In the conference and in this book we have asked scholars in Europeanist medieval studies, anthropology, and liturgical theology to focus their individual disciplinary lenses on Catholic ritual events, qua performance, in historical and/or ethnographic detail. Our aim has been to see how a set of deeply contextualized case studies can help all three fields to sharpen their interpretive and methodological tools for looking at questions of Catholicism as a lived faith of ritual practice. Each of the three fields stands to be productively challenged by the interpretive claims, methodological strategies, and text-reading practices of the others.

This particular mix of disciplines is, admittedly, unusual, given the generally quite secular stance of much anthropological research, given the faith position of Catholic theologians, and given the disparities of historical time period from which our collection of case studies come, from the Middle Ages to today. However, these exploratory essays, along with brief commentaries by scholars from related fields such as the sociology of religion and comparative theology, work to push scholarship on Catholic sacramentalism toward greater cultural depth and humane relevance. All our authors speak in the voice of their own disciplines, so that interdisciplinary connections—and sparks—might not take place in some vague middle ground but are always tethered to well-developed and well-theorized lines of inquiry.

RITUAL PRACTICE: THE VIEW FROM LITURGICAL THEOLOGY BY BRUCE T. MORRILL

The scholarly discipline of theology approaches the topic, "Practicing Catholic," from the inside, so to speak, since what distinguishes theologians from others who study religion (in such academic fields as religious studies, history, sociology, anthropology, philosophy, or psychology) is their explicit commitment to the Christian faith itself. A fundamental characteristic of that faith, nonetheless, causes theologians to draw heavily upon all those other disciplines for their work. Roman Catholic theologians apprehend in the biblical content as well as the liturgical, mystical, and ethical practices of Christian faith a view of the world that rejects its being divided into sacred and profane realms. This is a worldview shot through with paradox, as any observer of Roman Catholicism would most likely aver. Here is a religion rife with elaborate rituals, hierarchical authority figures, such distinctive edifices and precincts as cathedrals, basilicas, churches, convents and monasteries, as well as the cloistered inhabitants therein, and a panoply of devotional objects adorning households, hillsides, and human bodies. What can it mean to say that, strictly speaking, the categories of sacred and profane do not apply here?

The answer lies in a theological elaboration of the concept of sacramentality, which one liturgical theologian recently summarized in its "broad meaning" as the belief "that God is disclosed and discovered here and now on earth and in human life," a worldview characterized by "both . . . and" rather than "either . . . or" thinking, a good but fallen world that is at once the arena of creation and redemption.[1] This makes contemporary Catholic theology a scholarly discipline that, while grounded in a collection of divinely inspired texts (the Bible) and other normative documents (creeds, doctrine, rituals), is not limited to textual analysis (biblical exegesis, philosophical hermeneutics, study of the history of interpretations). The best of current theology, rather, employs as many theories from the humanities, social sciences, and physical sciences as show promise of shedding intellectual light on a faith that, in the famous phrase of Jesuit founder Saint Ignatius of Loyola, "finds God in all things." A brief historical overview of Roman Catholic theological tradition—one necessarily devoid of much nuance and prone to numerous caveats—can help set the stage for exploring the current state of theological scholarship (particularly sacramental and liturgical theology) regarding rite.

From its rise as the "queen of the sciences" in the newly founded universities of medieval Europe up to the present time, Roman Catholic theology has operated under an adage, its self-description as "faith seeking understanding" (*fides quaerens intellectum*). The phrase seems to have served academic theology well due not only to what might today be described as its "sacramental" harmonizing of *both* faith *and* reason but also its ability through the centuries to serve as a banner under which to wage intellectual battles with Protestant thought (perceived, to put it very simply, as opposing faith and reason), post-Enlightenment rationalism (opposing the intellectual relevance of faith at all), and now post modernism (opposing rational subjectivity). This Catholic insistence, however, on the compatibility of faith and reason—this patient confidence in salvation's coming about through the workings of creation and, especially through the human exercise of intellect and will—has roots far earlier than in the Middle Ages.

Since the earliest Christian centuries bishops (whose extant writings largely comprise our access to what became orthodox theology) optimistically insisted on the goodness of creation, on this creation's having come about and being sustained by the Logos or eternal Word of God, and on the incarnation (the taking on of flesh) of that eternal divine Word in the person of Jesus Christ for the redemption of a creation gone awry through humanity's sin. While much theologizing in the early Church took place in the liturgical contexts of preaching and catechetical instruction, thinkers such as Clement and Origen of Alexandria also wrote more speculative tracts, a hallmark of which was their identification of what we can roughly translate as reason (or intellect or rationality) with the divine revelation of Christ in Sacred Scripture. Creation might be fallen, but not beyond repair by the God whose Word pronounced it good from the start.

Abstracted from the context of preaching and celebrating the Church's rituals, this perspective on creation and redemption in the Middle Ages came to highlight the heart-warming wonder of the Word's taking flesh (incarnation) and the horrifying spectacle of the enfleshed Word's suffering death as divine satisfaction for human sin. In both popular piety (such as the Franciscan promotion of the crèche and the stations of the cross) and fine art (painting and sculpture), the predominant themes became the nativity and the crucifixion. In the scholastic theology that emerged from the late medieval period the principle of incarnation came to occupy much intellectual inquiry on the basis not only of Scripture but by means of theology's "handmaiden," philosophy (mostly neo-Platonism and Aristotelianism), dwelling on questions of form and matter, intellect and will. The abstract realms of ontology and metaphysics proved well suited to a faith whose content had come to focus on the principle of God's having taken on and redeemed the human condition. From the medieval synthesis, theological treatment of the sacraments followed from the doctrine of the incarnation, with the sacraments fitting into the plan of salvation as the means—instituted by Christ in his Church— whereby fallen humanity (and through them, all created things) are drawn into saving union with the Word-made-flesh.

This overly brief historical sketch can hopefully shed light on how and why Roman Catholic theology is still characterized in certain ecclesial-academic circles as "faith seeking understanding." The near universal hegemony of this Scholastic ("schoolmen's") approach to theology, however, has in recent decades begun to collapse. Contemporary dissatisfaction with the scholastic theology long regnant in seminary classrooms and college lecture halls has been primarily due to a new historical consciousness on the part of theologians who, especially since the middle of the past century, have come to recognize that the excessively abstract quality of typical Roman Catholic theology was rendering it irrelevant not only to the modern world in general but to Catholics themselves.[2] Put simply, there are no abstract Catholics. Given that historical fact, as well as the need to attend to socio-historical contexts, power-relations, and epochal events following from them, new methods for theology (drawing upon not only philosophy but the whole range of academic disciplines) now proliferate. To name just a few, these include feminist theology, womanist theology, liberation theology in the Southern hemisphere, political theology in the North, ecological theology, and—turning to our specific interests—liturgical theology.

With its origins in the rediscovery and study of early-church liturgical documents as well as experimentation with celebrating liturgies on their basis in certain monasteries of northwestern Europe in the late 1800s, the relatively young discipline of liturgical theology continues to seek clarity in not only its methodology but its very definition today. Liturgical theologians are fond of functioning under an adage of their own, *lex orandi, lex credendi*. This is a contemporary condensing of a theological principle pervasive in the writings of the Early Church Fathers which places the way in which the Church liturgically prays in a normative relationship with what the Church believes or, in other words, makes the Church's liturgy the source of its theology and the summit to which it returns. Contemporary liturgical scholars find the principle crystallized in a fifth-century text by Prosper of Aquitaine, *ut legem credendi lex statuat supplicandi* ("so that the law of prayer establishes the law of belief"), even as they continuously debate just exactly what this principle means in the life of the Church. Negatively, this tends to entail liturgical theologians rejecting the long-regnant Scholastic theology of the sacraments, which focuses primarily on doctrinal and metaphysical principles and only secondarily, at best, on the rituals themselves. Positively, liturgical theologians approach the topic on the basis of the history and elements of the Church's rites, with an increasing effort to study not merely the ritual texts but rites in practice and, moreover, how practicing the rites impacts how believers live the faith in their social contexts, and vice versa.

French theologian Louis-Marie Chauvet explains the methodological difference between classical Scholastic sacramental theology and contemporary sacramental-liturgical theology in terms of their points of departure. Chauvet observes that in the Scholastic manuals the treatise on the sacraments directly followed on the treatise on Christology, which for them entailed a metaphysical inquiry into the Church's belief that in Jesus the eternal Word of God took on a human nature (the hypostatic union). The starting point for sacramental theology thereby became the incarnation—more precisely, philosophical theorizing about the joining of divine and human natures—setting the framework for sacramental theology in terms of ontological and metaphysical inquiry into how God (divine being) is able to communicate through such materials as bread, wine, water, and oil. Chauvet's critique of this approach raises the deeper question of academic theology's purpose at all, the relevance of such theory to the actual practice of faith: "Rather than '*How* can God (it being understood that *we know who God is*) do such and such?' would it not be more in keeping with biblical revelation and especially with the 'scandal of the cross' to ask '*Of what God* are we speaking when we say that we have seen God in Jesus?' "[3] This makes the starting point for sacramental-liturgical theology not the wonder (mystery) of God's coming to join us in materiality (bodiliness) but, rather, the far more humbling but also ethically (personally) compelling marvel at the actual, *historical* way in which God did this, namely, in the first century Palestinian man Jesus, a Jewish prophet whose message—in word and deed—led to the human disaster of his execution and the divine vindication of his life-unto-death in the resurrection. In this approach, the starting point is what contemporary Catholic tradition has come to call the *paschal mystery*. This concept has biblical and patristic roots in theological reflection on the church's ritual celebrations of the mystery of faith that came through two lines of development, one emphasizing the sacraments as participation in the definitive event of salvation that was Jesus' death and resurrection, the other emphasizing how the sacraments immerse believers in the work of salvation that Christ's death and resurrection continues to realize in their lives and, ultimately, for the life of the world.

Contemporary liturgical theology's focus upon the paschal mystery does not abandon the Catholic belief of divine redemption through human bodily existence. What it does, however, is to shift the focus of this revelation primarily on the crucified Jesus' resurrection, that is, on God's having not only vindicated the life of Jesus but also raised that life to an unprecedented status *for humanity*. The import of the Christian belief that God raised Jesus bodily from the dead, therefore, entails the collapse of the sacred-profane dichotomy. The presence and action of the divine is not confined to certain (sacred) times or places separated from the normal (profane) landscape of human life in this world. The narratives of the Christian gospels along with the arguments and imagery found in the other writings of the New Testament proclaim the message that in the person and story of Jesus the religious means for communication (covenant) with the divine have been taken up and transformed. The purpose of sacred rituals is to reveal what the God of Jesus is bringing about in and through all of human activity and creation, namely, a participation in mutual loving service, in self-emptying sacrifice for justice and the life of others, in discovering the presence and action of God by reflecting upon the events of each human life and our lives together as histories in light of the paradigmatic texts (Scripture), and ritual actions shared in the Church's liturgy. Liturgy reveals the immanence of God (the sacred) in the ongoing life of humanity (the profane), but the latter not as an abstract historicity (the sheer fact of human bodily existence in time) but as concrete historical lives fashioned by human decisions, whether self-determined or (often tragically, if not unjustly) imposed. Recovery of this primordial Christian view of worship has led contemporary liturgical theologians to describe Christian liturgy as an engagement in the human pathos and divine ethos of life[4] and the juxtaposition of human religious symbols with the world-shattering divine Word revealed in the person and life of Jesus.[5] Christian liturgy is not a matter of taking believers out of the world for a moment but, rather, of immersing them more deeply in the mystery of God's paradoxical purpose for it over time.

Put differently, "In doing [the liturgy], the Church pursues its most essential purpose, which is to ensure the active presence of divine realities under the conditions of our present life—and that is what 'mystery' means."[6] With a concern for how biblical faith comes to be known and appropriated in the doing of the Church's rituals, liturgical theology has turned to the increasingly wide range of disciplines that study how symbol and language function within ritual and, moreover, how ritual functions in society. In its approximately first hundred years, that is, since circa 1870, liturgical theology tended to be a study of ritual books—their orations, rubrics, and commentaries—with an often misguided presumption that an analysis of the texts reveals not only the meaning of the rites in themselves but the impact they had on those who celebrated them. While that impressive corpus of work proved a fruitful and necessary beginning, its text-bound methods have proven ultimately insufficient. One need only witness all the controversies at present over the reformed rites of the Roman Catholic Church, let alone the way in which pastors and people alike take significant liberties with the official texts, to realize that the rituals Catholics (or any people) do, whether religious or secular, are not merely the matter of following a book. Thus, Jewish liturgical theologian Lawrence Hoffman[7] and, learning from him, Monsignor Kevin Irwin[8] have written theories on how context shapes texts, and vice versa.

Recently the burgeoning field of ritual studies, drawing on diverse disciplines, has offered increasing resources for liturgical theologians not only to explore the kind of participative knowledge believers obtain in the doing of both the Church's official rites and myriad popular devotions but also how various types of power—ecclesial, economic, political, familial, and so on—are negotiated in the performance of these rituals. Not surprisingly, liturgical theology today encompasses a range of questions about the practice and impact of the Church's sacramental and other rites, among such categories as the bodily nature of human existence and how this functions in both cosmos (nature) and society (history); the irreducible role of ritual for (shared) human knowledge and living; the distinctive content and function of liturgy in the life of the Church; and the complex web of power-relations (divine and human, intra- and extra-ecclesial) operative in the practice of the rites. These very sorts of theological questions unfold throughout this present book as it explores the practice of Catholicism in body, ritual, and contestation.

Medieval Studies Encounters Ritual Practice
by Joanna E. Ziegler

No mere editorial caprice is responsible for locating the section on medieval studies between theology and anthropology—between the two disciplines that in this book interpret the "living" practices and rituals of contemporary Catholicism. Even the word Catholic, central to our title, was not in use until after the Middle Ages. Catholic distinguishes the faith from the myriad Protestant denominations that emerged in the wake of the Reform movement of the sixteenth century. Before then, people were either Christian or not.

In this Introduction, medieval history finds itself, quite unusually then, in the midst of discussion and research on "the present." Although the field has been borrowing from other disciplines in the past two decades, the process has for the most part been unidirectional—*from* the social sciences *to* the medieval areas, prompting a fundamental change in how medievalists do history, especially as it concerns ritual. Our hope is that this book can furnish the space for a two-way conversation, a genuine dialogue, to take place.

We can ask how medieval history came to be central to a book about the present, "lived" nature of Catholicism. We can answer that question by charting in general terms the adaptation of social science methodologies to medieval studies. To put historical Christianity in dialogue with present Catholicism, we must go farther, though: to explore not only what medieval studies stands to learn from anthropology and theology, but what, in turn, it can offer those disciplines, particularly as regards the study of fully historical ritual practice. In such an exchange of views, each discipline and every approach must stand as equal to the other. The results may feel challenging, at times even disconcerting. In addition, to address the intense physicality of Catholicism—its bedrock in bodily experience—scholars must be willing to peer into its very core, which is the source of its supreme meaning and, paradoxically, its gravest danger. Both the dialogue and the subject at hand are potentially contentious.

Historians of Christianity are well aware of this paradox—but perhaps more than most scholars, they are not wary of it. Christianity has traditionally profited from elaborate embodied experiences in ritual, while at the same time standing in dread of the possible aftergrowth. The core of Catholicism is, after all, an incarnate God, and the rites that glorify it have been fittingly corporeal and sensual. Fred Paxton's essay in this volume brings to light the long history of affective and therapeutic song, music, and architecture to religious women's lives. Yet, historically the Church has feared the body perhaps more often than it has uplifted it, as Joanne Pierce's essay in medieval churching rituals shows. For the lush sensuality of the body is capable of steering the gaze away from the transcendental God back toward earthly realms, where the human being's "fallen" nature is drawn as apple is to ground.

Scholars, however, are no more comfortable with the outright unmediated physical, sensory nature of ritual experience—the body participating in ritual performance—as a realm of serious research inquiry. Everything about the body and the senses in the act of ritual—not the least of which is its unmistakable immediacy—puts academic credibility to the test, so hard won through "social scientific" methods. Throughout this book we interrogate the judiciousness of holding onto that convention.

A generation ago, the connection of medieval studies with theology and anthropology would have been unthinkable. In the early 1970s, medieval was an isolated historical "period" with fixed boundaries and governed by an internal set of customs, language, and procedures. Methods, perspectives, all the practices were hermetic, wrapped in the stolid (masculine) mantle of the European-based systems of archival and documentary analysis. All this would change in the 1970s, so radically that many of the older practitioners hardly recognized the emerging work as pertinent, or even medieval at all. In some ways, the divide was, of course, typically inter-generational. But something was different. The practice of medieval history for the first time in its lengthy historiography was yielding its distinctive identity to a really rather foreign modality—the social sciences, in particular, anthropology.

Recently, historian Philippe Buc[9] has argued that the impact of the social sciences has been virulent and, worse, has led the study of medieval ritual astray from an accurate representation of the data. While this is not the time to enter into Buc's aggressive formulation of the problem, an entire book devoted to *The Dangers of Ritual* (his title) is nonetheless patent testimony to the centrality of ritual to the study of the European Middle Ages.

It was anthropologist Victor Turner (1920–1983) who struck the mighty fortress of medieval studies hard.[10] His influence is well known, and has been covered well elsewhere.[11] What matters here is not so much Turner's particular take on ritual, as the nature of its impact on medievalists. Fascinated by ritual processes and much in tune with the intellectuals of the 1960s, Turner looked purposefully at wide-ranging social and cultural material for ritual, and what he saw was a dynamic, transformative, processual activity. Ritual lived, people acted and enacted it, and it changed them. It helped them grow up, move out, and contend with their world (as discussed in his famous work on rites of passage), and thus with their social and community identity. Ritual was society's way to respond to and manifest tension, ambiguity, and change, all part of the nature of social structures, where nothing is static. Turner's model for understanding ritual was thus dynamic *and performative*; it was inclusive, too, opening up areas for analysis hitherto restricted to institutional systems: from parades and games, to pilgrimages, and even subversive literature.[12] To a field such as medieval history with its eye firmly fixed on (male) clerical institutions, monarchical politics, and war—hierarchies without much contestation from below—the introduction of Turneresque realms of social inquiry was itself transgressive. The "world turned upside down" became as much a metaphor for the changes in medieval studies as it was the subject of them.[13] Even so, sociologically and anthropologically oriented definitions of ritual resonated well enough with key matters in medieval history to offer elucidative and translatable tools for analysis.

Our book thus stems from Turner's concepts of ritual as dramaturgy and political instrument or agent, but is also the legacy of three decades of research in medieval studies generally. After all, shifting attention from the liturgy of the Mass (once the sole locus of ritual) to civic displays, public debates, games, women's devotions, and all sorts of urban actions and spaces was a huge change in medieval history. Moreover, faced suddenly with legitimizing "foreign" or imported methodologies and grafting them onto the fiercely positivist modes of analysis, scholars early on in the period of change were occupied with defining ritual. Today, though, this matter, while still of some concern, is not as urgent as it once was, and scholars are more comfortable adopting looser definitions.[14]

Second, ritual received new life from the field of literary criticism and theatrical theory as performance. In her "Introduction to Performance Studies" Mary Suydam notes that literary criticism "has been increasingly unraveling and problematizing the once-tidy categories of text, author, editor, translator, and performer."[15] These two areas gave rise to the field now known as performance studies,[16] an enormously important body of theoretical work. In shifting the emphasis toward *doing*, action, toward sensory experience and even the experience of space, performance studies paved the way for a confident replacement of many of the core assumptions of medieval history that had commandeered the field since its incarnation in the nineteenth century: its empiricist/rationalist/objectivist foundation; its masculinist emphasis; the dominance of formal liturgy (i.e. the Mass); and its focus on institutional rather than social political realms. In short, ritual and performance studies—already growing in the light of social scientific models—opened scholars up to a very different past than their predecessors had seen.

As for research on "the body," Caroline Bynum's daring analyses of the gendered nature of medieval religious experience dismantled many of our assumptions about body, experience, and social identity.[17] It is nearly impossible to overestimate the impact of her work on the field—one should perhaps say fields—of medieval studies.[18] Bynum's work of the 1980s, as persuasive and commanding as it was, would nevertheless be cast into doubt by the postmodernists of the 1990s. This is a point worth reflecting on, for it explains something about the current fluid status of medieval studies in the academy.

While Bynum read prodigiously from devotional literature and was grounded in many of the procedures of analysis that traditional medieval history used (documentary, multilingual, textual), the nature of the documentation and the uncommon use of myriad artistic and iconographic sources (not to mention her conclusions regarding female devotion and its relationship to clerical power) gave the traditionalists pause. The generation that taught her largely rejects her. Documentarily grounded but in minor devotional literature? Women mystics hardly qualified to the generation raised in the aftermath of World War II of being worthy of study, let alone worthy of supporting a specialized branch of inquiry! Bynum would change all that, as time has proved. Yet, feminists, especially the revisionists of the 1990s, found her too objectivist, too lacking (too conservative) in the personal narratives that characterize so much postmodern writing. Bynum is not much interested in the construction of self, if by that we mean the self-consciousness of the author of the history as prime motive of interest. The practitioners of history in our deconstructivist era are as much the topic of the study as the ostensible subject; they are both subject and object. Bynum preserves greater distance of self from history.

The forces shaping self are fundamental to current historical academic practices. Specialists call this "constructing identity," for the notion of individual and self to emerge out of this framework is one that seeks to understand how power dynamics are structured and how they shape social identities. An instance of this postmodern thinking is Catherine Bell's prominent study, *Ritual: Perspectives and Dimensions*. She is clear about the need to begin with authorial presence:

It might seem logical to begin a book on the subject of ritual with an introduction to the data, namely, examples of rituals, and then proceed to examine the theories that have attempted to explain what rituals are and what they do. In actual fact, however, that apparently logical approach would probably prove to be more confusing for the simple reason that scholarship on ritual, as in many other areas, does not usually proceed so directly from data to theory. Most often, explicit theories or implicit assumptions lead scholars to find data that support or challenge these views. Hence, what counts as data will depend to a great extent on what one already has in mind, the problem that one is trying to solve.[19]

Commitment to authorial consciousness of self and "normative" historical concepts is especially striking for scholars working with women and other marginalized people. Researchers now see ritual less as expression and more as vehicle for the construction of social identities.

This book's chapters on medieval topics are heir to the last three decades of research into ritual.[20] Yet, our project goes farther. One of our aims is to activate the concept of practice within a performance model. We recognize the role of social construction and power relationships being played out quite literally in ritual movement and action. Gender still helps us understand the complex social dimensions of the medieval past; and we are cognizant of our authorial premises and voices. We are of the present moment. And, while acknowledging the authority of these perspectives at this time—gender, power, mentalities—we seek to set some new approaches in motion.

We are interested in thinking about performance itself as a way of understanding. This is what might be called an "experientialist" apprehension of knowledge—one that originates and is consummated in "right now," the presence and presentness of the physical and sensory immediacy of the performance, *for the performers as well as the authors who study them.* Our most difficult question has to do with grasping the nature of that knowledge, given and gained in direct sensory, spatial, kinesthetic occurrence at the moment of performance—not in the "after moments" of interpretation, which constitute another opportunity for understanding (such as the present study), *but at the time itself.* This is performance time, where actions are not symbols or constructed realities but are ends and meanings in themselves. This impression—which we return to in part VI—is what distinguishes our conception of "practice" from the Marxist and deconstructivist notions that precede and govern its current use.[21]

It is useful to take the word practice to mean the habitual, regular doing of an action in order to attain dexterity. The regularity, the doing of something over and over to obtain skill, this aspect of ritual can give medieval studies new questions to ask. This approach would emphasize more of the disciplined, habitual aspects of practice than practice theoreticians do. Practice can be seen more in the sense of practicing skills—such as scales on the piano, or drawing in perspective. Yet, since the practice we speak of is Catholic ritual practice, it occurs within faith, in that specific semantic field.

The physical, sensory element of performance can help to precisely locate the sort of knowledge that so often and so loosely is referred to as "bodily knowing." But, given its vagueness, this is a problematic term. With it, bodily experience is dichotomized from thought, as in mind *versus* body, sensory *versus* intellectual or rational content, or thinking *versus* feeling.[22] Practice, integral to performance, circumvents this dichotomy. Habitual doing is fully recognized in Eastern meditation practices as the source of "awareness." And, in the West, it is often seen as a wellspring of creativity. These are two manifestations of habitual in-body practice that are hardly severed from "the mind." More positively, a perspective on practice in this sense insists that there is no dichotomy between doing and knowing. This approach therefore has the potential to unravel one of the knottiest problems for students of ritual: to discern the connection between thought and action.

In this book we take up the really tough question of what, exactly, is the intellectual (and hence serious research) content of performance, of performed ritual—when performance is not entertainment; when performance unites participant and observer, when performance results from regularity of practice, when it manifests the most skillful degree of regular discipline that is ingrained in the body—and when it exists inside faith. What sort of participation is this, then? And what is our obligation as scholars to articulate its value as an academic matter?[23]

It is intriguing that for some contemporary anthropologists, discussed shortly, the living ritual of Catholicism is not only a rich "text" that yields insights into social systems and power relations but also can be encountered through participatory engagement—or practice—an experience that in itself can help to generate more culturally precise lines of research questions than would some "exterior," objectivist approaches to ritual. And, for the theologian, liturgist, and sacred musician, the participant in Catholicism is a believer, one who is—and is intended to be—transformed by the participation in the practice itself.

Whereas medievalists stand to make a distinctive contribution is in how they plumb the written records for evidence of ritual that is documentarily grounded, anthropologically sound, and physically practiced. In part II, writers do precisely this. The historical nature of their material constitutes a rich repository of information for all of us. The ritual bodies at issue no longer exist; we have mere residue, remembrances, of them in written texts and documents. To explore practice and performance of ritual in history thus means two things: one, to look at the *texts* with great powers of observation, as acute as those of an art connoisseur with a magnifying glass before an image.[24] They must look for form, visual form, not only for patterns or sequences of ritual, or for the identification of the players or the social/political meanings, but form—the appearance—as and in body. Two, we must ask, How best to narrate practice and performance? What style of writing can bring physical and sensory phenomena—embedded in history's archaic past—to life? Therese Schroeder-Sheker offers a rare instance—indeed a model—of this new academic practice. We take up the issue more fully in our book's last section: in retrieving a physically embodied ritual past, and in the ensuing act of writing responsibly and effectively about it, scholars have an exciting prospect of becoming both participant and researcher, observer and beholder, transformed in authentic ways by ritual performance—ways that partake of the interpretive strategies of anthropologists as they confront "living" data *and* ways that can yield insight into the "participative knowledge" (see Morrill, above) that lies at the heart of the theological worldview.

ON ANTHROPOLOGICAL APPROACHES TO CATHOLIC RITUAL *BY SUSAN RODGERS*

At first glance, cultural anthropology and Catholicism would seem seriously at odds, except in terms of traditionalist anthropology's tendency to turn the world into subject matter. Catholicism is a faith, one that proclaims a God, salvation, a messianic shape to human history, and the life, death, and resurrection of Jesus of Nazareth as revelatory of God's plans for the world. Anthropology by contrast often propounds a secularist worldview: the field is, after all, the study of human cultural worlds. Following the foundational work of Emile Durkheim on Australian Aboriginal worship of totemic spirits,[25] anthropology posits a human authorship to all God-talk, in all social locales and historical times. Anthropologists also invoke Durkheim to explain the cross-cultural presence of beliefs in supernaturals, and the prevalence across human space and time of heartfelt but apparently nonpractical ritualized actions directed toward those imagined beings and forces.[26] In religion, Durkheim famously contended, society is worshipping itself. Put more subtly, in *The Elementary Forms of the Religious Life* (1912) Durkheim asserted that the main Australian Aboriginal social group, the clan, first represented itself by creating an ancestral totem (e.g., a spirit reference to an animal). This totem was then sacralized: imagined to be a divine being, not the figment of the human imagination that Durkheim qua social scientist knew it to be. In anthropological and also sociological constructions of events, the clan members (e.g., the Green Parrots) come to look upon the purportedly ancient, origin-times totem, Green Parrot, as both their physical ancestor and protector. The human clan members will join together periodically to do ritual actions such as communal songs in praise of Green Parrot, in the process thus effectively "forgetting" the human hand in authoring this religious system of myth and ritual practice in the first place. In such rites, the parrot clanspeople would be worshipping Green Parrot but also the contours of their own social structure (the clan).

Durkheim took this to be an essentially functionalist arrangement: religious belief systems and rituals served at base to lend an aura of experientially, emotionally believable legitimacy to human-made social systems that would otherwise be vulnerable to cognitive and sociological collapse, over generational time. Clifford Geertz much later rephrased this set of Durkheimian insights to define religion as a ritual and belief system that joined ethos (a particular moral system, with its associated social organizational systems) to core worldview (i.e., a community's apprehension of reality "as it really is").[27] The faithful would come to fervently believe that *their own social universe*, with its "traditional" social organizational forms, was somehow the uniquely real one—even, the one set up by the divine. Religious rituals were key: they were the mechanism for catalyzing this "confusion" of ethos and worldview on a regular basis, for ceremonial participants.

Given anthropology's obviously secularist style of encountering religion, Catholicism emerges in such models as a topic of study, albeit an extraordinarily rich one in terms of key symbols and complex power relations within church hierarchies.[28] However, Catholicism's social reality in itself confounds such traditionalist theoretical approaches, at least in the hands of sensitive fieldworkers. The religion's historical nature and the revolutionary undercurrent from Christ's teaching about the powers of this world immediately make any mechanistic application of standard Durkheimian frameworks wildly problematic. Like any of the great world religions based on holy texts and anchored in the teachings of actual persons, Catholicism is hugely more complicated and intellectually sophisticated than any simple reading of its social legitimatory aspects would imply. And, Christ's counter-cultural stance vis-à-vis Roman imperial state power, His critiques of institutionalized religion, His focus on the poor (valorizing the very opposite of the power elite), and the sort of radical egalitarianism of His ministry recorded in the Gospels all go together to make Christianity of any historical variety a faith tradition that continually interrogates social science.

Luckily for anthropology, the field's signature commitment to conducting years-long ethnographic fieldwork in local languages and then reporting (to the extent possible) the community's own perception of reality has aided in keeping the discipline close to the untidy, often contradictory, lived worlds of religious believers and practitioners worldwide. In anthropological fieldwork, reliance on survey data or even on extensive interviews is never sufficient. Ethnography demands that the researcher gain serious access to the emic, or folk view of reality. In practical terms, this means that the fieldworker generally moves full-time to the community he or she is studying and gives up his own language on a day-to-day basis, to use the language or languages of the people being studied in all oral conversations. Importantly, fieldworkers are to combine such data-gathering and interpretive techniques as individual and group interviews, key informant interviews over many months, and textual analysis with full-scale participant observation. That is to say, if an anthropologist is studying a folk Catholic pilgrimage in the contemporary Philippines he or she should join the processions, acting always as a clearly identified researcher but seeking as well to generate study questions from the ritual experience itself. Anthropologists doing participant observation also put themselves in the "one down" position in relation to the people studied. That is, they do not come into the community as some sort of experts but rather as mere learners. When brought to the study of Catholicism, this research style inevitably lands the sensitive ethnographer right in the middle of the political, familial, emotional, and aesthetic "messiness" and vibrancy of any Catholic community, with its local squabbles, its resentments and warmth, its sacred objects and actions, and its alternately hapless and revelatory attempts to discern Christ's message, and Christ's body, for and in the here and now.

Given this built-in openness to the greater complexities of actual social worlds over passing social scientific theoretical constructs (all the while remaining heavily invested in the theoretical project), anthropology has gone through a range of interpretive course corrections, so to speak, to the old Durkheimian understandings of religion. This flexibility has opened up small spaces, at least, for illuminating anthropological study of Catholicism. The sub-field cannot be said to be large, but has promise. Many of the discipline-level theoretical course corrections have had to do specifically with ritual. Directly relevant to crafting a post-Durkheimian or at least a beyond-Durkheimian understanding of religion and religious ritual useful for studying Catholicism are three modes of analysis. One of these looks sharply at issues of power, social hierarchy, and resistance, within religious institutions and idea systems; a second attends to the ways in which religions and sacred rituals construct emotion, often in relation to healing practices; and a third mode of interpretation interrogates the ways "folk religion" in settings such as villages or minority enclaves in places like the Philippines can interrelate with conditions of structural poverty, nationalist discourse, and transnational flows of ideas and capital.

This entire range of research is also predicated on the post-Durkheimian realization that "religion" itself is not so much a human universal, but (qua concept) is an historical product of the interaction of societies with each other. Anthropologist Jane M. Atkinson provides an apt example.[29] The Wana people of Indonesia's upland Sulawesi had an intricate system of shamanistic worship but no concrete concept of "having a religion" until well into the Indonesian national era, post 1945. Then, information reached the Wana that more politically powerful lowland Sulawesians "had an *agama*," a world religion, in the form of Islam. Wana publics learned that proper agamas had such things as religious specialists, holy texts, and set rituals. By the 1970s the Indonesian state was expending considerable political resources to enforce the nationalist policy that all citizens must *beragama*, have agamas, to be both respectable humans and to be patriotic (and to demonstrate to the state that they were not Godless members of the outlawed Partai Komunis Indonesia, the PKI). The Indonesian state deemed people without formal agamas as *belum beragama*, "not yet having an agama," and thus in need of "upgrading," within Jakarta's *mission civilatrice*, which does indeed have echoes of Dutch colonialism in the Indies. In the late 1970s the Wana assiduously set about fashioning an agama for themselves and their outside state interlocutors, by compiling their ritual protocols into suitably modern-looking texts and by solemnizing their shamans as priests. In sum: anthropologists see the word religion itself as a product of history. Rite itself has similar historicity.

First, to frameworks stressing power and hierarchy. To outsiders it might seem that contemporary anthropologists are interested *only* in issues of power, domination, and resistance in their studies of religion, or indeed, any social system. Though this perception is an overstatement, it is true that questions about power have dominated the field since approximately the late 1970s. An older idea of "a culture" as a matter of consensually shared meanings gave way in thorough fashion at that time to Marxist-inspired and then Foucauldian conflict models. As a result, today an entity such as "Navaho culture" tends to be seen in anthropology as a loose, always changing set of negotiated meanings, in which social elites will probably tend to promote an ethos and worldview useful to their own political and economic interests, and various out-of-power groups will "carry" different visions of reality and will see the social world from the perspective of the margins. The structurally dispossessed will then negotiate religious meaning in relation to the canonical knowledge of the center. And, as I.M. Lewis argued, marginalized persons will sometimes "speak back to power" via charismatic religious languages and persona.[30] Lewis finds that persons on the edges of official religions employ prophetic language, trance states, demon possession, and various types of holy madness to claim sacred importance. Often these "languages" subtly undercut the authority of official priesthoods. Gananath Obeyesekere's *Medusa's Hair* added an intriguing use of Freudian psychoanalytic categories to this style of studying "holy madpeople."[31] Sociologist Max Weber had of course laid much of the groundwork for this style of interpreting religion, in his large-scale comparative religious histories.[32]

When this type of interpretive lens is turned on Catholicism, the results can be illuminating. Let two examples suffice. Not accidentally both draw on insights from feminist theory. Stanley Brandes notes that Catholic biblical imagery is marshaled together with a hierarchical arrangement of village space (domestic areas consigned to women and the feminine; the public plaza linked to men, the masculine, and the political) to yield a misogynistic worldview in Spanish towns in Andalusia.[33] The Fall of Man is laid to Eve, and to the Serpent, represented as aggressive, dangerous, and female. In this scheme of thought men must conserve their bodily essences, lest a rapacious woman leech them of their powers and health. Women are seductive, duplicitous, and potentially harmful to both grown men as sexual partners (who can be both hobbled physically by "semen depletion" and cuckolded) and to male infants (a fear of maternal infanticide is prominent, encoded into tales about a serpent seeking to kill the infant Jesus). Brandes sees Catholic folk myth as reinforcing sexual scripts and systematically disempowering women, through shaming. Doubtless, aspects of this complex of accusations and fears is present in numerous Catholic worlds, although it must be said that Brandes's style of interpretation here is overly programmatic. More nuanced are later anthropological treatments of power and resistance themes, where "the dispossessed" are recognized as actors in their own right, and the possibility that a subordinated group may mimic the social persona of their "betters" is acknowledged.[34]

A second example deals more explicitly with colonial state power relations with indigenous groups (of obvious importance to questions of conversion and colonialism). In *Moon, Sun, and Witches*, Irene Silverblatt (1987) traces the power trajectory of indigenous women from Quechua-speaking highland villages first in pre-Inca conquest times, then under the Inca kings and queens, then under the Spanish colonial state and the early Jesuit missions. Early on in this time line, villages had considerable gender equality, with women's pregnancy powers being associated with agricultural bounty and their farm labor publicly acknowledged. Older women were also feared and respected midwives, operating close to the dangerous powers of world creation and death. Under the imperial Inca state, in the villages a scheme of gender parallelism was promoted (sun versus moon; Venus-morning versus Venus-evening; Lord Earth counterposed to Mother Sea).[35] However, despite this seemingly benign gender complementarity, Quechua male chiefs served as middlemen to Inca rulers, and sometimes had to provide their daughters as tribute wives to the Inca king. Inca queens cited hierarchies of goddesses as part of their own claims to higher status than that of the village women.

With the arrival of the militarily even more powerful Spanish state and the missionary Catholicism that followed in its wake and participated in its privileges, village gender arrangements became even more hierarchical. Village women lost their status as full human persons under Spanish marital law; the Quechua midwives became redefined as witches and the sorts of healing cures they did became "satanic." In this new colonial, Christian framework, midwives could be punished or even put to death. But, drawing on the village sense for women's fecundity powers and their own professional accomplishments as healers, the midwives themselves rejected the negative aspects of the witchcraft "diagnosis" and exulted in the resistance potential of their role. In other words, they took the vocabulary of missionary Catholicism (which had itself been distorted by the state) and flung it back on the colonial power structure, criticizing it in prophetic ways. Similar power negotiations along the borderlands of states and indigenous communities during early Catholic conversion times have been documented in a number of recent historical and anthropological studies.[36]

A second line of post-Durkheimian and beyond-Marx anthropological research on religion touching directly on Catholic topics is to be found at the intersection of the scholarship on folk healing and the social construction of emotion. Many religions offer attractive scripts for bodily and spiritual "recovery" from serious illness and conditions of loss and mourning, no matter how powerful the local or transnational secular medical establishment might be. Classic anthropological studies of folk healing ceremonies laid the groundwork for new research in this area. Insights here in the newer studies include the following. First, that healing rituals worldwide tend to have highly dramatic storylines to them, playing on motifs of spiritual dangers to the "vulnerable" patient. These ceremonial dramas lead up to a catharsis in which healers suddenly restore the afflicted to life by defeating evil forces, or casting them out of the body. Second, that the ill person's bodily state is defined in the curing ritual in terms of macrocosmic/microcosmic models, with the patient's body being "like" a sick family, or a socially diseased village, or even an ill universe (e.g., a king's ailment thought to be reflected in earthquakes, with both "illnesses" taken as a sign of a failing state). Third, folk healing rituals can work to give voice to inter-society political relationships. For instance, soul loss in Quechua-speaking mountain villages in Peru sometimes indexes fears about migration to national, lowland cities.[37] Folk *curanderos* in highland settlements conduct divination and soul-recapture rituals for young migrants that subtly acknowledge these dilemmas of modernization. Such studies of healing ritual have informed recent studies of Catholic charismatic healing. Thomas Csordas's work is prominent here.[38]

A third broad type of recent anthropological inquiry into ritual and specially Catholic ritual concerns Catholic "folk traditions" (e.g., Corpus Christi processions in Mediterranean Europe). The term folk Catholicism is itself problematic, as it implies a blunt diffusion model of Catholic symbol and ritual practice from "center to periphery" and from church center to "local parish." Locality and center probably always mutually constitute each other in world religions, and in social scientific terms one pole is likely no more creative of religious meaning than the other. Contemporary anthropological attention to folk Catholicism (or, popular Catholicism) operates in more interesting theoretical territory than these older diffusion models.

At issue today are questions about how Catholic popular worship practices interrelate with political economy, with the rituals and meaning structures of nationalism, and with transnational flows of ideology and capital. Within such frameworks, one can ask, Exactly what systems of meaning are being bandied about in rituals such as street processions to saints? Historian of American Catholicism Robert Orsi helped set the stage for this sort of research in his *The Madonna of 115th Street: Faith and Community in Italian Harlem, 1880–1950*,[39] a study of "street Catholicism" and Italian-American devotional culture in relation to ethnic identity. In his prescient introduction to *Lived Religion in America: Toward a History of Practice*, Orsi advocates scholarly attention to this sort of informal Catholicism, not just to the religion of the official Church. The 1997 volume concerns Protestant America as well as Catholic experience, but Orsi's methodological messages are the same: "Religion comes into being in an ongoing, dynamic relationship to the realities of everyday life," and ritual practices such as penitential visits to grottos and healing shrines deserve respectful study open to these practices' intellectual and emotional depths.[40]

Orsi's *Thank You, St. Jude* demonstrates the potential of this historical approach (one close to an anthropological sensibility) for the study of Catholic healing, broadly construed.[41] Subtitled "Women's Devotion to the Patron Saint of Hopeless Causes," the book draws on letters that second- and third-generation American women from immigrant families penned to the shrine of St. Jude. These were often desperate missives in which the writers sought solace for such dilemmas as the demands of caring for a handicapped child without much family support, or life with an abusive or alcoholic husband, or pressure from relatives to be a "good Catholic wife" attending to progeny and household at the same time that all parties to the debate knew that the woman's salary from a job outside the home was needed to keep the family afloat economically. Orsi holds that the devotion to St. Jude (indeed, the women's very imagination of this saint as a friendly male presence in their home) helped these women to make subtle religious sense of what are in effect oppressive double bind situations having to do with gender hierarchy and national and international labor markets.

Some recent anthropological monographs attempt similar holistic interpretations of Catholic popular devotions but handle issues of agency differently than Orsi does. One such study, for instance, is Nancy Scheper-Hughes's *Death Without Weeping: The Violence of Everyday Life in Brazil*.[42] In this study of infant neglect and maternal despair (and women's emotional numbing) in a Brazilian shantytown, Scheper-Hughes reports a heartbreaking array of popular Catholic ideas and rituals that devastatingly poor households bring to a stark fact: young mothers living in shacks without running water are having more babies than they and the shantytown can possibly feed. The mothers at times will designate a sickly looking newborn as a special sort of child, an "angel baby" who seeks only to swiftly fly back to Heaven to adorn the throne of Jesus (i.e., to die, starved by their mother's hand). Scheper-Hughes first came upon this pattern of behavior and interpretation as a young Peace Corps volunteer in the 1960s; she returned as a medical anthropologist years later, trying to make sense of what she forthrightly calls "a horror." The young women typically considered themselves good mothers and they generally provided loving care to their "keeper" babies. The angel babies by contrast were aided in their supposed quest to leave this world by their mothers' refusal to feed them, to give them water, or even to talk to them. Placed in a hammock or on old rags in the back of the house, the babies soon died. They were given formal child funerals: a troop of youngsters would put the bodies in little white boxes and process out to the cemetery, carrying crosses. The mothers themselves claimed Mary-like suffering, in their attempts to handle their households. And, sometimes older children with serious illnesses would be brought to *curandera*, for curing. The children would sometimes be laid out on the ground in the shape of Christ on the Cross, as a sort of tableau of family suffering and sacrifice. Scheper-Hughes urges students of such seemingly very local re-interpretations of Catholic imagery and ritual to look beyond these families' immediate actions and circumstances to seek out the veiled causes of infant neglect and this form of mother love: she would have us look to aspects of the globalizing economy relating to Brazil's colonial-era history of plantation cropping of sugar; to state policies that lead to the neglect of illegal shantytowns; to gross disparities of wealth that underwrite the sort of profuse mother love that can be found in middle-class America versus the hunger-mad mother love these shantytown young women experience.

Such recent anthropological studies of Catholic ritual worldwide bespeak a large-scale turn away from programmatic formulations about religion's "functions" toward more historically grounded approaches open to issues of power and the reciprocal interconnections between ideologies of body, health, emotion, and social hierarchy—as animated by actual faith universes.

PLAN OF THE BOOK

Such points of contact between liturgical theology, medieval studies, and anthropology are potentially exhilarating. Taking these intersecting themes of liturgical power, ritual force, embodiment, contestation, and our search for productive interdisciplinary interpretive schemes into account in designing this volume, we present five sections: "Catholic Ritual: Practice in History," "Contemporary Ritual Practices of Healing," "Catholic Ritual as Political Practice," "Contemporary Mass Media as a Domain for Catholic Ritual Practice," and "Between Theory and Practice." Each includes a set of contextualized studies of rite, with each chapter speaking from a concrete disciplinary perspective. In each section, we pair one or several chapters with short Commentaries, written by researchers from complementary fields (e.g., sociology or religion). Our concluding section, an especially important one since it allows us to return to the contrapuntal use of academic prose and performance, unites reflections on the "Practicing Catholic" project as a whole by Holy Cross Director of the Chaplains Katherine McElaney with two theoretical chapters by Joanne Ziegler and Christopher Dustin. McElaney offered the homily at the Vespers (or Evening Prayer) held at the conclusion of the conference, crafting words to call to mindfulness the sort of interdisciplinarity and exchange between faith worlds and academics that she had experienced during the conference. Our book as a whole is designed to encourage debate about all these matters and to suggest new ways of appreciating Catholic ritual practice as the historical and sacred sort of action that it is.

PART II

Catholic Ritual: Practice in History

Joanna E. Ziegler

INTRODUCTION

The following four chapters take up one of the thorniest methodological problems in this study—how to retrieve the "presentness" of ritual performance in history, the "immediacy" of ritual, as Macy terms it. This aspect of ritual is surely the body. It is *my* body that walks, sings, or feels pain—no one else can experience those things for me. While words point to physical sensation, they are but abstractions only. It is individuals, after all, in their uniqueness, who experience sensation *in the body*. This, ritual's particularized embodiment and immediacy, constitutes the challenge to the scholars in Part II of this book, as they seek to understand this occurrence as an historical phenomenon.

The chapters that follow are not about the *history of* ritual, although each one is concerned with some piece of ritual's history. The history of ritual is a different project altogether. The scholars writing here have concerned themselves with the sensory experience of ritual, particularly the immediate and unrepeatable physicality of that experience. This objective is almost completely a matter of evidence, much more so even than historical inquiry is, almost by definition. As Macy discusses, to work through ritual's immediacy, it becomes a question of how to locate, retrieve, and faithfully represent the singular and essentially embodied nature of ritual.

Macy's study, "The Future of the Past: What Can History Teach Us about Symbol and Ritual?" reminds us just how elusive evidence is. The sources of ritual experience are limited, scarce, and incomplete. Macy offers many helpful questions for us to take up as we go about the search for sources, such as how did the evidence survive? Who wrote it, and how was it preserved? How much was preserved? Is it neutral? Beyond these questions, Macy looks long and hard at the words used to denote ritual, words that we, in the present, take for granted. "Believe it or not," he writes, "the earliest Christian never used the word 'ritual'." Thus concentrating on English speakers, Macy goes on to reveal that the words today for ritual—ritual, symbol, and sacrament—either did not exist, or have no equivalent in the past at all. For Macy, then, the words and terms for ritual have primarily to do with us, and, in turn, dictate the sort of evidence we find ourselves interested in discovering. "History is irrevocably present," Macy concludes.

Paxton's chapter, "Performing Death and Dying at Cluny in the High Middle Ages" is a powerful example of an historian who squarely faces these present interests but demonstrates that it is nonetheless possible to interact with the historical sources in a way that preserves both historical truth *and* present interests. This essay is an exemplary model for the discipline of history in our times, when many scholars are moving beyond the difficult density of postmodernism and the radical reductionism of the concept of self to mere subjectivity that this movement espoused. Paxton shows us that it is possible to write a history that is faithful to the immediate self in the present and faithful to the historical evidence, too.

Paxton's exploration of the customaries of Cluny that describe death, burial, and commemoration relies on the documentation but moves beyond it. This was not always true for him. His earliest analyses had not considered rhythm, motif, and even orchestration as "essentially performative events." It was his introduction to the "anthropology of ritual" and music-thanatology of Therese Schroeder-Sheker that gave Paxton "a way of seeing death at Cluny not just as Benedictine or Christian, but also as deeply human." His work has striven to locate and explore Cluniac death ritual as performance, stage direction, space and timetable, music, and even theater. It was Paxton's own personal exposure to prescriptive music, that put "meat" on the "bones" of ritual, as he says—not only for the monks, but for the scholar himself. At the Chalice of Repose (cf. Part III: Contemporary Ritual Practices of Healing), where he was teaching the history of Cluniac practices, Paxton began to sing, read aloud, and, as it were, absorb into his own body the musical practices he taught. Text, the written remains of the living history, migrated into the scholar's physical being via the vocalists and instrumentalists at the Chalice, thus making the text live in the present. Indeed Paxton's approach furnishes an impressive model of "embodiment" as interpretation, wherein the form and content of performed ritual merge with scholarly research.

There are, of course, instances of ritual embodiment that one would not wish to "practice," such as those studied by Pierce in her chapter, "Marginal Bodies: Liturgical Structures of Pain and Deliverance in the Middle Ages." Pierce explores the rites for the "churching" or purification and blessing of women after childbirth and the rites for the trials by ordeal, specifically, by hot iron and cold water. She has patent evidence for "the use of physical elements as mediatorial elements of God's presence with and self-communication to human being." Her sources are the prayer texts of the churching and ordeal *ordines* from an Austrian ritual book dating from the first half of the twelfth century, the Ritual of St. Florian. Pierce thus directly engages the precise matters that Macy alerts us to—whose *ordines* are these, and whose stories do they tell? Pierce's skillful, sensitive reading makes available new and crucial evidence about the physical immediacy and importance of "the body" to ritual. She also provides, albeit quite differently from Paxton, insight into how the past is of concern to the present. "Perhaps the most dynamic [issue] is the stress on the close relationship between God and creation, both the very 'ordinary' elements of the physical world as well as the human beings who increasingly influence its future."

Irene Silverblatt, in the final chapter "Race, Religion, and the Emerging Modern World," offers an anthropological perspective on how this troubling history concerns the present. On first reading, she seems occupied by quite a different set of objectives and terminologies from the other scholars in Part II. Yet, Silverblatt's exposition of "the racialized categories of the Spanish colonial world" illustrates Macy's point: that documentation itself—the historical sources—is fraught with ideology and manipulation. Moreover, although Silverblatt only adumbrates this, her study points up the ways the past and the present are parallel. Important to the readers of *Practicing Catholic*, it is through the history of embodied ritual—in this case, the shattering physical immediacy of torture—that the parallels come to life.

These chapters, in original ways, tell very different stories about our embodied interaction with the past—original because their approaches are neither traditional nor postmodern. These scholars do not fall into the traditionalist mode of justifying parallels of past with present by an "application of history to the present." But, just as importantly, they escape postmodernity's failure to acknowledge subjectivity and individuality in historical events. By being attentive to how ritual, at its very core, is about issues of personal embodiment, immediacy, and irreplaceability, these scholars pave the way for a history of embodied ritual history to be written.

CHAPTER 2

The Future of the Past: What Can the History Say about Symbol and Ritual?

Gary Macy

Sacraments are something one does, not something about which one speaks. To be more precise, a "sacrament" or even a "ritual" or a "ceremony" in the abstract are merely concepts, not at all what we actually celebrate. There are only concrete rituals, unrepeatable events that shape individuals by creating and recreating the socially constructed world in which they live. There are, for instance, no generic weddings; there is only my wedding, or my friend's wedding, or my daughter's wedding with its own unforgettable and unrepeatable sights and sounds and mishaps and gaffes and laughter and tears. Even if one gets married twice, each wedding is a unique, unrepeatable event; and so are all human ceremonies.

If this is true, what can an historian of Christian ritual and symbol possibly bring to the table in a discussion of events of such immediacy? Historians first of all study the past, and the past is also unrepeatable. Further, what historians describe is not and cannot be what really happened long ago. The twelfth century, for good or ill, will never come again and descriptions of the twelfth century are not the twelfth century as it was lived. The history of Christian symbol and ritual, then, describes things and actions which are not themselves either rituals or symbols, nor do rituals of the past in any case celebrate present life and concerns. Does, then, the past have any future, or indeed, even any present? Can the past shed any meaningful light on discussions of contemporary liturgy?

A closer look at history and at the history of Christian symbol and ritual will, I hope, convince readers that while what I have just claimed is true, history does provide a modest service to the present. Of course, this may just be special pleading, but I leave that for the reader to decide.

First of all, I would argue, history is never about the past. In fact, nothing about history is in the past. Every single history that historians write exists in the present. Every history that is still read, is read in the present. Moreover, every single piece of historical evidence (or at least evidence for that evidence) exists in the present; otherwise we could not possibly know about it. History, then, is irrevocably present. A few more points about the social shape of history-telling are well worth spotlighting, here at the outset, before moving on to important issues of terminology and translation, regarding ritual, symbol, and liturgy.

Second, history exists because of present interests. Somebody somewhere wants to know something about how they got to be who they are and why they are the way they are. A present concern prompts an investigation of the past. Without some present interest on the part of some present person, no history would be written at all.

So all history is the concern of the present; all history serves some current concern, no matter how obscure. This concern, moreover, is not in the abstract. This somebody who is interested in an historical question comes from a particular society with a particular viewpoint; this somebody has a gender; this somebody belongs to a particular economic group. Inevitably, these settings shape both the kind of questions this somebody asks and how they answer the questions.

History, if I may be so bold, turns out to be the stories that we tell ourselves so that we know better how we got to be who we are. So history depends a great deal on who "we" are. The story of the southwestern border between the United States and Mexico, where I live, is often told quite differently on different sides of that border, even when historians on both sides use exactly the same set of sources. This means that there is no one "history" of anything or anyone, there are only "histories" which tell the stories of different peoples who may or may not share the same memories.

But doesn't that mean that history is pure fiction? Surely history is not *just* stories, but facts based on evidence. Yes, and no. Yes, because historians do have a rigorous set of criteria and practices that are supposed to keep them from lying. No, because even these criteria and practices are hostage to inevitable problems.

First, evidence is often problematic. Sometimes there is far too little; and sometimes there is far too much. More than occasionally, historians find that there is just too little evidence to answer the questions they are asking; or at least to answer the questions truthfully. For instance, a friend of mine studies the families of Burgundy in the early Middle Ages. He came across the following description of Agnes, countess of Anjou, "she besieged the castle and took it, as was her custom."[1] At once, a thousand questions arise. Did she then normally lead an army, storm castles, and collect them for a hobby? Did many women do this? What did men think of this? What did other women think? What is going on here? The story we usually tell ourselves is that women of the time were helpless and oppressed and definitely did not knock over castles to pass the time. Maybe what we are telling ourselves is wrong. Actually Agnes produced a long line of extraordinary women, including her powerful and learned great-great-granddaughter, Eleanor of Aquitaine. Agnes may not have been the exception she seems at first sight.[2] However, this is the only reference we have of Agnes fighting and one of the few we have of women fighting. Are the references lost; deliberately destroyed? Or did they never exist? We may never know.

On the other hand, sometimes there is too much evidence. For example, the story is widely told (and believed) that veterans of the Vietnam War were spat upon when they returned home from war. The story has become important for certain groups in describing why the United States is the way it is. The problem is, the story may not be true. To check, one would have to review hundreds of newspaper stories, hundreds of feet of video footage from news reports, home videos where available and check hundreds of eyewitness accounts. Even then an incident could be missed. Sociologist Jerry Lembcke undertook this monumental task. He found no instances of returning Vietnam vets ever being spit upon. Does this settle the issue? Hardly; some despicable person somewhere may have spit on a returning vet; other equally disturbing incidents may have taken place. Lembcke notes that "given the passion of the times and the wide range of personalities attracted to the anti-war movement, it would be surprising if some activists had not directed their political emotions toward the men who fought the war." However, he concludes, "It is significant, though, that with all the research that has been done on the anti-war movement and the government's actions against it, no evidence has surfaced that anyone ever spat on a Vietnam veteran."[3] Maybe we have been telling ourselves a story about ourselves that is not quite true.

Finally, no evidence survives by accident. Every piece of parchment, every book, every monument, every grocery list survives because someone cared first to create it and then someone cared to preserve it. This is extremely important for documents from the first few centuries of Christianity. Only the wealthy were literate; only they could read; only they would care to own and preserve written documents. They decided what was worth keeping and what was not. Any history based on such biased evidence will be the history of the wealthy and literate. We don't know (and probably can't know) what the ordinary Christian of the second, third, or fourth century thought. They left no records. We only know what Justin Martyr or Origen of Alexandria or Augustine of Hippo said the ordinary people thought, which some other people thought it worth while preserving. Much of Augustine and most of Origen, for instance, is lost either through deliberate destruction or simple neglect.

All evidence, then, is tainted. Worse yet, all evidence is used selectively by historians, who all have agendas. When you read histories, then, even histories of Christian sacraments and liturgies, be suspicious. Good historians try to use all the sources that have survived and to use them judiciously. Bad historians pick and choose their sources to fit an already conceived agenda. Both kinds of historians, though, are limited by their own social, economic and political setting, by the limits of the evidence available and by the social, economic and political settings that created and preserved that evidence.

So what has any of this to do with liturgy, with the unrepeatable and immediate rituals that shape people's lives? Quite a bit, I would suggest.

One of the attributes of rituals that give them power is their antiquity, or at least their perceived antiquity. Christian rituals in particular are understood to be in continuity with a 2000-year history. We do what Christians have done before us, or so we wish to believe. We only know that, alas, based on what historians tell us earlier generations have done, and historians are working within all the limitations just mentioned.

This means that our understanding of our rituals will change depending on who the historians are and how they read the past; in short, how they preserve the memory of what we are doing in the rituals we perform. So, for instance, a generation ago the majority of historians of liturgy were clerical and male, today they are just as likely to be lay and female. Certainly this a shift that has already taken place both among professional theologians as well as in the practical, everyday workings of parishes around the country.[4] Clearly this shift will have an impact on the way in which histories of the liturgy are being written, although perhaps the impact of that change has not yet been felt.

Now let me move to some concrete examples of how the story of Christian rituals is presently changing. First, let us start with the word "ritual" itself. It is important to note that the earliest Christian never used the word "ritual." They never spoke English, so they couldn't, but more is at issue here. Greeks, Latins, Syrians, Copts, and Armenians used different words for this phenomenon. In the Western European tradition, the word used most often for ritual and symbol was "*sacramentum*." At least for English speakers in this tradition, there exist not only the words "ritual" and "symbol," but also the interesting and theologically loaded word, "sacrament." While this term is clearly a transliteration of the Latin, it cannot, in fact, be translated back into the Latin of the early or medieval church. There is no word in Latin from these periods that is the equivalent of the English word "sacrament" with its polemical overtones of Reformation and post-Reformation debates. This might seem almost a truism, but think of some of the consequences of this simple observation. First of all, medieval theologians used the word "*sacramentum*" far more inclusively than any English speaker can use the word "sacrament."

A few examples should suffice. When the great twelfth century theologian Hugh of St. Victor, wrote his monumental work, *De sacramentis christianae fidei*, he was not speaking of seven (or two or five) particular Christian rituals. He used the word "*sacramentum*" to refer to creation and redemption as well all the rituals and symbols which preceded the incarnation in both the periods of natural law and of Jewish law. The word as Hugh used it can mean something similar to the Greek, "*mysterion*," as well as symbol or ritual. Hugh also used "*sacramentum*" to describe individual Christian rituals, of course. Hugh defined "*sacramentum*" as "a corporeal or material element set before the senses without, representing by similitude and signifying by institution and containing by sanctification some invisible and spiritual grace."[5] As an example, Hugh gave the water that is used in baptism. Note that he did not give the ritual of baptism as an example, but just the water. Any thing, any action that God has used, or now uses, to sanctify humans is a "*sacramentum*." The word is very difficult to translate. It means "ritual" or "symbol" surely, but only those rituals and symbols that sanctify. To transliterate the word as "sacrament," as the only English translation of Hugh does, is very misleading. In English, "sacrament" refers only to very specific formal Christian rituals, a far narrower meaning than Hugh ever intended. It would make little sense, for instance, in Hugh's understanding of "*sacramentum*" to argue about how many *sacramenta* there might be.

Hugh of St. Victor not surprisingly has not been picked as a random example from Christian history. His writing and the writings of his school produced the most influential theology on symbol and ritual in the Middle Ages. An anonymous work from the school at St. Victor that depended heavily on Hugh's teaching is the so-called *Summa sententiarum*. Beginning in the late twelfth century, the description of the structure of Christian rituals contained in the *Summa* was copied by almost every medieval theologian. It appears, for instance in another and better known *Summa*, that of the Dominican friar, Tommaso d'Aquino. According to Thomas (and the *Summa sententiarum*) the "*sacramentum*" of the Eucharist consists of three elements, the *sacramentum tantum*, the *sacramentum et res* and the *res tantum*. Consider the weird translations that result when every use of the word *sacramentum* by Thomas is translated by sacrament in English. One example will suffice. "We can consider three things in this sacrament: namely, that which is sacrament only, and this is the bread and wine; that which is both reality and sacrament, to wit, Christ's true body; and lastly that which is reality only, namely the effect of this sacrament."[6] How many sacraments do we have in this one sacrament? Are sacraments then not reality? Are parts of the Eucharist not sacraments? The translation completely misses Thomas's point (and that of the *Summa sententiarum*).

Let's try another translation without the English word sacrament at all. "We should consider three things in this ritual; namely that which is the symbol alone, and this is the bread and wine; that which is both the reality signified by that symbol and which is itself a symbol, that is, Christ's true body; and lastly that which is the reality alone signified by the symbol, namely the effect of the ritual."

Sacramentum cannot mean sacrament here or one loses the whole meaning of what Thomas is saying. The point being made here, and it was made over and over again by medieval theologians, is that bread and wine are symbols and even the real presence is a symbol, a symbol of the unity in faith and love that make up the Christian community. The Eucharist both celebrates and empowers the faith and active love of the community.

Most importantly, the second translation demystifies the theology. We are no longer talking about some spiritual reality called "sacrament" that is different from ordinary human symbols and rituals. Indeed, it is precisely about human symbols and rituals (shared bread and wine) that Thomas and other medieval writers are talking. They use the same word, *sacramentum,* for Jewish and even pagan rituals and symbols. In short, any human symbol or ritual can be called a *sacramentum*; this is something one cannot say of sacraments. We are now back in a human world which really can embody the divine in ordinary human actions. The magic is gone; and with the magic, of course, some of the power.

The simple change in translation suggested above is part of a larger change, a change from a history of sacraments to a history of Christian symbol and ritual. A history of sacraments is looking for historical justification for a predetermined theological position that considers sacraments to be a reality different from other human symbols and rituals. A history of Christian symbol and ritual is looking for historical justification for a predetermined theological position that considers Christian symbols and rituals to be the use by Christians of basic human symbols and rituals, symbols and rituals shared with other communities. Of course, from the examples given above, this second interpretation would be arguably closer to what early Christian and medieval theologians had in mind when they spoke of *sacramenta*.

The relation of this issue to present liturgical practice can be demonstrated by the two simple questions, "Is the ritual of quincinera a sacrament?" "Is the ritual of quincinera a *sacramentum*?" If the answer to the second question is yes, then answering no to the first question becomes tricky. It is an issue that deserves serious discussion on the level of ritual performance. Who decides which rituals mediate God's grace?

Another word that deserves similar reconsideration is the Latin word *ordinatio*. Once again, the English transliteration, ordination, is far narrower than the Latin original upon which it is based. Historically, the words *ordo*, *ordinatio*, and *ordinare* had a far different meaning in the early Middle Ages than they would come to have in later centuries. The problem with references to ordination in the Middle Ages, in fact, lies precisely in the lack of precision with which that term was used. Yves Congar, in a brilliant exploration into the words *ordinare* and *ordinatio* suggests that particularly in the period before the thirteenth century, considerable diversity existed both over what constitutes an *ordinatio* and which states or *ordines* should be considered "clerical."[7]

Pierre van Beneden has argued that early Christians appropriated the language of "ordination" for use in their communities not so much from Roman law as from everyday usage. This "everyday" use of the terms *ordo* and *ordinare* continued throughout the Middle Ages as even a cursory glance at any thesaurus of medieval Latin will show.[8] *Ordo* could refer simply to one's state of life and *ordinare* would still be used in its original sense of providing order either in a political or metaphoric sense.[9] According to Pierre Marie Gy in an article on the ancient prayers of ordination, "at least in the patristic era, *ordinare* is greater than *consecrare* or *benedicere* and designates not only the prayer of ordination but all the ecclesial processes of which this was a part. The term *ordinatio* was applied in the high Middle Ages to kings, abbots, abbesses, and by imperial Christian law, to civil functionaries."[10] In fact, based on medieval examples given in the *Novum glossarium mediae latinitas*, the words *ordinatio* and *ordinare* were used to describe not only the ceremony and/or installation of bishops, priests, deacons, and subdeacons but also of porters, lectors, exorcists, acolytes, canons, abbots, abbesses, kings, queens, and empresses. The terms could also apply to the consecration or establishment of a religious order or of a monastery or even to admission to the religious life. So too, an *ordo* did not necessarily refer to a particular clerical state. Innocent III described canon lawyers as a separate *ordo* in 1199.[11] At least as late as the fourteenth century, *ordo* could also be used to designate the sacrament of extreme unction and marriage would be referred to as an *ordo* as late as the fifteenth century.[12]

According to Gerard Fransen in his study of ordination in medieval canon law, "For them [the medieval canonists] *ordinare*, *ordinatio* did not necessarily have a sacramental meaning. One calls *ordinatio* the election of a pope, the nomination of an archdeacon, the canonical establishment of a monk that he might administer a parish."[13] Early medieval sources discussing ordination cannot be read with the assumption that they are discussing the same institution that would emerge from either Lateran IV or Trent. In fact, as interesting as the question of what ordination comprised in the early Middle Ages is that of whom it encompassed. The Rule of Benedict used *ordinatio* frequently to refer to the installation of an abbot.[14] Abbots, monks and others entering the religious life were referred to as ordained throughout the early Middle Ages.[15] Kings and emperors were also considered to be ordained by themselves and/or by their contemporaries. According to Congar, " 'To be ordained' was the official formula of the Capetians for their coronation."[16] Pope Urban II in a letter of 1089 to Rainold, archbishop of Rheims, affirmed the archbishop's power to ordain the kings and queens of France.[17] In another example of the use of *ordinatio* for a queen, the *Annales Altahenses maiores* for the year 1043 described how King Henry led his bride to Mainz and here arranged for her to be consecrated queen, and then "having completed the days of ordination (*diebus ordinationis*) in Ingelheim, the region made preparations for the marriage."[18] The coronation rite contained in a Florentine sacramentary from the second half of the tenth century introduces the blessing of the Empress with the description "the ordination of the Empress at the entrance to the church."[19]

Kings and queens, emperors and empresses often considered themselves and were considered by their contemporaries to be validly ordained into an important *ordo* of the Church. To quote Henry Chadwick, "So Western a writer as Pope Leo the Great can tell the orthodox Greek emperor that he is invested not only with *imperium* but with a priestly office (*sacerdotium*) and that by the Holy Spirit he is preserved from all doctrinal error."[20] No doubt such claims were more impressive when backed up with an army; nevertheless, kingship (and queenship) represent an historical example of ecclesiastically supported ordination which later Roman Catholic theology would judge not to be ordination at all.

If the terms *ordo, ordinatio*, and *ordinare* did not necessarily entail "ordination" in the sense which Trent would later use the term, what exactly did it mean to "ordain" someone during this time? According to Cardinal

Congar, "The words *ordinare, ordinari, ordinatio* signified the fact of being designated and consecrated to take up a certain place, or better a certain function, *ordo*, in the community and at its service."[21]

Again, the interesting questions here are, "Have women ever been '*ordinata*'?" and "Have women ever been ordained?" There is a significant difference in the two questions. Once again, a history of ordination would be quite different from a history of *ordinatio*. Quite different theological assumptions underlie these two different histories, yet both would, presumably, use exactly the same evidence. A history of ordination might even claim that Christians never ordained women; a history of *ordinatio* could not make that claim.

Suppose that so far I have convinced you that quite different histories result from the different theological assumptions that one brings to the sources that make up that history. I might even have convinced you that a history of *sacramenta* and a history of *ordinatio* offer a better explanation of the Western tradition than a history of sacraments and of ordination. The question still remains "what possible relevance could this have to the actual performance of Christian symbols and rituals?"

I believe the answer lies in who one thinks one is and what one thinks one is doing when one participates in the rituals. Do we all have our own *ordines* in which we serve the Church; *ordines* that are equal and equally appreciated? Or are some of us channels of God's grace to and for the others? Do we receive our *ordo* in the community from the local community to serve the local community? Or do we obtain a metaphysical status from God that transcends the local community and commissions us to serve God wherever we are needed. Each of the understandings implied in these questions exists in Christian thought and the answers to these questions depend upon one's reading of the tradition and this, in turn, will depend on which traditions historians present to us.

One of the important points to make here is that our traditions are pluralistic. If one turns to the first millennium of the church as normative as Cardinal Yves Congar and, following his lead, Archbishop John Quinn of San Francisco tend to do,[22] then one would see the understandings of *sacramentum* and of *ordinatio* presented above as normative. If one turns to the later Middle Ages and particularly Trent as normative, then one will write histories of the seven sacraments and of ordination as discussed above. Arguments about which of these periods ought to be normative for the present and how these periods show be normative are very important theological issues.

Every one inherits, or "catches" to use Terrence Tilley's more accurate phrase, a tradition, an understanding of one's story.[23] One catches it through sermons, through schooling, but even more powerfully through symbol and ritual. One can simply accept the tradition one has inherited and pass it on uncritically. Or one can be suspicious, as I have suggested. What theological assumptions are behind these traditions? What periods, documents, and people are normative for this tradition? Where is the tradition coming from?

Most importantly, what tradition do I wish to pass on in my performance of rituals? What tradition do I see myself a part of when I participate in rituals? And here are the most important questions of all. For each participant in a ritual embodies a living tradition which he or she inevitably passes on to all those to whom the participant introduces the ritual. For this reason, every participant in ritual and every celebrant in a ritual has an obligation to understand and critically embrace the tradition in which they stand. We are who we remember ourselves to be, and we will become the selves our rituals celebrate. And here, I submit, historians can play a crucial role in determining which stories tell us who we have become and, therefore, who we wish to become.

Commentary: Ritual Efficacy: Cautionary Questions, Historical and Social Anthropological

Anthony Cashman

In his paper, "The Future of the Past," Gary Macy deftly shows us possible histories of the terms *sacramentum* and *ordinatio* and demonstrates that indeed, "our traditions are pluralistic"(p. 36). His larger implication here is that Catholics need information about their symbols and rituals and the variable theology behind them to make informed decisions about contemporary practices. According to Macy, "every participant in ritual and every celebrant in a ritual has an obligation to understand and critically embrace the tradition in which they stand" (p. 37). This is where the historian's craft can help shape religious understanding by "determining which stories tell us who we have become and therefore who we wish to become" (p. 37).

The idea of Catholic self-empowerment sounds promising, but for many contemporary American Catholics, the menacing clouds of doubt and frustration darken Macy's sunny outlook on the spiritual and ritual health of the Church. The individual freedom of contemporary American Catholics is paramount here. Much of the current scholarly debate on ritual practice centers on this question of freedom. How much autonomy do actors exhibit in their words and deeds within the ritual framework? Are people free to take their cues from historians and other cultural sources so that we can determine our own courses of action or are we more or less prisoners of our own historical dramas? To answer, one could place human endeavor on a spectrum, with one pole occupied by totally free, unconstrained, creative activity and the other pole characterized by socially and culturally determined behavior. Where then does ritual activity fall?

The anthropological approach of "practice theory" has arisen in recent years specifically in response to this knotty problem of the relationship of people's actions, especially in ritual contexts, to the social, cultural, and economic systems in which they act.[1] According to the practice-theory anthropologist Sherry Ortner, "the actor is not viewed as a free agent, engaged in unconstrained creativity on the one hand or manipulation on the other.. Rather, the actor is recognized as being heavily constrained by both internalized cultural parameters and external material and social limits."[2]

At the heart of this approach is the concept of the "cultural schema," (alternatively, Pierre Bourdieu's *habitus*). In simplified terms, the cultural schema is a person's way of organizing, interpreting, and acting upon the world. Practice theory holds that people are not entirely unconstrained when approaching cultural situations. In fact, actions are conditioned by schemas even as the schemas themselves undergo modification during and because of events.[3] The pull of tradition tends to lead ritual participants toward the pole of total constraint. This brings us back to Macy's arguments and to the basic question of people's abilities to effect changes in traditional symbols and rituals. Even armed with historical knowledge, how much can any of us change rituals and symbols within the context of the base tradition, or specifically within the context of the modern Catholic Church?

Practicing Catholics also need to confront a more worrisome issue regarding contemporary devotion—the ineffectiveness of rituals. While structural-functionalism fell out of fashion long ago, many scholars continue to assume the efficacy of ritual, specifically that it has the power to shape and reshape effectively the beliefs, attitudes, and feelings of its participants. Moreover, general readings of rituals or cultural events tend to miss multiple interpretations rather than illuminate them. Historians and anthropologists always need to examine the historical context of rituals, striving for what Clifford Geertz calls "thick description", in order to challenge the notion that rituals simply "work."[4]

Repetition, for example, is a key component of ritual. It inhibits change and tends to reinforce structure, so it serves as an important part of learning and enacting a ritual. As anthropologist Jack Goody notes, "It is not surprising, therefore, to find that ritual is so commonly seen as system-maintaining, group-maintaining, as eufunctional. But formality, repetitiveness also means culture lag and loss of meaning."[5] A ritual attempts to recreate itself over time, sometimes centuries even, while the social conditions that gave rise to the original enactment might have changed considerably. Ritual, in its search to reinforce structure, contains the seeds of its own degeneration.

So Macy is right on the money in his attempts to remind us of the plurality of meaning when it comes to ritual practice. Symbols and rituals do not usually mean the same things to different people in various situations. So, on reading Macy's insights, we can ask the following. In the end, will the possibilities of ritual practice matter? Do what Macy calls "caught" rituals still have the power to keep people connected to the Catholic Church? As people's social and cultural circumstances change, with ever-increasing rapidity, and along with them, their cultural schemas, how long can rituals which are hundreds or even thousands of years old still matter to most Catholics?

Because the Catholic faith is no longer compulsory as it was during the Christian Middle Ages, people often seek outside of the Church the freedom that they might not be able to find within. This might be precisely what explains an apparent paradox in a recent survey concerning attitudes, opinions, and practices of American Catholics. The poll, conducted by Gallup for the *National Catholic Reporter*, questioned American Catholics over a twelve-year period concluding in 1999. The survey found that "American Catholics tend to value 'core' aspects of the faith, such as the sacraments, the church's role in helping the poor and belief that Mary is the Mother of God."[6] Nevertheless, the study also determined that U.S. Catholics simply feel less connected and dependent on the institutional church.

In 1999, only 37 percent of the respondents attended compulsory weekly Mass, down seven percent from only twelve years before.[7] Controlled for generation, this data looks even bleaker, as only 27 percent of Post-Vatican II respondents (ages 18–38) said that they went to weekly Mass against 42 percent for Vatican II respondents (39–58) and 64 percent for Pre-Vatican II respondents (59+).[8] Since Mass includes the Eucharist, the most commonly practiced sacrament, and people are staying away from Mass in ever increasing numbers, it is clear that today's American Catholics are willing to do without this key sacrament on a regular basis. Thus, despite claims that the sacraments remain important to them, American Catholics are also becoming increasingly estranged from the Church's traditional ceremonies.

Therefore, in the end, there might be another way that historians can be useful to the modern faithful. But this requires a role that modern historians typically shun—that of prognosticators of the future. We should venture a guess to the question, What will happen to the ritual life of the American Catholic Church? From my perspective as an historian of ritual, the future does not look especially promising. If people are casting about trying to find their places and roles in a church whose practices seem to have trouble keeping up with the culture lag and loss of meaning to which all rituals are subject—at ever increasing rates—it's not hard to imagine that American Catholic churches will soon be like the Catholic churches of Western Europe: largely empty.

Author's note

A vigorous discussion followed my concluding comments. One respondent argued that my estimation of the ritual health of the Church was "simply wrong" while another, who identified himself as a Catholic priest, supported my position by expressing his concern that the U.S. Catholic Church was particularly failing its youngest parishioners through its indifference to their faith and ritual needs. This wide difference of opinion suggests an important observation. Writers and scholars should be careful about jumping to conclusions based on the health or difficulties of any single parish, a tendency that informed this particular discussion. Personal experiences are not adequate to assess the challenges facing the American Catholic Church. We must account for the limitations of our own subjectivity when examining ritual.

I experienced first-hand the constraints of personal perspective regarding the highs and lows of parish life when I was in graduate school and was a parishioner of Holy Cross Roman Catholic Church in Durham, North

Carolina. From my observations, almost all aspects of the ritual life of the parish seemed to enjoy remarkable participation. The church, which began as a Jesuit mission for African American Catholics, included a large number of recent converts who vigorously supported the parish and infused many of its activities with the vibrant practices of other faith traditions. Many of my fellow parishioners and I were unaware that underneath this healthy and harmonious façade, Hispanic members of the congregation felt as if they were being systematically squeezed out of the parish. They became so disaffected with the leadership and the ritual life of Holy Cross Church, namely the cessation of weekend bilingual services, that they staged a stunning public rejection of their membership, interrupting a weekend Mass and carrying off the church's statue of Our Lady of Guadalupe. Many of these parishioners relocated to another Catholic parish in Durham and never returned to Holy Cross Church, while evangelical Christian churches in the area boasted an increase in Hispanic participation.[9]

CHAPTER 3

Performing Death and Dying at Cluny in the High Middle Ages

Frederick S. Paxton

The liturgy of death and dying at the great Benedictine abbey of Cluny first caught my attention over 25 years ago. Returning time and again to the textual remains of Cluniac death rituals: translating, teaching, and writing about them, considering them from various points of view—the history of monasticism, the cure of the body and care of the soul, relations between the living and the dead, the anthropology of ritual and religion, contemporary practice—has revealed not just some of the ideas and beliefs to which they gave expression, but also something of the gestures, choreographed movements, and musical forms of the people who performed them. In this chapter, I would like to address some of these performative aspects of the Cluniac death ritual. I would like to begin, though, with a brief account of the role these texts have played in the history of music-thanatology, a contemporary musical-medical practice that uses voice and harp in the palliative care of the dying. We will then turn to the spaces in the monastic complex where the monks performed the death rites, and as to how they evolved over the course of the eleventh and twelfth centuries when Cluny reached the peak of its development. Finally, we will follow the death and funeral of a monk at Cluny as it unfolded in the infirmary, chapter house, churches, and cemetery, attending to the possible meanings of the ritual performance, and the ways in which its performative aspects organized—and affected—the participants.

CLUNY AND MUSIC-THANATOLOGY

Most of what we know about death at Cluny comes from the eleventh-century "customaries" of the monks Bernard and Ulrich.[1] The customaries preserve a record of nearly every aspect of life at Cluny, especially the complex round of services and duties that made up the heart and soul of Benedictine monasticism. For a master's thesis completed in 1980 under the direction of Caroline

Bynum at the University of Washington, I translated the chapters of the Cluniac customaries that concern death, burial, and commemoration of the dead; analyzed them for data on medieval attitudes toward death, particularly in the Benedictine tradition; and commented on such things as the overall structure of the rites, their liturgical and sacramental qualities, and what they implied about the relations of individual monks to the monastic community. I noted how rhythm, motif, and even orchestration shaped them, but I did not think of them as essentially performative events.[2]

Later, as a doctoral student at the University of California, Berkeley, I discovered the anthropology of ritual, in particular the work of Arnold van Gennep on *rites of passage*. Van Gennep noted, almost a century ago, that all rites accompanying a change of status—child to adult, single to married, and so on—tend to have a common tripartite structure, each phase of which shares certain common symbols and actions. People undergoing such rituals have first to leave behind their former state through rites of separation (pre-liminal rites). The rituals that follow address the 'liminal' phase of the process, that marks the transitional between what they were and what they will become (from the Latin word for 'threshold'). Post-liminal rites of incorporation help ease them into the community of those sharing their new status.[3] I also read Victor Turner, who extended van Gennep's analysis, arguing that the liminal phase of rites of passage could generate new social ideas and conditions, especially the phenomenon he labeled 'communitas,' a profound feeling of identification among those who have shared an experience of liminality, such as a pilgrimage.[4]

It had always seemed to me, and it still does, that a great deal of life at Cluny centered on death, and that this is nowhere more evident than in the rituals that developed there around the treatment of the dying and the dead. The anthropology of ritual provided a way of seeing death at Cluny not just as Benedictine or Christian, but also as deeply human. It situated the wonder I had felt the first time I read the customaries—at the care shown to the dying, the energy brought to bear on the transition from this life to the next, and importance of commemorating the dead through prayer and almsgiving—against a wider backdrop. The tendency of an emerging rite of passage to take shape in accordance with van Gennep's tripartite form also became an important methodological tool of the dissertation I wrote at Berkeley, which traced the history of death rituals in Latin Christianity up to the tenth century, when Cluny was founded.[5] After reporting on some of this research at an academic conference in 1984, I met Therese Schroeder-Sheker. Therese told me about her experiments in caring for the dying with harp and sacred music. Listening to my report, she had sensed that the Cluniac death ritual might be a historical precedent for the work she had been developing over the previous decade. She asked if I had realized that the Cluniacs actually sang people through the transition from this life to the next. I told her I had not. I knew, of course, that the monks chanted the psalms and antiphons that accompanied much of the ritual action, but I had not heard it as music, nor understood it as an essential feature of the rites, an agent as central and active as the blessings, prayers, gestures, and anointings.[6] We agreed to stay in touch.

Eight years later, Therese contacted me with the news that she was opening a school at St. Patrick Hospital, in Missoula, Montana, under the auspices of the Chalice of Repose Project, and with an offer to become a visiting faculty member. The school's purpose was to train students in the art of delivering prescriptive music to the dying, a contemplative clinical practice grounded in pre-modern music and spirituality that seeks to promote "a blessed death in the modern world."[7] Therese wanted me to introduce the students to the Cluniac tradition, which she saw as a historical touchstone for the kind of work for which they were training. I jumped at the chance. It is not often that a historian, not to mention a medievalist, gets an invitation to participate in a project that draws inspiration from his work. For the next eight years I spent a week each semester in Missoula, lecturing on the Cluniac rituals and the history of death and dying to people who were training to care for the dying through sung prayer. It was the most challenging teaching I have ever done.[8]

Teaching for the Chalice of Repose Project led me to change my approach to the Cluniac death rituals once again. The customaries of Bernard and Ulrich record every act and gesture of the ritual process, but in the abbreviated manner of stage directions. They say who did what and when, and they indicate what was said or sung, but not in full. The monks knew all the psalms and many of the prayers of the rituals by heart and referred to service books for the text of any they did not. Therefore, Bernard and Ulrich identified them simply by *incipit*, the three or four words with which they begin. Because of this, the customaries make the structure of the ritual process very clear, but they also obscure whole layers of meaning. They reveal the bones, but not the meat of the Cluniac response to death and dying. Without the words of the prayers and psalms, much of what was specifically Benedictine, Christian (and Catholic) about the rites remained hidden from view. So I set out to reconstruct the ritual in its entirety, inserting the missing words into Ulrich's text from medieval liturgical books that survive either in manuscripts or in editions produced since the seventeenth century, creating an edition, in Latin and English, of a text that never actually existed.

As I reconstructed the Cluniac death ritual, I explored with the students in Missoula the meanings of its prayers, antiphons, and psalms. In one exercise, we used some of the prayers as models, seeing if the students could express the spirituality that each brought to the Chalice of Repose Project in the ancient cadences of the Latin Church. In the last couple of years, we began to read the reconstructed ritual through out loud, and even to sing some of its more familiar elements. We did not perform it, but we got a sense of its length and character, its rhythms and motifs, its sounds and solemnity.

ARCHITECTURE, SOUND AND PERFORMANCE AT CLUNY

Even if we had performed the Cluniac rituals in Missoula, we would have had little sense of how they actually sounded, or what it was like to experience them, because the spaces in which and through which they took place were as important as what the monks did, said, or sang. Little can be said about the rites in the first hundred years or so of the abbey's existence, because the earliest customaries did not address responses to death and the architectural remains from the period are still obscure.[9] Things start getting clearer from the abbacy of Odilo (994–1049), who rebuilt the whole monastic complex except for the main church (known as Cluny II), which his predecessor, Abbot Mayeul, had dedicated in 981.[10] Kenneth Conant's hypothetical drawing of the monastic complex in the last years of Odilo's abbacy shows what it might have looked like to a rider approaching from the northeast. The apse and towers of the main church dominate the view, but the large dormitory building with the chapter house on the ground floor is also clearly visible, as is the small church known as the Lady Chapel (added ca. 1032–33) and Odilo's two-storied infirmary. The monastic cemetery lay just inside the boundary wall and extended from the infirmary to and around the apse of Cluny II.

By the end of Odilo's abbacy, the death rituals took place within a series of contiguous and interconnected spaces—the infirmary, the Lady Chapel, the chapter house, the main church, and the cemetery. The action began in the infirmary, when it looked as if a monk was entering the terminal phase of his life. The dying monk was helped to the chapter house and back, after which the whole community processed from the chapter house through the infirmary cloister for his anointing. If he received the viaticum at the same time, a priest would fetch the sacraments. As long as he lingered, servants and fellow monks would keep vigil at his bedside. When the monk was on the point of death, everyone ran from wherever they were in the enormous complex to gather around and see him through the final agony. After washing and dressing the corpse, a group of the same rank as the deceased would carry it on a bier to the church. After the next High Mass, they would all process together, one last time, to the cemetery for burial.

Odilo's successor, Abbot Hugh (1049–1109), transformed the spaces of the death rituals. In 1088, when he had just begun to lay out the foundations for Cluny III, which would be the largest church in Christendom until the rebuilding of St. Peter's in Rome during the Renaissance, he had already rebuilt and expanded the Lady Chapel and the infirmary, added a small chapel to the cemetery, and expanded the cemetery to over double its previous size. A change he instituted, moreover, consolidated the ritual process even more compactly in space than Odilo had. Bernard tells us that, where the body of a dead monk had previously been taken on its bier first to the Lady Chapel and then to the great church for vigils and mass, Hugh restricted it to the Lady Chapel.[11] Also, while the dead still lay around the apse of Cluny II, Hugh's plans meant that they would no longer do so around the apse of Cluny III.[12] Taken together, these changes suggest that Hugh, while as committed as Odilo to the care of the dying and the dead, had different ideas about where the death rituals should take place. At a time when the community was reaching its greatest size and contact with the world outside the walls was increasing, he may have wished to preserve their intimacy by containing them within the interior space of the monastery where the laity never went. He may also have wanted to separate the purely liturgical services that took place in the main church—the daily offices of the dead and the special masses and psalms sung for individuals after death—from the more physical experiences of dying, handling the corpse, and burial. In any case, once his changes were complete, the sick, the dying, and the dead would never leave the inner confines of the monastic complex bounded by the infirmary, cemetery, Lady Chapel, and chapter house.

Abbot Peter the Venerable (1122–56) oversaw a final layer of expansion. Peter modified Cluniac practices a bit in response to economic realities and the criticisms of the Cistercians, who objected to the use of gold and other luxury objects around the deathbed, but otherwise left them unchanged.[13] He also vigorously defended the commemoration of the dead from the attacks of critics like Peter of Bruys and Henry of Lausanne, who rejected the notion that they were of any benefit to the living or the dead.[14] Abbot Peter rebuilt the infirmary once again, this time as a grand three-storied hall. He also expanded the main cloister through what had been the nave of Cluny II and, apparently, turned the cemetery of the laity, which had occupied a space to the north of the apse of Cluny II for over a century and a half, over to other purposes. I do not know if that spelled the end of lay burials at Cluny. The most complete study of the subject does not cover the period of Peter's abbacy.[15]

What was it like to move through these spaces, to sing in them, to perform the rites for the dying and the dead? Not much is left of the medieval abbey. Only the south tower of the great transept survived the systematic destruction of the great church in the wake of the French revolution.[16] But there is no question that music was central to life, and death, at Cluny. Abbot Odo (927–42), left the text and music to some hymns he wrote as well as a statement of the importance of music at Cluny, which makes clear that it was, in the words of Manuel Pedro Ferreira, "a kind of sanctification, a projection of divine spirituality capable of touching, and moving, the souls of those who were present."[17] The ultimate expression of the Cluniac attitude to music, besides the chant that issued almost unceasingly from the choirs of monks, are the two beautifully carved capitals, which, along with six others, adorned a row of columns defining the ambulatory in the apse of Cluny III, and which are the most important surviving evidence for the decoration of the great church.[18] The two capitals, sculpted in very different styles, each represent four of the ancient musical modes in which ecclesiastical chant was composed. The capital "of the first four tones" is of particular interest. The representation of the third tone (the tonic of the phrygian mode) is of a figure—a layman, not a monk—playing a harp-like instrument, a psaltery or zither. Word play in the inscription that surrounds the figure makes it difficult to interpret. It reads: *tertius impingit Christumque resurgere fingit.* I have never been able to translate this adequately but it is something like "the third tone molds (or fashions an image of) Christ and fastens on (drives/pushes) [him] to resurrect."[19] Whatever it means, it clearly connects this mode with Christ's triumph over death. It may even mean that the Cluniacs believed that music in the phrygian mode participated in some way in the resurrection. The representation of the fourth tone (the tonic of the hypophrygian mode) is even more pertinent to our topic. Once again, it shows a layman, this time carrying a kind of yoke from which bells hang. He is also holding a bell and another hangs from his left arm. His head is bent over the yoke and his expression is sorrowful. The inscription reads: *succedit quartus simulans in carmine planctus* or "the fourth comes next, simulating lamentation in song."[20]

There is no evidence that the Cluniacs used instruments in the death ritual. The customaries mention only singing and the ringing of bells (by which they meant the bells of the church towers if not also ones like those in the sculpture of the fourth tone). But they clearly regarded music as an active force and an agent of great spiritual power. It is no longer possible to know exactly what their singing sounded like, but we can get closer to it in imagination by taking into account that the sacred spaces in which the rituals took place were designed as much for acoustic purposes as anything else. I learned this at first hand on a recent trip to the region. There was no place or opportunity to sing at Cluny when I visited, although I was tempted to let loose in the one remaining section of the great church, the south end of the great transept, whose Romanesque barrel vaults soared 60 feet above my head. Not far away however, at the Romanesque monastery of St. Philibert at Tournus, I got my chance. It was a late spring evening and most tourists had left the church. I was in a small "warming room" to the south of the west end of the church, from which it was possible to enter the cloister. I sang a hymn I had learned at the Chalice of Repose Project in Missoula. The sound of my voice rose up and around the vault, and back down again, almost immediately filling the room in a continuous rolling effect, whose diminishing echoes lingered for some moments after stopping. My voice was not the real instrument; the room was. I had just provided the wind that moved through the space. I thought to myself that the sound of voices singing for the dying or the dead, in the infirmary, the Lady Chapel, or the great churches of Cluny, must have been as impressive as anything heard on the planet at that time.

CLUNIAC DEATH RITUALS IN THEIR PERFORMATIVE CONTEXT

With the foregoing in mind, let us turn to the death ritual itself. Life at Cluny was organized around the daily performance of mass and the divine office, what the monks called "God's work," the *opus dei*. A death disrupted the daily round and created a fundamental tension. The liturgy must still be performed, day and night, but everyone was expected to be present at a monk's death, and to attend to him for some time both before and afterwards, so extraordinary measures were called for. If his agony was prolonged, for example, the monk who rang the hours would look in on the dying man before calling the monks to choir for the divine office, making adjustments if necessary so that they would not unnecessarily coincide.[21] After a monk died, the living shared with the recently deceased the liminal status of being outside normal time. Ulrich writes that "for as long as [a monk] lies unburied nothing may be done in the cloister, not talking or anything else, except psalms, until the funeral is over" and Bernard adds that no one may leave the monastery at any time during that period.[22] Throughout the ritual process, but especially while the community was shut off from the outside world, the monastery became a single performance space where everyone concentrated on the fate of the protagonist. They would continue to do so until his body was laid to rest and his soul was well on its way to the other world.

A dying monk himself initiated the ritual process. "Sensing the approach of death," he asked the prior or abbot to hear his confession. Then two brothers helped him walk along the arcade leading past the Lady Chapel to the chapter house, for a rite of mutual confession and absolution with the whole community. Bernard and Ulrich do not say much about this ceremony. Ulrich says only that the dying man forgave the brothers for their sins against him, and they did the same, after which the prior granted absolution. Bernard adds only that, at the end, "all bow deeply from their seats."[23] It is not clear exactly what he meant, but his remark indicates the importance of ritual bows and prostrations at Cluny, which gave every meeting and leave-taking a performative aspect.[24] But this first act of the ritual process set the tone for everything that follows. A successful passing depended on the clean separation of body and soul from this world. No untold sin and no ill will toward anyone would be allowed to distract the dying man or the community from successfully completing the work at hand.

The next act took place in the infirmary, where anointing with holy oil clarified the dying monk's body and senses just as the mutual confession and absolution had clarified his relations with the community. After helping him back to the infirmary, his companions laid him in a bed placed so that the congregation could gather in a circle around him. Carrying holy water and oil for the anointing and accompanied by others carrying a cross and two candlesticks, a priest then led the community in procession from the chapter house to the infirmary. There he prayed God that the dying monk be granted forgiveness for his sins and be worthy of entering into eternal life. He then anointed him seven times—on the eyes, ears, lips, nose, hands, feet, and groin—as the congregation chanted the seven penitential psalms, with antiphons.[25]

An antiphon is a line or two of chant that precedes the singing of a psalm and, in a sense, introduces it. Drawn from the psalm itself or from another scriptural text, antiphons offer many possibilities for adding to the musical and performative aspects of the liturgy. The antiphons that introduced the seven penitential psalms during the anointing of the dying at Cluny exhibit a particularly subtle artistry. While two of them appear in anointing rituals from the ninth century on and the rest turn up in various settings in high and late medieval manuscripts, their use as a group for this occasion appears to be unique. They comprised, in effect, a dramatic accompaniment to the ritual action.

The first antiphon is freely adapted from lines three to five of psalm six, the first of the seven penitential psalms, which it introduces, and strikes the central theme: "Heal me, Lord, for my bones are troubled and my soul is troubled exceedingly; but turn, Lord, and deliver my soul." The second introduces a narrative from the Gospel of John (4:46–47): "There was an official whose son was ill at Capernaum. When he heard that Jesus had come to Galilee, he asked him to heal his son." The third draws first-person dialogue from the different, yet similar, story of the centurion in Matthew (8:6–7): "Lord, my servant is lying paralyzed at home, in terrible distress" they sang; followed by Jesus' words "Amen I say to you, I will come and heal him." The gospel stories refer to physical cures and the return of health, but the place of the anointing within the death ritual at Cluny, as a preparation for the agony and *transitus*, makes it clear that the cure sought at this time was of the soul, not of the body. The fourth antiphon, which is freely adapted from verses three and nineteen of psalm 50, which it introduces, is presented as the voice of the dying monk: "Do not despise a contrite and humbled heart, O God, but according to thy great mercy, have mercy on me." The fifth antiphon goes back to John (4:49–50, 53) for the completion of the scene: " 'Lord, come down and heal my son before he dies.' Jesus said to him, 'Go, your son lives'; and he himself believed and all his household." The sixth returns to Matthew (8:8) for the famous words of the centurion, "Lord, I am not worthy to have you come under my roof; but only say the word and my servant will be healed." The final antiphon is a passage from Luke (4:40), which, even in its imagery, suggests the ending of a drama: "Now when the sun was setting, all those who had any that were sick with various diseases brought them to Jesus, and they were cured." Although the story in John clearly concerns the centurion's son (*filius*) and the Latin term *puer* in Matthew is translated as "servant" in English renderings, a better translation here (and in the previous citation from Matthew) would be "but only say the word and my son will be healed," since the dramatic action is clearly meant to be unified and continuous. As the priest performed the seven anointings, and the congregation sang psalms of penitence, the monks of Cluny used antiphons to weave two different Gospel stories into a single narrative about the healing power of Jesus.

At the completion of the anointing ritual, the congregation left the infirmary, some staying on to keep watch over the dying man, day and night, while a brother sang the hours to him and read from the accounts of the Passion of Christ. When his death seemed imminent, the most important part of the ritual began. As Ulrich writes, "infirmary servants who are well trained and highly skilled in such matters, after seeing that the hour of his departure is at hand, spread a hair shirt out, sprinkle ashes on it from above, raise the sick man from his bed, and lower him onto it." Bernard adds that the ashes were sprinkled in the shape of a cross.[26] Then, one of the servants struck a wooden tablet against the door of the cloister over and over. According to Ulrich, "because this sound means that someone may be about to die, all the brothers run to the infirmary immediately upon hearing it." The only other time that they were allowed to run was in case of a fire. As they ran, the monks chanted the *Credo* over and over "so that brotherly faith will bring aid to the one about to make his departure," writes Ulrich. The chanting of the *Credo* while gathering at the bedside of a dying monk seems to have been a specifically Cluniac innovation. It was also one of the most successful, showing up in customaries and ritual books for the rest of the Middle Ages.[27]

Once assembled in a circle around the dying man, they began to chant a litany. Starting with the throne of heaven itself, they worked their way downward, calling on God the father, the son, and the Holy Spirit; then on Mary, the archangels, the patriarchs and the prophets; and finally on John the Baptist, the apostles, and all the holy martyrs and confessors. They beseeched each in turn to pray for the dying man. Ideally, his death would occur with the attention of all the heavenly hosts focused on him. Once he had died, servants rang the bells of the church. Most of the monks then left the infirmary, reassembling in the choir of the Lady Chapel to sing Vespers and Matins of the Dead. In the meantime, others prepared his body for burial. After washing it and sewing it into a shroud made from the monastic habit, they carried it to the main church or the Lady Chapel, and set it on a stand near the altar.

Except during mass or the divine office, some of the congregation remain by the bier continually chanting psalms until the burial; prayer, either spoken or sung, surrounded the monk's physical remains at all times. After supper and Compline, the congregation began a long night of vigils. Dividing the night into three parts, the right choir kept the first watch, the left the second, and the boys and their masters the last, after morning Matins. Each group sang a third of the psalter (50 psalms). The next day, after Prime and Terce, they sang the morning mass in his name. "Everyone should be there," says Ulrich, "so that they can offer it for him."

The procession to the cemetery began after Sext and High Mass. Attendants passed candles out to everyone. Then, as the procession moved toward the cemetery, all the bells began to ring and the community intoned psalm 113, *In exitu Israhel*, which calls to mind the exodus of the Israelites from Egypt. With the beautiful antiphon that introduced it, *In paradisum deducant te angeli*, "May angels lead you into paradise," this psalm had been sung at funeral processions since the beginnings of Christian ritual practice in the Latin Church.[28] As a pair, the antiphon and psalm express confident expectation that God will lead the soul of the dead man out of captivity in this world and into the Promised Land. The procession with the body from church to grave symbolized the soul's journey from this world to the next, for the congregation that accompanied the body on earth also symbolized the heavenly hosts who would lead the dead monk's soul into paradise.

Ulrich says that the monks formed a circle around the gravesite, while Bernard suggests that they recreated their position in the choir as if they were inside the church.[29] As they sang psalms from the office of the dead, the priest blessed the grave and the pallbearers lowered the bier down into it. The priest then censed the body, sprinkled holy water onto it, and after tossing a handful of dirt down into the grave, said the prayers that ended the ceremony. When the psalmody ended, and the priest turned away from the grave, the candles were extinguished, and the bells, which had been ringing continuously since the procession set out for the cemetery, stopped. The community returned in procession to the church, chanting the penitential psalms, which they finished prostrate before the altar. The gates of the monastery reopened at last. Commemorative services of masses and psalms, plus gifts of food and clothing for the poor, would begin immediately and continue for some time—intensely at first, and then diminishing over time, like echoes of a chant, until the dead monk became no more than a name among the thousands in the great necrology—but the main performance was over.[30]

Cluniac death rituals in the High Middle Ages were a peculiar expression of centuries of development in the Latin liturgy. In general, they represent the rite of passage that had evolved in Western Christendom to ease the transition between this world and the next, which filled out the tripartite structure of all such rites with the specifics of medieval theology and spiritual anthropology. In the highly controlled environment of Cluniac monasticism, the Latin death rituals reached their most elaborate form. In a community of as many as three hundred monks, the death of any one of them engaged them all. They prepared the dying in body and soul. They aided them during their agony and death. They accompanied their remains until they were safely laid to rest and their souls, as well, until they had been duly incorporated into the ranks of the faithful departed. They spoke to and with the dying. They spoke to God for them. They sang to them, and for them, in spaces designed for maximum acoustic effect. And they did all this upon multiple stages—infirmary, chapter house, chapel, and cemetery—moving between them in formal processions, and playing and replaying the cosmic drama of salvation in the individual drama of each soul's passing.

Commentary: No Time for Dying

Edward H. Thompson, Jr.

> *To every thing there is a season, and a time for every purpose under heaven:*
> *A time to be born and a time to die.*
>
> *Ecclesiastes 3:1*

The secularization of life has gradually stripped away the authority of religious interpretation and charged other social institutions with the responsibility to define a good life. This social transformation has been discussed by many, but few have addressed the secularization of death. It is not fashionable. Dying and death trigger avoidance in societies founded within the Protestant ethos and on the belief that to die is to have not fought hard enough to live.[1] Right now, people living in Western cultures practically deny all aspects of dying and death. From euphemisms like "life insurance" instead of "death award," to obituaries buried on back pages and not mentioning the cause of death, to hospices and palliative care settings hiding the dying from sight, to the craft of funeral directors masking the body with cosmetics to seem more lifelike and then artfully directing the wake and burial as if it was live theatre, to small, flat, concealed headstones replacing older slate and marble orchard cemeteries; death has been nearly banished from the ordinary and everyday aspects of people's lives. Not witnessed firsthand, not discussed, and certainly not understood, dying and death have become frightening yet more rationally acknowledged.

By contrast, when dying and death remain integrated within a faith tradition, they can be understood to be ordinary events, even part of a divine plan. Dying is normalized. Whether framed by medieval Christianity, Shinto traditions in Japan, or the Navajo's way of life, the taken-for-granted perspective of many faith traditions makes dying and death a stage in a process that continues to the afterlife. This commonplace acceptance of dying and death as a "natural" stage in a long life course that continues in an afterlife is what has been displaced; in our modern, secularized world bereft of ultimate meaning, and in which the belief in an afterlife no longer provides solace,[2] our community's dying rituals have become organized by a medical-legal rationality. The importance of leave-taking rituals in facing death and facing death communally as a passage has been replaced. Dying and death have been given over to professionals to manage, partly because people expect medicine to intervene to conquer death and to prolong life, and because most people are relieved to have family members' dying supervised in a hospital setting.[3] This brief essay is designed to review this unoriginal observation and argues that there is a marked similarity in the *function* of the Benedictine monastery's death performances during the Middle Ages and European Americans' elaborately orchestrated time for dying in modern hospitals, nursing homes, and hospices.

IMAGES OF DEATH

Every culture has a mythology, the repertoire of stories about what it means to be human; it has its own image of death, and the image is intimately bound to the prevailing concepts of (spiritual and bodily) health. Constructed by the dominant social institutions and ever-present myths, the meaning of death reflects the soul of the community, and with membership in a community generally comes acceptance of its death system and rituals. Our own contemporary image of death as failed health has deep roots that both precede and evolve from the "natural death" interpretation that the medieval Benedictine monks took for granted.

Aries[4] and Illich suggest that distinct stages mark the historical development of Western culture's contemporary image of death. The initial stage was made evident with the emergence of Christianity as a cultural force. From the fourth century onward, the Church resisted an old pagan "dance of the dead" tradition in which (naked) crowds danced on tombs affirming the joy of being alive. The devotional dance with dead ancestors was "an encounter between the living and those who were already dead,"[5] likely carried over from deep-seated pagan myths that the bones of the dead were the resting places of holy spirits, and dust of their graves warded off or cured sickness.[6] Likened to a seed, in these agricultural communities death was taken as a transformation that involved going down into the darkness and rebirth. Dancing with the dead was experienced as an occasion for the renewal of life, and as Illich noted, for a thousand years cemeteries and, as often, Church floors were ritual dance floors, despite the frequency of ecclesiastical prohibitions. The "dance of the dead" era conceived death as the result of an outside agent—a witch, enemy, or murderous ancestor, for example. And the ceremony of dancing on tombs seems to have served as a primitive form of preventive medicine as much as a pagan and early Christian spiritual tradition.

By the fourteenth century, the Church had acquired enough cultural capital and resources to establish Christian doctrine as the moral code, as well as institutions devoted to caring for the poor, sick and dying members of the congregation. Most healers were in religious orders. Bodies were envisioned as the vehicles of a soul, and death was regarded as the personal intervention of God to reclaim the soul. The prior understanding of death as a malevolent intervention is replaced with a thesis that death is sovereign, a natural bodily outcome coexisting with an immortal soul. Death marked the end of biological life and the beginning of an eternity in heaven or hell. Monastic infirmaries and hostels became the chosen providers of medical and spiritual care, reflective of the dual missions the monasteries had assumed. Portrayed by the hourglass, death defines a transition point for the soul, not an ending. This newer understanding of death is what frames Paxton's review of the death rituals of the Benedictine monks at Cluny. The entire monastery "became a single performance space" for the monks' death rituals to assure a "clean separation of body and soul from this world".

The next distinct image of death in Western culture appears with the emergence of a bourgeois class, and bears the distinction "bourgeois death." The class equality in mortality that characterized most of the Middle Ages came to an end as those who could pay physicians to keep death away did so. This made dying a private matter, something negotiable with a healer. Privilege allowed greater numbers of people to negotiate a time for dying by using a physician as a death-delayer. The prolongation of life by those who could afford it reframed the meaning of death into "timely" versus "untimely," and efforts to prolong life marks the beginning of our medicalization of death.

The meaning of death was modestly transformed again in the nineteenth and twentieth centuries, this time into an "unnatural" loss of life. Physicians, hospitals, and public health officials were expected to excise all determinants of death, and using every therapy available, untimely and preventable deaths were to be stopped. This effort to postpone death was quite successful: A century ago, just 4 percent of the U.S. population was aged sixty-five and over. And what became new was the concentrated medicalization of all stages of life, from birth to death bed. Postponing death, a secular type of salvation, was promised by the medical enterprise.[7] Death no longer was an event to be accepted; it became an unnatural outcome, even for the old. Now discussed as one or multiple biological system "failures" by the attending physician when the case is presented in the following morning's clinical rounds, the meaning of death has become sterilized of its social and spiritual connections.

Managing the Time for Dying

Ironically, most North Americans believe in life after death and the worthiness of spiritual interventions as they approach their death.[8] Thus we have a conundrum. As hospitals and physicians became responsible for all those who were critically ill and dying, their practices imposed on society a place for dying and form of dying that ignores the social and spiritual needs of the sick and dying.[9] The practice of medicine ritualized care in ways that ignore the comfort and spiritual work evident among Benedictine monks' caregiving and death performances.[10] As much as hospitals obscure the meaningfulness of a deathbed vigil,[11] and commercial nursing *homes* and funeral *homes* strip away the importance of the private time customs of long gatherings of relatives and friends to say farewell;[12] in postmodern Western cultures, most people choose to be not intimately connected to death and the dying. People prefer minimal involvement in death rites and choose to relegate the death to experts—to the hospital staff at the last stages of life, to the mortician, and to memorial services or the church to organize a funeral ritual.

Deaths are, nevertheless, jarring—to the professional caregiving staff, their dying patients and the significant others, as well as to the Benedictine monks. Deaths require "time work." Because the scene of dying has shifted to custodial care hospitals and nursing homes, death in an institution is now prevalent. And it is routinized. In contemporary America, the death bed scene has all but been eliminated. Relatives are infrequently present when death occurs, and hardly ever request to see the corpse before it is removed to the funeral home. Hospitals and nursing homes have constructed elaborate strategies to manage the time for dying and patients' dying trajectories. Last hours in an institution center on the staff's "empty" time that a death watch entails, and the caregiving staff prefers not to be present at death and having to face an unpleasant "last look". The provision of religious ceremonies is more or less standardized; as the dying person nears death, it is the timing of when to call a chaplain of the correct faith that demands attention. The call may be too late or too early; either is an error that upsets rhythms. Special announcement rituals, not unlike the clapping of boards or ringing of bells in Middle Age monasteries, also are needed during the death watch and immediately after the death to "usher" family and friends on the premises who want to take their "last look" prior to and after the death. Requests for post-death looks are problematic, because they prolong the corpse's presence and thwart reinstating order in staff's work schedules.

In Middle Age monasteries, dying brethren and their deaths were equally disruptive. As Paxton's summary of the rituals within the Benedictine monastery revealed, when death became imminent the whole monastic community was summoned. The monks congregated around their dying brethren to use prayer and song to " 'unbind' the pain and provide the departing with spiritual nourishment for the journey to the beyond."[13] This involved death watch that went uninterrupted until the death, which meant everyday life in the monastery came to a standstill. After the death rites—when the corpse was wrapped in a shroud, the dead brethren prayed for again, and burial in the monastic cemetery after an elaborate funeral ceremony—the sentimental order of the Benedictines' ascetic lifestyle that had been suspended was reinstated by including the dead in all intercessionary prayers. Thus, ironically similar to American hospitals and nursing homes, the function of the dying and death rituals was to bond together the work community of brethren.

The differences are manifest. The monks attended to the dying monk's spiritual and bodily needs and their own subjective experience in a communal manner. As Risse summarized, "One of the most important functions of the Benedictine monastery was the preparation for death, involving sick brethren who failed to recover."[14] Today, we have made no time or space for dying in our lives. Existing dying rituals and funeral rites cut off the dying and their significant others from being able to manage with (sacred) ceremonies the existential concerns that arise in the face of death. Yet existential concerns do arise. According to one contemporary philosopher:

> Death is the rock upon which all systems shipwreck. It is the unknowable. It is the question for which there is no answer, and the one we've been looking for most of all. It is the great, primal mythic question, the great terror.[15]

My reading of Paxton suggests to me that since the time of the Middle Age monasteries, the pendulum has swung nearly the full extent of its arc away from how monks integrated death into everyday life. The institutionalized ways in which death is denied certainly maintain medicine as the authoritative social institution and support our postmodern way of life. But they ignore the communal and spiritual significance of someone dying. Are we at a turning point in our culture's organization of dying and death? Are we ready to make time and space for the dying?

Marginal Bodies: Liturgical Structures of Pain and Deliverance in the Middle Ages

Joanne M. Pierce

INTRODUCTION

From the first century, Christianity has stressed the importance of the body and of the physical elements of creation in its theology of salvation. As time went on, this stress moved in paradoxical directions simultaneously: a sense of asceticism with an emphasis on control of the body and its "misleading" appetites, out of control as a result of what would be defined as original sin (influenced by forms of Hellenistic dualism); combined with an insistence on the physical resurrection of the body and the essential capacity of the physical word to mediate the presence of the divine (rooted in the initial Christian experience of the Incarnation). Additional "world-view" elements are added to the praxis of Christianity in the west as its practitioners reflect on their lived experience, and as Christianity spread out of the Mediterranean basin north of the Alps: what has been called the "rediscovery" of the Old Testament and the reintroduction of reflection on the scriptures and practice of the Old Testament and their influence on Christian life in late antiquity and the early Middle Ages; and the impact of the non-Hellenistic "world views" of the Northern European peoples on their adoption and lived experience of Christianity.

The purpose of this chapter is to use the texts of two early medieval liturgies as lenses through which to shed light on early medieval theologies of the body and "physicality" in western Christian liturgy. These are the rite for the "churching," or purification/blessing of women after childbirth; and the rites for the trials by ordeal, specifically, the trials by hot iron and cold water. Both of these rituals focus on the body, and the use of physical elements as mediatorial elements of God's presence with and self-communication to human beings.

The rites for trial by ordeal are unfamiliar ones to the twenty-first century Catholic, since the church's involvement in trial by ordeal was officially ended by the legislation of the Fourth Lateran Council (1215).[1] The rites for the churching of women after childbirth, later renamed in the Catholic church as the Blessing of Women after Childbirth, gradually fell into disuse during the course of the twentieth century (as a last vestige in the United States, the Catholic custom held that the mother did not attend the baptism of her new baby). Since the Second Vatican Council (1962–65), the rite has been reformulated into a blessing of the parents at the child's baptism, as well as a series of parental and family blessings after the birth or adoption of a child, found in the Book of Blessings.[2]

TEXTS

For this discussion, the prayer tests of both the churching and ordeal *ordines* will be taken from an Austrian ritual book dating form the first half of the twelfth century: the Ritual of St. Florian.[3] Prepared for the community of Augustinian canons at the monastery of St. Florian (near Linz), it contains at least some prayer material dating from the tenth and eleventh centuries, and follows the same organizational plan as other regional rituals and pontificals compiled during the same period.

CHURCHING

The ordo for the "churching" of women after childbirth is usually given a variation of the title "The Introduction of a Woman into Church after Childbirth" in medieval manuscripts.[4] Only in a few is the rite referred to as a "Purification." However, purification is one of the theological themes expressed in these early texts of the rite, as well as those of thanksgiving, blessing, penitence, and celebration. A full history of the rite is yet to be written,[5] but it does seem clear that one element in its institution is the ritual reappropriation of the Old Testament, both in terms of allegory as well as real or attributed roots of some Christian ritual practice. Here, the key text is Lev 12:2–5; which ascribes 40 days of ritual impurity to a new mother after the birth of a male, and 80 days after the birth of a female. This kind of ritual impurity has been described as "physical impurity," akin to menstruation or nocturnal emissions, rather than the more serious "moral impurity." The purification ablutions and/or offerings are "mechanical" and free from the "stigma" that a moral offense would carry.[6]

Already in the mid-fourth century, we find echoes of this text reincorporated into the liturgical life of at least one Christian community. In the Egyptian church order *The Canons of Hippolytus* (ca. 340 CE), new mothers are at one point directed to stay outside of the church for 40 days if the baby is male, 80 days if the baby is female; however, it seems that some women did attend church during that time, for the text continues "If she enters the church, she is to pray with the catechumens."[7] Traditionally, catechumens were viewed as members of the community whose prayer had not been fully purified by baptism; interestingly, midwives, too, were expected to sit with them. Other texts from late antiquity and the early Middle Ages offer contradictory evidence on this physical impurity and restrictions on the new mother returning to church, although Gregory the Great (d. 604) in his letters to Augustine of Canterbury is very clear that the Leviticus text is to be taken allegorically, and if "a woman [were] to enter church and return thanks the very hour of her delivery, she would do nothing wrong" since (unlike the pleasure of sex) childbirth is not a sin, although the pain associated with it is understood as the penalty imposed on Eve from God.[8]

The actual churching rite in the Florian ritual, as in some other medieval liturgical books, is preceded by a short *ordo* entitled *Benedictio mulieris post partum*, or "Blessing of a woman [immediately] after childbirth."[9] This rite is actually somewhat longer than the more "formal" churching rite that follows, and sheds additional light on the themes of the body and deliverance under discussion here. Note the illustration (f. 76v) in the contemporary Austrian ritual from the Benedictine monastery of Lambach,[10] published in the Franz edition of the St. Florian ritual: A priest and an acolyte stand at the foot of the bed, in which the new mother reclines. In the foreground, the baby lies in a small crib, attended by another woman, presumably the midwife.[11]

The rite begins with a short set of psalm versicles, with the themes of calling for God's assistance in the face of trial, as well as the theme of praising God: Psalms 112/13 (*Laudate pueri*) and 127/8 (*Beati omnes*), followed by the Lord's prayer and other single psalm versicles.[12] A first short collect follows, requesting that God lead this "your servant" (*famulam tuam*) to freedom and give her health. As in many individual medieval rites, the Prologue of the Gospel of John is then read, followed by yet another prayer addressed to God "who commands life and death and who is the physician of souls."

The rite is closed by a short blessing of the woman herself. The invocation asks that the Lord might cleanse her from all impurities of body by a heavenly (or celestial) blessing in the name of the Father and the Son and the Holy Spirit. Here we see the theme of bodily impurity explicitly raised, perhaps not so surprising given the pain and, most importantly, the shedding of blood at the childbirth that had just taken place in this same chamber.[13]

The prayer texts from the Florian ritual book used during the churching rite emphasize some of these same theological themes.[14] Other contemporary texts begin with rubrics noting that the woman, holding a lighted candle, is met by the priest and an acolyte at the door of the church, for example, the Lambach ritual.[15] After introductory verses, the priest is directed to take her by the right hand and literally lead her into the church (usually up to or near the altar). This rite does not contain these rubrics, but begins with two psalms, the penitential Psalm 50/1 (*Miserere mei*) and Psalm 120/1 (*Levavi oculos*), both requesting mercy and help from God.[16] These are followed by a brief series of short versicles,[17] all connected by the themes of blessing, protection, and thanksgiving and reinforced in this specific context by diverse references to children, grandchildren, as well as divine guardianship of one's "coming in and going out." The first following prayer text makes another scriptural reference: to the incarnation of the Son and the presentation of Jesus in the temple (Lk 2:22–38). The prayer goes on to request the purification of the new mother's feelings or thoughts (*mentibus*) as she is herself presented to God.[18] The wording seems to have been suggested by the wording of the second prayer, a collect seen frequently in medieval liturgy: the *Aufer a nobis*.[19] The text reads:

> Take away from us our sins, O Lord, we beseech You, that we may enter with pure minds into the Holy of Holies.[20]

This prayer again requests that the Lord remove "our" sins that we might merit to enter "the holy of holies" with "pure minds" or feelings (*mentibus*). Once more, note the combination of spiritual purification with the theme of entering into a holy place, here, the church building. A final psalm versicle also refers to the believer's reliance on God's help.[21]

Observations

Taken together as two ritual "moments" marking childbirth in the early Middle Ages, these *ordines* provide a perspective on at least the "official" and "public" understandings of the theology and meaning of this important event.[22] Thanksgiving for deliverance and acknowledgement of God's help are evident in both. However, the blessing rite in the birth chamber adds additional elements: a stress on the woman's physical health as part of this deliverance, and an explicit statement on her physical "impurities" (although these are not listed by name). The churching rite, which would take place 30 to 40 days later, does not refer to physical purification, but instead moves to a stress on spiritual purification for a re-entrance into the holy place, the church building itself. It is important to note that this theme in the *Aufer a nobis* prayer would be repeated by the priest on his own behalf every time he began the celebration of Mass. Intertwined with this is a thread of thanksgiving to the Lord for his help, and a sense of joy in the birth of the child, perhaps seen most clearly in the versicles.

TRIALS BY ORDEAL

Various trials by ordeal were in use during the early centuries of the western Middle Ages; all seem to have been used as a kind of "court of last resort," in the case of accusations founded on little, if any, corroborating evidence (e.g. adultery). The origins appear to have Germanic roots, although there are some Old Testament parallels as well (e.g. Gideon's fleece).[23] These liturgical trials by ordeal were usually prefaced by an intense period of preparation by the accused: separation from family and friends, fasting, and a solitary vigil the night before.[24]

There have been a variety of studies done on their history and meaning. While, for example, some have interpreted the ordeal rites as a form of "psychological bombardment,"[25] one of the most recent pieces provides a compelling argument that their apparent brutality in modern eyes obscures what may in fact have been the original intention of recourse to these trials "of last resort": a preference for (or even bias toward) the vindication of those accused without significant substantiation.[26] With these differing views of "deliverance" in mind, I would like to examine two of the most "physical" trials: the trial by hot iron, and the trial by cold water.[27]

Hot Iron

The trial by hot iron involved an important physical test of innocence.[28] The one-to-three pound piece of iron used in these trials was set aside for this ritual; one text describes how an eleventh-century abbot was compelled to request another trial iron form the local bishop after a monk of the monastery had used theirs for a "profane use."[29] The accused would be required to hold[30] this "sacred" hot iron that had been ritually blessed and heated for a specific length of time, for example, the time it took for the presiding priest to say mass before the trial took place.[31] The hand would then be bound, and examined after a period of days (often three days) for evidence of pus, damaged flesh, or any evidence of a lasting wound. A wounded hand was evidence of guilt; an undamaged hand, of innocence.

The Florian ordo demonstrates how seriously the rite was taken.[32] First comes the celebration of Mass. The priest is directed to vest fully for Mass, and meet the accused in the atrium of the church with, among other holy objects, the gospel book and the relics of the patron saints (*patrocinia sanctorum*).[33] The first blessing is that of the place itself, since it will be the locus for the manifestation of the truth and God's judgment. Then Mass begins, with a reading from Isaiah (Is 55:6–7: seek the Lord while he may be found; let the wicked man forsake his way; the Lord will have compassion on him) and a reading from the gospel of Mark (Mk 11:22–5: have faith; mountain remove itself to the sea; forgive others and your father in heaven will forgive your sins). The offertory verse is Ps 129/130, the *De profundis* (often associated with funerals; here, a cry for help from God). At communion, the accused is addressed directly by the priest, and warned not to approach the altar or communicate if he or she (or they) "have done or consented or have knowledge what has been done." Then the accused is given communion (under the species of both bread and wine) with these words: "May the body and blood of our Lord Jesus Christ be to you today *ad comprobationem*."[34]

At the end of mass, the priest and the accused go to the place of the trial, and the accused is sprinkled with holy water, and a formula similar to the communion formula is recited: "May this water be to you today *ad comprobationem*." Next, the iron itself is blessed, first with a trinitarian invocation, and then with a prayer containing several scriptural references to the use of fire by God: Moses and the burning bush (Ex 3); the column of fire preceding the people of Israel (Ex 13:21–2); and the fire of the Holy Spirit kindled in the hearts of the Apostles (i.e. at Pentecost; Acts 2). A second blessing of the iron follows, immediately before it is placed in the fire. Though there are no rubrics to indicate it, one can infer that the iron was placed in the fire at that time. As it heats, several prayers are recited: the seven penitential psalms, the Our Father, versicles, the Credo, three more psalms, and the *Gloria patri*. A series of six more prayer texts follows (petitioning God's just judgment in the case). Finally the accused is exorcised with a prayer text including two more scriptural references: the three young men in the fiery furnace (Dan 3:19–26), and Susanna falsely accused (Dan 13). The Prologue of the Gospel of John is read (John 1:1–18), and the last text is the final blessing of the now-heated iron, commending that it might discern in the accused "the true and just judgment of God."

Cold Water

The trial by cold water also depended on an interpretation of God's judgment through an intervention with a certain twist of nature. The accused would be bound hand and foot, often bent over a wooden staff inscribed with psalm verses, and dropped into a pond, river, or other location providing cold water.[35] Here, if the accused sank, his[36] innocence would be demonstrated; if the accused floated, then guilt. The reasoning here is that the water would "reject" a guilty person, and not "receive" him into its depths; thus, in some medieval commentaries, presumably acting against its "nature" as understood by society and the church.[37]

In the Florian ritual book, the prayer texts for this rite stress the themes of the physicality of water, and its "creaturely" obedience and submission to *God*.[38] The ordo itself strikes the reader as more formal; it is lengthy and includes a series of substantial prayer texts for the "swearing in" (*adiuratio*) and blessing of the water. As in the other rites, this one begins with a series of versicles and responses, followed by a triple *Gloria patri*, the *Kyrie eleison*, and a formidable litany of the saints,[39] among them the falsely accused Susanna mentioned in the hot iron rite above. Three psalms are then recited (Ps 28/29, *Afferte Domino*; Ps 67/68, *Exurgat*, and Ps 9, *Mirabilia*), and the triple *Gloria patri* is repeated.

The first prayer is the same prayer text as the last of the six (read as the iron heated) in the trial by hot iron,[40] and is followed by another admonition to the water. Here, the nature of water as a creature of God is stressed, with many scriptural examples (not, however, in strict order of the books of the Bible) of how water has obeyed God in the past, or has acted as God's agent, for example. Christ's walking on water (Mt 14:22–33; Mk 6:45–52; John 6:16–21), his baptism in water (Mt 3:13–17; Mk 1:9–11; Lk 3:21–2; John 1:29–34), and the division of the waters for the people of Israel at the Red Sea (Ex 14:15–29). The water is then warned about judging the accused justly (or his representative/proxy[41]), not considering guilt of any other sin, but only of this crime.[42] A second "abjuring" of water follows, composed on a similar pattern: scriptural "reminders" of water's past obedience to the Lord, for example, the cleansing of the world in the Flood and the sparing of Noah (Gen 6–8); Israel walking through the Red Sea (Ex 14) and being provided water from the rock (Ex 17:1–7); Christ's changing of water into wine (John 2:1–11) and the water and blood that poured from his side at the crucifixion (John 19:34); and the role of water mixed in with communion wine; and a warning to the water to reject the accused if guilty. A third text takes baptism as its theme: the water that baptized Christ and all Christians is now commanded to reject the accused just as it had accepted him at his own baptism. However, the water is then commanded to accept (i.e. let sink) the accused if he is innocent in the face of any demonic forces by the merits of John the Baptist.

Next comes a series of blessing prayers for the water. Four are unique to this ordo; the last two also appear in the ordo for hot iron. Again, the Prologue from the Gospel of John is read, and a consecration formula parallel to that for the hot iron accompanied by a short but interesting blessing close this section of the ordo: *Benedictio dei patris et filii et spiritus sancti descendat et maneat super hanc fluentem aquam ad discernendum in ea uerum iudicium dei* (the true judgment of God).

The final text in this ordo is addressed to the accused himself. It takes the form of another *adiuratio*, and stresses the witness and intervention of numerous scriptural figures, a kind of prose recapitulation of the litany of the saints earlier in the rite. Many figures are invoked: Christ, the Trinity, angels, archangels, all saints; the Day of Judgment itself; the 24 elders (Rev 4:4); the four evangelists, the twelve apostles and twelve prophets; all the saints (again), martyrs, confessors, virgins; principalities, powers, dominations, virtues, thrones, cherubim, seraphim, all the "hidden heavens" (cf. Col 1:16); Shadrach, Meshah, and Abdengo (Dan 3:19–26); the 144 thousand (Rev 7:4); Mary, all the "holy people of God," and lastly, "through that baptism which the priest of God requested over you." The final phrases are a warning to the accused: that if he is guilty in any way of the crime,[43] the water will not accept him nor will any "misdeed" prevail against its rejection of him. The prayer closes with a short doxology addressed to Christ.

Observations

The theme of deliverance runs through all of these very physical, though very different, *ordines*. However, this concept of deliverance accents this physicality in various ways. This is clear in a careful consideration of the ordeal rites.

The liturgies for the trials, like those for childbirth, focus on the split, as well as the connection, between body and soul. However, this corporal/spiritual distinction is not limited to the human body, but also extends to wider creation as well; here, the physical elements of iron and water are viewed, really expected, to function in obedience as spiritual instruments of God their Creator. The ritual piece of iron is addressed in the third person, and is in a real way put under oath to give evidence justly and correctly. It is reminded of the ways that God has used it (i.e. fire and iron) to reveal Godself in the scriptures, and these reminders are intended to prompt the heated iron to present-day obedience. It is commanded to refrain from producing its usual physical injury (according to its physical nature) in the case of an innocent man or woman as testimony to the injustice of the accusation levied against him or her.

The water is treated in an even more solemn fashion. The formality of this rite is enhanced by the opening with the litany of the saints, traditionally used on major liturgical occasions. The water is addressed several times, and reminded of several scriptural occasions on which God has made use of this important elemental creature. Perhaps the crucial difference between the water and the fire is the use of water as a sacramental/salvific element: it purifies (the Flood), sustains physical life (water from the rock), and is a special servant of Christ (walks on water, changes it into wine). For Christians, it serves as a conduit of salvation in both baptism and in the eucharist (water is mixed with wine at the beginning of the eucharistic rite, paralleling both the water and blood that flows from the side of Christ at the crucifixion, as well as the mixture of human and divine that took place at his incarnation). Thus, not only is it a creature of God and obedient to his will, but water serves even more fully as a means of a sacramental/incarnational mediation between God and humanity than does the hot iron. In addition, note the striking difference in the results expected from the water: unlike the iron, water is expected to act against its then-expected physical nature to demonstrate guilt, not innocence. Since the sinking into water indicates its "acceptance," and since that acceptance has already taken place once at the accused's baptism, the guilty man will be "rejected" by the water by floating.

CONCLUSION

These early medieval rites for childbirth and trial by ordeal clearly show a number of intricate levels of physicality in their various expressions of deliverance: from the pain of childbirth, and through pain, to vindication (or condemnation). The interaction between notions of physical and spiritual purity and innocence is evident in a close examination of the contents of these *ordines*; however, the theological themes expressed in these rites show a "thick" texture that belies what might seem to be an easy initial reading. Purification is not the only, or even the major, focus of the childbirth rites, although requests for bodily and spiritual purity are explicitly mentioned in the texts. And the trial liturgies, especially the *ordo* for the trial by cold water, express more than a request for a manifestation of God's judgment through a painful ordeal. They are themselves based on a more profound understanding of God's intimate connection with the elements of nature (rooted in scripture), and a creation/incarnation/sacrament continuum, most evident in the formal and detailed rite for cold water. Again, the theme of deliverance runs throughout these texts; most seem to express a preference (implicit or explicit) for the vindication of the accused, rather than confirmation of guilt.

These early medieval rites seem at first glance to be completely out of synch with the lived Catholicism of the early twenty-first century. No one would argue for an ahistorical reinsertion of these twelfth-century structures in today's Catholic life. However, a close examination of the theological themes that are expressed in the scriptural and prayer texts do provide a fresh and perhaps unexpected perspective on issues that are of concern to Catholics, and other Christians, today. Perhaps the most dynamic is the stress on the close relationship between God and creation, both the very "ordinary" elements of the physical world as well as the human beings who increasingly influence its future. The creation-incarnation-mediation axis is clearly seen in these liturgies of deliverance that deal with bodies "in the margin," suspended between life and death, pain and joy, and shadowed by doubt and fear. Perhaps some of these insights from our shared early medieval tradition can serve to engage us today, as we ponder our stewardship and responsibilities in the contemporary world so different from theirs, in our own reflection on the sacrality, the meaning and the limits of this complex world and the human body that shapes and is shaped by it.

Commentary: Body-Critical
Embodiment

Jennifer Knust

According to Joanne Pierce, during the medieval period, the stress on the importance of the body "moved in paradoxical directions simultaneously." First, there was an emphasis on the necessary control of the body with its "misleading" appetites. Second, there was an insistence that the body would be resurrected and, therefore, that the created, physical world, including the human body, "mediate[s] the presence of the divine." Pierce has nicely and succinctly stated what I believe to be a fundamental tension, not only within medieval Christianity, but also within Christianity in its infancy, the period I study most intensely in my own work. There is a tension in much of early Christian discourse between an affirmation of the human body, its privileged place in salvation, and a deeply felt ambivalence about the possibility that our bodies, especially our bodily desires, will betray us. This tension is summed up by Paul, himself a proponent of the theory of physical resurrection. On the one hand, Paul argued that all of creation "groans in labor pains" as creation and Christian together wait for the bodily redemption that is to come. On the other, he claims that brothers and sisters in Christ can and should overcome flesh altogether. Thus, Paul called for a kind of body-critical embodiment: the followers of Jesus remain in their bodies, but by following Christ, their bodies have been transformed into something new and different. Paul longed for a resurrection body that could replace these limited, corrupted bodies subject to sin and death, yet he insisted that the body and creation were to be included in the redemption to come. Similarly, as Pierce demonstrates, the churching of women and trials by ordeal expressed a paradoxical body-critical embodiment: creation is celebrated and affirmed, yes, but pain and wounding participate in the vindication. Theologically, these rites "focus on the spilt, as well as the connection, between body and soul," while extending this connection to include the wider creation. Creation and bodies were welcomed into Christian liturgy and thought in striking ways, with practical implications for both, believer and priest.

According to Nancy Jay, the opposition between sacrificial purity and the pollution of childbirth is a common feature of societies that practice a system of patrilineal descent, a system "in which women give birth to children but have no descendants."[1] In societies with matrilineal descent, maternity alone is sufficient to determine who "owns" the offspring. Patrilineal descent, by contrast, requires an intervening ritual to demonstrate the paternal tie since biological paternity is less obvious or certain than biological maternity. Jay argues that blood sacrifice can serve this function. By interpreting sacrificial killing as purposeful, "rational," and pleasing to the divine, suggesting that childbirth is an irrational, uncontrollable, polluting act designed to produce heirs for men, and allowing only men to officiate, sacrificial cults celebrate paternal ties. As Jay notes, Christian churches, medieval and otherwise, did not include actual blood sacrifice among their practices, yet sacrifice is present symbolically in the form of the Eucharist. Christian churches were and are organized according to a system of patrilineal descent. She explains, "[the Christian church] is a truly perfect 'eternal line of patrilineal descent,' in which, as it were, authority descends from father to father, through the 'one Son made perfect forever,' in a line no longer directly dependent on women's reproductive powers for continuity."[2] The churching of women seems to support Jay's analysis: childbirth was interpreted as inherently polluting by a church and a culture that celebrated the blood sacrifice of Jesus, the Son of God, on a regular basis.

The evidence Pierce offers suggests that provisions designed to address the "ritual impurity" of childbirth may be more complex than Jay allows, but churching does imply a particular understanding of gender. Why did medieval women require the intervention of a male priest to reassure and purify them? Why were the midwife and the mother herself understood to be incapable of dealing with the inevitable "impurities" involved in childbirth? Why was the new mother viewed as so dangerous that she needed to remain outside the church for forty days? Why did her reentrance into the community require an elaborate ritual performed by a male priest? Of course, one does not have to interpret the churching rites as exclusively negative for women. Perhaps they were intended to reassure faithful women during the painful and potentially life-threatening process of giving birth. Perhaps the 47-day span between childbirth and reentering the church was designed to give new mothers a well-deserved rest. An emphasis on thanksgiving prevails in both of these *ordines*, as Pierce notes. Also, beliefs about ritual impurity were counterbalanced by an emphasis on the necessity of spiritual purity for the mother and the priest alike. Nevertheless, the woman is clearly construed as passive in this process—she is a victim of Eve's original sin and a vessel of ritual impurity that she herself cannot control or remove—while the male priest is viewed as an active mediator between the woman and God. The male priest can consecrate the sacrifice (the Eucharist), but the woman can only be a passive recipient both of God's grace and of the priest's benevolent intervention on her behalf.

The trial by hot iron and the trial by cold water offer remarkable examples of the (orthodox) Christian insistence that creation is good and plays a part in God's redemptive plan: God created matter, matter must obey God's decrees. Here inanimate matter was understood to be more trustworthy than human witnesses. Still, the judicial application of burning or drowning is hardly a bodily affirming practice in the end. Vindication may have been the goal but torture was the instrument. Moreover, the theological meaning of these rituals—created matter is good and subject to the command of God the creator—is not the only meaning here. As Catherine Bell has argued, ritualization does not simply enact belief; ritual enforces certain social relations while excluding others.[3] Thus, it may be possible to detect some of the pressing social concerns of the medieval church by examining these trials. Since I am not a scholar of medieval liturgy, I will offer a few initial suggestions by comparing these medieval trials to material with which I am more familiar, the Roman custom of torturing slaves and a very early mention of a trial by ordeal in a Christian source, the test of the water of the conviction of the Lord given to the Holy Couple in the apocryphal work the *Protevangelium Iacobi*.

According to Pierce's analysis, anyone accused of a crime could be subjected to a trial by ordeal as a last ditch effort to establish the truth of the matter. The Romans took a different approach: bodily torture was to be applied exclusively to slaves and other low-status persons. Torture was intended not to establish the guilt or innocence of the slave, the one tortured, but to ensure the validity of slave testimony regarding someone or something else entirely. Torture was applied to elicit the testimony of slaves against their masters, verifying a truth that had already been established and as a final step in the judicial process. As in the medieval trials by ordeal, the judicious use of slave torture was a method of last resort; it was designed to confirm guilt or innocence that was already assumed to be present. This judicious use of torture had an important side effect, however: it reemphasized the supposedly great divide between slaves and masters. Masters, properly educated and from "good" families, were expected to give accurate testimony. When their testimony was in doubt, their slaves could be brought forward to give evidence against them under torture. Slaves were not given the same presumption of honor. Roman law presupposed that the application of pain was necessary to ensure that slaves would tell the truth. Thus, status was repeatedly and painfully dramatized in ancient Roman legal proceedings.[4]

Medieval trials by ordeal figured status quite differently, offering no directions regarding the social status of the accused. Perhaps this willingness to injure the physical bodies of Christians, regardless of status, can be linked to the belief that the suffering and death of Jesus was redemptive. The torture and death of Jesus, as well as the martyrs who died in imitation of him, brought honor rather than shame.[5] Further evidence for this rather different understanding of the relationship between status and the application of bodily pain can be found in the test of the water of the conviction of the Lord, as described in the popular second-century apocryphal work the *Protevangelium Iacobi* (PI). According to the PI, Mary was raised in the temple as a virgin. When the news of her miraculous pregnancy reached the priest, he assumed that Joseph, her betrothed, had violated her. He resolved to determine the truth by administering a test involving consecrated water: if either Mary or Joseph had engaged in sexual immorality, drinking this water would cause their skin to erupt with tell-tale sores; if not, their skin would remain pure. When they remained whole, the priest concluded, "If the Lord God has not revealed your sins, neither do I judge you," and he sent them off rejoicing (16.1).

There are several similarities between this fanciful story and the rites that Pierce examines: Mary and Joseph were suspected of sexual immorality yet protested their innocence. In an effort to clear them, a religious authority administered water consecrated to serve God's purpose. When their bodies remained clean, the priest was satisfied and their innocence was accepted. The water and the physical bodies of the accused settled what their verbal testimony could not. God's creation was viewed as capable of outing the sin, even when the subjects themselves were determined to remain reticent. The test could be applied even to a man of high standing and his betrothed. Nevertheless, social relationships were dramatized by Christian practices as well. While the torture of slaves emphasized the (presumed) good character of masters, the trials by ordeal emphasized the role of priest as God-ordained adjudicator over everyone, irrespective of social status, and even over creation. God is just, creation is good, and the priest alone understands how to convince creation to do its part in determining guilt or innocence. The boundaries drawn here are between priest and people rather than master and slave. Profound theological claims about the goodness of creation, the bodily integrity of the innocent, and God's mercy also had profound implications regarding the appropriate role of the church as the court of last resort and of the priest as uniquely capable of administering God's justice.

As Pierce has demonstrated, the blessing in the birth chamber and the ritual churching of women offer striking evidence of the welcoming of bodies and bodily concerns into medieval Christian liturgy. The churching rites and the trials are linked in their expression of a paradoxical relationship between bodies, creation, pain, and God's goodness. They are also linked by a concern for the centrality of the church and its chosen representatives, the male priests, in articulating God's will. Priests are viewed as uniquely qualified to handle the problems of body and soul. Their intervention is required at the bedside of women during childbirth, at the return of new mothers to the church, when further evidence is required of guilt or innocence, and when creation needs to be reminded of God's mandates. In the "creation-incarnation-mediation axis," priests are the pivot points, capable of dealing with bodies "in the margins" because they are viewed as very much at the center.

Race, Religion, and the Emerging Modern World: Indians, Incas, and Conspiracy Stories in Colonial Peru

Irene Silverblatt

In 1639 Lima witnessed a Gran Auto de Fe, a public ceremony of judgment, exhibiting the punishments meted out to accused heretics, either reconciled or damned. During this auto Manuel Bautista Perez, convicted of secretly practicing Judaism and refusing to confess his crime, was burned at the stake. The day after, Ana Maria de Contreras, an accused witch, was whipped, shorn, and humiliated—stripped to the waste and led around Lima atop a mule. Manuel Bautista Perez and Ana Maria de Contreras had something else in common besides the fact that they were convicted heretics: they were both accused of having an unholy relationship with native Andeans.

I will be using their very tragic histories as an entree into Spanish cultural politics and colony-making—the cultural changes at the heart of Spain's efforts to convert the Andean region into a dependent Viceroyalty. Spain's imperial enterprise was built by fashioning the new social beings at the core of colonial political economy: (1) the racialized triad—Indian, Spaniard, Black; and (2) the bureaucratized-beings—created by and establishing the institutions of state to implement that remarkable social and cultural metamorphosis.

The Spanish Empire was at the vanguard of state-making in the early modern world. Spain built the most modern bureaucratic apparatus of the times as it set about establishing colonies in the New World; and, in the process, it created the boilerplate for race-thinking in Europe and the Americas.

Castilian monarchs, learning from the obstacles to absolutist control encountered on the Iberian Peninsula, kept the colonies (at least in principle) under a tight rein with political institutions ensuring the supremacy of royal authority over both settlers and natives. They also brought renowned measures to investigate the beliefs and ethics of their colonial subjects—the

Spanish Inquisition, which set up its Lima office at the end of the sixteenth century. Although it could not stand in judgment over natives (that was a diocesan affair), the Inquisition was the only royal institution with authority over all of the Spanish empire's colonies and kingdoms—with offices in Castille, the Philippines, Mexico, Columbia, Basque country, Catalunia— pretty much wherever Spanish settlements could be found. And it was a *state* bureaucracy: the Spanish Inquisition was not under the supervision of the Church or of Rome, but of the Crown. With jurisdiction over pivotal dimensions of religious life—in a country in which Catholicism was akin to a nationalist ideology—the Spanish Inquisition was a commanding political presence. And, as befitted one of the most advanced bureaucracies of its day, the Spanish Inquisition generated an amazing amount of paperwork. Much of this presentation will be based on the Lima tribunal's record-keeping compulsions.[1]

One of the Lima Inquisition's most important functions was to clarify cultural blame: to specify and bring to judgment those among the Viceroyalty's inhabitants, who held contrary beliefs or engaged in life practices perceived to threaten the colonial state. Inquisitors legitimized the ensuing imprisonments, infamous torture sessions, and punishments, not only by appeals to God and religious orthodoxy, but by appeals to reasons of state, national security, and the public's well-being. In the middle of the seventeenth century, Inquisitors expressed deep-seated fears that Peru's moral fabric—and political stability—were being undermined by two principal culprits: hidden Jews, glossed frequently as New Christian /merchant/Portuguese, and the colony's ubiquitous witches. Both, according to Tribunal calculations, had significant ties to Peru's indigenous or slave populations, and their purported relationships, crossing the racialized divides of colonial rule, point to confused fears, a conspiratorial bent, as well as to broader struggles over political and social legitimacy.

Manuel Bautista Perez was one of Peru's wealthiest merchants, with networks from Africa to the Amazon. In prison for over five years before being executed, Perez, a New Christian—or convert of Jewish or moorish ancestry—was executed by order of the Lima office for secretly following Jewish beliefs and refusing to confess them. (Had he confessed and repented, his life would have been spared. Yet he refused.) The auto of 1639 was the bloodiest in Lima's inquisitorial history; it was the auto when members of the so-called "conspiracion grande" or great (Jewish) conspiracy were punished. Perez was one of eleven executed for crimes in some way associated with Judaising; another 62 admitted guilt and were penanced. The Inquisition's head office in Madrid was actually aghast at this broad sweep of arrests and at the harsh sentences imposed by its underlings. Accordingly, the Supreme Council demanded that the Lima tribunal justify its actions. They did so by appealing to the dangers New Christians posed, not only to the ethical foundation of the colony, but to its very political security.[2]

The Lima tribunal's take on the Jewish menace elaborated a familiar set of charges, but with a twist appropriate to the emerging social conditions of a global, colonial order: New Christians usurped trade and merchandising to the detriment of Castilians; New Christians committed treachery through alliances with Spain's foreign foes; New Christians committed treachery through alliances with the potential enemies within (Indians and Black slaves), and New Christians were able to plot treachery because of their remarkable ability to conspire in secret languages. The character of seventeenth century conspiracies had a long history, but it was chiseled in the geo-politics of new world empire. These anti-New Christian beliefs were not universal. We should remember that conflicting sentiments toward New Christians vied for prominence in Peru in the 1620s and 1630s. On the one hand, the wealthiest New Christian merchants, en route to becoming colonial aristocrats, were championed in the highest places of ecclesiastical and secular government. At the same time, however, Lima's inquisitors were appalled that men of suspect origins were entering the highest places of ecclesiastic and secular government. The Lima tribunal, spearheaded by the Inquisitor Juan de Manozca, began to step up its campaign against New Christians. They were bolstered in this endeavor by Spain's purity of blood laws—decrees stating that "stains" of Jewish and Moorish ancestry were inherited for generations. So, when stories began to spread about the growing number of hidden Jews living in the Viceroyalty, Lima's Inquisitors came to the fore, promising to find a cure for this "plague" that was devouring Peru.

This "plague," we discover, had several facets—all contributing to a growing Viceregal anxiety over conspiracy. One was economic, and we find that in line with stereotype, New Christians were accused of economic chicanery.

> They wrote to Madrid, since about six or eight years, it is said that many [New Christians] have found a footing in Peru . . . commanding almost exclusively all the commerce of the kingdom; they owned all the dry goods stores; and monopolized the retail trade and traffic so that from gold brocade to sackcloth, and from diamond to cumin seed, and from the lowest black slave from Guinea to the most precious pearl passes through their hands.[3] "A Castilian of pure stock," they added, "has not a ghost of a chance."[4]

These anxieties over a colonial economic conspiracy were compounded by political concerns. Again in line with stereotype, New Christians were accused of treachery. Not only were New Christians accused of allying themselves with Castile's international rivals in the Americas, the Dutch and English, they stood accused of conspiring with slaves and *indios* to oust the conquerors. Blacks and Indians, new to Catholicism, were ripe for sedition the Viceroys feared, and particularly so since New Christians were determined to undermine the "simple people's" faith.[5]

New Christians were said to communicate their heresies in the thriving mercantile spaces of colonial life. Here Indians, Blacks, and New Christians could engage in illicit conversation; moreover they could do so secretly, for all were conversant in languages unintelligible to Old Christian ears. In fact "they could speak their languages in front of Old Christians, and Old Christians wouldn't have a clue"—or so went the charges.[6]

> [It was] a secret language . . . [and] Old Christians just heard normal words, not that out-of-the-ordinary language, [and New Christians spoke with] duplicity and scheming, so that the prisoner and the rest of his ancestry and kin could converse about conspiracies and heresies.[7]

Not only did Spanish conspiracy theories presume rather fantastic linguistic infiltrations between Indians, Africans, and Jews, but they made customs of indigenous or African origin into heretical Judaic rituals. Manuel Bautista Perez stood accused of practicing rather exotic Jewish rituals with tobacco and cola nut.

According to testimony, when Manuel Bautista would give his *compadre* and fellow Jew, tobacco, he would say, taking it with his fingers and pressing it to his nostrils, senor compadre, this tobacco is very good and he would scatter it on the ground or blow on it. Then the compadre would say to Manuel Bautista Perez, isn't there some *colilla* to drink with water (a root or fruit from Guinea, which becomes sweet by drinking water after putting it in the mouth) and Manuel Bautista Perez would order his servants to bring it.

And as if to reenforce the Jewish derivations of taking tobacco and drinking colilla the witness added, "the compadre and Manuel Bautista would then speak to each other in a language only understood among themselves, talking about the Law of Moses."[8] Of course, Manuel Bautista Perez emphatically denied these allegations. He strongly objected to charges that he made ritual offerings to the god of the old testament, let alone with cultural artifacts from South America and Africa. He was, however, the head of an international trading enterprise whose agents traversed the globe—including Africa and the Andes.

How striking that goods associated with processes at the heart of Spain's colonial endeavor, the conquest of *indios* and the expansion of the African slave trade, were conflated with the practices of Judaism. Global commerce and cheap labor anchored Spain's colonial enterprise, and New Christians along with Indians and African slaves were key figures in this equation. At least according to stereotype, New Christians dominated international trade; and in keeping with colonial reality, Indians and Blacks embodied the Viceroyalty's sources of cheap labor. Both groups were needed for the success of Spain's global endeavors and both were distrusted. New Christian merchants, slaves, and colonized Indian vassals were outside of the traditional institutions that had structured life in the Iberian Peninsula before colonialism began to change the rules. In different cultural and economic ways, each signaled the novel social relations of the emerging modern world. This version of cultural finger pointing hints at the tensions animating nascent modern/colonial economics and politics, as well as the tensions animating the cultural order on which they both rested. Manuel Bautista Perez was inscribed by the social contradictions of his times, contradictions that pit appeals to lineage and traditional hierarchy against appeals to worthiness based on a modern order rooted in commercial wealth. This renowned, prosperous, and powerful merchant surely felt that aristocracy, or at least full "Spanish" status, was his due. Of course, Manuel Bautista Perez believed in and defended the legitimacy of a political structure that enslaved *negros* and coerced Indian labor; but, he also believed in the right of good Christian subjects, regardless of ancestry, to be justly recognized for their contributions to nation/empire and church. It was in this regard that he challenged Castile's racial definition of Jewishness and of Spanishness, along with its accompanying social hierarchy governed by purity of blood laws and an aristocratic ethos.

*　*　*

Magistrates pursuing the "conspiracion grande" were appalled by another failing running deep in the Viceregal character: its attraction to native life. Writing to the Supreme Council in Madrid, the Inquisitor Juan de Manozca, who oversaw the 1639 auto, bemoaned the colony's abysmal lack of faith. He assessed Peru as a degraded country and, in his letter, blamed Peru's degradation on the ubiquity of witches, nearly always women, who were immersed in the customs and lore of the colony's uncivilized natives. To Inquisitor Manozca's chagrin, things native were becoming increasingly prominent in the witchcraft repertoire. By the time Ana Maria de Contreras (the accused witch sharing the scaffold with Manuel Bautista Perez in the auto of 1639) was penanced, even the Inca had made an appearance.

A novel edict of faith posted on Peruvian Church doors during lent of 1629 tells much of the story; unlike every other edict read in every church throughout the Spanish empire, it contained this warning of

> weak women, given to superstitions . . . who do not doubt . . . their adoration of the devil . . . [T]hey invoke and adore him . . . and wait for images . . . of what they want [to know] for which the aforesaid women . . . go to the countryside and . . . drink certain potions of herbs and roots, called *achuma* and *chamico*, and *coca* with which they deceive and stupefy the senses and the illusions and fantastic representations that they have, they judge and proclaim afterwards to be revelations or to be a sure sign of what will happen in the future.[9]

This emphasis on the dangers of witchcraft was highly unusual. In the eyes of most historians, the Spanish Inquisition tended to minimize the perils associated with witchcraft, not emphasize them. What stands out, then, in the edict, in letters of concern sent to Madrid, as well as in the trial transcripts is the Inquisitors' anxiety over the lure of Indian customs, Indian dress, Indian remedies, even Indian language, for women who were not.[10]

Peru's accused witches came from a host of backgrounds: there were witches of Spanish descent, either born in the peninsula or in the growing

South American cities of Lima or Potosi; *mestiza* witches, *mulatas*, and black witches (slave and free) and *sambas*, of black and Indian ancestry. Witches' special skills addressed the daily stuff of life—in love and justice: they could foretell if much missed husbands would be coming on the next fleet; they could ensure that lovers remain passionate; that royal officers be impeded from carrying out a sentence; or eventually, it was said, they could ensure that the Inquisitors themselves were stymied.[11]

In the Lima Inquisition's early years, women accused of conjuring with saints and holy water—along with the Tablets of Moses and the Tribes of Israel—were also condemned for "speaking in Indian," and, more damaging, for actively seeking native "witches" to assist in "sorcery" sessions.[12] Cusco royalty, however, first appear in the trial of Ana Maria de Contreras, who shared the scaffold with Manuel Bautista Perez in the auto-de-fe of 1639. This *mulata* slave explained that the great numbers of women who sought her out, lavishing money and food, pushed her return to old "deceits and tricks." Ana Maria de Contreras's "deceits and tricks", included "having worshiped the mountain peaks and rocks in memory and signification of the Inca and his wife."[13]

Castaneda's trial indicates something about a "witch's" clientele. Ana had an extensive following of women "of all social conditions and ranks." Witnesses called them "*tapadas*," women who would, without apparent shame or concern, promenade around the city masked by very carefully and seductively draped veils. Lima's *tapadas* were notorious: they were serenaded in poetry, were the object of royal denunciations, and were strongly censured by the Church. *Tapadas* found themselves the object of bans in Spain as well as in Lima. However, they were perceived to be most dangerous in the colonial capital, condemned by secular and religious authorities for "enjoying improper liberty, promoting public scandal and disgrace." The hazards they presented to civilized living seemed to grow (at least symbolically) with the complexity of colonial politics and culture.[14] We encounter *tapadas* in colonial witchcraft trials throughout the century. Flaunting, as they did, the political and culture hierarchies at the heart of the colonial enterprise, it should not be surprising, then, that "witchcraft" involving *tapadas* could get blamed for inciting all kinds of political havoc. Nor should it be surprising that authorities either could not or did not have the will to carry out their obligations to arrest them.[15]

By midcentury, every woman charged with witchcraft included Indian objects in her repertoire. Coca was the central ingredient of conjuring rites; and along with more conventional figures, saints and credos we find the Inca, and sometimes the Coya or Inca Queen. For example, Dona Maria de Cordoba's coca readings—always conducted with several friends, "*maestras*," (teacher/mentors), and relatives of the person to be healed—were built around deciphering images made from wads of coca leaf. Although she denied ever praying to the devil or even seeing his figure in her porcelain bowl,[16] she did claim to venerate the Inca as the king of the pagan Indians who lived in the Andes before the coming of Spaniards. In the early seventeenth century, Peru's clerics determined that the Inca, the queen, and their entire court were "condemned to an eternity in hell for worshiping the devil in guacas."[17] Witches, however, drew on these "gentile" powers for insight and strength: "I conjure you with the *palla* (noblewoman) and with your ancestors, with the idols whom you believed in, my father, I drink to you with this wine, [and] with this coca that you used in your sorcery.[18]

By now coca was irrevocably tied to what were *colonial* concepts of Indian and Inca. For before the Spanish conquest, most native peoples living in the Andes did not consider themselves to be the Inca's descendants; many, in fact, detested the Inca for usurping their labor, lands, and political sovereignty. Nor did they consider themselves part of one encompassing ethnic group—like "Indian." Notwithstanding, some colonial Peruvians were transforming that pre-Columbian past. Painting Indians/Inca in broad strokes and making coca the key to a merging Indian/Inca domain, they were making significant changes to the conceptualization of Andean history: they were creating the category Indian.

The colonial Inca, promising fortune and dominion over human beings, was infused with powers grounded in the magic the colonizing world had foisted on native experience. The Inca and his entourage sparked colonial imaginations and his powers seemed to grow as Spanish control was in decline. During the middle decades of the seventeenth century and the years to follow, the strength of Spanish imperial dominion was battered by internal dissension, economic downturns, and foreign challenges. This is when the Inca's authority in love, luck, and even government blossomed. Ana Maria de Ulloa, in prayers to fix the outcome of a civic trial, implored, "O my coca, o my princess, o my Inca, I beg you, since for you nothing was impossible. . . ."[19]

Catholic missionaries, "extirpators of idolatry" (equivalent to Inquisitors, but over native heresies) twinned Indian idol worship with witchcraft, and once clerics found witchcraft in native religious practices, they were quick to discern *indias* doing the devil's work. Native women were assumed capable of the darkest of witchcraft, of using black arts to cause death.[20] With anxiety over witchcraft on the rise, Churchmen feared that women's heresies—Indian and non-Indian—were beginning to crisscross cultural boundaries; all the more reason to see non-Indian women, turning to Indian habits, as a growing danger to the colonial enterprise.

Missionaries also made an explicit connection between the New Christian threat and Church campaigns to extirpate idolatry. First of all, clergy clearly understood the struggle with New Christians in Europe to have been a rehearsal for idolatry campaigns in the Americas. Second, royal officials were ever wary that Peru's fifth column of New Christians/hidden Jews would form allegiances with "Indian" subjects to overthrow the empire.[21] And that, in turn, only enhanced the cachet of native Peruvians and their perceived power as the potential "enemies within". Indeed, during the period when witchcraft and Jewish heresies loomed as threats, clerics and royal authorities were increasingly concerned that natives were abandoning Christianity, and returning to the idolatrous, pagan ways of the ancestors. Of course, idolatry, they reckoned, was the first step in the slippery slope to sedition.

To tie this together: Inquisitor Manozca's anxieties over witchcraft and "Indianness" and over New Christian ties with Indians were concerns regarding the cultural work of Spanish hegemony. Colonial rule, inscribed in cultural terms and through cultural hierarchies, was menaced, or so the Inquisitors thought, by witchcraft ideologies and New Christian conspiracies that reached into the heart of imperial cultural politics. The imagined threats of colonial witchcraft and New Christian sabotage swelled as they absorbed fears surrounding idolatries, native subversions, the allegiance of slaves, and the power of foreign enemies. And vice-versa.

Peru's inquisitors intertwined stereotypes of New Christians, Indians, African slaves, and women as part of an etiology of fear and blame. This etiology was built on a racialized vision that confused nationalist sentiments, religion, and the caste-categories of colonial rule. It also promoted some of the irrationalities that have accompanied the modern age—irrationalities made all the more dangerous by their coating in the rhetoric of reason and in the rhetoric of reasons of state. Seventeenth-century Peru provides an extraordinary example of how fears—in this instance—about New Christians, witches, and Indians could coalesce, develop, and ultimately balloon into absurd conspiracy theories—all with the help of government officials.

This is a cautionary tale.

PART III

Contemporary Ritual Practices
of Healing

Bruce T. Morrill, S.J.

INTRODUCTION

The following three chapters of *Practicing Catholic* put into practice several of Gary Macy's insights from chapter 2, the most comprehensive of which being the recognition that ritual, symbol, or liturgy are terms referring not to abstract principles but, rather, to actual events performed in human time and space. As with any attempt at rethinking terms and methodology, Therese Schroeder-Sheker's and my own chapters here require the courage of our convictions. In our case, we share the conviction that performances (concrete enactments) of ministry, music, spiritual discipline, and ritual, themselves constitute a type of scholarship, that such professional but also (necessarily) personally integrated and engaged pastoral work, historically and theoretically informed, contributes not only to the tradition(s) of Catholicism but also to various disciplines in the academy. A challenge to the ever-tenacious protocols of modern academia, our efforts to convey in the form of book chapters what has occurred "in motion," that is, as praxis, have necessitated the enlistment of memory, narrative, and selected theoretical tools so as to provide descriptions and analyses of the multiple dimensions (bodily and spiritual, human and divine, conserving and constructive) of Catholic faith practiced in contemporary ministries for the sick and dying.

Harpist, singer, and composer Therese Schroeder-Sheker made her Carnegie Hall debut in 1980 and has numerous recordings, films, compositions, and scholarly publications to her credit. She also founded the Chalice of Repose Project and the palliative medical field of music-thanatology (both of which she describes in chapter 6 which follows). With three decades of experience in the care of the dying and an equal amount of time recording and concertizing internationally for the very-much living, she has integrated the scholarly, artistic, medical-clinical, and prayerful into one vigorous though complex life and life-work. Her opening session at the Practicing Catholic conference integrated the harp, voice, and shruti box in a scholarly, artistic, and spiritual presentation on music-thanatology and the clinical, pastoral, and educational work of the Chalice of Repose Project. During her session she artfully merged the three norms for concert, lecture, and homily into a comprehensive and captivating performance. Combining the informational with the experiential, the audience was left with a transformative experience on the performative aspects of music-thanatology as they relate to historical ritual embedded within the texts of monastic medicine and the personal identity of the speaker who chooses, in the present era she characterizes as institutionally difficult and unsettled, to be a practicing Catholic.

Just as Schroeder-Sheker's musical-pastoral praxis exemplifies Macy's argument for (religious) tradition as a matter always of present commitment in relation to a perspectival, and thus contested, past, so my two chapters (7 and 8) on the current rites of the Pastoral Care of the Sick and the Sacrament of Anointing the Sick amount to another inquiry into Roman Catholic ritual, in all its bodiliness and contestation. Here issues specific to rites that are officially promulgated and sanctioned in the Church come into play, but so do an array of other observations concerning history, anthropology, theology, and pastoral theory-and-practice in a certain North American context. Whereas Schroeder-Sheker consciously goes about her work as a lay person, albeit in the monastic, mode she suggestively calls "contemplative musicianship"; my institutional identity both as a priest in the Roman Catholic Church and a professor in an American university require my own consideration of methodological issues as I attempt to do theology in what may amount to an original mode in its own right, a sort of twenty-first century (critical) mystagogy.

Commentator Judith Marie Kubicki, C.S.S.F., a specialist in liturgical music, explores ways that performative language theory can be applied to the sort of music thanatology that Schroeder-Sheker does. Kubicki then goes on to discuss issues of sickness and the vulnerable body, in Catholic faith lives, via her comments on Morrill's two, linked papers.

CHAPTER 6

The *Vox Feminae*: Choosing and Being as Christian Form and Praxis

Therese Schroeder–Sheker

The readers of this anthology will understand, because my session in the *Practicing Catholic* conference was laced with voice and harp, we cannot publish the contents of that evening without having produced a recording or documentary film. However, in this article, I attempt something new, a departure from systematic scholarship, from musicology or theology, liturgy or history. For the same reasons, I have not written a medical or clinical treatise on the principles of prescriptive music used in the care of the dying, nor the historical practices at Cluny. (I have done those things in detail elsewhere).[1] Risking the periphery, and this is consistent with living or dying, here I have written something with a wide circumference and a different voice. Through narration and reflection, memory and discernment, I change key from archival scholarship and send out something which I hope will be a theological and hermeneutical poetry of living and dying made more whole through risk, through feeling forward into the unknown. To that end, I have written a meditative essay on the *vox feminae*, the strongest and most authentic element I am and have as an artist, clinician, teacher, and a practicing Catholic.

The palette the Maker has given us is full-spectrum, and I love the choices given to us even though I am forever (clumsily) learning how to *be with and in* some of the variances and intricacies of darkness and light. *Chiaroscuro* is one of the ways possible for someone committed to maintaining the tensions of opposites, and that is what life with harp is all about: holding opposites under thousands of pounds of torque. In maintaining the tension of opposites, in our particular practice in the Chalice of Repose, we are attempting to liberate living and dying, sickness and health, and other experiences as well, from the tightly defined terms and criteria of the late twentieth-century practice of biomedicine. In doing so, one tries to re-unite these experiences with one another, re-integrate them back into the fullness of the life cycle. Together, these pairs offer us ways that are more whole, for even illness has its mystery in God's design and in the assignments given to each of us in becoming more fully human. While this is thought-provoking, uncomfortable and unsettling "stuff," it is soul-renewing when done *first*, within our own private lives. Some would say this discomfort is a mandate, saving us from our own tendencies to the lukewarm mediocrity that can settle in before we even notice.

I am attempting to describe that which can appear new and radical, yet strangely, we are together gazing at a way of being that has been available to the world for long centuries. Gradually, we see, sense, and learn that this commitment to a new kind of conversion and integration (and the resultant interpenetrating working together of the transformed head, heart, and hands) emerges as a core element in the orientation and commitment I have called *contemplative musicianship.* As such, on-going personal *metanoia* is the foundational music-thanatology spiritual *praxis* from which our clinical and pastoral work with the needs of the dying derives its integrity, strength, and efficacy. Dying to our old ways, the habituated and unconscious ones that are brambled and fruitless, and becoming new, in Christ, in an increasingly burning faithfulness, disorients and re-orients the musician-clinician. He or she must in fact draw the prescriptive music *de profundis,* out of the depths (of the human body), reflected through their more or less individualized soul and spirit, including newly alive capacities for thinking, feeling, and willing. How can we serve the dying patient *if we ourselves haven't first risked a series of inner deaths?*

If the humanly organized person of body, soul, and spirit is a sordid mess, if we are habituated in lying, cheating, stealing, maiming, and so on, the musical pharmaceutical which the vulnerable patient in pain receives from the musician-clinician delivering prescriptive music is darkened or lifeless. As such, the notion of right livelihood is then eclipsed and our notes fall on the ground as so many fraudulent sound bites masquerading as more. In other words, *how* we are really matters; it determines the quality of living, streaming music. Especially with the current scandals in the Church and betrayals in the world of corporate finance, this burning necessity of being called to honesty, of calling ourselves to honesty, to inter-connectedness and congruency, is of paramount importance.

The performative element I am describing, and the power of prescriptive music which is delivered live at the bedside of the dying patient, is validated to a degree under very specific criteria. The music-thanatologist makes a personal commitment to make the effort, over years of continual work and prayer, reflection and forgiveness, receptivity and courage, false and true starts, diversions and distractions, to gradually bring the inner world and outer life to such conversion and authenticity that they might gradually become more transparent and single, closer to one unified whole. This unity cannot be conferred with a certificate or a graduate degree; it is a life-work.

In the Pauline sense, or in the sense of the Russian *staretz,* there are times when this commitment to *metanoia* involves, quite literally, being a fool, making a choice or choices that the world will scorn, that the worldly hate, and that leave the personal pocket poorer. Yet this holy foolishness, if it lauds the Gospel over success, allows one an inner integrity. We could say, at another level, that music-thanatology with its core commitment to *metanoia* 'embraces' the *sacrament of failure*, for that fruitfulness (and not *success*) is traditionally considered one of the surest ways to God. The point of monasticism is that saints are not born, they are made. They come into being gradually, through constant pruning and the cycle of the changing seasons. Holiness slowly blossoms if we fall down *and* get up; over and over, we remember and forget, forget and remember—it's the hierarchy of humility to ascend by falling. We fall from or walk or crawl from or run from direct contact with grace and yet—*Damascus!*—through grace, we get back up and choose once more to be in deeper relationship with the God of love.

This healing praxis and eschatological vision, reflective of the *intelligence of the heart*, is central to a vision of an *interiorized monasticism* and is essential to a life-work called music-thanatology. I am saying, on one level, that monasticism has long been here for the laity, for every person of prayer is *called*, but more than ever, a renewal is available for those who are very much in the world but not of it. *Metanoia* and consciously embodied Christian practices more than ever can be "about" healing a modern tendency to fragmentation, compartmentalization, and abstraction. However, embodiment issues are complex; both my *raison d'être* and methodology are profoundly theological; I think on my knees. Jesus was not prone to abstractions, but could and did distill the messiness of our lives and "see through" our divided elements in a new and living way.

The nature of harp is very physical, touching, and enigmatic. In a strange combination of strength and tenderness, the harpist is called to subvert and disarm listeners through an intimate, substantive, spiritually and emotionally naked music which invites listeners (doers and receivers) to abandon distractions and re-embrace essentials. We draw upon the already existing enthusiasm, the warmth of God within, residing in the human breast, allowed and encouraged to breathe in harmony, and bring this forward into profoundly practical monastic practices whose first stirrings emerged in the world of Judaism. The practices I have remembered, studied, loved, extended, renewed, and hope to embody (and learn by heart) are especially rooted in monasticism, both east and west. They are central to the historical visions of Benedictine, Cistercian, and Franciscan spiritualities, and before that, within the intrinsic and powerful Jewish legacy from which Christianity so naturally and providentially comes into being. Many of these Judeo-Christian legacies are mystical, practical, musical, merciful, and intrinsically imbedded within rather than explained by the canons of monastic medicine and all the liturgical arts and sacred texts of both traditions. This is especially true for music-thanatology.

This mystical transparency, hard won today through ongoing *metanoia*, encourages us to allow a living God to become inscribed in our innermost lives, hearts, and minds. This speaks to the practices of silence and a form of prayer that begins with listening, comes to flower in listening and responding, of knowing that *we are heard*, and seeks the courage to share human suffering. We do not avoid it and in many cases cannot; we go all the way through personal and collective suffering, not around it, when and where it is present, and hold it until it eventually becomes praise. This is not to prettify life, to make things more comfortable, more pleasant, for that would be egocentric and self-serving; we do so because we are called *to transform that which is less into something that is more*. A Eucharistic people lives transubstantiation as the deepest mystery of human existence, and so the world is an altar. We are called to transform all our sordid messiness into that which is more true, more beautiful, and more good. In so doing, we draw attention and intention to what already is and to that which can be rediscovered and renewed. The Psalms say that *this way is fire-tried*, so it is traditional. But, our practice is not "about" traditional institutions so much as it is "inside" sacraments and sacramentals which faithfully and creatively unify us in and with the God with whom we have an intimate personal relationship, and that God many of us call Christ. There is a great deal of personal responsibility in this picture, as opposed to collective following or bargaining. Yet the Christ I am seeking is very large, beyond institutions, embracing and belonging to many. Though I may not be one whom others want to own as their own, I do claim my Catholic identity and the life in and of the Eucharist which is so vital.

Contemplative Musicianship

I begin with a suite called *The Prayers from the Four Directions*. The East Indian *shruti* box, though comparatively unknown to American Christians, plays a central role in making *heart* available in new ways. Please allow me to explain.

The *shruti* box is a hand-held bellows, essentially a kind of exterior lung. It is the size of a hefty book, such as the *Jerusalem Bible*, and quieter, sweeter, and milder than a bagpipe. When air moves through pressure on the reeds inside the bellows, the cycles of inspiration and expiration create a drone, a sustain without meter, weaving together a sonic structure that can hold or frame the singer, praying through and beyond time. This un-metered music, sound breathing and expanding outside of time, ushers in a possibility fraught with liminal meaning and fecundity. But make no mistake! The air being drawn into the bellows by the right hand of the singer moves the soul into *kairotic* time, where heartbeat and breath are the essentials linking an eschatological self to God and community. In that corridor, the singer responds to this sonic framework and its overtones with freely flowing, highly ornamented melody.

The title of the suite at issue here isn't an oblique reference to Native American indigenous ways of praying so much as it hints at four different directions of the globe, and by extension, *ways of being*. These ways of being and modes of perception rise from vastly different religious cultures and time periods. But all four of these sung prayers make audible a vernacular of intimacy, and highlight the *vox feminae*, or the woman's voice. This suite is composed of ancient Irish, medieval French, modern Hindu, and contemporary

Israeli themes, and the melodies are reflected through the lens of grief, devotion, longing, and joy. The singer is stripped bare of pretense, by choice and by vocation. Each tradition is present in unique particularity, attends a different gesture and meaning, and yet all four remain rooted in common sonic ground: the framework of the perfect fifth, with the *d* as the fundamental experience, bedrock, and home. Within that fifth, it is possible to soar and glide on melodic line in and out of major and minor modes and scales, and in so doing, make audible different qualities of light. But that is just the beginning.

The suite begins, develops, always returns to, and ends with the ancient Irish *sean nos* singing tradition of *keening*, a particularly feminine, embodied, generative, and transformative way of *being with grief*. Though *sean nos* singers are both male and female (for the musical imagination and cognition required to ornament a melodic line beautifully is not gendered), *keening* is a particularly feminine gift. I say "feminine" because it seems to be a musical term which describes, in addition to a specific kind of singing style, a spiritual-emotional capacity for a gestation period, a different kind of pregnancy and holding, insemination through sorrow, and this period of containment is a kind of witnessing and is as necessary for the renewal of life as is a biological pregnancy. Certainly, this mystical and feminine capacity is also available to men, especially, for example, with the Hassidic *niggun* or air. But, historically, more often than not, women have keened in public and in private, for themselves and for strangers. In the Irish *sean nos* tradition, the principal voices of keening are those of women.

When we keen, we stay wholly *with* the experience of grief and *inside it* (or we accept that *it* lives in *us*) until gradually, at a certain moment or hour, the loss that once pierced the heart, even into immobility, turning us into lead, has become softened, melted, and transformed by the re-organizing power of sound (sung prayer). That which we have been holding in the darkness becomes *something else*. Keening takes courage; for in grief, one jumps off the side of a very steep mountain, a dive with no end, and the tears might never stop if we let them once begin. Yet when we keen, we deepen and expand our previous human dimensions. In a particularly concentrated form of prayer, we make room for something quickened, wholly new. And keening, in the ancient Irish tradition, is prayer, not psychodrama or social drama, not hysterics or theatrics. Keening is a prayer of healing.

THIS TENDER GAIN: THE MYSTICAL PREGNANCY

What is born of this keening? This mystical pregnancy? Not a new child, but *a new adult*, in the form of a being endowed with a new capacity. By consciously dying while we are still awake, surrendering, we are reborn with a new capacity, a tender gain, a gift for which one would not ordinarily pray or seek but by which many are eventually blessed and oftentimes healed. Once we have grieved and sung and prayed through the greatest possible losses and traumas, and waken to find ourselves still very much alive, one could with humility and awe whisper that there is little left to fear. Once having looked fear, or rather, fear of death, in the heart or in the eye, we are more whole, certain of resurrection and multiple resurrections, because we have lived it. Living and dying are re-woven as a unified whole, and though curing is not always possible, a major healing has taken place.

As the Irish term implies, *sean nos* is an old way. Old ways take time, and yet "time taken" has a double meaning and is paradoxical because taking time ultimately gives time. The old, traditional ways of keening are unrelated to the medicalization of death or perhaps stand in marked contrast to it, for the *sean nos* tradition of keening is profoundly Christian, incarnational, embodied. It protects living and dying as a comprehensive unified sweep moving toward the same reality, not mutually exclusive of one another. Unified, they anticipate the glory of the upcoming *dies natalis*. Death will one day come to each and every person, and if we are sensitive, we realize it comes to us many times, interiorly, during the course of a biography. Entering grief is a kind of death, a kind of sepulcher; re-entering life after profound mourning is a kind of resurrection. In taking time, the *sean nos* tradition of *keening* frees us from the qualities of time that leave one bound and shackled, unfree. When you are singing this intensely, the past is real, but all that remains is this present moment, and with this presence of being, we choose to greet, cultivate, and protect the future. Keening also involves silence and sound in equal power.

It is not insignificant that the highly ornamented melody and refrain of the *sean nos* tradition reflects unique elements of a particular singer's soul as well as body, constitution, temperament, nervous system, laryngeal apparatus, biographical journey and more. No two *sean nos* singers lean on or metamorphose a melody in quite the same way, and with the passing of a great *sean nos* singer who may know hundreds of airs, a certain tradition sleeps. In keening, the melody, most often of intense beauty, is repeated many times, bearing the impress of the heartbeat, pulse, and respiratory cycles. Thus ensouled and humanized, the song takes on a new energy or life, eventually ceases being representative of a single (traumatic) event or memory and becomes instead, a *new capacity*. This is how the wound becomes luminous. What was once initially a major invasion, a most difficult life event or experience, causing cramp and defense necessities, rips us open. The place of the lance eventually congeals, encrusts, hardens, dries, begins to shift, the crust turns to dust, falls away, leaving a scar, and eventually, this scar becomes our beautiful human patina, a humanized alchemical gold. The place or condition of the original grief metamorphoses as an open corridor, a source of light. We remain open after having been cracked open, *if healing takes place*. This *keening*, this *song*, wholly and uniquely *ours*, becomes a current of sheer radiance meant to be freely given away. Few people remain numb or unmoved in the presence of authentic keening, and its language transcends our differences. Keening makes heart audible, perceptible, and available.

After having had the privilege of learning repertoire from many different cultures and time periods, I would have to say that few nations have the capacity to transform sorrow, anger, or injustice into the searing beauty that is experienced in the true Irish or Hassidic air, melodic ensoulments of particular times, places, sets of conditions, and series of events. True, the singing of, in this case, the Irish air reflects the memory and vigor of the singer's inner life, and I would like to develop this history a little more deeply.

In the *sean nos* manner of *keening* an air, and the thematic example I live in the suite I'm describing on paper, a solitary young woman who has just lost her first-born child takes the whole of the experience of death and loss and acknowledges that it is not only linked to an exterior, historical event which others, too, may share. It is also embodied. To the extent that the experience of loss/grief is embodied, it is intensely personal and unique, private and yet universal. This composite experience is rooted and sounding within her very body, not only in her soul or mind, at which point, she begins to emit a sound, a body wail, beginning down low in the gut and *ascending* into the region of the chest and heart. This wail that comes from loss moves up the spine, her unique spine, emerges into the air as a *one-of-a-kind never-to-be-repeated* song. The wails start out in a kind of difficult breathing, little, awful gasps clutching pitch. The wails, with each inhalation, become larger, longer, and more melodic. The one keening sings with body, soul, and spirit, *each repetition calling forth something into existence*, and in keening, the singer expresses the unadulterated grief which has left a hollow echoing place inside her body and heart. It is an empty space that nothing and no one can replace, *for we are not replaceable*, but it is true that time and grace can bring healing. Slowly, like burnished gold shining in a darkness, that which was once traumatic emptiness can in fact become *a clearing*—a gifted space receptive for that which is wholly new. The theological point here is that *keening is kenotic, self-emptying*.

Consciously sending the grief out of the body, via the larynx, through the medium of air, is nothing less than *a sound arrow*, is a kind of sung *kenosis*. Instead of using a bow and arrow as an implement of war, used to project something far into a distance with a specific target in mind, the keening singer reaches with unseen hands into the depths of the ensouled body and pulls out the pain, flinging it high into the heavens, offering it to God, because, in times of horror, that's all we have to give.

The whole activity, in the Irish tradition, has multiple layers of spirituality involved, and these can be carried to greater or lesser degree, depending on the human capacity. Nevertheless, to the extent that the meditative content of the keening is kept in solidarity with Christ and Mary, greater and deeper degrees of healing occur.

Since keening can be a particularly concentrated form of prayer, the sound arrow freely departing from the depths of the body effects a body-and-soul *clearing*. The loss becomes gain, time becomes space, immobility of grief becomes rooted strength, and the wound becomes a clearing of tremendous fecundity. It took only a few hours to write this, but it has taken years to understand the process and can take weeks and months of keening in order for healing and the renewal of life to occur.

In the Irish keening theme involved here, called an *Alleluia*, the tension of opposites is the source of the fecundity. The young mother sings because her first-born child has died. She reflects upon every loss of life, from wars and famines, betrayals and illness, and prays despite her rage and trauma for the strength to accept what has happened. Even if we do not want or understand what has come to be, it involves a mystery. To the Christian, living and dying are so profoundly bound together in an indissoluble fecundity that reversals usher in all the new possibilities. The singer keens for as long as it takes for the prayer of mourning to become the praise song. To do this, she prays in at least two ways, one Marian, the other, Christic. She remembers and links up with Mary, the mother of Jesus. She keens, often rocking as she sings, for as long as it takes, and she links, via heartbeat, to Mary's experience, how she stood holy vigil, and experienced fully and violently an agony and the loss of her first-born child.

Though this notion of solidarity can be taken in the wrong way, it is also the heart of the matter. The singer also can keen a witnessing because she remembers Christ on the Cross, remembering the crucifixion *as His complete, voluntary, kenotic self-emptying.* This in fact became the doorway to a whole new world, and our life today as Christians and Catholics. The keening or the song continues until the singer can weave all the losses together, bind them, offer them on an altar of impossible mystery, and because of it, come out the other side, in a new clearing. *The mourning becomes praise.* The meditation deepens until the young mother can imagine holding the Christ child. The two keening praxes (offering/surrendering and kenosis or self-emptying) reflect something of a voluntary crucifixion and a conscious resurrection, on a far smaller scale. Two themes from the Gospels will make this kind of prayer clear: "*Not my will, but Thy will*," and "*I must decrease so that He will increase.*"

Traditionally, *sean nos* melodies were very original and, at times, transmitted orally, from singer to singer, from elders to the younger singers, but never notated or fixed on paper, for this would deny many of the unique particularities which make keening truthful. In recent years, however, this reticence has been laid down and some of the great keening themes have been preserved as gestures and indications in free, almost ekphonetic notational styles. (For the same reasons and more, the mystical songs of the Hassidic world only grace the singer under certain conditions, and are not 'fixed' in print because they are alive and living. This is true for the Native American Indian medicine song as well). Hopefully, this publishing urge to precipitation will be remembered by musicology as something that still must be contextualized, remain linked to all the interior possibilities and spiritual practices of the tradition from which it arises. The soul of the work then continues to give others life.

So this reflection has hopefully modeled a way of being. In contemplative musicianship, we are not only concerned with the final product of musical professionalism, *many right notes*, which, in numerous ways, is a technical procedure. In contemplative musicianship, we take the artistic and spiritual time that is needed to look into the nature and meaning of layered musical realities, acknowledge the inter-connectedness of these deeper strata, and search for, acknowledge, affirm, and articulate the ways in which sound affects and effects life, in all its cycles.

This contemplative orientation suggests not only that we search and journey, but that we become open in a radical (rooted) way. *We allow music to change and transform us. We allow the lives and deaths of our patients, strangers and loved ones, to change and transform us.* We allow our failures and fruitfulness and those of our students, colleagues, and unknown strangers to change and transform us. We allow the betrayals and martyrdoms, glories and mysteries to change and transform us—and, insofar as we can grapple with the mystery of evil, we come to forgive and remember, and ask God to help us find the strength to walk our talk. In that regard, I would like to risk a story to illustrate a few of the challenges of the performative element in spiritual practices.

Totally Disarmed: The Choir of Witnessing

In the hospital, as the clinical supervisor for a large, multi-institutional music-thanatology practice, I experienced a young, lactating, 16-year old unwed mother with fresh milk bursting from her body. The milk had only moments before left the tracks of dampened patches on her blouse, which is usually a source of joy and wonder for the new mother. Instead, in this hour, everything was reversed. Her son was dying, and already, there was no cortical activity. We watched, witnessed, and participated as she entered into a sudden and trauma-induced keening that comes with the death of a first-born. No one taught her this expression—it seemed as if two weeks earlier she was a laughing girl and this day she was fully a woman. Keening is an innate and normal response to that which is unexpected and impossible. All nursing and physician staff startled as she broke into an agonal, spontaneous wailing.

A sensitive male nurse, anticipating what was to come with the morning light, had somehow found a rocking chair the night before and had it ready and waiting for Meredith in the intensive care unit. She sat holding the lifeless body of her newborn son who, in an end-of-life extubation, had, layer after layer, been disconnected from life-support systems and had died slowly. His leave-taking in the arms of his mother was slow; it took place over the course of the next two hours, right before our eyes. We witnessed her grief and his *transitus* as his perfectly round head changed color from a fleshy peach blossom pink to a cool blue, and as she unwillingly, unexpectedly had to die to her life as a mother. No masks here. Completely transparent, she wailed and heaved, grieving with all of the strength and vulnerability of her youthful body and soul, now tempered and made "as if" ancient in the space of a day.

The sound of her keening effected and quickened the whole staff because the grief was so blatantly honest. Keening takes *space*, the larger the space, the better. To be sure, there is *no* physical space available in an intensive care unit, such as they are, equipped with the technological apparatus of biomedicine. Add to this our harps, and the needs of the day, and you have a more-than-full spectrum. Yet invisibly, the power of her wailing conveyed unadulterated authority, like Moses commanding the Red Sea to open. The concrete hospital congestion that comes with intimidating technology evaporated and a clearing occurred, at least emotionally. The urgently needed social space manifested sensitively and immediately. Though there were other patients nearby, down the hall, in nearby cubicles, and the census was high, no one sought to silence or dampen the sound of her grief. She sat and rocked, keening a strange, deep, throaty, loud, moaning, rising and falling song, instinctively repeating her own tracks in this *one-of-a-kind, never-to-be-sought-out medicine song* that was forever unique to her totality as a woman, a mother, and lover. In thirty years, it remains the most difficult death-bed vigil I have ever attended or played.

Only some forty-five or fifty minutes into this vigil, I turned slightly from them, mother and son, the student interns, and my harp, only to be taken aback in heart by what I discovered directly behind us. There stood an entire host of equally young soon-to-be mothers, a silent choir of magnificent import. No boys or men stood in their ranks. Most were in very advanced stages of pregnancy. At least fifteen women, all of them her peers from the local group home that had given her so much support during her pregnancy, were leaning in solidarity on the oversized windows, hands raised on the glass as if ready to touch, comfort and anoint both mother and child, their eyes streaming silent tears. No conversations were taking place. No words were exchanged, but their presence was powerful. Each time Meredith looked up from her son's still face, she saw them. Each woman in various expressions of containment witnessed the sorrow of a very new mother and held her own life-filled belly and anguished heart in reserve strength for the matter at hand. These acts were so courageous, not one of them turned away because the sights, sounds, and smells were too difficult or too close to the bone (though they surely were). An infant's death is the most difficult. They risked everything in friendship, a kind of communion most needed, and I was amazed at their gifts.

They didn't avoid her pain; it was the opposite. They walked with her, every step of the way, to the bitter end (with no end) and for the time following, no matter what it cost them. What would have happened if other immediate groups had been able to rally *en toto* and respond with such powerful disarmament at Dachau, Ravensbrück, Wounded Knee, or Cape Town? The implications were stunning then and now, and asked all of us to consider our own mediocrities in many new ways.

That day, instead of coming home exhausted, demoralized, or perhaps tempted to leave clinical practice because it was too hard, some blessed opposite opened up, for me, and for other clinicians as well. We were stunned by the love extended between virtual strangers, and the courageous compassion embodied in the entire course of events. That keening was so authentic it could have flattened an army, but instead, it was holy, *set apart*, protected by all, as if for a brief day the medical setting had become transformed and emerged as a sanctuary for completion. This *intensified living* changed life in ICU for a good while. Years later, nurses still talked about that community experience of Tyler's dying, of the bold young women, and the much intensified, accelerated living that had taken place that day, a day when the unit was aptly named. Tyler's primary care nurse taught in our classrooms years later and said that the entire experience remained as one of the moments that re-defined, deepened, and ennobled the nursing personnel and professional commitments. The role that sound, prescriptive music, and keening played, the rhythm of the rocking chair guided by the sustain of the harps, cannot be measured in double blinds. Nevertheless, it weighed in heavily on the side of shared and individual experiences of the transformation (and healing) of grief. This article is not the right forum to describe what and how we delivered prescriptive music for the mother and the child in this situation. I'm choosing rather to emphasize the phenomenology of the embodiment processes, incarnational and excarnational, the miraculous shift of social space that occurs when people are open, when we listen and respond and allow. These become the community experiences of death, the reality of death as part of the fullness of life, and the power of the keening sound arrow or *saeta*.

The Chalice of Repose Project: Thirty Years of Vigil

Our Chalice of Repose Project with its ancillary School of Music-Thanatology makes contributions in these regards to the field of palliative medicine. It has garnered respect and collaboration from a wide spectrum of professionals and organizations in the arts, sciences, humanities, the media, and philanthropy. The Chalice has grounded music-thanatology in the world essentially by being faithful to the very clear essentials of its original vision. Through various forms of pedagogical models and internship programs, rigorously educated musician-clinicians who met the requirements for certification in the field have been bringing prescriptive music to the bed-side of dying patients. This has happened in every psycho-social setting: hospitals, hospices, geriatric homes, parishes, prisons, private homes, and various long-term facilities.

The work of music-thanatology began thirty years ago when I was an orderly and had instinctively climbed into bed in order to hold a man who was dying of emphysema. He was dying desperately, thrashing, clutching, and grasping. I held him in midwifery position and sang to him until he died; as we began to breathe together, he rested into my body as if it fit like a glove. He trusted me, the struggle dissipated, and he died very peacefully, with the *Mass of the Blessed Virgin Mary* and the *Adoro te devote* and the *Salve Regina* sending him back into his deepest self, and then, soon, to his Maker. That moment so long ago was a practical response of courtesy, and, in retrospect, natural to anyone who has been raised in a praying community and in a community where death has continually been a community event.

While this chapter is not the place to review our history in detail, nor to relate the steps that were involved in becoming a formal profession and a sub-specialty of palliative medicine,[2] I must mention this first death-bed vigil very briefly, because the dual themes of embodiment and performance found there are ever-present in our *Ur-vigil* and have accompanied our students in formation. There is a way of knowing, sensing, and responding with every fiber of your being to the possibility that true *encounter* is a moment where we also meet God. This has burned itself into my reason for everything, including joy.

I have always retained the Pauline language of body, soul, and spirit, and coupling this with the fact that Christianity is the religion of incarnation, it seemed that there had to be a way of being with medicine, music, and spiri-tuality that can take all these nuances into account. Simply doing something, even if it involves music or ritual or art, isn't (to me) necessarily a sign of embodiment. Just look at medical and nursing procedures, many musical performances, and even, sadly, love-making, and one must admit that it is possible to be adept in some ways while still entirely absent amidst great activity. So I use the term *embodiment* advisedly, thoughtfully, to indicate something that is so much a part of our conscious selves, after metanoia, after multiple metanoias, that the resultant activities bear the unmistakable stamp of a more unified and transformed thinking, feeling, and willing, or, as they say in poetry, an awakened head, hands, and heart. In other words, the inner transformative deaths are not about human potential and personal growth. Rather, they can prepare us for service, and bring us back home to a greater good which can be experienced widely in community, regardless of the named or identities of many constituencies we serve.

As a medical modality, music-thanatology is available for anyone in pain, anyone who suffers, and one need only make the referral or request to be a recipient of this service. (The majority of patients identify themselves as hav-ing no religious affiliation). But I'll risk the complexities—I have observed that it is impossible to sustain the work of music-thanatology without being involved in some kind of daily prayer, meditation, or worship praxis.

Fast-forwarding to more recent times, a few clinical details might flesh out the picture for readers. During the 32 years of our work, with voice and harp, many thousands of death bed vigils have been attended by our clinical teams wherever the Chalice of Repose Project has been located, and by extension, wherever our certified graduates are now placed in medical settings through-out the world. My colleagues and I have been present to tens of thousands of patients and their families. The work of music-thanatology has been solely dedicated to serving the physical and spiritual needs of the dying with this prescriptive music, which is always delivered live at the bed side. No pre-recorded music is used, and the two terms (prescriptive music and recorded music) both have their place and beauty, but are antithetical in our discipline.

Music-thanatology is a contemplative practice with clinical applications, and has its historical roots in a number of crucial areas, but a primary one is the Western Christian vision of monastic medicine. This flourished in whole new ways during the eleventh century at the Benedictine monastery of Cluny in France. I would like to emphasize several things here from my previous work[3] that are particularly germane to this anthology.

The Cluniac customaries are a spiritual gold mine for anyone with a moral imagination. These texts are by no means our only intellectual or spiritual sources, and the Benedictines never mention harp or "prescriptive music"; those and many other critical elements are my contributions and discoveries, the ones that went on to constitute the field of music-thanatology. We study these texts, *not to reproduce rituals*, but because the Benedictine world— being a world of ritual—modeled something comprehensive. They practiced a way of being with sickness and health, dying and becoming, that embraced the body, the soul, and the spirit, individually and collectively. As such, their monastic infirmaries anticipated what we now call palliative medicine by eight hundred years, and to everyone's benefit. My colleagues and I still re-read the customaries because they are wisdom texts; we read them and are renewed.

Be that as it may, every group and every effort has its rituals, but people define ritual differently in the professional disciplines of anthropology, liturgy, psychology, theology, and so forth. We've been very careful, during the entire thirty years, to be respectful of the role of the chaplain, the minister, priest, or rabbi in the medical setting, so there will be no question of usurping professional boundaries. *We do not reproduce rituals*, and we do not reproduce Cluniac rituals at the bedside of the dying patient. However, the spiritual power and spirituality of the work is undeniable, and in the sense that is widest, we have hundreds of little ritual acts of professionalism, ritual acts of kindness, ritual acts of clinical and pastoral care, musical preparation and delivery, and so forth. To the degree that these become formalized, observed, their symbols, meanings, and terms deepen and expand our lives, we, too, in a modern and ecumenical way, are daily involved in both ritual and performance practice. One of our most poignant rituals is silent, but has effected change.

In our medical records, we do not record that Mr. Smith died at twelve hundred hours today. Rather, we always say and write: Mr. Smith made his *transitus* at noon today; stressing movement as something natural and organic. A second ritual occurs at the weekly clinical discussions, where we begin with the naming of those whom we have attended upon and who had made their *transitus* during that period of seven days, in the previous years, for however many years we have been in practice. Some weeks, many names are read and it takes several minutes; other weeks, few names are read. But always, we make an attempt to honor them, remember them in our daily lives, hold their faces up in our memories, and link the communities of the living and the dead, bringing our gratitude for their lives and their last gifts into consciousness during the work of the day. A third ritual is practiced by many to different degrees. Before we go to sleep at night, many of us try to hold up in our memories the faces of those whom we have attended that day, and each clinician, in their own way, takes that life and human being with them into the threshold of sleep. I pray that they are given what they need, and that their loved ones will be comforted.

A New and Living Way

The Chalice of Repose Project, both graduate level school and clinical practice, is located in Mt. Angel, Oregon, a center of monastic spirituality for over one hundred years. Here we have secured a permanent home for a small but beautiful clinic-sanctuary for the delivery of prescriptive music, the first of its kind in the world, as well as a second building for offices and faculty. While we are expanding with some ten collaborative projects nationally and internationally, a core dimension of our fourth decade is the return to that which is human scale. A life of harp and voice is one of intimacy. Our work began with the central values of bringing beauty, intimacy, and reverence into the medical setting, into the lives and deaths of our patients, into palliative care. The early monastic infirmaries were beautiful sanctuaries; so our clinic today is also beautiful.

Now, in addition to the concert tours, I see patients daily, consult for hospitals nationwide, and teach some fifty international graduate students enrolled in our educational program. Many days, I work in a nearby monastic infirmary where most of the patients are in their nineties. We are also developing an interdisciplinary master's degree program for The Catholic University of America. On the one hand, this is significant growth, but none of this will work unless we maintain the interiority. So it seems right to say: I cannot think of a single time when any inner death did not result in further growth. Going all the way through something, sustaining at all odds, over and over, becomes a capacity, a source of luminosity, and this is the gold that grief has taught and given me. Most of my colleagues and I have been her apprentices; but this also allows us to know true joy. Being broken, we are broken open, whether broken-hearted, broken in spirit, or broken in body. Each massive diminishment is a massive clearing; I do not wish to be broken, but am musical enough to squint and see/hear God's signature in every bolt of lightning, calm breeze, or downpour that shakes the sleep from my eyes. To the extent that I can live any day in a more balanced way, and live from the combined fruit of head, heart, and hands, all three in continual metanoia, I might be starting to approach something like a Christian life, a *Judeo-Christian life*— I try to remember that from which we have come.

In Conclusion

Practices spiritual, musical, clinical, intellectual, religious, and artistic necessarily become, through repetition, deeply embodied. To the degree that embodied practices *become* conscious and *are* performative, these specific practices cease being merely activities, pure action, and emerge, over time, as new capacities. To the degree that the embodied practices which have become capacities are ritualized in public liturgy or evangelical expressions springing directly from the teachings of the Gospels, we stand inside ways and mean of prodigious delicacy, creativity, complexity, and connection. These exteriorized, performative ways and means link all three time streams—past, present, and future—and the people who pray, praise, love, and forgive inside, around, and beyond time with the mystical body of Christ. It is this greater unity of historical catholic practices to which I was early called and in which I have repeatedly, despite struggle and challenge, rupture and erosion, found spiritual home and inexhaustible source of fecundity. The purpose of this effort has been to reflect upon some of the most poignant how's and why's of the artist/clinician's world, and to model those integrated particularities by translating the world of music and sung prayer, health and illness, living and dying, suffering and joy, into a world of pure text. In so doing, I have worn both heart and mind in equal voice upon a freely billowing sleeve, believing transparency to be the first and most foundational of all the listening-responding practices bequeathed to us from Christ. Personally, through study, work, reflection, rest, and prayer, cherishing silence as much as music, I have come to see myself as both an inheritor and a practitioner of a generative and polyphonic way, living as if inside a string quartet made in heaven: *catholic, mystical, practical, and sound.*

Practicing the Pastoral Care of the Sick: The Sacramental Body in Liturgical Motion

Bruce T. Morrill, S.J.

INTRODUCTION: SEARCHING FOR A METHOD BOTH ACADEMIC AND PASTORAL

In my contribution to the introduction of this present book I reported how liturgical theology holds the actual practice of the rites of the Church to be its primary subject matter. Liturgical theology is in the midst of a methodological quest as it seeks to do theology not merely as book-bound ideas but, rather, as an argument constructed from the historically situated praxis of Christian faith, centered in the liturgy as "the summit toward which the activity of the Church is directed" and "the font from which all her power flows."[1] This places liturgical theology in the age-old problem of the relationship between theory and practice. Given the faith-perspective within which liturgical theology operates, theory has a normative dimension, and practice, a pastoral character—and both of these, moreover, an ecclesial nature. This, at times, makes for a volatile mix of ingredients. In attempting to move beyond the mere study of texts to the actual performance of rites in contexts, the liturgical theologian does not approach the ritual practices of the faithful as an external observer-analyst but, rather, as a member-participant and (in my own case) as an ordained pastoral leader. Whether ordained or lay, the liturgical theologian's scholarly writing includes a faith-commitment to the observed tradition being analyzed, a vocation to promoting the tradition of the Church's sacramental worship. To teach, discuss, or write about such material in this way in the contemporary academy poses difficult but unavoidable questions: What are the ethical boundaries of this type of academic endeavor, given the pastoral situation of the actual subject matter?

What responsibility does the theologian have to orthodoxy, given the normative dimension of the theoretical pursuit? How can and does the liturgical theologian's work include a constructive dimension, an effort to make the tradition a living reality by drawing on resources from history to meet the pastoral needs of today?

No mere quest for "relevance," the liturgical theologian's passionate desire, as a scholar and believer, to study and theorize about actual practice has required methodological experimentation. Over the past decade I have developed a term paper for my undergraduate introductory course in Catholicism requiring the students to go see what actual communities of worship are doing. Only in that way can they study liturgy as lived religious tradition. This approach requires an articulation of principles for guiding the interpretation of liturgical performances, including attention to the ambiguities and benefits of participant-observation.[2] With my graduate theological students, a self-selecting group, I am able to presume fundamental knowledge of the rites, as well as a commitment to pastoral ministry. In classes spanning the spectrum of Catholic sacramental rituals, I have groups prepare and present the rites themselves so as to get practical experience of them, motivating further historical and theological study. This method is along the lines of Victor Turner's performance-as-anthropology approach, with students gaining affective and intellectual insights into a given ritual by assuming roles within a (safely) framed field of play.[3] But what if another situation presents itself: a special event that occurs both as part of the actual ongoing life of a community and an event explicitly meant to provide an element of performance within the overall work of an academic conference? How does one do this, as priest and professor in the context of a college community, without transgressing modern boundaries of faith and academy, private and public?

Attending to performance requires narrative. The next section of this chapter will recount how I went about constructing and executing a liturgy that could (1) engage believers as a rite of the Church, (2) explore new possibilities for that rite, and (3) contribute an element of original liturgical performance for the benefit of an array of scholars at a conference on Catholic ritual practices.

The Emergence of a Specific Performance of the Pastoral Care of the Sick

As explained in the Introduction to this book, one of the methodological principles for the "Practicing Catholic" conference was the inclusion of performance not as mere decoration or entertainment but, rather, as integral a scholarly contribution as the academic papers. To think of practice in terms of "Ritual, Body, and Contestation in Catholic Faith" brought to mind for us the highly original work of liturgical dance choreographer Robert VerEecke, S.J., who for decades has been exploring the movement of the body in liturgy. VerEecke's acceptance of our initially vague request quickly ushered into the development of the conference an element of contestation that proved generative of an even larger practical, that is, pastoral and liturgical, undertaking on the Holy Cross campus.

That Roman Catholics, or Christians more generally, in history have included dance in a variety of forms and contexts—not only liturgical but also mystical[4]—over centuries of practicing the faith is a story rife with contestation. Prelates in the early church condemned such activity, especially by women, as did other councils down the ages. Still, forms of dance have continued in scattered times and places up to the present, not to mention processions and movement with incense and the like. Since the middle of the twentieth century choreographers have been creating dances based on classical, folk, modern, and free-expression forms of this art. Their performance has largely been met with discomfort on the part of clergy and laity, although not universally so. After observing decades of experimentation in churches, convents, cathedrals, and colleges, the Vatican and their episcopal minions have published statements effectively condemning such dance in the context of the Church's liturgical rites. The status of dance in the liturgy, however, remains ambiguous, indeed, a quintessential example of contestation over meaning, purpose, and power. From the side of those condemning dance in worship comes apprehension over eroticism, ambiguity of meaning in the movement, and evidence for often contrived and poorly performed instances of dance in specific liturgies. Those who promote the incorporation of dance in liturgy admit to the Scylla of amateurism and the Charybdis of presentations so polished in form and execution as to feel external to the communal action of the rite.[5] Inviting VerEecke and his Boston Liturgical Dance Ensemble, then, to perform during the conference would not be a matter of including a standard form of contemporary Catholic practice. Indeed, as we pursued the possibility, some of the pastoral-liturgical staff at Holy Cross expressed strong reservations.

Arguments over the appropriate purpose for dance during the Mass at the conference, a Mass that would also be part of the regular weekend worship of the College community, led me to raise a more fundamental question concerning our objectives for this ritual event: Were we indeed falling into the trap of including dance as a showpiece, so to speak, something to make the Mass special? A review of objectives for the entire initiative was in order. Were the reasons for such a Mass a combination of obligation (a weekend conference that would coincide with the Lord's Day, a compulsory day of worship for the Roman Catholic participants), aesthetics (the beauty of the College's 900-seat chapel, world-renowned organ, and VerEecke's dance company), and the desire for ample performance during an academic conference devoted to ritual and the body? If so, then in some way the tail still seemed to be wagging the dog, so to speak, leading me to pose a more fundamental question: What sort of liturgy would really be integral to the conference, coinciding with some of the specific content of the conference's scholarly papers and other performances? Equally, if not fundamentally more, important: What sort of liturgy might provide a genuine service to the life of the College community, the wider Roman Catholic environs and, thereby, to Catholicism as practiced tradition? This latter pushed aside, in my opinion, any unexamined inclination to "put on a show" for the conference. It also generated the new educational situation for liturgical theology to which I alluded above, neither a matter of taking a group of students and scholars to observe and participate in some liturgy happening outside the framework of our academic setting nor enlisting all in an explicitly defined play-exercise of some one or other of the Church's rites. It dawned on me that here was an opportunity to *do* liturgical theology by undertaking an original pastoral-liturgical initiative that would enact an official rite of the Church in a way that might also advance the viability of its practice for and within Roman Catholicism.

One of the constellations of papers and performances that had emerged in planning "Practicing Catholic" concerned health crises past and present: childbirth, sickness, chronic illness, and death. In light of this compelling thematic convergence, I had already decided to make as my academic-theological contribution a study of the official Roman Catholic ritual, Pastoral Care of the Sick: Rites of Anointing and Viaticum.[6] While related to one another within a larger *ordo* of pastoral-liturgical ministry to ailing believers, Anointing and Viaticum are distinct sacraments serving specific purposes for the sick and the dying. The pastoral problem perduring some two decades since the establishment of the current ritual is the conflation, not only by poorly informed laity but also by far too many clergy, of *both* sacraments into "last rites" at the "hour of death." To explore this still-unsettled contemporary Roman Catholic rite by means not only of research in the library, but ministry in the chapel seemed a prime *theological* opportunity to me, one which could expose Roman Catholics and non-Catholic academicians alike to a still only emerging phase of one of the Church's sacramental traditions. A brief word of history concerning that tradition, then, is in order.

Viaticum is Christianity's original sacrament of the dying, a special celebration of the Eucharist (within the context of either a Mass or a briefer ritual) for supporting the dying believer as s/he makes the passage from life in this world to the next.[7] In the early Church the ministration of the Eucharist with prayers and blessings especially suited to the process of dying was the last liturgical act to be celebrated in the life of a person. Viaticum literally meant "food for the journey." Only after the eighth century did changes in the theological understanding of "sacrament," in general, and the forgiveness of sin, in particular, converge to displace Viaticum as the "last rites" for the dying with another of the ancient ritual traditions of the Church, the Anointing of the Sick. With this shift in practice came a change in language for that rite, from *Unctio Infirmorum* (Anointing of the Sick) to *Extrema Unctio* (Last Anointing [before death]). The liturgical reform mandated by the Second Vatican Council restored Viaticum as the proper sacrament for the dying, while Anointing, on the other hand, is for the sacramental strengthening of any person "whose health is seriously impaired by sickness or old age," including not only those physically afflicted but also people suffering with serious mental illness.[8] The Sacrament of Anointing, moreover, is repeatable for a given person (as opposed to the once-off practice of the former Extreme Unction). Rather than being a sacrament isolated at the deathbed, a ministration between the priest and the dying person amounting to his sealing the latter's immanent mortal demise, the Rite of Anointing has been restored as a liturgical celebration best performed in some communal context, drawing a circle of believers around the sick person under the ritual leadership of the priest as soon as a person, with the help of medical professionals, pastoral ministers, family and friends, discerns one's health to be in serious danger. The communal and processual character of Anointing is the key to understanding why the reformed sacrament is situated in the much larger complex of supportive rituals, pastoral visitations, and catechetical formation that together comprise the entire rite, entitled "The Pastoral Care of the Sick." One final aspect of the reformed Sacrament of Anointing that contributed to my proposing its enactment within our conference is the option of ministering the sacrament to numerous individuals during a Mass with an assembled local community.

My experience at Holy Cross certainly indicated that the meaning and practice of this sacrament is currently a matter of significant contestation. When early on I shared with the steering committee of the Center for Religion, Ethics, and Culture (CREC) our plans to do this liturgy during the conference, one professor expressed bewilderment over who at the College might desire the sacrament, while another was concerned that those who did come forth might be inappropriately put on display. With the support of the Director of the Chaplain's Office we were able to persuade the committee, and I began planning.

Putting the Rite into Practice: An Original Pastoral Performance

First, I was able to reconnoiter with Bob VerEecke, who warmly greeted the news that the liturgy during the conference would be a ritual Mass for the anointing of the sick. He had significant prior experience choreographing movement for such liturgies. The key, VerEecke explained, lay in recognizing that the liturgy is about healing whole persons; thus, the body in motion comprises the primary symbol. His work would need both to create gestures in service to those who would be anointed and to incorporate these in larger movements capable of drawing the entire assembly into what he poetically called "the circle of healing." A further concern I raised was the desire that the ritual of anointing not function in too great an isolation from the other (usual) parts of the Roman Mass, a sort of extra event disjointedly inserted. Crucial to avoiding this problem would be multivalent (that is, by words and gestures) connections between the Liturgy of the Word (scriptural proclamations and preaching), the Liturgy of Anointing, and finally the Liturgy of the Eucharist.

What would make the bodily connections much greater, we both agreed, would be VerEecke's choreographing a series of processions throughout the

Mass: the Entrance Procession (typical for every Mass), a procession accompanying the sick forward from the pews into the sanctuary for the Sacrament of Anointing, and the Communion Procession. Working with processions promised several benefits. Processions are without doubt the most common form of liturgical movement (or dance) in the historical and contemporary practice of Catholicism. Thus, while many in the assembly might be uncomfortable or unfamiliar with liturgical dancers within Mass, their processional function would situate their artistic activity in places where overt bodily movement is readily expected.[9] In addition, procession is a linear form of movement designed to pass through the entire assembly—an action best suited to the long, tall, and narrow architectural features of the Holy Cross chapel. Finally, we agreed that the music would need to help unify the liturgy. Liturgical composer Andrew Witchger has quite beautifully set the entire Rite of Anointing to music, with parts for the presiding celebrant, choir, cantor, and assembly. Musically unifying the processions would be two versions of Marty Haughen's "Shepherd Me, O God," the first a litany for accompanying the Entrance Procession and continuing through the entire Introductory Rite, and the second, the complete text of Psalm 23, for accompanying the Communion Procession. Plans for the liturgy were sufficiently in place.

The larger task was to conceive a pastoral strategy for ensuring that the Mass for the Anointing of the Sick, scheduled for Saturday afternoon, October 19, 2002, not take place in a vacuum but, rather, constitute a genuine service to the Holy Cross College community, as well as perhaps the wider local environment, the Roman Catholic Diocese of Worcester. I enlisted the help of Suzanne Dwinell, R.N., a graduate student of mine in the pastoral ministry program at Boston College, who works both in the emergency ward of one of Worcester's hospitals and as the parish nurse[10] in one of the city's Catholic churches. Suzanne has had extensive contact with Holy Cross students in both contexts over the years. Together we developed what we came to call our Pastoral Program in relation to the Mass for Anointing the Sick.

The official Roman Catholic rite of the Pastoral Care of the Sick entails a variety of activities including Visits to the Sick (which include scriptural reading, reflection, prayer, and blessings—all of which can be done by laity as well as clergy), Communion of the Sick (again, a work open to lay ministers of the Eucharist), as well as Anointing of the Sick (requiring a priest). This entire complex of pastoral-liturgical activity presumes a combination of fixed (daily, weekly) and flexible time-patterns and a context of people's houses or apartments, nursing homes, hospitals—all in relation to local parishes. A college campus, Suzanne and I readily recognized, is a different environment, both spatial and temporal. We fashioned for the students a Pastoral Program characterized by a series of weekly meetings, fitted into the fall semester, with the Ritual Mass of Anointing as the climactic, central event. For faculty and staff, as well as local alumni we would offer a similar series of lunchtime sessions. In order to craft the entire Pastoral Program, as well as to publicize it, we would work with leaders involved with all those constituencies: the Office of the College Chaplains, the Office of Student Life, the Director of Counseling Services, and the Jesuit moderator of the Alumni Sodality. One further group I decided to involve would entail a new bridging of the pastoral-academic divide, namely, students enrolled in my fall seminar in the Religious Studies Department, entitled "Solidarity in Suffering: Sacrament, Word, and Ethics."

I had constructed the course in relation to the "Practicing Catholic" conference by setting up a series of units alternating between theology that addresses social-systemic realities of suffering and theology found in the Church's pastoral-liturgical ministry. I would give the students an option of participating in the Pastoral Program for Anointing, wherein they would participate in all phases of the project and write a reflection-type paper integrating elements of the experience with related readings from the course. This constituted a new approach to my *doing* liturgical theology in an academic course, namely, students' participation in an actual pastoral-liturgical initiative (one done in "real time," as it were). Suzanne and I would rely on these students to advise us on how to go about reaching potential participants in the program, and I would mentor their involvement in it. As things turned out, three of the students chose to pursue this option and ended up playing highly active roles in the pastoral process.

I decided to model our Pastoral Program on another rite of the Roman Catholic Church, indeed one of the most revolutionary and successful in the wake of Vatican II: the Rite of Christian Initiation of Adults (RCIA). Drawing on initiatory practices that reached their zenith in the fourth century of the Church, the RCIA is a four-staged pastoral rite comprised of Inquiry and Evangelization (inviting potential neophytes), the Catechumenate (a long period of spiritual, liturgical, ethical, and doctrinal formation), the Sacraments of Initiation (the climactic joint-celebration of the Baptism, Confirmation, and Eucharist, usually at the annual Easter Vigil), and Mystagogy (a brief period of theological reflection on the sacramental mysteries the newly initiated have experienced). Implementation of the RCIA entails ordained pastors, trained parish catechists, individual sponsors for each neophyte, as well as periodic support from and interaction with others in the local faith community. It should not be difficult to imagine what a vital force this ritual process has become in the annual life of American Catholic parishes.

My (theological) theory was that, just as the aesthetically elaborate celebration of the Sacraments of Initiation at the Easter Vigil constitutes a ritual climax that is nonetheless dependent for its pastoral effectiveness on the other three stages of the Rite, so too our elaborate communal celebration of the Sacrament of Anointing within Mass at Holy Cross could be significantly enhanced by similar stages of formative pastoral engagement. Thus, we would begin the fall term with two weeks of Inquiry and Evangelization, using flyers, announcements at weekend Masses (presented by students to students), and letters to all students, faculty, and staff, explaining the current theology and practice of the Rite of Anointing and inviting all to a series of four, one-hour sessions leading up to the Mass on October 19. The latter would comprise the Catechetical phase, which the students advised Suzanne and me to hold for students on Tuesday evenings after dinner-time. I announced and scheduled a similar series of lunchtime sessions for the non-student population (faculty, staff, and alumni). Following the Mass in late October, we would have a Mystagogical session, an opportunity for all involved in the process to reflect, pray, and share about what had been experienced. The remainder of this section will recount the first two stages of the process, while the Mass for the Anointing of the Sick, given its ritual magnitude in the process, shall warrant a subsequent section of its own.

Since many readers of this present book may have little familiarity with the contemporary Roman Catholic sacrament of anointing, I am reprinting here the entire content of the brochure we produced as a tool for evangelizing (that is, introducing and inviting) the general student population. The text draws heavily on the rite of the Pastoral Care of the Sick (including verbatim, nos. 1, 5, 6, 7, and 108), an approach we considered catechetically responsible. A couple of students advised me to entitle the outer panel of the brochure, "Are You Suffering?"—a blunt approach I myself would not have conceived, let alone pursued, but for the assurances of the students. That panel opened to an inner one reading, "An Invitation to the Holy Cross Student Body." Then came the three panels of text:

Human Sickness and Suffering

Suffering and illness have always been among the greatest problems that trouble the human spirit. Our faith helps us to grasp more deeply the mystery of suffering and to bear our pain with greater courage. The gospels witness to the fact that Jesus associated with many who were sick and suffering and showed great compassion and love for them and their families and friends.

Jesus and his disciples made a point of touching and anointing the sick. They imposed hands upon them as they prayed for God's healing strength: "They cast out many demons, and anointed with oil many who were sick and cured them" (Mark 6:13). *The Church carries on this tradition through the Sacrament of the Anointing of the Sick.*

Who is Invited to this Sacrament?

The rite for anointing within Mass may be used to anoint a number of people within the same celebration. The rite is appropriate for large gatherings where the sick and people suffering from chronic illnesses, such as asthma, anxiety, arthritis, depression, eating disorders, and other life-altering conditions, can assemble. The nature of one's illness, disease, or condition need not be disclosed to anyone.

A Ritual Mass for Anointing the Sick will be celebrated on campus in the Saint Joseph Chapel on Saturday, October 19th, 4:30 p.m. Catholic students who feel called to the sacrament are warmly invited to join fellow members of the Holy Cross community (faculty, staff, alumni/ae) participating in the special liturgy that day.

Celebrating the Sacrament of Anointing within Mass

"Are any among you suffering? They should pray. . . . Are any among you sick? They should call for the elders of the church and have them pray over them, anointing them with oil in the name of the Lord. The prayer of faith will save the sick, and the Lord will raise them up; and anyone who has committed sins will be forgiven" (James 5:13–15). Those who are seriously or chronically ill need the special help of God's grace. Christ strengthens those who are dealing with various illnesses or conditions, providing them with the strongest means of support. The celebration of this sacrament consists especially in the laying on of hands by the priests of the Church, the offering of the prayers of faith, and the anointing of the sick with oil made holy by God's blessing. This rite signifies the grace of the sacrament and confers it. This sacrament gives the grace of the Holy Spirit to those who are sick. By this grace the whole person is saved, sustained by trust in God, and strengthened to bear difficulty with new strength and courage.

In the anointing of the sick, which includes the prayer of faith, faith itself is manifested. The sick person will be saved by this and the faith of the Church, which looks back to the death and resurrection of Christ, the source of the sacrament's power, and looks ahead to the future kingdom that is pledged in the sacrament.

Period of Preparation

So as to help those of us who will be receiving this sacrament to celebrate more fully, the College is offering a period of preparation. This will include four, one-hour sessions. These sessions will entail presentations on the Scripture and tradition of the sacrament, faith sharing, and prayer. Follow-up sessions will be offered after the celebration of the sacrament. The first session will take place on Tuesday, September 17th, 7:30 p.m., in Smith Hall 303.

Contact

[Here were provided contact information for Morrill and Dwinell, as well as acknowledgement of the College Chaplaincy's and CREC's sponsorship of the program and, finally, citation of the pamphlets extensive quotation and paraphrasing from the Rites of the Catholic Church, "Pastoral Care of the Sick: Rites of Anointing and Viaticum."]

The four, one-hour sessions took place on the successive Tuesday evenings, with a half dozen students proving to be regular participants, along with a number of other students who attended one or two of the sessions. I did not want these sessions to be the sort of classes woefully typical in American Catholic parishes—lectures followed by questions or small group discussions with some little prayer added at the end. Learning again from the RCIA, with its model Celebration of the Word of God setting a "context of prayer" for "catechetical or instructional meetings,"[11] I designed these catechetical gatherings as liturgical actions, opened and concluded with ritual-greetings and blessings. Essential to good liturgy is a space characterized by silence and song. Students took leadership roles for the readings and music, as well as the instructional component and shared reflection. As for pastoral counseling in relation to the sacramental ritual, some students came to see me privately in my office to discuss their personal discernment about being anointed.

In the end, two Holy Cross students presented themselves for Anointing at the Mass on October 19th in Saint Joseph Chapel. They were among a total of thirteen people anointed during that liturgy. A couple of faculty members came forward for anointing at the Mass. In addition, Suzanne had proposed the Mass to various people with whom she works as a parish nurse. There also was the touching case of the student who helped one of her parents to discern the call to be anointed at the liturgy.

CELEBRATING THE MASS FOR ANOINTING THE SICK

Approximately two hundred people assembled for the Ritual Mass for Anointing the Sick on that late Saturday afternoon. For the Entrance Rite, as a way of getting all the assembled bodies joined not only in song and silence but also movement, Bob VerEecke invited all to join in simple arm gestures accompanying the Kyrie: first, a gesture of arms upward, then a reaching outward, and then finally both arms extended outward from the waist, with palms opened upward. The entrance procession was led by the six liturgical dancers (whose movements included the gestures to be used in the Kyrie), then followed the acolytes and reader (Holy Cross students), master of ceremonies (VerEecke), and the presiding minister (myself). A cantor sang Haughen's series of five invocations for healing, to which choir and assembly responded antiphonally, "Shepherd me, O God."[12] The first set can serve here as a sample: "Through the trials that form us [Shepherd me, O God] . . . Through the times that test us [Shepherd me, O God] . . . You who rule creation, show us your salvation, when we face temptation [Shepherd me, O God]." The dancers moved in the aisles in front of the altar rail on each side, doing a diagonal cross motion over the head and down the front of the body, which VerEecke conceived as an image of sheltering. This crossing-and-sheltering gesture would recur throughout the liturgy, especially in accompanying those to be anointed. Once in place at the head of the sanctuary I led the Introductory Rite, finishing with the Opening Prayer from the Roman Ritual:

> God of compassion you take every family under your care and know our physical and spiritual needs. Transform our weakness by the strength of your grace and confirm in us your covenant, so that we may grow in faith and love. We ask this through our Lord Jesus Christ your Son, who lives and reigns with you and the Holy Spirit, one God forever and ever.

These and all the prayers of the liturgy were chanted, a practice that brings solemn dignity to the liturgy by infusing a metered rhythm, along with melody, into the ritual action.

The Liturgy of the Word comprised a New Testament reading, the responsorial psalm, the Gospel reading, and the homily (preaching). The first reading from the Book of Revelation (21:1–7) proclaimed the vision of "a new heaven and a new earth . . . God's dwelling . . . with the human race," when God "shall wipe every tear from their eyes, and there shall be no more death or mourning, crying out or pain, for the former world has passed away." The cantor and choir led the assembly in Psalm 25, "To You, O Lord, I lift my soul," whose verses ask God to reveal the divine ways of truth, confidently proclaiming trust in God's goodness, the hope of the faithful. The Gospel, selected by our Tuesday evening Catechetical group, was Mark 2:1–12. Four people bearing a paralyzed friend are unable to get through a dense crowd around Jesus and therefore open the roof and lower the man to him. "When Jesus saw their faith, he said to the paralytic, 'Child, your sins are forgiven.' " This sparks a contest for the religious elders, with Jesus demonstrating his authority by finally commanding the paralytic to stand, take his mat, and go home. This he does, causing the awestruck crowd to glorify God, "saying, 'We have never seen anything like this.' " I drew on words and images from both the gospel passage and the entire liturgy in preaching the homily:

How greatly we desire to see Jesus. This deep and often urgent desire of Christians down the ages has been carried perhaps as fervently in music as in any other way our bodies can raise up our souls to God and to one another, grasping each others' hands, begging for that word of Grace.

How eagerly and earnestly we desire to see him. And yet we know those moments when we would say in a very different vein, like the people at the end of this story, that we have never seen anything like this. Maybe you're like me and you say, "Well, that's a really pretty story there, a nice story in the Gospel, that quaint little opening in the roof and all." And scripture scholars might help us know, "Well, it really wasn't tiles they removed on that roof; it was probably a mud construction." And we can have a very nice time looking at the story, only to end up thinking: "But we have never seen anything like this!"

Have you?

Still we know that something of the truth in this story is within our own hearts and in the lives of people with which God has privileged our lives as friends and families and loved ones. And we know it also at times in people that we don't even recognize among us. As Professor Rafael taught us today [see chapter 12] about the dynamics of the crowd, the ecstasy of the crowd, in the Philippines, he brought us this image of a woman, sitting on the curb, in a moment . . . the cell phone. Even in people like that, images, pictures, parables come to life and we know something of the deepest longings and yearnings of people, and we know that in ourselves and one another this is our great desire, to see the face of God. And for you and for me who are Christians in this assembly, that is to say how greatly we desire to see Jesus.

And we have.

As many as are the people in this room who could and would tell their stories of the encounter or of the yearning for it, the desire to see him, there are also as many people perhaps who could tell the story of seeing that desire in their sister or brother. The one who cannot move now, flat out on his back: that's where they saw the face of God. That's where they saw Jesus. Maybe even in the places that people said God couldn't possibly be: "God doesn't want to go there! We've got some pretty good conceptions of what God is like. In fact we've got some firm notions, and we've got this image and that, high and above, resplendent, luminously bright." And yet the moments in your life and mine when most likely we see the face of God is not unlike the faith of these four people who carried in a friend, a sister or a brother, a loved one, because they said, "We love you, and we see God in you, even in your courage, even in your faithfulness, even when you don't gloss over and pretend that you're not afraid or discouraged or could use some renewal, some love—and in your remarkable honesty you let God know that too."

If this morning Professor Macy helped us even briefly to reflect on what the term sacrament means, that is, the history of the concept, he taught us as well that it must mean something now in the present tense if it's going to mean anything at all. I would propose that the sacraments with which we live are the living sisters and brothers, people that we know and people we've never met and all those in between, who are, in the words of the great Flemish theologian Edward Schillebeeckx, the human face of God. It's not so much a matter of objects and, in the end of the day dare I say (at least in the preaching), it is not so much the rituals per se. The sacraments are the living, breathing people whom, when we receive the gift from God, we are privileged to recognize as the very face of the divine.

Jesus did.

And eventually, gifted with the same Spirit with which he was baptized, so did his followers too—haltingly, off and on. That's their story, that's my story, and that's your story too.

Perhaps another yearning is: Enough already, enough! I've had it. The Revelation of John, a new heaven's and a new earth? Okay, yes, it's time. Please, by all means, it's time.

But until in God's own time the fullness of that new creation is revealed, what we have is a profoundly special and powerful gift that Jesus lauds today in this story: the gift of our faith that sees in moments, that sees in instances, that expects that God will show us God's faithful presence out there in the crowd, and across the bed, and downstairs, and wherever the very face of God be known. And we need finally, then, these ritual sacraments to help us recognize this faith, living on a sheer promise. We have the Lord's promise that when we together as the body of Christ, assembled in that Spirit, honestly and truthfully celebrate the faith of those whose lives at this moment are a struggle with some illness and of those who are there to bring them and help them and save them and raise them up, then there it is! There's the glimmer. There's the moment. There's the sacrament of the in-breaking of the Kingdom of God.

The invitation that the Lord extends to us in this evening's liturgy is an invitation to those buoyed by the faith of all of us assembled here, all of us who have come through the doors, under the roof, an invitation to step forward and receive that gift of faith and of strengthening which is only and already an acknowledgment and raising up of the faith that perhaps we can't even speak. And so the invitation to this Roman Catholic Sacrament of the Anointing of the Sick is extended to anyone who discerns and knows in his or her life now that his or her condition of health of body and of mind poses a challenge, needs God's help, might require some new renegotiation, because: "I want to move forward. I don't want to be stuck. I don't want to be flat out on my back. And even if it's not a matter of moving my body differently than it did before, I'll know I'm moving nonetheless."

And so we move—and not just in any old way. Not slumping and shuffling toward the Kingdom, but with the artistic help of a very talented liturgical choreographer, dancers, musicians, but, most importantly, one another. We invite and call forward those whom the Lord now desires to strengthen and to raise up.

At the conclusion of the homily I returned to the chair and allowed for a minute of silent reflection.

Then began the Liturgy of Anointing. I asked that all who wished to be anointed step into the center aisle and stand at the end of their pew. One of the dancers would walk each person up into the front of the sanctuary to seats arranged there. As the dozen or so people were brought forth, instrumentalists repeatedly played the antiphon that the choir and assembly would be singing in response to the Litany that begins the rite. Upon seating the individual, each dancer blessed the person with the "sheltering" gesture that had been introduced in the Entrance Procession (diagonally crossing one arm over the person's head and then drawing the arm down in front of the body). VerEecke later told me this was his favorite movement in that liturgy, a gesture at once simple and transparent, bespeaking shelter and protection. For me the entire processional movement of the dancers with those to be anointed, including the blessing-gesture, was crucial for symbolizing that the sick are not external to the liturgical assembly—as if objects to be acted upon—but members from within who become a sign (sacrament) to all, in a mutually affective relationship of faith. After the liturgy people described for me how the dancers reduced the divisions in the cavernous chapel space, enhancing the sense of membership in the worshiping assembly and their solidarity with the sick.

The entire Liturgy of Anointing was sung, using Witchger's score.[13] The Litany was a series of invocations for God's strengthening and giving peace to the sick and those who care for them, to which choir and assembly responded, "Lord, have mercy." The music then turned melodic and dance-like for the Thanksgiving Prayer over the Oil of the Sick [*Olio Infirmorium*]. I sang each stanza, recounting the history of God's mercy and redemption toward humanity, to which all responded repeatedly, "Blessed be God, blessed be God, blessed be God, who heals us in Christ." Five of the dancers were stationed in the sanctuary and front crossing-aisle. They spun gracefully from side to side, arms raised in quiet exuberance each time the antiphon was sung. VerEecke had designed this gesture as a counterpoint to the interior-reflective quality of the movement accompanying "Shepherd Me, O God." As the blessing was sung and danced, the sixth dancer carried the glass container of oil up the aisle through the assembly to me, where I received it with the ritual's prayer: "Almighty God, come to our aid and sanctify this oil which has been set apart for healing your people. May the prayer of faith and the anointing with oil free them from every affliction. We ask this through Christ our Lord."

Father VerEecke and I then anointed the sick, each of us ministering to about half of the dozen of them in the sanctuary. We approached each person, dipping the fingers of our right hands in dishes of the oil, imposed the person's head for a moment of silent prayer before signing the forehead, "Through this holy anointing may the Lord in his love and mercy help you with the grace of the Holy Spirit." Then, onto the person's palms, resting open in the lap, we signed more oil, "May the Lord who frees you from sin save you and raise you up." As we anointed, the choir and assembly sang softly Witchger's antiphon, "Trust in the Lord, be strong. Be brave, trust in the Lord." Having finished, I returned to my chair and chanted the Prayer After Anointing: "Father in heaven, through this holy anointing grant our brothers and sisters comfort in their suffering. When they are afraid, give them courage, when afflicted, give them patience, when dejected, afford them hope, and when alone, assure them of the support of your holy people. We ask this through Christ our Lord." The choir and assembly responded by repeating the exuberant "Blessed Be God" antiphon until the dancers had accompanied all of those who had been anointed back to their seats in the nave.

The Liturgy of the Eucharist proceeded as usual. The special preface to the Eucharistic Prayer for the Mass of Anointing thanks God for having "revealed to us in Christ the healer [God's] unfailing power and steadfast compassion." During the Communion Rite, as people processed forward to share the sacramental food and drink in front of the sanctuary, the instrumentalists and then gradually also the choir introduced the refrain to Haughen's setting of Psalm 23, "Shepherd me, O God, from all my wants, from all my fears, from death into life." Once all had received the sacrament and returned to their seats the dancers presented in the sanctuary (which had been cleared by that point of as much furniture as possible) VerEecke's final and fullest dance-expression for the Mass. This dance drew upon key gestures that had appeared in the Entrance Procession and Procession with the Sick, augmenting them into a complete program for leading all in meditative reflection after communion. I concluded with the post-communion prayer: "Lord, through these sacraments you offer us the gift of healing. May this grace bear fruit among us and make us strong in your service. We ask this through Christ our Lord." The Mass concluded with the customary final blessing.

CONCLUSIONS, PASTORAL, AND ACADEMIC

Three tasks remain by way of conclusion: first, to describe how the students and I brought our Pastoral Program to completion in the weeks following the Mass of Anointing; second, to revisit questions of methodology; and third, to note the numerous types of contestation evident in this entire pastoral-academic initiative for engaging ritual and body in Catholic faith.

Further scholarly (theological) analysis of the rite and its contexts will unfold in greater depth in chapter 8.

The fourth and last stage of the Pastoral Program I had conceived in relation to the Mass of Anointing was Mystagogy, a time for reflecting upon and learning from the sacramental liturgy we had experienced. It seemed wise to me that I not rush this closure to the process but, rather, give all of us a week or so before gathering one last time as a group. When we did so it was in the context of sharing dinner together, which we ourselves prepared. Prayer and reading from Scripture framed the meal and informal discussion we shared, offering individual reflections, insights, and even a few questions that emerged from the celebration of the Mass with Anointing. While respecting the pastoral boundaries of the sharing, I can report that the students who had been anointed described powerful experiences of sustained peace and assurance. Perhaps more significant than specific comments about the Mass, however, was the clearly evident bond among the group that had only deepened through the celebration of the sacrament and our concluding meal together.

That entire pastoral initiative, again, was integral to two academic endeavors: the majority of students in "Suffering in Solidarity" opting to make the project part of their theological work in the course, and the ritual-performance of the Mass of Anointing as part of the interdisciplinary conference, "Practicing Catholic." Here I shall assay some methodological reflections in relation to each.

The students in the seminar expressed how helpful the actual pastoral engagement of the rite had been to their study of the history and current practices of Catholicism's liturgical ministry to the sick, dying, and bereaved. It is otherwise quite difficult for young adults to grasp not only the issues at stake in those practices but also the potential of the reformed rites of the Church. Here the normative and pastoral dimensions of liturgical theology come into play. The post-Vatican II rites of Catholicism operate on the principle that participation in them brings about personal encounter with the crucified-and-risen Christ. Reading or arguing about this principle generally does not amount to much if people have not experienced something of it in practice.

The other academic constituency of the project comprised the professors, graduate students, and pastoral professionals who came to Holy Cross to participate in the conference. In the end several professors and performers, across all the disciplines involved, expressed how the conference had proven to be a unique scholarly experience in comparison to all others in their careers. The integration in "real time" of performances that were clearly related to the historical, social-scientific, and theological subject matter of the conference seemed to contribute to the depth of conversations and quick growth in trust and mutual-confidence experienced among the participants. One professor at the conference wisely averred that the value in interdisciplinary conferences such as this resides in the unique impact the experience has on each individual, which can only play itself out in each person's life and further scholarship, as those subsequently unfold in their several contexts. There is great truth in that statement. I leave open the question, nonetheless, of whether the pursuit of mechanisms for evaluating and transmitting outcomes in such endeavors is possible, especially in light of Joanna Ziegler's essay in the conclusion to this book.

Finally, noteworthy are the numerous forms of contestation that this Pastoral Project in conjunction with the Anointing of the Sick Within Mass evinced. The status of religious practice in relationship to the still-regnant hegemony of post-Enlightenment rationalism in modern academia remains problematic in not only secular and post-religiously affiliated institutions but also in the more than 200 Roman Catholic affiliated universities and colleges in the United States. The problematic tension between religious mission and academic freedom is evident not only in ideological struggles between schools and the Church hierarchy but within the college communities themselves. A stellar example of the latter is the anxiousness on the part of religious studies or theology faculty that their (academic) work not be identified with that of campus ministers. Must the praxis of faith be considered only in the category of "Student Services" (along with such entities as health care, counseling, etc.) the college or university provides? Can the Catholic college or university's liturgical programming provide not only comfort to students, faculty, and staff but also challenges to their conceptions of worship spaces (e.g., chapels), actions (e.g., liturgical dance), and rites (e.g., the Pastoral Care of the Sick) and, thus, contribute to the growth of the Church's tradition? Then there remains the methodological challenges and ongoing identity crisis for the young discipline of liturgical theology itself, the parameters of which I have sketched in this book's Introduction. It seems that finding ways responsibly and productively to integrate observations from pastoral engagement into the method and content of writing theologically about the Church's liturgy comprises an important agenda.

"Practicing Catholic" ends up constituting a programmatic question for the professor and author of liturgical theology, perhaps even more poignantly for one who is also a priest in the Church. To do this *theology* (in contrast to history or religious studies) requires finding ways to bridge the worlds of students, fellow theologians, academic colleagues (believers and non-believers), and members of the Church (both ordained and lay), which altogether contribute to the content of the liturgical-theological enterprise itself. In the next chapter I attempt one such theological exercise in relation to the Church's pastoral-liturgical ministry to the sick, building upon the ritual process I have described here.

CHAPTER 8

Christ the Healer: An Investigation of Contemporary Liturgical, Pastoral, and Biblical Approaches

Bruce T. Morrill, S.J.

INTRODUCTION

Father, all-powerful and ever-living God,
we do well always and everywhere to give you thanks,
for you have revealed to us in Christ the healer
your unfailing power and steadfast love.

In the splendor of his rising
your Son conquered suffering and death
and bequeathed to us his promise
of a new and glorious world,
where no bodily pain will afflict us
and no anguish of spirit.

Through your gift of the Spirit
you bless us, even now,
with comfort and healing,
strength and hope,
forgiveness and peace.

Pastoral Care of the Sick: Rites of Annointing and Viaticum (1983)

In Catholicism the sacraments are properly understood and practiced as manifestations of Christ's redemptive action in the lives of believers and for the life of the world.[1] This is not to say that the ritual sacraments are the exclusive means of practicing the faith. They are, rather, meant to be tangible experiences, through highly condensed symbols, revealing Christ's active presence in all dimensions of life. The key to the reform and renewal in

Roman Catholic sacramental theology over the past several decades has been an effort to shift how the faithful—clergy and laity alike—fundamentally conceive of sacraments, a shift from receiving them as holy *things* to sharing them as graced *events* revealing the active presence of the Spirit of the Risen Christ amidst an assembled community of faith.

Situating the liturgical sacraments thus in a broader pastoral context, however, is not meant to reduce them to a merely expressive function. While sacramental celebrations find their concrete effectiveness (their "fruitfulness," to use language from the tradition) through their strategic roles in specific pastoral situations, they not only draw upon the assembled people's experiences but also make a further, unique contribution to them. Traditionally the Church speaks of this in terms of grace, a profoundly biblical word designating the merciful favor of God toward humanity and, in the New Testament, this as definitely given in and through the person and mission of Jesus, the Christ. Commissioned by the risen Christ to carry on this mission in the power of his (Holy) Spirit, the Church brings an effective Word into history, to people living in particular times and places.

Drawing on New Testament texts, Christian tradition describes the genuine difference grace makes in human lives by employing medicinal, economic, and legal metaphors: salvation, redemption, and justification, respectively. For the Sacrament of Anointing the Sick the medicinal dimension, obviously, is primary. With its etymological roots in *salus*, the Latin word for health, salvation shares that root with another English word, salve (medicinal ointment). Both terms, as liturgical theologian Susan Wood has noted, thereby imply bringing about health and wholeness.[2] For Christians this is a bodily and spiritual reality. The effects of sin (which ultimately reside in death) are, speaking again metaphorically, both interior and exterior. The Eucharistic preface mentioned earlier, invoking Christ (the very title means "anointed one") as healer, frames Jesus' death and resurrection in terms of the assured promise of final deliverance from bodily and spiritual affliction, a promise which nonetheless can be sacramentally experienced presently as "comfort and healing, strength and hope, forgiveness and peace." The Sacrament of Anointing the Sick, especially when celebrated with an assembly of the local faithful, is meant to make, through word and symbolic gesture, an effective difference in the lives of those who are experiencing the turmoil—physical, psychological, spiritual, and social—that sickness or declining health brings about for them and those around them.

At the Ritual Mass for Anointing the Sick the presiding bishop or priest may introduce the liturgy with the words, "Christ is always present when we gather in his name; today we welcome him especially as physician and healer."[3] Building on the preceding chapter of this book, the liturgical-theological question for further exploration here concerns how that offer of healing might be heard in the late-modern context of American Catholicism. Indeed, I find "Christ the Healer" at present to be a highly ambiguous Roman Catholic symbol. The ambiguity lies not only in the psycho-social and religious connotations of the markedly fluid term, "healing," but also in the current approaches—biblical, doctrinal, and popular—people take in attempting to understand the person and mission, "Christ."

Recall how in chapter 7 I described the resistance with which my initial proposal for a Ritual Mass for Anointing the Sick was met by some of the faculty and staff at Holy Cross. That contestation concerning the sacrament's meaning and practice led me to observe and reflect upon the ways in which Catholics—on that campus, in the region, and even in the Jesuit order—employ healing as a religious concept. In this chapter I begin by describing and briefly analyzing a few such scenarios in order to return once more to the ritual text of the Sacrament of Anointing the Sick to see what correlations might exist between the official and popular notions of sacramental healing and the understandings of healing people demonstrated in those other situations. Catholic notions of healing—popular and official, pastoral and liturgical—bear with them notions about Christ, however explicitly or implicitly held. The last major section of this chapter, then, will briefly survey a few of the current scholarly approaches to Jesus as healer in Scripture and tradition, seeking insight into how the Gospel stories of healing proclaimed in the rite might be heard in relation to the sacramental healing being celebrated. The conclusion will proffer observations in support of the ongoing practice of this tradition in Catholic fait.

The Rhetoric of Healing: Scenarios from the Contemporary Church

First Scenario: At the beginning of the 2002 fall term at Holy Cross, its Jesuit president designated September 14, the College's titular feast on the Church calendar, a "Day of Community Healing." The day's purpose, as reported in the student newspaper, was "to help mend the wounds of the past year's violence still painful in the hearts of many."[4] The previous academic year had begun with the suicide of a student, followed immediately by the terror of September 11. At the other end of the school year, the final weekend in the spring term brought an unprecedented homicide of one student by another, a violent fight in the early Sunday-morning hours during which one young man allegedly inflicted blows to the head that resulted in the other's death later that day. The College's response was to hold a "Mass of Healing" on the following evening and to instruct faculty to work with class deans in considering distraught individual students' requests for exemptions from final exams. The long summer recess intervened, followed by the President's call in September for the "Day of Community Healing" on the feast of the Triumph of the Holy Cross.

The day had two main events, a "memorial service" and a picnic. The student newspaper reported attendance at the memorial service at a mere "100 students, faculty, and family members" out of a possible 2700 students and 500 faculty and staff. The president, as reported in the article, spoke in terms of transformation, calling on the assembly "to transform those terrible events into something meaningful and life affirming." The mother of the slain student, the newspaper reported, explained "what healing meant for her and what lessons can be learned from the tragic death of her son": (1) stop asking "why," since there is no ultimate explanation for the tragedy; (2) live in such a way as to have hope and peace when tragedy occurs; and (3) live in preparation for eternal life in heaven. Finally, she reported her consolation in knowing that the donation of her son's organs had saved six lives, a scholarship established in his name will help educate others, and his death brought together family and friends.

Second Scenario: For six years I had been helping in a suburban parish in the Archdiocese of Boston, approximately two thousand members served by one priest and a small lay staff, by presiding at one Mass per weekend. During the last week of June, 2002, the Archbishop removed the pastor due to a man's allegation that this priest had molested him as a child 35 years ago. A nun on the staff undertook the administration of the parish. In the ensuing weeks she collected scores of letters of encouragement from the parishioners to deliver to the secluded pastor. As the month's anniversary (her words) of his removal neared, she organized a "Healing Mass" to be held on a Tuesday evening in the parish church, at which she asked me to preside and preach. I asked her what she meant by a "Healing Mass," and she said she found the parishioners in need of comfort but, moreover, she wanted to videotape the liturgy to send as encouragement to the pastor. She left the selection of scriptural passages to me, and I preached on a passage from Jesus' farewell discourse in the Gospel of John (15:9–17) in terms of "our deep longing for truth." Approximately 150 attended on the muggy July evening.

Earlier that year a group of parishioners had formed a "response group" to the Archdiocesan sexual abuse crisis. In the early fall, 2002, the group attempted a letter-writing campaign to the Archbishop, calling for fair treatment of alleged victims and abusers, as well as the wider faithful. In their written invitation to fellow parishioners, they exhorted all to "remain united in our faith and in our prayers . . . to resolve this crisis," and articulated this objective: "By taking this action, of writing a letter, it becomes a part of our healing process and hopefully it can make a difference."

Third Scenario: The College of the Holy Cross is an apostolate of the New England Province of the Society of Jesus (the Jesuits), of which I am a member. In the fall of 2002 our provincial superior wrote a series of letters in light of the Church crisis. His second letter concerned "the experience of victims," including not only (but, nonetheless, first) those abused by clergy but also the Jesuits' own experience, as well. "I believe we need to enter into solidarity with victims not only as members of a Eucharistic community who wish to be healers, but also as men in need of healing ourselves."[5] He described healing as a "long journey" in which victims tell their stories in safe environments; shame, fear, and isolation are replaced by hope and confidence; and the possibility of forgiveness can at least be dreamed. Healing, he instructed, comes through "graced relationships," replacing the tendency to persevere through loss alone, which often results in bitterness and despair. The graced alternative, he argued, is to join Jesus' call "to make the windings [sic] straight and the rough ways smooth (Lk 3:5)."

Brief Analysis of the Scenarios: I have rehearsed these pastoral vignettes in the hope of some insight into the context in which the Church's perhaps most obvious official rite of healing, the Anointing of the Sick, might take place. Considering these popular symbolic notions of "healing," rather than an exclusive focus on the official ritual texts, seems all the more necessary since I have found American Catholic clergy and laity profoundly lacking in knowledge of the content and structure of the reform of the sacrament of anointing. Indeed, my pastoral and classroom experience leads me to think that most Roman Catholics not only do not understand anointing within the entire rite of the Pastoral Care of the Sick, they in fact cling to the pre-Vatican II (medieval-tridentine) titles for this sacrament, Extreme Unction or Last Rites, which terminology in fact appears nowhere in the ritual text that has been functioning officially in the Roman Catholic Church now for some twenty years.

Ritual theorists might aver that a couple of decades constitute a short period of time in the ongoing practice of a religious cultic tradition. The point would be well taken. My point here is that one must take into serious consideration the popular uses of the word "healing" in the above scenarios when one questions how these clergy and laity perceive or understand healing to take place ritually, whether by means of sacramental liturgy or not, in the Church. It would seem that "healing" among these well-educated U.S. Catholics connotes a social process entailing: (1) a crisis—including physical and/or psychological violence, a breach in community coherence and power relations, and a serious questioning of ultimate meaning—and (2) subsequent efforts to transform the situation, that is, for people to change how they perceive themselves individually and collectively so as to recover a sense of wholeness or rightness in their worldview. Ritual (especially the Mass, a point to be considered further) plays a fundamental role in the pursuit of transformation, serving both a salvific function—situating the current crisis in the larger narrative of Christ—and a redemptive one—exhorting believers to activities that will benefit the social entity as a whole and/or the disadvantaged therein.

At the time I was first attempting this description and analysis a professor of psychology shared with me his dissatisfaction with popular uses of the word healing. He cautioned that the current widespread pattern of calling people to "heal" in such situations sets them up for pain and frustration in pursuing an ill-defined goal. In other words, when students are in shock over a homicide or suicide among their numbers, or citizens are terrorized by the events of September 11, or priests and parishioners are demoralized by scandals of sex and authority in the Church, their pain may well end up compounded by feelings of failure and guilt when, after having done the activity of "healing" to which their professional leaders exhorted them, they do not in fact find themselves much transformed at all. One wonders whether this therapeutic insight might not be relevant to the fact that such a small number of the community participated in the "Day of Healing" in the first scenario, as well as the "Healing Mass" in the second. It may well also be relevant to the slowness of so many American Catholics to understand and embrace the reformed sacrament of anointing, to which we now turn.

THE ANOINTING OF THE SICK: CONTESTATION IN THE PASTORAL THEOLOGY OF A SACRAMENT

From the outset the General Introduction to the Pastoral Care of the Sick, places suffering and illness in relation to both the entire human condition and Christ's words and actions. Christ's words reveal "that sickness has meaning and value for [the sick persons'] salvation and for the salvation of the world," while the biblical stories of his healing of the sick reveal his "[love] for them in their illness." Faith in this Christ "helps them to grasp more deeply the mystery of suffering and to bear their pain with greater courage."[6] A vocational dimension to this sacrament is thus established from the start. The Introduction provides the substantive content for the ensuing rhetoric of strengthening and comfort, saving and "raising up," that pervades the instructional and ritual texts of the entire rite. Suffering believers are strengthened to strive against illness so as to be able to contribute to the good of society and the Church. They are, moreover, *in their very infirmity* to function as sacraments (living signs or witnesses) of the Gospel by joining their sufferings to Christ's "for the salvation of the world," reminding "others of the essential or higher things" of life, and "show[ing] that our mortal life must be redeemed through the mystery of Christ's death and resurrection."[7]

The purpose of the sacrament of anointing, especially in light of the rite's expectation that religious education, pastoral visitations, and a variety of rituals suited to individual and communal circumstances will be practiced, is not only to grace suffering believers with gifts that enable them to renegotiate (transform) their lives in relation to their illness. It is also to grace (transform) the community with greater faith through their interaction with the sick and suffering, who become living witnesses for them of a crucial dimension of the Gospel, namely, that in the raising up of the lowly God's reign is known. In an overwhelmingly consumerist culture that glamorizes largely unattainable images of youthful beauty to the detriment of compassionate attention to the ill and aged, the Pastoral Care of the Sick brings a much needed vision and practical program for helping Catholics embrace the Gospel. The rite's recurrent call for communal celebrations of the sacrament[8] makes pastoral sense not only for the strengthening of the sick and those who care for them but also for the ongoing conversion (transformation) of the entire community of faith.

Such are the basics of the ministry of this sacrament, as reformed after Vatican II on the basis of sources from the first eight Christian centuries and implemented for its renewal in the contemporary context. The actual practice here in the United States, as already mentioned earlier, is another matter. During my year at Holy Cross, I encountered what may well be representative attitudes toward the sacrament of anointing among working, middle, and upper class American Catholics. Recall from chapter 7 how my students and I had distributed the educational flyer explaining the theology and current practice of the sacrament of anointing, along with some of them making short presentations on our Pastoral Initiative for this sacrament at all Masses one weekend. I had distributed a similar letter of explanation and invitation to all faculty and staff of the College.

I realize that multiple factors contribute to the attractiveness of a pastoral initiative in a particular community. The notable, recurrent feedback I received on or around the scheduled first catechetical gathering, however, included people's strong perception of the sacrament as relevant only to the deathbed, despite all our efforts to educate to the contrary. People were not receptive to the written quotations from the reformed rite, with its clear articulation of the sacrament as being for the benefit of those suffering from chronic or recurring illnesses, nor to its encouragement for communal celebrations. My conversations with a staff member in her forties and a student in his twenties were almost identical: "Father, for people this sacrament is what the priest does to somebody who is dying. It's the Last Rites. And that's it." More than one of my fellow clergy told me how bemused they were at my "trying to do something" with Extreme Unction or the Last Rites. The consistent language of the rite's instructions and rituals bespeak healing and strengthening, comfort and pardon through the ministration of Christ as healer, savior, messiah, and physician. These people, on the contrary, seemed adamant in perceiving the sacrament only as providing a final forgiveness of sins at the last possible moment of earthly life.

All of this led me to wonder how Roman Catholics on that campus, whether young, middle-aged or old, cleric or lay, *do* think about healing in the context of the Church—in the community, its ministers, and the person of Christ. That question caused my attentiveness to the pastoral-ecclesial scenarios, with their rhetoric of healing, that I recounted earlier in this section. On initial reflection, at least, the sorts of words and objectives voiced in those situations seem consistent with those of the Sacrament of Anointing and the Pastoral Care of the Sick: Healing is sought not individualistically but amidst the community of faith; healing is a matter of transforming people's perceptions of a critical or painful situation by means of making it somehow meaningful; healing comes through doing actions that, even if only as verbal protest, seek to enact change in the situation; healing in some way invokes Christ (e.g., his death and resurrection, his service to others); healing is needed when communal relations, whether vertical or horizontal or both, are somehow broken off, eliciting the need for reconciliation and forgiveness not only among people but with God. This very list, however, could be applied and substantiated in reference to the rite of the Pastoral Care of the Sick, although a couple of factors crucial to the rite would need to be added: the drawing upon ancient biblical symbols of anointing and hand-laying, and the necessity of acknowledging Christ's presence to suffering and sickness as *sacramentally* manifested in individuals in relationship to the entire community of faith, that is, as revealing the mystery of his life, death, and resurrection (the paschal mystery) as the healing source of meaning for their lives in these particular circumstances.

That last point, however, raises one further difference between the first three scenarios and situations pertinent to the Pastoral Care of the Sick: the criteria for identifying who needs healing. Nobody in those three scenarios invoked the term "sickness." Whatever needed healing was due to some breakdown in social or interpersonal relations, placing the authority structures of the community's institutions (e.g., the Church, the College, the ordained priesthood, the civil, criminal, and judicial systems) in play, if not in question. In case of the Pastoral Care of the Sick, the recognition that somebody needs anointing has a highly personal dimension. The rite specifies that a given individual needs to be afflicted by either a serious illness or significant debilitation in old age, and calls on pastoral ministers and health care professionals to help the given individual discern whether anointing is suitable.[9]

With the rite cautioning against both undue scrupulosity that would withhold anointing, on the one hand, and indiscriminate anointing of large numbers, on the other,[10] the question of criteria for the suitability of individuals for sacramental anointing remains one of the thorniest challenges in implementing the reform of this sacrament. Theologian Charles Gusmer shows great wisdom in his primary criterion for this pastoral question: "[I]t is not so much the person's medical condition that is determinative. It is rather the 'religious' condition, a spiritual powerlessness, the crisis that illness represents in the life of an ailing Christian as regards communication with self, others, and God."[11] Compounding the problem of discernment, I would argue, is the fact that Catholics in mainstream America largely view sickness as private and, whether in explicit or inchoate ways, shameful. Such feelings can easily work against a person's desire to be part of a communal celebration of the sacrament which, as I have noted above, singles out the sick and elderly as sacramental signs of faith amidst the larger assembly. All of this would seem, indeed, to contribute to conflicting views about the meaning and purpose of the sacrament of anointing in contemporary Catholic communities.

The contestation concerning the appropriate practice of the Rite of Anointing resides, however, not only in the social, cultural, and ecclesial perspectives people bring to a sacrament engaging sickness and healing. Important as well is how Catholics, clergy and laity, perceive the image of Christ. Who is the Christ being invoked as healer? If individual alienation or communal anomy are what contemporary Catholics seek healing *from*, then what are they being saved *for*, that is, what is the positive meaning brought by Christ? How does healing fit into his saving mission for humanity?

THE HEALING CHRIST:
SCRIPTURE AND TRADITION

The above analysis or approach to healing in the contemporary practice of Catholicism has basically focused on what theologians and official Church teaching call tradition, that is, the content of the doctrine and rites of the Church (as promulgated by the magisterium or teaching office), as well as the processes whereby the doctrine and rites develop in and through history. Vatican II (1962–65) was a ground-breaking council in its endorsement of this processual notion of tradition, trusting that the definite content of doctrine is nonetheless part of a continuous unfolding of the depths of divine truth. Also crucial to the Council's agenda of reform and renewal was its preeminent desire that the reading of Scripture become a crucial aspect of Catholic theology and popular practice. Abandoning certain Counter-Reformation dualistic views of scripture and tradition, the Council promoted an integral relationship between the two, even giving priority to the word of God over the magisterium.[12]

The pastoral and theological impact envisioned, and slowly being realized, by the renewed engagement of the Bible in the practice of Catholic tradition cannot be understated. The Council's mandate that the proclamation of Scripture be integral to the liturgy (a primary form of the tradition) has changed the content, tenor, and length of sacramental celebrations. Whereas prior to the Council liturgical reading from Scripture was cursorily done (if at all), often in an unintelligible language, the Mass and other sacraments now include substantial and sustained readings, focused around the gospels and other New Testament texts, but also drawing from the Old Testament, especially the Psalms. For any Catholic intellectually and emotionally willing and capable of engagement in the Liturgy of the Word during the celebration of Mass or other rites, gospel stories of Jesus' words and actions contribute to their image of the Christ who is salvifically present in the sacramental ritual.

Concerning the Pastoral Care of the Sick and sacrament of anointing, when the General Introduction explains the rite in terms of "Christ's words" revealing the "meaning and value" of people's sickness "for their own salvation and the salvation of the world," or of Christ "during his life" visiting and healing the sick and "lov[ing] them in their illness,"[13] we can reasonably ask how such large concepts might be filled with narrative content. A few typologies of Christ can be drawn from contemporary Catholic tradition and current biblical scholarship.

Christ the Priest: As noted at the outset and at other points in this chapter, the Rite of Anointing refers to Christ as healer and draws upon the imagery of healing narratives from the gospels. The Church doctrinally locates Christ's institution of the sacrament, however, in the Letter of James, a pseudonymous work attributed to an apostle, probably written at the end the first century:

> Is any among you sick? He should summon the presbyters of the church, and
> they should pray over him and anoint [him] with oil in the name of the Lord,
> and the prayer of faith will save the sick person, and the Lord will raise him up.
> If he has committed any sins, he will be forgiven. (James 5:14–15)[14]

While discussion of the scholarly exegesis of that text as well as its association
with the sacrament of anointing in the Church's history are beyond the scope
of this present chapter, the official Church teaching (doctrine) concerning
this biblical text in relation to the present sacrament can be summarized as
follows: Christ instituted the priesthood for his church at supper on the eve
of his execution and by sending the Holy Spirit upon the twelve apostles in
the wake of his resurrection.[15] The power to heal and forgive sins resides in
Christ, the high priest who, in turn, has given that power to his apostles and
their successors (bishops and presbyters) as priests. Such a view of the origins,
authority, and exercise of priestly ministry in the Church can easily foster a
highly restricted view of the ministry to sacramental healing in the Church,
namely, that priests are called in to forgive the sins of the faithful on their
deathbeds. Hence the persistent view of clergy and laity that I encountered in
my recent pastoral effort with the reformed rite: one which perpetuates asso-
ciating anointing with the dying, not the sick, and with the work of an individual priest, not an entire community of faith, is not, in the end, all that
surprising. Christ the Healer, in this widespread Catholic paradigm, is Christ
the Priest, the divine-man with power to forgive and save people for eternal
life in heaven.

Christ the Sacrament: Where, however, does that leave all those allusions to
Christ's healing works in the gospels that pervade the sacrament of anointing and the Pastoral Care of the Sick? Here the other christological strain in
the reformed ecclesiology of Vatican II, namely, Christ the primordial sacrament of the encounter with God, comes into play. Formulated in the influential work of Edward Schillebeeckx, as well as by expert theological advisers
at the Council, the paradigm "Christ the Sacrament" locates the origins
of the seven ritual sacraments and, indeed, the foundation of the church,
not primarily in certain words or actions of Jesus but in his entire person
and mission. Jesus' words and actions, his association with the marginalized and his preaching of God's reign, his faithfulness to the Spirit's call
even unto death, and God's raising him up in the power of that Spirit altogether amount to his being the very human, bodily manifestation—that is,
the *sacrament*—of God's saving will in and for human history. This fundamental sacramental insight led Schillebeeckx into a decade of New
Testament research resulting in a massive, albeit controversial, liberationist
Christology.[16]

Biblical Scholarship: Jesus, Prophet and Healer: The strongly biblical turn in
Schillebeeckx's work is a prime example of Vatican II's call for Scripture's

integral role in Catholic theology coming to fruition. Whatever the given question they might be addressing, most Catholic theologians today ground their work in an investigation of pertinent biblical material, critically availing themselves of the research and writing of biblical scholars.

If we look to contemporary New Testament scholarship concerning Christ as healer, two different basic approaches present themselves. Using analysis free of what they consider the ideological distortions of Christian doctrine, "historical Jesus" scholars seek to satisfy the insatiable modern desire to know "what really happened," as well as how Jesus and his contemporaries themselves understood what he said and did. These scholars draw upon research methodologies and outcomes from a broad array of social sciences (archeology, anthropology, history, political science, economics, and the like), in efforts that might fairly be described as textual deconstructions opening into historical reconstructions. The other approach, one that garners far less media attention, continues to seek what Jesus meant to himself and others in the narrative structures of the Gospels themselves, especially as these culminate in Jesus' death and resurrection. While also making use of historical, anthropological, and archeological findings, these scholars look for answers to who Jesus was and what happened in his life within the narrative frameworks of the New Testament texts themselves. The difference between the two approaches, both in fundamental principle and various outcomes, is significant and, not surprisingly, the polemics rage. Nonetheless, I believe liturgical theology can benefit from the research and writing emerging from both camps.

The most academically respected of the first, historical Jesus-type of scholars win praise from a wide range of their colleagues, even their adversaries, for their exhaustive study of the socio-historical context of Jesus and his mission. It would seem that no Christian (Roman Catholic) theologian of whatever specialty can dispense with the assurance that one's theology is connected in some way to the earthly person and work of Jesus. The doggedness of Catholic faith in the incarnation would seem to demand it, not out of mere curiosity, but in order that the prophetic, transformative, salvific potential of what Jesus said and did in such a different environment long ago might not be lost on believers today. The pastoral question of how the sacrament of anointing can function as a saving encounter with Christ in the Church today is a stellar example of liturgical theology's need for such scholarly biblical input. If the intention of the rite is, as I have repeatedly quoted it, for the sick to receive consolation, strength, and even a sense of mission *from Christ* and, moreover, if the current practice of its various rituals includes proclaiming gospel passages about cleansed lepers (Mk 1:40–44; Mt 8:2–4; Lk 5:12–14), stopped hemorrhages (Mk 5:25–34; Mt 9:18–22; Lk 8:43–48), and restored paralytics (Mk 2:1–12; Mt 9:2–8; Lk 5, 18–26), then greater insight into the circumstances and implications—social, cultural, religious—of those stories cannot but shed significant light on the theological meaning and pastoral benefit of the sacramental-liturgical action taking place in the present.

For all the strangeness that details, and in some cases, the total story, of gospel healing accounts present to late-modern readers, their incongruence with a technological worldview can nonetheless reflect back some important knowledge people have generally lost in their valorization of scientific, medical progress: Sickness and health are not simply objective realities, not merely somatic entities; rather, as New Testament scholars have come to learn from anthropologists (medical and otherwise), illness is a comprehensive social condition, if not a status, that results from a person's coming down with a disease.[17] As John Dominic Crossan has argued, "Society (and its systemic structures) can not only exacerbate the *illness* that follows from a *disease*, it can create the *sickness* that leads to *disease*"[18] The challenge for modern readers of the gospels is to learn what pre-modern peasants and indigenous peoples have known to this very day, namely, the difference between *healing an illness* and *curing a disease*, as well as how these two are entwined. Learning about the social dimension of disease (the somatic symptoms or processes making a person sick) and illness (the sickness as it functions in the total life of the person—physically, psychologically, interpersonally, economically) brings a much needed perspective on the comprehensive situations of the sick people populating the gospel narratives, as well as how gospel accounts of Jesus performing healing marvels are not at all beyond the historical pale. Furthermore, this line of scholarship presses the recognition that Jesus' healings and exorcisms, far from being isolated feats, were ritual events reorienting Jesus himself, those whom he healed, and others who acknowledged the miracles into a new social context, which Jesus called the reign of God. Deliverance from sickness includes a realignment of social relations and statuses, human and transcendent.

The controversial question in light of such biblical scholarship concerns interpretation. Among the most contested positions is that of Crossan (notably, a Roman Catholic), who portrays the Galilean peasant Jesus as a wandering cynic dispensing a socially radical wisdom. Magic and meal were at the heart of Jesus' program, Crossan determines, because the way Jesus went about healing people and practicing an utterly open table fellowship struck at the heart of ancient Mediterranean society's system of honor and shame, patronage and clientage, creating in its place a kingdom of "nobodies." The marginalized people with whom Jesus dined and among whom he performed miracles lived in the "schizoid position of a colonial people," stressed-out, as it were, physically, psychologically, and socially. Jesus' exorcisms and other cures must be understood under those human conditions wherein acts of magic help oppressed people feel secure or relieved and exorcisms amount to "individuated symbolic revolution."[19] Stevan Davies, another gospel historical deconstructionist, on the other hand, criticizes Crossan and other colleagues for uncritically projecting onto the texts their own worldview, a bias for a coherent, meaningful world from a teacher, only to produce a plethora of diverse interpretations: Jesus as a political revolutionary, a reactionary Pharisee, or a sort of cynic. Davies argues that the place to meet Jesus on his own historical ground is his healing activity, wherein he exudes the characteristic psychological behavior of a *medium* or, to use the ancient Jewish paradigm for such a medium, a spirit-possessed prophet.[20]

But to what end such historical precision (concerning healing) and specu-lation (concerning Jesus and his followers)? And has Jesus' own end, that is, his death by execution, no significance for the meaning of his prophetic work, as these and others conclude?[21] While such scholarship helps us avoid projecting our worldview onto ancient Palestine, raises the human complex-ity of sickness and health, and even forges an important link between Jesus' miracles and his radical table fellowship, the question remains as to whether and *how* anybody could give oneself over to this Jesus now. For theology and pastoral practice recent historical Jesus scholarship reaches a limit: affirming the historicity of Jesus' miracles by methods functioning outside the narrative structures of the gospels ends up producing theories about Jesus' work at too great a distance from what I believe Leander Keck rightly calls "the offense of the Gospel,"[22] namely, its proclamation of Jesus as the crucified Jewish prophet whom God has raised from the dead, making him a life-giving Spirit capable of animating our lives today. Although one might look to more recent, multivolume works by biblical scholars promoting a narrative-textual–based approach to the historical Jesus,[23] I turn, finally, to one from 1970s, a lithe, original work abounding in insights that, when read in the light of the findings of those more recent massive volumes, seems to have been ahead of its time.

In *To Heal and To Reveal: The Prophetic Vocation According to Luke,* Paul Minear acknowledges how difficult it is for modern readers to grasp Luke's message about Jesus, as well as about *the church* as the historical successor of his mission. Indeed it is impossible without undertaking the hard work of trying to apprehend the consciousness or worldview that Jesus and his first followers lived (the "reign of God"), which is at odds with virtually every tenet of modernity. This is the consciousness of God calling people to repen-tance, to break away from the pattern of lording authority over others, of expecting might (political, religious, economic, professional) to make right and, in its place, embracing the pattern of Jesus' prophetic life of self-emptying (kenotic) service. For Jesus these local, specific acts of God's deliv-erance of the forsaken amount to nothing less than the cosmic overthrow of the dominion of evil, of sin, of Satan. This worldview of Jesus is a paradoxi-cal one, given to disclosure not by analytic argument but parabolic words and deeds, of which the definitive one was his crucifixion.

The offense of the Gospel lies, then, not in Jesus' performance of healings or exorcisms per se but, rather, in how those miracles help to reveal some-thing far more world-shattering, namely, the origin and kind of authority Jesus was inaugurating and the decision it demanded: "[W]e will not grasp how healing meant revealing, and how revealing meant healing, without grasping the mystery of how weakness had become the channel of God's power."[24] Jesus' taking the latter all the way to his death makes the crucifix-ion, along with the resurrection, the definitive realization of this divine power exercised through humility in suffering, service to the lowest, the revelation that the dominion of evil is not ultimately in charge. Jesus' death and glorification sealed with authority the prophetic implications of his miracles, table service, and teachings, which he clearly intended as applicable "to all types of human associations, whether political or economic or religious . . . constitut[ing] nothing less than the most revolutionary form of liberation from every kind of servitude."[25] Freedom resides in the awareness that in taking on this "from the bottom up" approach in whatever situations of urgent need, believers experience the invisible God's immanence in visible human actions. Belief in this fusion of the human and divine, the visible and invisible, is evident in Luke's disinclination to separate what modern interpreters would identify as the objective and subjective factors in the miracle accounts.

The immense question remains, of course, whether and on what terms believers might embrace and practice the life of faith this gospel envisions. Minear's challenging response:

> Any reentry into Luke's world presupposes and requires a world view the oppo-site of the 'flat-earthers,' those radical secularists whose earth is limited to one dimension; it requires a world view which gives absolute primacy to the reality of God and his governance of man's affairs. Moreover, we will never reenter the world of the prophets unless we concede that God actually has available various means of communication with his people, means which explode the firmness and fixity of those patterns of thought by which we have domesticated the anar-chies of history, making ourselves slaves of immanence in the process.[26]

I would propose that the understanding of Christian sacraments and liturgy outlined at the outset of this chapter, of their revelatory function for the practice of faith as a comprehensive way of life, of their engagement of the biblical word with the symbolic enactment of the paschal mystery, amounts to one such world-transforming means of communication between God and people. Sacramental liturgy, when understood and practiced not as quantified portions of grace dispensed inside sacred boundaries but as graced events dis-closing God's active will amidst those hungering for it, has as its very purpose the making visible in and to human bodiliness the invisible mystery of salva-tion. Liturgy can only have such a healing and revealing force if members of the Church, clergy and laity alike, give themselves over to the divine author-ity hidden in its unblinking openness to biblical proclamation, its tradition-based symbolism, its irreducible musicality of rhythmic sound and silence, its attentiveness to the real, live human story in which it occurs—in a word—to its ritual promise of disclosing what could not otherwise be known.

Conclusion: Practicing Tradition

If Catholic liturgical tradition is to go forward as a living, formative practice then it will have to come from a deep sense of need, not a need to perpetu-ate hierarchy or cultural niceties or ancient symbols for their own sake, let alone to assuage guilt before divine retribution, but from a deep need for the gospel to come alive, to make a salvific difference at a given place and time for actual people. It would seem that the reformed sacrament of anointing, as part of the entire pastoral-liturgical rite of the Pastoral Care of the Sick, is both symptomatic of the social, cultural, and religious challenges to the renewal of the church's liturgical practice, as well as an opportunity for discovering the liturgy's transformative power in the Christian community when the biblical, ritual, and pastoral dimensions of a rite are put into play.

Beneficial practice of this sacrament demands that its subjects, the sick and elderly, not be approached as abstract souls but as persons who have reached a moment of crisis involving all dimensions of human life—psychological, physical, interpersonal, social, familial, economic, religious, and spiritual. Discerning the appropriateness of sacramental anointing is a matter of determining that a person realizes that life will not or cannot go on as it has, that one needs the salvific support of Christ to renegotiate one's place in the world and in the presence of God. Failing that fundamental theological insight, which as we have seen in this chapter finds ample support in scripture and tradition, the sacrament cannot but remain mired in the misconception of its being "Last Rites," a hastily timed curative to the departing soul, a gesture moving entirely in one direction from the priest to the passive recipient. Both the gospels and the reformed rite, however, see in the sick person a living sign, a sacrament, an event disclosing the truth Christianity finds in suffering.

Human misery, shame, guilt, or fear do not glorify God; rather, seeking the presence and action of Christ in and with the suffering—or for the sick person, in one's own suffering—occasions a moment for sharing his disclosure of divine solidarity therein. Liturgically enacted, such a sacramental encounter compels ongoing pastoral engagement with the sick person in a genuine exchange of gifts, human and divine, grounded in the assurance of God's exultation of the crucified one. Such pastoral-liturgical practice brings to the central ritual of Catholicism, the Eucharist, an intense lived knowledge of the paschal mystery, the pattern of Christ's life, death, and resurrection. This experience of and with the sick, this experience at the margins, sheds light on what matters most at the center of the Catholic religion—as seems only fitting, given the gospels' portrayal of Jesus the healer.

Commentary: Embodiment, Integration, and Authenticity: Keys to Reshaping the Catholic Sacramental Imagination

Judith Marie Kubicki, C.S.S.F.

Both Therese Schroeder-Sheker and Bruce Morrill, S.J. provide the reader with an abundance of vivid images and engaging ideas regarding sacramentality and healing. Such richness allows for a limited response to the key foundational principles offered by means of story, analysis, and reflection throughout the three chapters. They include the importance of working toward the integration of body, mind, and spirit, the inestimable value of authentic performance, and the challenge these insights pose for the revitalization of the celebration of sacraments of healing.

Therese Schroeder-Sheker's "The Vox Feminae: Choosing and Being as Christian Form and Praxis" offers stories of ritual performance that illuminate the sacramentality of daily life. Two sections are particularly powerful in their impact: her reflections on the vocation of the music-thanatologist and the story of Meredith's keening in response to the death of her newborn son, Tyler. Both highlight embodiment and integration as part of the healing process and emerge from a sacramental vision of life.

Schroeder-Sheker's description of the ministry of the music-thanatologist invites comparisons with that of the icon painter. In both cases the musical performance and the icon become windows that provide the possibility for glimpsing the divine. The artist as either musician or painter observes a spiritual regimen such as prayer and fasting that enables metanoia or change of heart. Inner conversion is requisite for the performance of the music and the painting of the icon. In the case at hand, the performance of the music emerges from a life journey of conversion that is holistic—its goal is the full integration of body, mind, and spirit. Such integration allows God's healing to shine through the music-thanatologist who embodies that wholeness to which God is calling the dying person.

Applying J.L. Austin's performative language theory to musical performance can assist in identifying what the performance aspects of music-thanatology accomplish. To use Austin's terminology, the illocutionary force of singing allows the musician to *do something* in the act of singing. Those same principles can be applied *mutatis mutandis* to music-thanatology. In this instance, the musical performance creates a state of affairs and situates participants in a sonic environment that invites contemplative openness. In other words, the musical performance provides sonic structures within which healing and reconciliation can occur by promoting openness, heightening awareness, and enabling receptivity—all qualities that orient a person to perceiving the sacramentality of life and experiencing God's healing and integrative action.[1]

This "accomplishing of an action" was poignantly illustrated in the story of Meredith and Tyler. In the absolute depths of her grief at the loss of her newborn son, Meredith loses herself in the sacred act of "keening." By giving herself over totally to the unimaginable grief that fills her entire being, her inner groaning finds a voice in a wailing of almost superhuman proportions. In that very act of keening, voice becomes the intersection of body and spirit. This embodiment of grief is response, expression, and means of healing her deep sorrow. Indeed, keening is a step toward healing not only for Meredith, but for the hospital staff and the other young pregnant women who stand in silent vigil to her response to this tragedy.

Schroeder-Sheker's stories challenge us in a dramatic way to reflect on our own ways-of-being with those who suffer gravely or mortally. How can our sacramental rites of healing promote that authentic integration of body and spirit that opens up a person to God's healing? Schroeder-Sheker's story graphically illustrates that it cannot be accomplished by simply rewriting prayers in the ritual books, but by exploring the potential for music, silence, and personal presence to enhance an experience of God's healing touch—a touch that is more often soul wrenching and life changing than many of us would be willing to admit.

In "Practicing the Pastoral Care of the Sick: The Sacramental Body in Liturgical Motion," Bruce Morrill not only provides a model for doing liturgical theology that addresses the issues of academics. He also raises issues that have practical and pastoral implications for liturgical performance. His performative approach to learning and his adaptation of the Rite of Christian Initiation of Adults (RCIA) model for preparing participants for the Sacrament of the Anointing of the Sick suggests several creative possibilities for revitalizing the sacramental rites of healing. Furthermore, Morrill's success with the RCIA encourages more creative and extensive implementation of that model in yet other celebrations of sacramental rites.

Perhaps it is the image of the dancer in Morrill's narrative that best illustrates the centrality of embodiment, not so much as a focus on the physical, but as an instance of the integration of body, mind, and spirit. By means of motion and gesture, the dancers delineate space, energize ritual action, and gather the assembly into a unified whole. One of Morrill's acknowledged concerns was that all of the elements of the liturgy celebrated during the conference be experienced as integral to the lives of the various communities involved. By attending to that concern, the liturgy as he describes it, possesses an authenticity that engages the participants, not on the level of demonstration or show, but as authentic worship that involves body, mind, and spirit. It is the same kind of authenticity demanded of the music thanatologist and expressed by Meredith's keening. In the case of the celebration of the Sacrament of the Anointing of the Sick for the conference, the dancers are both integrated into the rite, the space, and the community even as they serve to integrate all of these aspects. The result is an authentic expression of ministry through this art form.

In chapter 8, entitled "Christ the Healer: An Investigation of Contemporary Liturgical, Pastoral, and Biblical Approaches," Bruce Morrill builds a theological case for an issue that he raised in chapter 7. Earlier, he reported his discovery that despite Vatican II, the great majority of Catholics, both clergy and lay, continue to imagine the Sacrament of the Anointing of the Sick, not as it has been promulgated by the reform, but as the former sacrament of the dying, that is, Extreme Unction. In other words, he locates a key failure of the reform of the Pastoral Care of the Sick, not in poorly constructed or enacted rituals, but in the Catholic imagination formed by an official emphasis on the first of three possible typologies of Christ, Christ the Priest. The other two are Christ the Sacrament and Jesus the Prophet and Healer. Morrill points out that the Church locates its doctrinal support of the sacrament of the sick in the Letter of James rather than in the Gospel stories of Christ as healer. This strategy effectively directs the imagination to view the ministry of healing as the sole responsibility of the priest. Such a focus effectively dispenses with a need for the type of community participation envisioned in the Pastoral Care of the Sick. This is a particularly telling observation. The current preoccupation of Vatican documents with protecting and clearly delineating the role of the priest, particularly in regard to the sacramental rites, does not bode well for rectifying this situation.

Morrill convincingly argues that the typologies of Christ the Sacrament and Jesus the Prophet and Healer have not yet begun to shape the imagination of the average Catholic. Both have influenced the construction of the reformed rites and the perspectives of academic theologians, but they are yet largely untapped resources in the larger Church. Morrill's insightful interpretation of the three typologies is useful for understanding, not only the failure of the Catholic imagination to grasp the paradigm shift intended by the reform in regard to the Sacrament of the Anointing of the Sick, but also in regard to the Sacrament of Reconciliation. Nevertheless, Morrill is acutely aware that this is not the whole story.

Morrill raises a further issue that needs serious consideration if we are to construct rituals that truly celebrate God's healing of human be-ing. Ultimately whether the sick avail themselves of the sacrament depends on a faith in and a desire for the healing power of Jesus Christ. No amount of ritual reform or liturgical planning will necessarily inspire anyone to present themselves for this sacramental ministry. Morrill acknowledges this when he insists that sacramental liturgy needs to be understood and practiced as God's activity among those hungering for it. It is the hungering of the person for this healing, a realization that "life will not or cannot go on as it has [and] that one needs the salvific support of Christ to renegotiate one's place in the world and in the presence of God." Here Morrill's reference to Paul Minear's work is especially helpful. In both chapter 7 and 8, Morrill provides guidance for how both the theologian and the pastoral minister might assist the sick in coming to this recognition of hunger for God's presence or need for Christ's salvific grace. Again, the RCIA model is an obvious untapped resource for this ministry.

Morrill's important distinction between healing an illness and curing a disease raises a further challenge to the formation (or re-formation) of the Catholic imagination. Deliverance from illness requires a more integrative approach that includes the renegotiation of relations with the community, God, and self. That is why the rites presume a communal setting. Nevertheless, Morrill's identification of the valorization of science and medical progress as major influences on that formation needs to be acknowledged and dealt with more creatively in the Pastoral Care of the Sick. This is an area that needs further exploration and development. Since our contemporary context does not place value on weakness, it is difficult for us to imagine a position of vulnerability as potentially advantageous on any level. Yet, the mystery of the Cross reveals that weakness is a channel of God's offer of grace to humankind. Therefore, despite the successes that the medical profession may achieve in curing disease, there remains a critical need for the Church to concern itself with the healing of illness—that coming to wholeness that is at the heart of the Christian journey. Morrill's analysis challenges the Church to assume a more prophetic voice in pointing out the inadequacy of an approach to suffering that does not go beyond the competencies of science.

Finally, Morrill's reading of the "General Introduction to Pastoral Care of the Sick" highlights important insights that have yet to catch the imagination of most clergy and laity when it comes to viewing illness from a perspective of faith. While one of the purposes of anointing the sick is to give comfort and strength to the sick, there is another, often forgotten dimension. It is the fact that the sick themselves, in their very infirmity, function as sacraments, that is, as living signs of the action of God in their lives. The community's presence, to the sick, thereby becomes an opportunity for the community to be transformed by the witness of those who suffer in their midst. The story of the silent community of witnesses to Meredith's keening in chapter 6 expressed that truth profoundly. Where is this notion active and alive in the Catholic imagination?

Surely a tension will always exist between creativity and ritual practice within cultural and social structures that are continually evolving and changing. Both Schroeder-Sheker and Morrill offer important insights for negotiating that tension. As with any human activity involving symbol, sacramental celebrations of anointing are critical for enabling the community and the sick members within them to weave and reweave identity and relationships threatened by serious illness. The three chapters in this section raise up the importance of reimagining authentic theological meanings through an integration that is both expressed and experienced as embodied.

PART IV

Catholic Ritual as Political Practice

Susan Rodgers

INTRODUCTION

Anthropologists, scholars of various disciplines employing ethnographic fieldwork in their studies, and theologians and activists exploring liberationist approaches to poverty and social oppression all generally join together in seeing religious discourse as something that exists within political structures. Yet, many such observers also see the major world religions from Islam to Christianity to Buddhism to sometimes transcend politics, to transformative effect (for individuals, occasionally even for societies). The three essays in this section of the volume deal with the politics of Catholic Christianity's diverse faith messages, communal fiestas and saints processions, and 'things' (saints cards, for instance, held tight by many Latino/a Catholics, in sometimes troubled immigration journeys toward America). The first article, by historian and ethnographer of North Indian Catholicism Mathew Schmalz, touches on issues of narrativity and historical memory among Untouchables converted to Catholicism. Schmalz asks: Among extremely low-status Chamar caste tanners of leather in a predominantly Muslim and Hindi area of India, what does it mean to see history through Catholic storytelling lenses? How is anti-Chamar violence apprehended, among such converts? Concretely, how was the death of a local visionary understood in a radically domesticated Catholic story culture where redemption, hope, and the bodily presence of God in the world have all been deeply inflected for caste memories of profound social hierarchy?

The second essay, by anthropologist Daniel Goldstein, looks at another political (and of course religious and faith-inflected) valence of contemporary Catholicism in the non-Western world: Catholicism's many uses as a code for social group identity. Goldstein describes a community of rural-to-urban migrants to a desperately poor shantytown section of Cochabamba, Bolivia.

Some are converting (in rather unstable ways) from Catholicism to Evangelical Protestantism—a growing trend in much of Latin America, where the emotional immediacy of evangelical worship and its relative avoidance of heavy-handed church hierarchy of the sort familiar from the institutional Catholic Latin American churches lead some long-time Catholics to flee the faith. In the shantytown at issue here, folkloric renditions of what had been an "old Catholic fiesta," a yearly procession to a saint, is being embraced in cagey ways by a diverse constituency: new Evangelicals and "old Catholics" alike. Goldstein plumbs the stories the fiesta participants tell, about why they "still" join in the ritual procession.

The third article looks at a related storytelling phenomenon, this time among Latino/a Americans: theologian Roberto Goizueta listens to "popular Catholicism" among these faithful, to see how they construct not only political community but a sort of depth aesthetics of faith, within a largely doubting Anglo (and Protestant) contemporary America. Goizueta argues that Latino/a popular faith practices make serious theological claims: that such actions as fiestas and such objects as santos statues proclaim God's active presence in the lived world of believers; that the richness and material abundance of the faith objects of home altars show God's grace among his people; that a language of suffering and hope tied to immigrant journeys and poverty animate Latino/a Catholic stories, beyond the official Mass per se.

Taken together this set of three essays suggest a promising research agenda for Catholic studies, seen globally. There is, of course, the official Vatican promotion of "inculturation" of the Gospel message through such means as the use of local musical ensembles in worship, or the incorporation of local, festive costume into Catholic ritual practice. These three essays suggest that much more is afoot when diverse social communities outside Anglo Euroamerica appropriate "the Catholic" on their own terms. Conversion seems to go in two directions, as Vicente Rafael documented so deftly in his study of the Jesuits in northern Luzon in the Philippines, *Contracting Colonialism: Translation and Christian Conversion in Tagalog Society under Early Spanish Rule.*[1] Rafael finds that the early Jesuits imagined that they were converting the Tagalog, through what turned out to be surprisingly popular practices such as going to confession. But, the Tagalog "converts" were seeing confession and in fact all the major ritual practices of Spanish Catholicism in terms of their own language ideologies, which stressed the magic of "powerful words" and the utility of debt relationships with wealthy mentor figures, who could be manipulated to provide food and succor to the poor. Two-way conversions along the borderlands of European Catholicism and "the converted peoples" have probably often occurred, and deserve even more research. Also of obvious interest and promise is the Catholicism of the squatter settlement, the Untouchable community, the shantytown, as medical anthropologist Nancy Scheper-Hughes has shown in such surprising ways in her study of infant neglect in northeast Brazil, *Death without Weeping: The Violence of Everyday Life in Brazil.*[2] In that book

Scheper-Hughes shows how a sort of poverty-constrained popular Catholicism works to provide near hunger-mad, impoverished young mothers with a vocabulary of "Mary-like suffering," when they systematically deny food and water to selected infants, whom they deem "angel babies" who seek to quickly leave this world and fly back to the throne of Jesus (that is, to die by their mother's hand).

The Death of Comrade Moti: Practicing Catholic Untouchable Rage in a North Indian Village

Mathew N. Schmalz*

INTRODUCTION

There's a strange thing about a village: the walls have ears. But it's not just a village's walls, but its trees and plants have ears as well—even the wind has ears.

Mudrarakshasa, Dandavidhena, *21*

The District of Ballia, bordering Bihar in the state of Uttar Pradesh in north India, is an area of legend, rumor and ridicule. Chandrashekar, a former prime minister, came from Ballia, as does one of North India's most notorious criminals, Mukhtar Ansari—although in Ballia it is Mukhtar who is considered to be the hero while Chandrashekar is branded the real criminal. Stereotypes of Ballia abound: villagers in the district are either rustic louts, or conniving scoundrels, who speak Hindi and Bhojpuri with a lilting effeminate cadence; Ballia as a district is wild, lawless, caste ridden, and backward. Ballia then is a place of and for stories, if for no other reason than it seems to have a rather special place in the popular North Indian imagination. In this article, I consider North Indian Catholic storytelling as a particular mode of Catholic performance—specifically, as a cultural site for practicing Catholic Untouchable rage. This understanding of Catholic performance usefully expands the definition of Catholic ritual practice.

Ballia is in the eastern most part of what is often called the Hindu heartland—a rather misleading label since the area is also home to the majority of India's Muslims. But within this predominately Hindu and Muslim area are pockets of Catholics, one of the legacies of Capuchin missionary activity in the 1950s.[1] These Catholic converts came from the Chamar caste of tanners. The word "Chamar" is derived from the Sanskrit word for "skin" and Chamars remove and eat the carcasses of dead animals as part of their traditional caste duties. Members of the Chamar caste are considered to be Untouchable for their occupation renders them so polluting that even their shadow is considered to have the power to defile. They live in huts of thatch and bamboo in colonies separated from the main village, and are often denied access to wells and are instead forced to drink water from the rivers and ponds where they bathe. Many of the women serve as midwives and are expected to care for women after childbirth and are particularly required to clean the feces of these women by hand. Conversion to Catholicism did little to change these fundamental elements of Chamar life, although it did lead to many converts being summarily expelled from the governing bodies of their caste and clan.

The Ballia story that this article will relate concerns a community of Catholic Chamars in a village that I will call Shantinagar. Shantinagar has long been considered a stronghold of the landowning Bhumihar caste that the untouchable Chamars serve. Chamars, both Catholic and Hindu, and other members of low and Untouchable castes are largely consigned to a life of manual labor, working in the fields during the wheat harvests, for which they earn one bundle of wheat for every sixteen they gather. Caste violence is a constant threat, often employed to keep manual laborers in their place. While the story we will consider involves caste violence and the Catholic Chamar community, the story also concerns Shantinagar's Catholic mission, originally established by a Canadian Capuchin priest in 1949 before conversions to Catholicism began in earnest. Today the mission is set off from the main road that runs north from Varanasi. The mission compound has the only Hindi medium school in the area that admits Untouchables as well as a medical dispensary. The mission's church displays a large picture of Christ sitting in the full lotus position—a depiction of Christ as the supreme *guru* that became popular in North Indian Catholicism in the 1980s.[2] All the buildings of the mission are painted red as are all Catholic institutional buildings in North India. The mission also has a cemetery where Catholics are buried, according to local custom, with only a cross of dried mud to mark their graves.

It is within this context of poverty and caste violence, that Catholic Untouchables tell their stories of resistance.[3] Through the performance of narrative, the Chamar Catholics of Shantinagar rework and reimagine a different context for their lives. But the tactics of narrative are not totally divorced from more aggressive means of protest, for some thirty years ago resistance to caste domination erupted into violence in Shantinagar and the surrounding villages. One story told about this period is that of the death of Comrade Moti, an Untouchable revolutionary who was reputed to have been the leader of the revolt. We will learn about Comrade Moti and his death as related to me by a man named Ujagir.[4] Ujagir is both a Chamar and a Catholic and it is this dual identity that gives shape and texture to his recollection of "The Death of Comrade Moti." Beginning with his account of the revolt, we will see how Ujagir portrays Comrade Moti's efforts to organize Untouchables against the landowners, an effort that ends in Comrade Moti's death. In moving next to consider to what extent Moti's tale can be considered "history," we will compare Ujagir's narrative to other accounts of caste violence in Uttar Pradesh, and especially probe how "The Death of Comrade Moti" draws upon themes in the "Naxalite movement," a movement espousing revolutionary violence that takes its name from the peasant uprising in the Bengali district of Naxalbari in the late 1960s. I will argue that Ujagir's rendering of "The Death of Comrade Moti" is best understood not as history but as a didactic and exemplary narrative. Indeed, in its broad outlines, Ujagir's account of Comrade Moti uses tropes that would be familiar to North Indian authors who have written politically inspired fiction concerning low-caste resistance to domination. In framing our discussion with quotations from the Hindi author Mudrarakshasa's *Dandavidhana* [The Criminal Code],[5] we can see how Ujagir, as an Untouchable, charts a revolutionary trajectory for the aspirations of his community. Yet when juxtaposed to Mudrarakshasa's subtle use of Hindu themes, we can also see how Ujagir's narrative incorporates Catholic understandings of the tragic dimension of human existence emphasized in the mystery of the cross and crucifixion. Ujagir's "The Death of Comrade Moti" intertwines the themes of revolution and sacrificial atonement in a narrative performance that reimagines the Untouchable Catholic body.

THE DEATH OF COMRADE MOTI

You blood-soaked, dictatorial, government dogs. Shoot me! Then there'll be a revolution of blood-letting.

Mudrarakshasa, Dandairdhana, *73*

Ujagir, now about 40 years old, converted to Catholicism in his youth. He recalls that his decision was an act of protest against caste Hinduism, for Hinduism was certainly responsible for the indignities he and his family suffered as Untouchables. When he converted, however, he found that his new religious identity did not fully remove the stain of Untouchability. Indeed, not only was he still considered to be Untouchable but his own Chamar caste had outcasted him—a decision that was only rescinded a decade ago. Not surprisingly, Ujagir's identity has always been defined against his understanding of caste Hinduism. And so he often tells stories that ridicule Hindu practices and beliefs.[6] For example, he states that Ravana, the chief villain of the epic *Ramayana*, was a great revolutionary and that the pure, chaste Sita, wife to Ravana's enemy Ram, actually longed to give Ravana a son instead of living in servitude to her husband. But more often than not, Ujagir reflects upon Untouchable identity, particularly the reasons why Untouchables have been subjugated for countless generations. Once Ujagir mentioned to me that after Adam and Eve were expelled from the Garden of Eden, they were forced to work the land. But after many generations, the land began to be dominated by the Bhumihar caste—a fact that for Ujagir gave proof to Christian conceptions of the effects of original sin. Bhumihars defined Chamars as Untouchable and forced them to subsist on meager rations of coarse grain. According to Ujagir, Chamars became so weakened that they were never able to develop the intellectual capacity to understand their oppression, let alone develop the strength to resist it. Untouchables then need to be taught, to be instructed and inspired to take what is rightfully theirs. They need a teacher and a leader. But according to Ujagir, in the early 1970s, one such man came to the Ballia District to educate Untouchables about the true nature of their condition. That man's name was Comrade Moti, and what follows is his story.

THE RESISTANCE BEGINS

In the early 1970s, a wedding procession was traveling from Shantinagar to a neighboring village. The procession stopped for the night and the Untouchables, who served as musicians and palanquin bearers, were eating their dinner separately from the groom's party. As they were eating, a young man emerged from the darkness and came to speak with them. Assuming the man belonged to a high caste, the Untouchables addressed him respectfully as "Babuji," an appellation that literally means "Father," and said that they had come from the village of Shantinagar in Ballia District. The man told them that his name was Moti and that he was also a member of an Untouchable caste. Moti then inquired about the conditions in Shantinagar, and the Untouchables recounted their tales of suffering: their women were taken as concubines by the landowners, bonded labor was the only recourse to pay dowry for marriage, they were Untouchable, forced to keep a safe distance from higher castes, prohibited from wearing gold and other adornments, and forced to sit on the ground as a sign of deference even before the children of the landowners. But in addition to this social ostracism, the Untouchables told Moti, they lived on the margins of subsistence. The famines of the mid-sixties had reduced many families to a reliance on rations of spoiled rice flour, supplemented by a drink flavored with sugar cane and tobacco. The discussion lasted for hours, with Moti explaining that the lot of Untouchables could only be changed by violent resistance. Moti then asked whether he could come to their village. The Untouchables in the wedding party eagerly asked him to come and they met him at the Shantinagar bus stand at 5:00 p.m. the next day.

When Moti arrived in Shantinagar, he explained that he was a member of a revolutionary Naxalite cell from Bihar and that he intended to train the villagers to resist the landlords. Comrade Moti, as he was soon called, formed a small cadre and in secret taught the villagers to use their scythes, usually used for harvesting wheat, as weapons and to make molotov cocktails. Ujagir recounts how Comrade Moti changed his location every night. Untouchable families, however, were more than eager to give him food and shelter. But realizing how little the villagers had, Moti fasted for days at a time, lest he become a burden to those he had some to liberate. Soon, other members of his Naxalite cell joined him, with a man named Devamuni prominent among them.

Several weeks passed and the villagers and Comrade Moti formed a strong bond. As their first act of resistance, Moti and his comrades led a procession of three thousand villagers who broke into a landlord's granary and carried off foodstuffs for their hungry families. Violence soon followed: several landlords were killed by the scythe and another landlord was thrown into his blazing granary after it had been set afire by a molotov cocktail.

As the resistance began to build, the Catholic mission at Shantinagar came under suspicion. At that time, the Catholic mission was more than twenty years old and had passed from the Canadian Capuchins into the charge of the Indian Missionary Society, a Catholic religious order composed exclusively of Indian priests and brothers. After an Easter Vigil Mass, some Catholics were returning to their homes and lighting firecrackers as they went. The sounds, so similar to rifle fire, attracted the attention of some henchmen of the landowners, who reportedly thought that there was some military training going on in the mission compound to support the budding insurrection. They followed some Catholics, waylaid them, and marched them to the house of a prominent landowner, where they were detained and the police contacted. The Catholics were summarily beaten and jailed after the police accepted a bribe from the landowner. It was not until special letters were sent to powerful political figures, that the Catholics were finally released from prison.

Suspicion about the Catholic Church's role in the matter abated when the mission's priest became more actively involved in countering the insurrection. The priest was named Father Premanand, and hailed from Kerala. According to Ujagir, Father Premanand was particularly respected by the local Catholic community for organizing both flood and drought relief when local governmental efforts proved to be ineffectual. Father Premanand was also a communist, as are a good number of priests from Kerala where a communist government has ruled off and on for many decades. Ujagir felt particularly close to Father Premanand and informed Comrade Moti that in the mission he would have an ally. As Ujagir recounts, Moti came to the mission one night to talk with the Catholic priest. Both men first sparred with each other in English and a variety of Indian languages. While Father Premanand supported some of Moti's goals, he condemned the use of violence and swore to tell the police of Moti's presence. The priest was true to his word and, as Ujagir asserts, made a complaint to the Superintendent of Police identifying Moti as the leader of the insurrection. Father Premanand also gave the police their first and only description of Moti: a short man, wearing kurta–pajama, with a light beard. Paramilitary units were soon dispatched by the Uttar Pradesh State Government and camped at the Shantinagar mission while they attempted to quell the uprising and capture Comrade Moti. The landlords also took to their own defense and hired mercenaries to lie in wait along village paths and press tenant-laborers for information. While they tortured and killed some innocent Chamars in this search, the Untouchable community never revealed Comrade Moti's location.

BETRAYAL AND MURDER

Over the weeks the violence continued. But as the resistance grew, so too did dissention in the Naxalite cadre. Devamuni, one of Moti's comrades from Bihar, challenged Moti's leadership of the struggle—saying that they needed money to buy weapons. Rumor had it that Devamuni was actually a dacoit, a simple thief and brigand. In any case, Devamuni had already broken the discipline of the cadre by drinking *daru*, a home brewed country liquor. And so it happened one night that Devamuni came to the house of a member of the swineherd Dusadh caste and asked for some *daru*. The Dusadh recognized Devamuni and informed the landlords who bribed him to put a tranquilizer into Devamuni's liquor. Once Devamuni was incapacitated, he was bound and revived. The landlords then beat and tortured him. Then, in Ujagir's words, strung him up like a pig, castrated him and finally shot him to death. But before Devamuni died, he told the landlords where Comrade Moti was hiding.

When the landlords captured Comrade Moti, they began to beat him. As they struck him, they asked, "Where's your village?" "India!" Shouted Comrade Moti. "What is the name of your village?," they asked again. "India!" Comrade Moti shouted. As they beat him, Moti began to shout the slogans "Long live the revolution! Long live Charu Mazumdar!" But as much as they beat him, they only seemed to stiffen his resistance until he finally lost consciousness. The landlords then reported to the police that the leader of the uprising had been killed. When the police arrived on the scene, Comrade Moti had regained consciousness. But since the report had stated emphatically that the leader of the revolt had been killed, it was now necessary to finish the job and so the landowners shot Comrade Moti dead.

THE DISCIPLES

Although Comrade Moti was killed, some of his closest companions did survive the Shantinagar insurrection by posing as itinerant manual laborers. Shivlochan, Moti's closest comrade who escaped as Moti was being tortured by the landowners, hid out in a neighboring village named Balgar. In Balgar, Shivlochan became enamored with a low-caste woman and began an affair with her. According to Ujagir, Shivlochan also longed to revivify the resistance, and when a small shipment of contraband arms arrived from Bihar, he planned to act. But Shivlochan's lover was playing a "double game," as Ujagir describes it, and also counted landowners as bedmates who would be suitably generous according to her whims. And so, Shivlochan's lover turned him in to the landowners who summarily made an example of him by cutting off his head with a scythe. Shivmochan, another member of Moti's original cadre, was also eventually revealed to the Bhumihars, but not through a conscious act of betrayal. According to Ujagir, Shivmochan had taken refugee in a sympathetic Untouchable colony in a village near Shantinagar. Two old women from the colony, however, broke the wall of silence surrounding Shivmochan by discussing him as they sat in the fields to do their evening "latrine." Evidently, their discussion was within earshot of someone who immediately informed the landowners. Shivmochan was not beheaded as was his comrade Shivlochan. Instead, Shivmochan was simply shot dead.

Suryabali was another member of Moti's Naxalite cell who had escaped across the Ganges river to Bihar after Moti's death. Suryabali, however, had continued to be in contact with an Untouchable named Chakauri who lived in Shantinagar. Several years after Moti's death, Suryabali decided to return to Shantinagar for a very specific task: to kill a Bhumihar named Radhashyam, who was particularly despised for reportedly taking an Untouchable woman to his bed every night. According to Ujagir, Chakauri made preparations by charting Radhashyam's movements and soon Suryabali arrived with two comrades to carry out the attack. Ujagir explains that Suryabali had brought a homemade "bomb" that he planned to throw at Radhashyam. But while the attack was carefully timed, Suryabali apparently needed strong doses of *daru* to fortify his resolve. And so, instead of surprising Radhashyam and killing him instantly, Suryabali jumped out from behind a stand of trees and taunted him before throwing his homemade explosive. This delay gave Radhashyam time to react to Suryabali's advance and dodge the bomb. In the haze after the explosion, Suryabali and Chakauri escaped across the Ganges river but not without some Bhumihars in hot pursuit. The Bhumihars then spread the word that some Muslims had attacked a Hindu on the other side of the river. According to Ujagir, Suryabali's flight was no match for the speed of a rumor. Suryabali was soon caught and, like Devamuni before him, was trussed up like a pig, castrated, and finally killed.

But even with the deaths of Shivlochan, Shivmochan, and Suryabali, the reverberations of the insurrection continued in Shantinagar and the surrounding villages. Devanath and Siddhi were two brothers who lived in Shantinagar and participated in the resistance, without ever being identified and arrested by the police. According to Ujagir, a number of years after the uprising, Devanath began to stockpile pistols and rifles to begin to talk about killing a number of prominent landowners. But the landowners discovered the plot and flushed out Devanath by setting fire to his thatch roof. As Devanath ran from his home, Siddhi was with him. The landowners, tackled Devanath and then put a pistol to his head and pulled the trigger. The killers then escaped under the cover of the smoke pouring from Devanath's burning home.

Siddhi, Devanath's brother, was not harmed during the attack and, Ujagir added, had a good look at the killers. But when confronted by the Superintendent of Police, he refused to identify any of the attackers, because

he feared retribution. This fear of the landowners led Siddhi to Shantinagar's
Catholic mission, where he asked for sanctuary until the danger passed.
According to Ujagir, the mission's superior refused to offer Siddhi any assistance. But as Siddhi walked away, a new priest, recently assigned to the mission, came and said that Siddhi could remain at the mission, as long as he
kept a low profile. The new priest was from South India as was his superior.
But unlike the mission's superior, the new priest was from an Untouchable
caste. After the death of Devanath, Ujagir says ironically that "peace"
(*shanti*) descended upon Shantinagar—a peace that remains to this day and
one that continues to allow Untouchable servitude and exploitation.

HISTORICAL FRAGMENTS

*No matter how ramshackle the thatched roof, no matter how faded the mud
walls that cup a narrow parcel of land like pale and sickly hands, if a
human being lives there, then that hut does have a history, even if it is a history of brokenness and ruin.*

Mudrarakshasa, Dandavidhana, *106–7*

I tape-recorded my interviews with Ujagir late at night at the Catholic mission
in Shantinagar. The entire Comrade Moti narrative ran approximately two
hours. Periodically, I would travel to Varanasi where I would hand the tapes
over to Vikas Chandra Pandey, a Bhojpuri poet and native of the Arrah
District, who transcribed Ujagir's Hindi and Bhojpuri. When Vikas delivered
to me the Hindi transcription of "The Death of Comrade Moti," I asked him
what he thought about the narrative. Never one to mince words, Vikas said
quite matter of factly and directly that Ujagir was making me into a
"*chutiya*," a "fool" or, more literally, a "cunt." Vikas pointed to the absurdity
of Ujagir's purported eyewitness accounts of the insurrection and its aftermath.
Even when Ujagir was not presenting events he claimed to witness, Vikas
argued that the stories of bombs, beheadings and chases were simply too
dramatic to be believed.

Ujagir would always reject any characterization of his narrative as simply
another tall-tale from the village and instead would insist that his narrative of
Moti's death constituted "history" (*itihas*). But history, especially within the
context of contemporary India, is complex and does not necessarily lend itself
to the familiar techniques of historical research. In "Defense of the
Fragment," Gayendra Pandey reflects upon the difficulties of retrieving a
conventional historical narrative from the context of Indian communal
violence.[7] In commenting upon his research on recent Hindu-Muslim riots,
Pandey argues that most Indian historiography has taken violence to be an
"aberration" within the broad sweep of the Indian struggle for independence
and beyond.[8] The specificity and complexity of the cultures of class, religious,
or caste minorities are also taken to be aberrations themselves since they cannot be readily assimilated into contemporary Hindu nationalist discourse.[9]

Pandey also quite rightly points out that official records of violence hardly provide a firm basis for any kind of historical reflection. Not only are the official records often skewed by the interests of the authorities who maintain them, in some cases they simply do not exist at all, as Pandey learned during research on communal violence in Bhalpur in 1989.[10] For Pandey, to engage subaltern history is fundamentally to deal with fragments.

Similar difficulties confronted me in my research on the Catholicism in Shantinagar. Indian Christianity, especially with regard to Untouchables, is a very politically sensitive area of research. Catholicism, in particular, is often viewed as an anti-national force associated with colonial or imperial domination.[11] Moreover, caste is always an explosive issue in Indian society and political violence; while commonplace in India, is usually not understood to be something that foreigners should research. To consult official records pertaining to the insurgency would have raised a great deal of suspicion, even in the unlikely event that I would have been given access to consult local archives and found that any documentation was retained. In the records of Shantinagar's Catholic mission, there were several letters referring to a "peasant uprising" in general terms, and one addressed to local political leaders asking for the release of the arrested Catholics, but nothing about the specifics of the revolt and certainly nothing about Comrade Moti. But the very nature of a narrative of political violence told by Untouchable Catholics will be not only be fragmentary but often deliberately fragmented or embellished in relation to the context in which it is performed. But since Ujagir presents "The Death of Comrade Moti" as history, we will begin by relating it to various fragments of the history that it contains, a discussion that will move us from understanding "The Death of Comrade Moti" as a subaltern memory of resistance to a narrative of mourning and rage.

THE NAXALITE MOVEMENT

Within contemporary India, the term "Naxalite" is used quite commonly to refer to diverse forms of Marxist inspired violence and resistance. For example, the highly organized People's War Group in Andhra Pradesh is called "Naxalite" as are the various makeshift peasant militias who battle private armies of the landowners in Bihar. Of course, Ujagir himself describes Comrade Moti and his cadre as "Naxalite." This is a particularly evocative label, coming as it does from the peasant uprising in the area surrounding Naxalbari in West Bengal in 1967. This revolt began with 150 villagers carrying away grain from granaries and then escalated to a protracted violent confrontation between peasants and landowners. West Bengal Communists who believed that party members in government were not aiding the revolt soon formed the Communist Party of India, Marxist-Leninist (CPI-ML) under the leadership of Charu Mazumdar. Naxalite ideology was predominately Maoist, although its vocabulary drew liberally from various forms of Soviet Marxism. For Naxalites, India was "semi-feudal, semi-colonial," a description deployed by Mao Zedong in his descriptions of Chinese society.[12]

To overturn this regressive order, peasants needed to be educated to claim what was theirs. But, perhaps more importantly, violence needed to be deployed ruthlessly to eliminate class enemies, particularly the landowning "kulak" class, who were complicit in or actively maintained peasant subordination. While Rabindra Ray has described the Naxalite worldview as essentially "nihilistic," there is a very strong theme within Naxalite discourse that violence in itself is transformative.[13]

Apart from his liberal but most certainly deliberate use of the title "comrade" and Moti's dying reference to Charu Mazumdar, Ujagir's narrative does not draw upon specific terminology employed by Naxalite idealogues and their cadres. He does not use the words "kulak," "class enemy," or "annihilation campaign" in Russian, English, or in any discernable Hindi or Bengali equivalent. But in its broad outlines, "The Death of Comrade Moti" does indeed articulate crucial Naxalite themes. While Ujagir does not use the term "cadre," it is clear that Comrade Moti's group is a cell organized within a revolutionary Marxist framework. In the aftermath of the Naxalbari revolt, for example, CPI-ML activists traveled the country-side in secret organizing peasants into resistance cells, much as Moti attempted to organize manual laborers in the Shantinagar area. As in Naxalbari, the first act of protest in Shantinagar was a collective repossession of grain that the landowners had refused to distribute equitably. In the narrative of the Shantinagar resistance and its aftermath, violence is not indiscriminate but is instead consciously directed toward members of the Bhumihar caste, who are, without question, the "class enemies." And so, we see that as the resistance grows, Untouchables under Comrade Moti develop the qualities necessary for their own emancipation. Principle among these qualities is solidarity—something made impossible by the system of manual and bonded labor. But what is symbolically most important in the narrative is how Untouchables use the tools of their servitude as their instruments of vengeance. Comrade Moti trains laborers to use the scythe as a weapon—perhaps following the admonition of the Naxalite leader Charu Mazumdar that peasants use the primitive weapons available to them to attack their oppressors. And so, not only is the story of the death of Comrade Moti a tale of violent revolutionary struggle, it is also clearly didactic. Not only does Comrade Moti teach Untouchables about the means they must employ to overcome their oppression, he himself embodies the qualities necessary if Untouchables are ever to succeed in their struggle for liberation.

SHERPUR CONNECTIONS

The most well-known incident of caste violence near Shantinagar involved Sherpur, a village about twenty miles south in the neighboring Ghazipur district. Unlike many incidents of caste violence in eastern Uttar Pradesh, the violence in Sherpur has been the subject of substantive efforts at historical research. In *Direct Attacks on Rural Poverty*, Prabhu Ghate initially examines the structural dynamics of low-caste subordination in Ghazipur District.

Ghate diagrams the failure of land reform and homesteading acts designed to lessen low-caste dependence upon tenancy and sharecropping. Ghate trains his analysis particularly upon the *harwahi* system in which low-caste and Untouchables are indebted or "tied" to the landowners as cultivators and servants often from generation to generation.[14] Ghate writes in part as an activist, struggling to envision approaches to rural poverty that would allow low-caste and Untouchable families greater economic autonomy. As part of his work, Ghate, along with his colleague B. N. Juyal, settled in Sherpur and wrote "The Sherpur Journal" as an addendum to his larger discussion of poverty in the Ghazipur District.[15]

Ghate's "The Sherpur Journal," which is in essence a short quasi-ethnographic account of the circumstances surrounding the violence in Sherpur, has many thematic similarities to Ujagir's account of the Shantinagar revolt and its reverberations. As in parts of Ujagir's narrative, the violence begins with an altercation between an Untouchable laborer and a Bhumihar. According to Ghate and Juyal's account, an Untouchable laborer, Radheyshyam left his Bhumihar master, Paras Raj, to work on another landowner's field. Paras Raj then publicly beat Radheyshyam and his sister. The next night, April 26, 1976, two Bhumihar landowners were killed in their homes. In retaliation, the Bhumihars killed Radheyshyam and another Untouchable and then put Sherpur's entire Untouchable colony to the torch, while beating and raping the residents. Interestingly, Ghate states that Radheyshyam was publicly executed in "feudal style,"[16] which is a rather euphemistic way of talking about either a shot to the head or beheading, acts that often provide the most dramatic moments in Ujagir's narrative of the events surrounding and following Comrade Moti's death. As in Ujagir's narratives as well, the police play either an indeterminate or adversarial role: Ghate and Juyal, for example, mention that Sherpur was a Bhumihar village "absolutely" and that any police or government official posted there had "to live and work on their [the Bhumihar's] terms."[17] But in spite of the fact that Ghate and Juyal were "on the ground" during the Sherpur violence, their account is wholly based upon discussions in the village, no official records are consulted at all, even though *Direct Attacks on Rural Poverty* as a whole draws upon a substantial amount of economic data. The closest "The Sherpur Journal" comes to any kind of directed political commentary is by observing that the "Naxalite bogey" was evoked by the government in order to place the blame on forces outside the village, and to pressure an unnamed Untouchable official who was nominally responsible for law and order in this part of the Ghazipur district.[18]

In his discussions with me, Ujagir did mention Sherpur often as an example of the cruelty of the Bhumihar landowners. But one night during our discussions, Ujagir became much more specific about Sherpur and stated that a Naxalite cadre had passed from Bihar to Sherpur through Shantingar. While Ghate and Juyal, state that there were no Naxalites involved in the Sherpur violence, only "criminal elements" who sought to capitalize on the violence, Ujagir maintained that the Naxalites were indeed involved in Sherpur, although he failed to mention any specifics. And so, for Ujagir, Sherpur is linked with Shantinagar and "The Death of Comrade Moti" in a continuing narrative of Untouchable resistance and Bhumihar domination.

DISJUNCTIONS AND FRAGMENTS

Perhaps the most suggestive study of a narrative of violence in North India is Shahid Amin's *Event, Memory and Metaphor*.[19] A member of the influential subaltern-collective of Indian historians, Amin focuses his attention on the nationalistic resonances of the destruction of a police station in the town of Chauri Chaura, in the Gorakhpur District. In charting the trajectory of the narrative of Chauri Chaura from 1922 to 1992, Amin examines how that specific act of violence has been represented as an anti-type to the broad sweep of non-violent Gandhian nationalistic resistance to British rule. For Amin, history itself is as much metaphor as it is "fact" for to examine the multiple resonances of a particular historical event is to engage numerous disjunctions between the accounts of contending groups that invest an event with meaning. Within this framework, as Amin's subaltern colleague Dipesh Chakrabarty might put it, history itself is often an "artifice" because it is so inflected by the concerns of the parties who seek to write it.[20] But perhaps, finally, whether Comrade Moti actually existed is not the central issue—for in any case, we all employ particular narrative tropes when we describe a friend, lover, or hero. "The Death of Comrade Moti" then is not a tall tale, but a story of longing and tragedy—made all the more poignant perhaps by its idealized and romantic symbolic tones and resonances.

PRACTICING CATHOLIC RAGE

When are you people finally going to give up this habit of belittling yourselves? Why don't you people feel that you are human beings too, and have a right to equality?

Mudrarakshasa, Dandavidhana, *130*

While some might say that "The Death of Comrade Moti" is a tall-tale rather than history, still others might see it as exclusively enmeshed within a North Indian Untouchable political sensibility, rather than as narrative that also reflects the Catholic Christian identity of Ujagir himself. Perhaps the most influential North Indian narrative of political violence is a Hindi work of fiction *Dandavidhana* [The Criminal Code], by Mudrarakshasa. In comparing Ujagir's "The Death of Comrade Moti" to Mudrarakshasa's *Dandavidhana*, we can indeed see how the former is replete with North Indian narrative tropes. But also through this comparison, we can see how Mudraraskasa invests fictional narrative with Hindu themes related to the god Shiva while Ujagir draws upon the sacrificial death of Jesus Christ. Indeed, Ujagir's "The

Death of Comrade Moti" is both a mythic creation and a dirge for Catholic Untouchable dreams.

Mudrarakshasa's *Dandavidhana* and the Death of Comrade Moti

A literary editor and social activist, Subhash Chandra first published *Dandavidhana* [The Criminal Code] in 1987 under the pseudonym "Mudrarakshasa." *Dandavidhana* concerns caste violence in a fictional North Indian village of Bhudra. The narrative begins with the landowners summoning low-caste women for "labor at night," for which the women receive an extra bundle of wheat in exchange for their "honor." When members of the low castes protest to the police, they are beaten by the landowners and violence quickly escalates.

Written in a clear and crisp Hindi prose suitable for a rural audience, *Dandavidhana* presents three characters that have clear symbolic resonances. Master Bhuraylal is a communist activist who organizes Bhudra's manual laborers to revolt. But Master Bhuraylal perhaps is more effective as a rhetorician than as a revolutionary, and his confrontations with the police are full of bluster proclaiming how his death will provide the seed for true revolution; a vain claim that Bhuraylal continues to make even in the face of his actual death at the hands of the police at the novel's end. The second key character is Bedana, a member of the Mushaher caste who have the duty to catch rats after which they may lay claim to the grain the rats have hoarded. As Robert A. Hueckstedt observes in his commentary on his English translation of *Dandavidhana*,[21] Bedana is much like the Hindu god Shiva: he is the Lord of Animals and is addressed as *bam bhole*, a phrase also used for Shiva. Of course, Shiva is preeminently the god of destruction, whose dance destroys and then recreates the universe. Bedana's violence against the landowners, especially his killing of the lead landowner, leads to the destruction of Bhudra itself. While Hueckstedt argues that the message of the novel is primarily political in its satire of communist activists and its valorization of villagers such as Bedana, it does have a strong religious subtext. The third crucial character is Bishan, a poet and song writer who is associated with Bhuraylal's activists and the ordinary villagers. When Bishan returns to Bhudra at the end of the novel, his feet are covered in ash—which is yet another sign of Shiva, the god who covers himself in ash. Within Hindu mythology, the ash of Shiva is generative for it is from ash that the universe is reborn. In *Dandavidhana*, there is thus a strong sense of how violence and destruction are part of the cyclical death and rebirth of the universe. Throughout the novel, Mudrarakshasa makes reference to the stories that surround any Indian village and asks the reader to attend to the stories that lie hidden in the ramshackle huts of the poor and oppressed. At the very end of the novel, Bishan is prompted to create another song, for it is only through story and song that the narratives of the oppressed can be told.

"The Death of Comrade Moti" has strong narrative similarities to Mudrarakshasa's *Dandavidhana*. Throughout the "The Death of Comrade Moti," there are dramatic rhetorical flourishes, though perhaps lacking in irony found in *Dandavidhana*. Descriptions of the plight of Untouchables are similar in both works—from the strains of manual labor to the sexual exploitation of Untouchable women. Deaths and executions are public and not subject to any investigation or legal action, while there is simultaneously a bureaucratic concern with filing the appropriate papers. The police are not only complicit in the violence directed against the low-castes, they actively abet it. In both *Dandavidhana* and "The Death of Comrade Moti," villagers alternate between fear and murderous rage. And in both narratives, the violence ends without any tangible gains being achieved.

Ujagir's "The Death of Comrade Moti," however, is much more self-consciously didactic or moralizing than Mudrarakshasa's *Dandavidhana*. What initially characterizes the story of Comrade Moti's death is its use of reversal—particularly reversals of common themes and characteristics associated with Untouchable identity. According to Ujagir, Chamars are not only fearful of all those who stand above them, they are also mentally backward, having been denied the basic foodstuffs necessary to build strength of mind and body. Comrade Moti is inserted into the narrative as a symbol of the strength that can be developed by Untouchables who have a revolutionary vision and commitment. Indeed, Comrade Moti goes without food for days as if to emphasize that revolutionary struggle alone can provide vigor and sustenance.

If Moti stands as an idealized revolutionary figure, those who seek to assume his mantle fail to embody his heroic qualities. Shivlochan and Shivmochan do not maintain appropriate discipline and allow either their sexuality or their need to talk overwhelm their commitment to resistance. Suryabali too could not control himself and his appetite for liquor and prideful boasting leads to his downfall. While Devanath might be brave, he is incompetent. Siddhi, however, is a coward who did not have the courage to identify his brother's killers. Villagers as a whole fail to support those who follow Moti, either because Moti's disciples are not worthy of allegiance or because the villagers are simply paralyzed by fear. Women, in particular, are represented as both witting and unwitting agents of the landowners. Indeed, as Ujagir describes village life, the Bhumihar landowners have eyes and ears everywhere. It is in this vein as well that the strong castist tones of the narrative become clear. The original Shantinagar resistance is betrayed by a member of the Dusadh caste, a rival of the area's Chamars and a group who raise pigs. Accordingly, Moti's unfaithful comrade Devamuni is treated like a pig and slaughtered, only after his masculinity is taken away by castration. Through these portrayals, Ujagir quite consciously emphasizes pervasive North Indian stereotypes of Untouchables who are often seen as deceitful and opportunistic, with raging appetites for sex and liquor.[22] Central then to Comrade Moti's symbolic significance is that he comes from the outside, from Bihar, for it is his status as an outsider that brings into sharp relief the life of degradation experienced by those Untouchables he has come to lead.

While "The Death of Comrade Moti" is an idealized vision of the tactics that both Catholics and Untouchables must use if they are ever to change their lives, it is also a profoundly tragic narrative that shows how often acts of resistance by Untouchables fail. And it is in its tragic aspect that the death of Comrade Moti has its most Catholic Christian resonance. If in *Dandavidhana* the primary theme is the cyclical movement of death and regeneration, in "The Death of Comrade Moti" the theme is sacrificial example and atonement. In Ujagir's narrative, it is only Comrade Moti who dies speaking words of resistance for his is a self-conscious sacrifice for the oppressed. Most of the villagers Ujagir portrays are fearful, and those who eventually decide to take up arms are killed quickly without any opportunity for dramatic denunciations of their killers. Most importantly, the resistance takes place during the Easter season and as Ujagir concludes his narrative, he spreads his arms to show how Comrade Moti died—for Moti extends his arms outward as he is shot by the police and landowners. Not only was Moti betrayed by his own "Judas," Devamuni, but in death the outlines of Moti body assumes a cruciform shape. Ujagir's narrative of the death of Comrade Moti then is not simply a story of resistance. Instead, it is also a powerful effort to reimagine the Untouchable body in an explicitly Christian form.

Rage and Mourning

While Comrade Moti is the Christ figure in Ujagir's narrative of the Shantinagar resistance, the Catholic community and mission have a far more ambiguous status. Ujagir emphasizes the revolutionary commitment of Comrade Moti and his comrades—a commitment that stood in stark contrast not only to the conduct of the mission, which houses the paramilitary forces deployed against the insurrection, but also to the conduct of the Catholic community. It is Father Premanand who provides the description of Moti to the police and the Catholics themselves become involved in the whole affair by means of a strange and unfortunate coincidence. While the landowners suspected that Catholicism was a revolutionary movement, the reality was that Catholics were only unwitting players in the drama of caste violence. Of course, in the aftermath of the resistance, it is a high-caste priest who denies sanctuary to Siddhi in contradistinction to the low-caste priest who is sympathetic to the cause of Shantinagar's poor. While at one time the mission spearheaded rural development projects and food distribution, it had severely curtailed such efforts because the priests believed that Catholic Untouchables were becoming too dependent upon outside aid. In Ujagir's view, this represented a fundamental betrayal of Catholicism's mission in Shantinagar since Catholic Untouchables were subsequently left to their own devices to deal with the twin stigmas of their Untouchable and Catholic identities. Ujagir's narrative of Comrade Moti's death is thus intended to spur Catholics to a more aggressive and self-conscious form of political struggle. The portrayal of Comrade Moti's cruciform body, hands outstretched as it is pierced by bullets, is a call to join a redemptive struggle waged through revolutionary violence and martyrdom.

"The Death of Comrade Moti" is also a narrative infused with rage. In our discussions surrounding his narratives of resistance, Ujagir would become enraged with the suggestion that Catholics and Untouchables could better their lot through political action and non-violent resistance. For Ujagir, the entire system is rigged: landowners resist land reform and subvert the political process while Catholicism has long given up any claims to privileges for the poor, focusing instead on efforts "to fit in" to Indian culture by bringing high-caste customs into the mission's religious life.[23] In Ujagir's words only "a river of blood" (*khun ki nadi*) can wash away the stain of caste and oppression. During a meeting of the Catholic *panchayat*, a governing body for the Shantinagar Catholic community, Ujagir evoked the image of Comrade Moti to shame the Catholic community into a more assertive political role. But Ujagir's impassioned speech was not well received and, as Ujagir will readily admit, there is no Untouchable insurgency in his area of Ballia District. As much as Ujagir longs for revolution, he also knows that it will never come. When Ujagir does tell the story of Comrade Moti, he most often does so in the darkness, with his few friends as they sit together after sunset to drink their home-brewed liquor. In such fragmented performances for his fragmented community, Ujagir attempts to frame a larger mythic narrative in which Comrade Moti becomes the embodiment of Untouchable and Catholic longings. Perhaps then it is appropriate that the story of Comrade Moti ends in death, for "The Death of Comrade Moti" has finally become a dirge, filled with rage and mourning for those lost Untouchable and Catholic dreams.

PERFORMANCE

Bring fire, Father, bring fire. Let me burn my house down. That is why my heart is so restless.

Mudrarakshasa, Dandavidhana, *153*

Of course, one of Ujagir's most eager listeners was me. And there were many nights when Ujagir and I stayed up for hours as he regaled me with his tales of caste violence and dreams of redemption. "The Death of Comrade Moti," along with the other political tales he would tell, was intended not only to inform, but to evoke a solidarity with the Catholic Untouchable struggle—a solidarity that Ujagir hoped would find expression in my publications. The transcripts of my Hindi interviews with him numbered over three hundred pages as I reviewed them as I left Shantinagar to move to Varanasi in preparation for leaving India.

Two weeks before my planned departure, I went for an interview with an Indian charismatic healer to her two-room flat in a military cantonment in the city of Varanasi. The guards let me pass through the gate and as I sat down to begin the interview, military intelligence arrived, detained me and then turned me over to the local police. After being rather mildly interrogated,

I was released. Several days later, the CID, the Indian equivalent of the FBI, came to my apartment in Varanasi and presented me with documents for a legal case they planned to bring against me for violating the terms of my research visa. I immediately sought legal council and received a strong admonition from a lawyer I consulted that I should turn over all my interview tapes and transcripts to the Superintendent of Police—who would obviously see that there was nothing inappropriate about my research.

When considering the "appropriateness" of my research, my mind immediately turned to Ujagir and his stories about Comrade Moti. At that time, it seemed to me that if any one in authority were to hear or read Ujagir's quite expansive reflections upon the necessity of violence, it might very well confirm many of the suspicions the Indian government has about the Catholic Church's work with Untouchables. In any case, I was already cautious since, as is common for many researchers in India, the police had already made inquiries about me and, in times past, had rather conspicuously opened my mail. And so, faced with the possibility of turning over to the police the tapes and transcripts of my interviews with Ujagir, I decided to destroy any written or audio record of his most polemical comments.

As things turned out, no case was brought against me. When a priest from the Shantinagar mission came to see me before I left India, his view was that I had spent far too much time in the village and that my reaction to the circumstances was as a rather rash decision brought on by the coming summer heat. Of course, as one study of ethnographers discovered,[24] one of the deepest preoccupations of fieldworkers is with the potential "burning" of their notes—a combination of both fear and self-destructive longing that would curiously resonate in North India, and especially in the pages of a narrative like *Dandavidhana* where the poet Bishan articulates the connection between death and regeneration by singing about burning his own house down. But in retrospect it is clear how much Ujagir succeeded in evoking a strong resonance in me with his story "The Death of Comrade Moti". For both Ujagir and me, in very different ways, "The Death of Comrade Moti" was a narrative of longing and rage that evoked shame and guilt. Moreover, for me individually, "The Death of Comrade Moti," especially in its description of the arrest of the mission's Catholics, was also a parable about the dark and strange twists of coincidence. Ujagir spoke of the destruction of the physical body of Comrade Moti, a destruction that had the power to redeem not only the material conditions of Untouchables but also the very character of Untouchables themselves. Ujagir had hoped that I too would "perform" this narrative by sharing the story of Comrade Moti and Catholic Untouchables with an audience far removed from the wheat fields of North India. But, for me, the performance of the narrative of "The Death of Comrade Moti" had its most immediate expression in the physical destruction of my own body of research for it was through that conscious act that I thought, strangely and paradoxically, that my own research could be redeemed. For me, as well as for Ujagir, the narrative "The Death of Comrade Moti" is still performed in a memory of rage and mourning.

The Customs of the Faithful: Evangelicals and the Politics of Catholic Fiesta in Bolivia

Daniel M. Goldstein

In Bolivia, folkloric dancing represents a kind of national resource, central to Bolivian national culture and identity. In the early 1950s, the Bolivian state declared folkloric music and dancing to be elements of the nation's official cultural patrimony, cataloging varieties of "folk" performance and issuing decrees naming these dances property of the Bolivian nation (and, by extension, of the Bolivian state).[1] In particular, the city of Oruro, site of Bolivia's annual folkloric Carnaval, gained recognition for its prowess in musical and dance performance, and in 1970 a governmental decree named Oruro the "folklore capital of Bolivia."[2] Such declarations, of course, are predicated on the idea of Bolivia as a predominantly Catholic nation, one in which national culture is derived explicitly from performances dedicated to Catholic saints and keyed to the Catholic ritual calendar.[3] Oruro's Carnaval is particularly well-suited to the task of representing the Catholic nation: Oruro was an important center of the Bolivian mining industry, long the economic backbone of the nation, and Carnaval was held annually to honor the Virgin of the Mineshaft, the patron deity of the region.[4] Even as they have become emblematic of the Bolivian nation, however, the popularity and visual appeal of Carnaval dances like the *Diablada* and the equally familiar *Morenada* have made them available for appropriation by others. The globalization of these dances—their expropriation and performance by non-Bolivians in international performance contexts—is viewed by some Bolivians as a threat to national identity, as the ownership of Bolivia's national cultural patrimony appears to fall under foreign control.

Meanwhile, within Bolivia itself but outside of the "folklore capital" of Oruro, Carnaval has provided a model for a variety of local festivals performed on numerous occasions, often to honor the patron Saints of towns and regions throughout the country. For example, in Villa Sebastián Pagador, one of the so-called "marginal barrios" (*barrios marginales*) on the outskirts of the city of Cochabamba, barrio residents are active performers of Bolivian national folklore in their own local performance events. Specifically, in their annual Saint's Day festival, the *fiesta de San Miguel*, barrio residents perform the famed dances of the nation's Carnaval, presenting their barrio fiesta as a satellite Carnaval in an attempt to claim Bolivian national culture as their own and to assert their membership in the Bolivian nation. Migrants from Oruro to the valley city of Cochabamba, the residents of Villa Pagador have been marginalized by virtue of their poverty and illegal occupation of the lands on which their homes are built, and so lack the resources and the mechanisms to transform their circumstances, to gain a political voice in municipal or national politics, or to attract development assistance into their community. By asserting a claim to being owners and originators of Bolivian national folkloric culture, residents of Villa Pagador consolidate their locality as a specific kind of community, one based on homogeneity of Oruro origins and command of national folklore, giving them hope of overcoming their marginalization and achieving a better quality of life in their neighborhood.

Complicating matters, however, is the fact that not everyone in this sup-posedly Roman Catholic community is, in fact, Catholic. Bolivia, like other countries throughout Latin America, has been experiencing steady evange-lization by North American Protestant churches among its populace, which have had marked success in recent decades.[5] Since its founding, Villa Pagador has been characterized by a high degree of religious heterogeneity, with a large number (perhaps as many as 50 percent) of barrio residents identifying as evangelical Protestants, attending one of seven evangelical churches in the community. For these Christians, as they call themselves, the dancing, drinking, and what they term "pagan" religiosity of the barrio fiesta are unac-ceptable, their churches proscribing participation in any such debauch. Nevertheless, for many of these same people the fiesta de San Miguel in Villa Pagador represents an expression of "their culture," an attachment to which even evangelical conversion cannot easily erase. Additionally, many of these evangelicals recognize the political salience of the fiesta as a mechanism for consolidating and performing collective identity in the barrio, and so are loath to condemn it out of hand. Barrio Catholics, on the other hand, resent-ful of the evangelicals' perceived aloofness and lack of commitment to the local community, describe evangelical Christianity as a form of foreign inter-vention aimed to undercut Bolivian national sovereignty, while also being disruptive of community-formation practices at the local level. In Villa Pagador, the production of a homogeneous and unified community on the basis of folkloric identity is predicated on the subordination of other forms of collective identification within the barrio, along with the erasure of actually existing religious heterogeneity that threatens to undermine collective solidarity.[6]

These kinds of tensions surrounding the performance of Catholic festivity problematize any functionalist notion of popular cultural performance, in

which "community" is viewed as the spontaneous outcome of festive enactment, or in which festival performance is regarded simply as a means of
reproducing social order and resolving conflict.[7] Rather, the fiesta emerges
here as contested and contradictory: Though it has political significance as an
instrument of community creation and representation, it operates in a context containing more condemnatory voices that regard festive behavior as
"sinful." Nor can the barrio fiesta be understood within the finite context of
what anthropologists might identify as "the local community"; the fiesta is
only interpretable in terms of its relationship with broader, national forms of
cultural performance and identity, within a globalizing context. In this scenario, as Guss suggests,[8] the fiesta is best understood as a set of "important
dramatizations that enable participants to understand, criticize, and even
change the worlds in which they live. . . . These public displays provide
forums in which communities can reflect upon their own realities."[9] They
also (echoing a point made clearly in Mendoza's work on *danza* performance
in Cuzco, Peru) enable fiesta practitioners to assert alternative versions of
reality, creating new meanings through festive performance.[10] In addition,
by establishing connections between marginalized localities and national
cultural identity, festive performance enables its practitioners to make claims
to national belonging and significance, though these may require the subordination of dissenting voices within the locality itself.

EVANGELICALS AND THE POLITICS OF COMMUNITY
IN VILLA PAGADOR

Doña Carmen was a young woman at the time of this story, and still a Catholic,
as her family had always been. But she married Don Arturo, and he was a
Christian, having converted to the Baptist Church (later he switched, ultimately
becoming pastor of the UCE) as a young man. They lived in Cochabamba,
along with some of Arturo's extended family, including her elderly father-in-
law—a recovering alcoholic, a former Franciscan catechist, and now himself a
recently converted Christian as well.

But Doña Carmen stuck to her faith as a Catholic. She didn't like the way the
men in her church drank too much *chicha*, and so she wasn't too crazy about fiestas and the like; but she loved the Saints and the *virgencitas*. She had a collection
of *Santos* in her room, in fact, framed images hung on the walls and small robed
figurines: San Miguel, San Francisco de Asis, San Ignacio de Loyola, all the
famous Santos of her church. She even had a few larger statuettes of some of her
favorites. To her these were holy objects, physical embodiments of the Santos
themselves, incarnations of God. And she wouldn't give them up, no matter how
much her husband or father-in-law tried to disabuse her of her faith in them.

Then one night, Doña Carmen had a dream. In it, the Lord came to her and
told her to give up the Santos, to leave the pagan ways and to come into the
evangelio, His true church. Doña Carmen woke in a sweat, confused. She told
her father-in-law of the dream, and he nodded with comprehension.

A short time later, her father-in-law brought home a new saint. Carmen was
surprised by this gift, but pleased nevertheless. It was one of the big Santos,

almost life-sized, and her father-in-law said he had gotten it from a man in Arani who makes these Santos for the church. Carmen was delighted. But her father-in-law turned to her and said, "Let me show you just what your Santo is made of." Then, picking up a metal shovel that he used for gardening, he turned and smashed the Santo right in its mid-section. Horrified, Carmen watched as he continued to beat the Santo as it lay on the ground, until its head came off and rolled to the side.

Doña Carmen, in tears, regarded the shattered Santo lying in pieces at her feet. In amazement, she realized that the Santo was made of plaster, that at its core it was only a broomstick with a head stuck on the end, molded hands and feet dangling from loosely draped apparel. She was stunned. And suddenly, as if a light shone upon her, she realized that she had been living in darkness, and she turned toward the light with open arms, and she stepped into the light. Later, she destroyed the rest of her collection of Santos, and began to learn more about the evangelio.

Now, when she tells the story, she laughs warmly at the ignorance of a young girl who thought that her Santos were divine beings, incarnations of God.

Villa Sebastián Pagador was founded in 1977 by a group of migrants from Bolivia's *altiplano* department of Oruro, whose capital city of Oruro hosts the nation's annual Carnaval celebration.[11] Shortly after the barrio's founding, the residents of Villa Pagador were invited by people in neighboring Valle Hermoso to participate in a fiesta dedicated to the local patron saint, San Miguel (the archangel Michael). The pagadoreños put together their own troupe to dance the Morenada, and in 1979 danced for the first time in the San Miguel fiesta. Following this initial participation, pagadoreños began to manifest an increasingly strong presence in the fiesta, eventually taking organizational authority away from their neighbors in Valle Hermoso and claiming the fiesta for their own. Pagadoreños who serve as fiesta sponsors and participants publicly express a strong faith in San Miguel, their patron Saint who, believers say, will reward them for their devotion, which they perform in the fiesta.

Though Villa Pagador was initially founded on land given to the settlers by the municipal government of Cochabamba, subsequent waves of migrants settling in Villa Pagador built their homes illegally, on land not intended for urban habitation.[12] As a result of their illegal settlement, barrio residents found themselves barred from membership in the city, symbolized by their lack of basic infrastructure and services, and reflected in their lack of formal channels by which to express their grievances to city authorities.[13] In this climate of illegality and exclusion, the fiesta de San Miguel began to take on more explicitly political significance. Barrio leaders and residents began a program of what might be called festive political persuasion: They began to deploy the fiesta as a mechanism to dramatize their belonging to the Bolivian nation, from which they felt unfairly excluded, and then used this belonging to make claims on the city and its representatives. As *orureños*, barrio residents asserted, they were not illegal settlers but, indeed, the owners and originators of Bolivia's national culture itself. Presenting themselves in this manner allowed the pagadoreños to assert their own centrality to the Bolivian nation, arguing that despite their migration and illegal settlement they remained an outpost of Bolivian national identity, an "island of Oruro" (in the words of one fiesta sponsor) in diaspora. As such, their exclusion from the benefits of national belonging was illegitimate and in need of transformation.[14]

In addition, barrio leaders recognized from the first that to achieve political integration and physical improvements in Villa Pagador, they would have to be able to mobilize a large group of people to put pressure on the government and agitate for change. The appeal to Oruro origins through festive performance was thus also aimed internally, at pagadoreños themselves, to consolidate the barrio as a unified community. Like good functionalists, the leaders of Villa Pagador believed that a fiesta could serve to build community, in the sense of forging unity among a group of people sharing common goals and concerns. By hosting a fiesta in which the Oruro migrants could come together and perform folkloric dances associated with Oruro and Carnaval, barrio leaders hoped to consolidate a spirit of community among the transplanted orureños. This community, the leaders believed, could subsequently be mobilized in pursuit of more explicitly political and development-oriented goals, and provide a base of support in efforts to transform barrio life. Unity and collective solidarity thus became goals of fiesta planners, seeking to mobilize the barrio population through the fiesta and transfer this energy to other ends.

As folklore and the San Miguel fiesta have been used locally to produce and perform community, mobilizing people on the basis of shared Oruro origins and culture, community solidarity has been threatened by the presence of evangelical Christians, who are proscribed from fiesta participation by the strictures of their faiths. Their critique of drinking, dancing, and the general devotion to Saints expressed in San Miguel offers a potent challenge to local efforts to construct community on the basis of shared mastery (by virtue of being Oruro natives) of national culture. At the same time, the power of this culture, both politically and in terms of its hold over individual lives and identities, competes with this critique, creating dissonance for those caught between these two faiths and their expressive practices.

In Bolivia, as in other Latin American nations whose syncretic Catholicism dates back to the Spanish conquest, evangelical Christianity is often regarded as a foreign threat to national unity and cultural identity. Although most evangelical churches in Latin America today are led by Latin Americans, many Catholics still regard the evangelical presence as a foreign (and specifically, North American) intrusion.[15] Despite often violent persecution at the hands of resentful Catholics operating in both official and unofficial capacities,[16] evangelical Protestant denominations (a broad category of diverse faiths that in Bolivia includes literally hundreds of different sects[17]) have experienced remarkable success in attracting converts to their churches. This is attributable to a variety of reasons, social as well as theological.[18] One factor that attracts people to the evangelical church is its prohibition of the consumption of alcoholic beverages. This is particularly appealing to women, who find sober men at the evangelical churches, many of whom profess a commitment to the churches' efforts to discourage domestic violence and extramarital affairs.[19] This is in marked contrast to the activities of the Catholic Church, whose rituals frequently involve the consumption of alcohol.[20] Marriage is also easier within the evangelical church: In urban Bolivia, many Catholic couples have to settle for civil marriage, often waiting years to save up the resources to pay for a religious wedding (and the obligatory party that follows it) in the Catholic Church.[21] At a deeper level, evangelical Protestantism (and particularly Pentecostalism, its most popular variant in Latin America) is particularly appealing in urbanizing Latin America, where it seems to promise community and a sense of belonging to people experiencing the disruptive effects of migration and the economic and physical insecurity of life on the urban periphery.[22] The churches provide settings of camaraderie and mutual support, echoing if not replacing the affective ties and systems of reciprocity that many congregants recall or imagine from their lives in the countryside. Additionally, with its emphasis on individual conversion and the creation of a personal relationship with the Lord, evangelicalism offers benefits that the large, hierarchical Catholic Church cannot.[23] Stoll's observation captures the appeal of evangelicalism to people in Villa Pagador: "In societies whose economies are being globalized, whose traditional social structures have heaved apart, where people must fend for themselves in hostile new environments, how can a single, centralized religious hierarchy satisfy a newly individuated population whose members need to chart their own courses?"[24]

The community of belonging that the evangelical churches offer competes with the secular or nominally Catholic political community in Villa Pagador. Many Catholics in the barrio recognize this as a potential source of division in the collective solidarity that they value so highly. Some complain that the evangelicals have their "eyes on the sky" (as one friend put it), and have turned their backs on the more worldly concerns of their neighbors in the barrio. They defend their festive practices (including the consumption of alcoholic beverages) as a necessary component in building solidarity among community members, and point to the "traditional" role of drinking in rural festive practices as evidence of the ways in which alcohol can foster intimate relationships of friendship, community, and mutual concern. Along similar lines, Catholics in Pagador regard evangelicals as having abandoned the larger struggles for political integration and physical improvements in barrio infrastructure. (This accusation resonates with Martin's observation that Pentecostalism "fosters a contempt for the world and that includes the political struggle in which the world is so constantly engaged."[25]) As we will see below, the belief by Catholics that evangelicals have detached themselves from the worldly concerns of the here and now is reinforced by the evangelicals' ambivalence towards the barrio's principal community-building event, the fiesta de San Miguel.

The question of religious identity in Villa Pagador begins with the founding of the barrio itself. Among the original group of settlers, there is today disagreement over what the religious affiliations of the founders were. Certainly there were a fair number of Catholics among the 156 people who received the original land grant from the municipality on the southeast side of the city. Eleuterio Mayta, the founder of the San Miguel fiesta in Villa Pagador, and Fausto Huanca, one of the earliest fiesta participants and a guide to others, were both Catholics, conspiring to create the fiesta shortly after the founding of the barrio.[26] Other founders of the barrio, including Ausencio Lopez and Bonifacio Villca, were also Catholic, though both of these men converted to the evangelio later in life. Nevertheless, others among the original founders group insist that the barrio was created exclusively by evangelical Christians. Arturo Avaroa, for example, my next-door neighbor and a pastor of the UCE (*Unión Cristiana Evangélica*) Church, claims that: "When we were initiating settlement here, the work was done by a group composed entirely of evangelicals (*creyentes evangélicos*). We didn't have a single unbeliever (*incrédulo*, i.e., Catholic) among us." According to Don Arturo, these Christians were members of different evangelical churches, principally Baptists, Pentecostals, and the UCE, and he was appointed by Ausencio Lopez to be "spiritual director" of the community, coordinating the worship of God between these denominations. He claims that the barrio was highly unified in the first years after its founding because of the shared religious faith of the population; only later, he says, as the barrio grew and many more Catholics began to move in, did the resulting "mix of believers and non-believers" lead to an attenuation of this unity. Some Catholics in the barrio contest the authenticity of the religious commitments of these first evangelical founders. Eulogio Ramirez, leader of a neighborhood political organization, says that many people who came to Villa Pagador recognized that evangelicals were in charge of the distribution of lots in the new barrio, and so conveniently converted to evangelical Christianity in order to be allowed to settle in Villa Pagador.

Whatever the case, the fact remains that a large number of evangelicals participated in the initial settlement of Villa Pagador (something not at all typical of new barrios in Cochabamba), and left a lasting imprint on the religious identity of the community. The importance of the evangelical faiths in Villa Pagador can be seen in the geography of the barrio itself. On the barrio's main plaza, as on all plazas in Spanish America, there is a church; but in Villa Pagador it is not a Catholic but an evangelical Christian church. (The Catholic church is a few blocks away, abutting the main football field where the main *demostración* of San Miguel is performed.) The church on the plaza, today dedicated to the UCE, was built in 1983, after five years of open-air services attended by virtually all the evangelicals in Pagador. Since then the evangelical presence in Villa Pagador has been a constant in barrio life. With time and steady evangelization this Christian presence has diversified beyond the original three denominations, and today in Villa Pagador, in addition to the UCE, Baptist, and Pentecostal Churches, there are strong contingents of

Seventh Day Adventists, Jehovah's Witnesses, Mormons, and Assemblies of God. The Pentecostal church was remodeled in 2001 and today is a massive temple that towers above the barrio, dwarfing the white-walled Catholic church a few hundred yards down the street.[27] Estimates vary, but some people claim that as many as half of the barrio's total current population are evangelical Christians.

In such an environment, it is odd that a Catholic Saint's Day festival should have become such a significant icon of barrio identity. It is also rather amazing that the fiesta not only has survived but flourished and grown in size and participation over the course of the last 20 to 25 years, given the powerful critique of fiesta practice offered by evangelicals in Villa Pagador. Barrio evangelicals condemn the fiesta de San Miguel for the massive consumption of alcohol (principally in the form of homemade corn beer, or *chicha*) that takes place over the three to five days of the celebration. Furthermore, evangelicals are highly critical of folkloric dancing, for the Protestant churches forbid dancing of any kind, particularly the gyrating, embodied movements of some of the more sexualized Carnival dances (e.g., the *Caporales* dance, in which women wear folklorized *cholita* [indigenous female] costumes that include very short skirts). In terms of Church doctrine, evangelicals denounce any form of what they call "idolatry," the adoration of "graven images" or physical depictions of God. Evangelicals are highly critical of the often grotesque, bloodied images of Jesus on the cross that are commonly found in Catholic churches in Latin America; their own churches are extremely bare of any symbolism or adornment, and in some one must look hard even to find a cross (in the UCE church it is painted on the ceiling). Nor do the evangelical churches permit the worship of saints, which they see as false idols standing between man and Jesus Christ, the one true God. Indeed, many evangelicals articulate their objections to what they call the "paganism" of the Catholic Church, and like good ethnologists can recite the history of Catholic syncretism dating back to the colonization of the Incas, to prove that contemporary Catholicism is not a "pure" (i.e., strictly biblical, or fundamentalist) religion. Evangelicals in the barrio interpret the San Miguel fiesta as a pagan celebration of a pre-Christian deity. The adoration of the Saint, embodied in a large oil painting that hangs in the chapel at which the fiesta's entry parade terminates, is criticized by evangelicals as the most vulgar form of idol-worship.

Despite this strong condemnation, however, evangelicals in Villa Pagador have an ambivalent relationship with the fiesta de San Miguel. Most evangelicals were born and raised in the Catholic Church, undergoing conversion only after migration to the city, and as youths themselves participated in fiestas and Saint's Day celebrations in their *pueblos*. Thus many evangelicals have a strong personal attachment to the cultural practices of the altiplano, including the dancing and carousing intrinsic to both the Carnaval de Oruro and the fiesta de San Miguel. Additionally, as some studies have shown,[28] membership in the evangelical church is often a temporary position for Andean people, who frequently switch back and forth from one church to another in the course of a lifetime. Men especially will temporarily leave the evangelical church, often around fiesta time. The Catholic priest in Villa Pagador told me stories about the sorry, drunken sots who every year would literally crawl on hands and knees into his church around the time of the San Miguel fiesta, begging his forgiveness and asking to be allowed back into the congregation. He of course would consent, only to see these men return to the evangelical church after the fiesta had ended. For others in Villa Pagador belonging to an evangelical church may be a political stance, as Don Eulogio suggested earlier on: Some joined to gain access to land in the barrio, others to advance a local political career. My *compadres* Nestor and Juana frequently claimed to be evangelical Christians, though they rarely attended church (Nestor is an active political aspirant in barrio affairs). When it came time to baptize their son Oswaldo, the ceremony was performed in their house rather than in the church, and my wife and I were named the boy's *padrinos* (godparents), though the institution of *compadrazgo* (ritual co-parenthood) is not formally allowed in the evangelical churches.[29]

Thus there is a fair degree of fluidity in church membership and religious affiliation, with tenuous ties to the *evangelio* weakening further around fiesta time, when the call of what people refer to as "custom" (*costumbre*) for some becomes overwhelmingly powerful. The story of my friend Tito illustrates the conundrum that many evangelicals in Villa Pagador face, when confronted by the contradiction that exists between present faith and historical custom:

> *30 October 1995*—We went for lunch at Nestor and Juana's, to eat the last of the chickens that had survived yesterday's party, which had followed Oswaldo's baptism. Tito was at their house when we arrived.
>
> I had last seen Tito a month before, when I spotted him dancing in the fiesta de San Miguel. I was surprised to see him dancing, because I knew him to be an evangelical Christian, a member of the Baptist church. Standing with Nestor at the time, I pointed Tito out to him, as the entrada passed before his house. "Isn't that Tito dancing there?" I asked. "Yes," said Nestor. I hesitated. "What's he doing?" I finally asked. Nestor shrugged. "*Está pecando, pues.*" He's sinning, I guess.
>
> So at lunch, I took the opportunity to ask Tito about his participation in the fiesta. Tito says he is not a *devoto* of the Santo. Rather, he dances because it is his culture to dance, his *cultura* and his *costumbre*. Because they dance in the pueblos, though he personally did not. He is from Turku, *provincia* Carangas, near the border with Chile, which makes him a *fronterizo* (a frontiersman), a *moreno* (someone with dark skin), and he dances the Morenada. A lot of people from his pueblo live in Villa Pagador; most of those are evangelicals, and most of them dance in the fiesta. They also will drink a cup or two, but not to excess. Why? "Because it's our custom to. We don't want to give up our *cultura*." But what does the Church say about that? "Well, the Church says it's a sin to dance." Yet you dance? "Yes."
>
> I looked at Tito with a questioning smile, and he looked down at his plate. Nestor turned to me. "To tell you the truth," he said, "Tito is kind of confused about the whole situation."

At another level, many evangelicals in the barrio, despite their articulate condemnation of the sinfulness of fiesta practice, recognize the cultural and political importance of San Miguel as it relates to the collective identity and political struggles of Villa Pagador. Particularly for local leaders, engaged in a variety of strategies for producing a community on the basis of an attachment to Oruro, the role of the fiesta in constituting this identity is not something they are willing to cast aside. Oruro is not Oruro without folklore, and Villa Pagador cannot be Villa Pagador without the fiesta de San Miguel as an expression of the folkloric Oruro identity of barrio residents. This recognition requires some barrio representatives to wear two hats, balancing their evangelical commitments against their political loyalties to the barrio. This is the case for Arturo Avaroa, who is quoted above as a founder and first spiritual leader of Villa Pagador. Don Arturo has also served as president of the barrio's water committee, an organization that successfully lobbied external agencies to bring potable water service into the barrio, and so is well acquainted with the goals and techniques of community politics in Villa Pagador. In his testimony below, the contradictions that these dual roles place on him is evident:

Daniel: And what do the evangelicals say about the fiesta de San Miguel?

Don Arturo: Well, it's a custom—I am speaking now as a leader—that has to be continued, until the Lord returns. We can't say to them [the Catholics], "No. Don't do it." But it is our obligation to tell them that the Lord does not like idolatry. Idolatry is not good. No, it always brings harm. Do you see?

Daniel: Mm hmm.

Don Arturo: It brings harm because when there is a fiesta, when people devote themselves to drinking, nothing good comes of it. Nothing good comes of it. And if we are to speak at the doctrinal level, it is not pleasing to God. Because God is against idolatry. When He created the first fathers of the *evangelio,* of the Israelites, the first thing the Lord told them was to destroy all the idols, made by the hands of men. Because these hands, they are not clean. They are stained with sin. That's the truth. How am I going to make my own god and worship it? A god that can't hear, that can't see, that can't feel, that doesn't do anything? Do you understand me?

Daniel: Yes.

Don Arturo: That's the thing. The only one that can hear us, that can understand us, is the Lord Jesus Christ.

Daniel: But at the cultural level, so to speak, it seems to me that the dances are very important to the people of the *altiplano.*

Don Arturo: Well. Now I am going to speak as an *orureño*! (laughs)

Daniel: (laughs) Please do!

Don Arturo: The culture of the altiplano is very different from the culture of the jungle, and of the valley. Today the valley has become infected (*contagiado*) with the culture of the *altiplano.* And the culture of the *altiplano*—I'm generalizing here—is the center of all fiestas, in the city of Oruro itself. That is where it all began, many years ago. That's where the famous fiestas of Carnival were formed and created.

Daniel: In the city?

Don Arturo: In the city. And it's from there that all these orureños are coming. It's not really a fiesta of the city, it's a fiesta of the mines, that's where it was created. And it's been getting bigger, and it's been infecting [other places]. (Laughs) And Oruro, therefore, is always called the folkloric city.

Daniel: And they couldn't create a miniature Oruro here without Carnaval.

Don Arturo: Without the fiesta. And this year, have you seen: It's almost exactly like Oruro. No? (Laughs). That's the thing about these cultures. They are very different.

Daniel: And the people have maintained this culture.

Don Arturo: Yes. And that's a good thing, no? It's a good thing. . . . Because the *altiplano* person is in love with his culture, and he's in love with his land. That's how it is.

CONCLUSION

The strategy adopted by barrio leaders and folklore experts to construct their community as an "island of Oruro" was based on that department's (and that city's) national identity as the "folklore capital of Bolivia," site of the nation's Carnaval. In Villa Pagador, people trade on the currency of national folklore to imagine publicly their collective selves through collective cultural performance. By positioning themselves as the true bearers of the national cultural patrimony, the owners and originators of Bolivia's national culture, the people of Villa Pagador seek an instrument to engage the attention of the national state and the local municipality, transforming their "marginal barrio" into a nationally significant location and in the process contesting their own marginalization from Bolivian national life. The fiesta de San Miguel has a central role to play in the creation, reproduction, and public representation of Villa Pagador as a particular kind of community on the margins of Cochabamba.

Despite this importance, the fiesta is not uncritically received in the community, nor can it be understood as unproblematically reproducing the structure or organization of the community that practices it. Rather, the fiesta is a highly contested terrain, fraught with ambiguities and contradictions. For some it is an annual occasion for a bacchanalian release from the stresses of daily life; for others, it is a sinful debauch that nevertheless draws them in by rekindling memories of the past and the cultural attachments of another time. For still others, the fiesta is a political instrument, conditionally tolerated because of its powerful role as producer and symbol of local collective identity. For the many evangelicals that reside in Villa Pagador, their commitments to the community-formation project in the barrio contradict their commitments to their faith, requiring them to conceal their condemnation of the fiesta and hence tacitly participate in the production of an idea of community predicated upon sin. The religious heterogeneity of Villa Pagador is disguised by a folkloric veneer, a spectacle produced, in part, for the consumption of others.

Making Christ Credible: U.S. Latino/a Popular Catholicism and the Liberating Nearness of God

Roberto S. Goizueta

In the early stages of its development, the Latin American liberation theology movement exhibited a certain degree of skepticism about the possible role of popular religion in the liberation struggle. Because popular religion in general, and popular Catholicism in particular, was not explicitly or directly political in either its expressions or its intent, some liberation theologians were openly derisive of popular religion, perceiving it as an ideological (in the Marxist sense) diversion from the liberation struggle. In more recent years, as the ambiguities of the liberation struggle itself have become more evident, liberation theologians in Latin America and elsewhere have come to a renewed appreciation of popular religion as a source of hope and empowerment for the poor. Among the theologians who have emphasized the positive role of popular religion and have thus attempted to broaden the understanding of "liberation" are U.S. Latino/a theologians.

In this chapter, I would like to examine U.S. Hispanic popular Catholicism as a source of empowerment that exercises a subversive, countercultural role in the lives of U.S. Hispanics. That role derives not from any explicitly political function but precisely from the fact that popular religious practices do *not* have such a function, that is, from the fact that in a U.S. society which identifies value with utility, popular religious practices emphasize the *intrinsic* value of created existence as the place where we meet God. Likewise, in a society where life is understood in individualistic terms, the religious faith of Latinos/as emphasizes the inherently relational character of all life, a relationality that is never abstract but is mediated through our concrete, everyday activities in the world. Ultimately, it is God's intimate love for and nearness to us in the person of Jesus Christ—as encountered in everyday life—that makes survival possible in an alien, threatening environment.

Because Jesus Christ walks with us, we can dare to hope and trust in the future. Far from limiting or suffocating our freedom, God's solidarity with us is the source of our freedom. And that solidarity is not just "known" or "believed"; it is felt, sensed, and experienced. Creation and human life are understood as intrinsically symbolic in that they make present the transcendent in a palpable, historical, and material way.

U.S. Latino/a popular Catholicism thus reflects an understanding of symbol that is different from modern Western notions of symbol. It is precisely in this non-modern notion of symbol that the liberating character of popular Catholicism is rooted, for the symbolic structure of popular Catholicism reflects a holistic, organic worldview fundamentally different from that of post-Enlightenment rationalism. Consequently, before examining the liberating character of popular Catholicism we should examine the particular history of Latin American Catholicism as still influenced by a non-modern, or pre-modern worldview.

IBERIAN CHRISTIANITY AND ANGLO-CATHOLICISM

As distinct from the Catholicism that was implanted in the English colonies to the north, Latin American Catholicism had its roots in medieval Christianity and baroque Iberian Catholicism. Neither Spain nor its American colonies would experience the full impact of the Protestant Reformation for several generations. As historian William Christian has noted, the medieval Christian worldview and faith were not seriously threatened in Spain "until . . . the late eighteenth century."[1] Consequently, unlike Catholics in northern Europe, Iberian Catholics—and, *a fortiori*, Catholics in the distant Spanish colonies of America—did not yet feel the pressure to define their own beliefs over against the Protestant reformers' beliefs.[2] Indeed, the principal menace to Iberian Catholicism had not been Protestantism but the Islamic faith that had only recently been finally "expelled" from the peninsula with the *reconquista* and the unification of Spain under the monarchs Fernando and Isabel. In northern Europe, on the other hand, increasing divisions *within* Christianity placed those Christian loyal to Rome in the position of having to define their "orthodox" faith *over against* the beliefs of the Protestant "heretics." The need for confessional precision and maximum doctrinal clarity was not nearly as pressing in areas where "Catholic" and "Christian" continued to be essentially interchangeable terms.[3]

These historical differences have had numerous implications for the evolution of Catholicism in Latin America and in the United States. Some of these implications have been examined by Orlando Espín, who himself notes that the Iberian Christianity brought by the Spanish to Latin America "was medieval and pre-Tridentine, and it was planted in the Americas approximately two generations before Trent's opening session."[4] He then outlines the significance of this difference: "While this faith was defined by traditional creedal beliefs as passed down through the Church's magisterium, those beliefs were expressed primarily in and through symbol and rite, through devotions and liturgical practices . . . The teaching of the gospel did not usually occur through the spoken, magisterial word, but through the symbolic, 'performative' word."[5] As yet, in their everyday lives, Christians did not clearly distinguish religious beliefs from devotional practices; both were assumed to be integral dimensions of the Tradition. Espín avers that "until 1546 *traditio* included, without much reflective distinction *at the everyday level*, both the contents of Scripture and the dogmatic declarations of the councils of antiquity, as well as devotional practices (that often had a more ancient history than, for example, Chalcedon's Christological definitions)."[6] According to Espín, the clear distinction between dogma and worship did not become crystallized until the Council of Trent, yet "on this side of the Atlantic the Church was at least in its second generation, and it took approximately another century for Trent's theology and decrees to appear and become operative in our ecclesiastical scene."[7] Liturgical theologian Mark Francis observes that "during its formative period and even after the struggle for independence from Spain, Catholicism in Latin America never underwent the systematic standardization that was brought about by the Council of Trent elsewhere in the Catholic world. North American Catholicism, for example, was largely dominated by clergy drawn from European ethnic groups who immigrated to this country along with their people in the nineteenth century and who were inspired by the norms and centralized pastoral practices of Tridentine Catholicism. In contrast, Hispanic Catholics, except perhaps those from large cities, have never been historically so influenced. The first period of evangelization of Latin America antedates the Council of Trent; and even after the decrees and norms established by the council were promulgated in Europe, their implementation was slow and sporadic, even into the nineteenth century."[8]

"JUST" A SYMBOL?

As Catholicism in the United States becomes increasingly *Pan*-American, the historical argument of scholars like Espín and Francis becomes increasingly relevant for understanding our context both theologically and pastorally. For instance, the different histories help explain why U.S. Latino/a Catholics, being of little real interest to either liberal or conservative "mainstream" Catholics, are generally invisible to scholars of "American Catholicism," whether these scholars are liberal or conservative; Euro-American Catholics in the United States, whether liberal or conservative, share an essentially post-Enlightenment, modern worldview that tends to view Latino/a Catholicism with suspicion.

Ironically, the reasons for the suspicion are similar to those which legitimated anti-Catholic, nativist sentiments *against* Euro-American Catholics not long ago. In both cases, the modern prejudice against anything "medieval" (the word itself connoting "backwardness") has engendered violent reactions against those groups whose religious practices are perceived as superstitious and infantile—precisely because they resemble non-rationalistic, pre-modern forms of religious practice. Thus, if today Irish-American Catholics deprecate Mexican-American Catholics, it is because these latter embody a type of Catholic religiosity similar to that which Irish-American Catholics have long been trying mightily to live down, so as to be accepted as full-fledged members of our "modern" society. Arguing that the prejudice against medieval Christianity is based on the anachronistic assumption that medieval Christianity was identical with post-Tridentine Roman Catholicism, historian Gary Macy has perceptively diagnosed the problem facing Hispanic Catholics in the United States: "If the Church in the Middle Ages was tyrannical, corrupt, and immoral, and the Church in the Middle Ages was (and is) Roman Catholic, then Roman Catholics are immoral, corrupt, and tyrannical. Hispanics, as mostly Roman Catholics, can therefore be expected to be devious, immoral, lazy, technologically underdeveloped, and ignorant."[9] If in the first half of the twentieth century Catholics as a whole were the objects of this modern prejudice, today it is Hispanic Catholics who are often stigmatized by a thoroughly assimilated U.S. Catholic establishment that has also assimilated the modern prejudice against the Middle Ages.

I do not mean to suggest, of course, that U.S. Latino/a popular Catholicism can simply be equated with medieval Christianity, which it of course cannot, or that we can or should somehow return to some romanticized version of medieval Christianity—which was, after all, also characterized by a great deal of horrific violence, oppression, and corruption. Yet an understanding of the historical influences of medieval Christianity on Latino/a popular Catholicism is helpful for understanding how Latino/a popular Catholicism functions as a source of identity, resistance, and empowerment in a Hispanic community that is not yet fully assimilated.

To suggest, as I have above, that U.S. Latino/a popular Catholicism reflects an understanding of religious faith rooted primarily in symbols and practices does not yet fully explain, however, the marginal character of popular Catholicism in the U.S. Church and society, for that assertion begs further questions. What precisely do Hispanics *mean* by the terms "symbol," "ritual," or "religious practices"? It is here, in differing *notions* of symbolic expression, that we find the source of conflict and, hopefully, the possibility of mutual understanding and unity.

The understanding of religious symbols and practices inherent in the medieval Christianity and baroque Catholicism brought to the Americas by the Spaniards in the fifteenth, sixteenth and seventeenth centuries differs radically from the rationalistic, modern notion of symbol that, I will suggest, has influenced Christianity since the late Middle Ages and became normative in the wake of the Protestant Reformation, the Council of Trent, the Catholic Reformation, and the neo-scholastic theologies that reached their apex in the nineteenth century. As the Catholic philosopher Louis Dupré has observed, the roots of this key difference can be traced back to the rise of nominalism in the late Middle Ages. Medieval Christianity had a unified, profoundly sacramental view of the cosmos; creation everywhere revealed the abiding presence of its Creator, a living presence that infused all creation with meaning. In turn, "the *kosmos* included humans as an integral though unique part of itself."[10] As the place where one encountered the living, transcendent God, all creation was *intrinsically* symbolic; that is, creation made the transcendent God present in time and space for us, here and now. All creation was thus assumed to be intrinsically meaningful and intelligible; the Sacred would be encountered, not "above" or "outside" creation, but in and through creation.

This organic, sacramental worldview was brilliantly articulated in the writings of St. Thomas Aquinas (despite the distortions to which those writings would be subjected by later, neo-scholastic theologians). And it would endure in the religious practices of medieval Christians. To them, matter mattered. Religious life was sensually rich; the believer encountered God in the physical environment, through the five senses. The Christian faith of the Middle Ages was firmly anchored in the body: the body of the cosmos, the body of the person, the Body of Christ. Contrary to the modern stereotype of the medieval Christian as having a dualistic worldview antithetical to the human body, the Christian of the Middle Ages "assumed the flesh to be the instrument of salvation" and "the cultivation of bodily experience as a place for encounter with meaning, a locus of redemption."[11] Of course, as in every age, the view of the body was also profoundly ambiguous and conflicted.[12] This organic, intrinsically symbolic worldview also implied a particular understanding of the relationship between the individual person and the cosmos: the person was *integrally* related to the rest of creation and its Creator. Knowledge of reality thus implied *relationship*; it is through *inter*personal *inter*action that we could come to know God, ourselves, other persons, and creation.

According to Dupré, this organic, holistic, integral, sacramental worldview began to break down during the late Middle Ages. Afraid that too intimate a connection with material creation would compromise God's absolute transcendence, nominalist theologians such as William of Ockham "effectively removed God from creation. Ineffable in being and inscrutable in his designs, God withdrew from the original synthesis altogether. The divine became relegated to a supernatural sphere separate from nature, with which it retained no more than a causal, external link. This removal of transcendence fundamentally affected the conveyance of meaning. Whereas previously meaning had been established in the very act of creation by a wise God, it now fell upon the human mind to interpret a cosmos, the person became its source of meaning."[13]

The nominalist assertion of God's autonomy and freedom from creation had, however, a further implication: creation itself was now autonomous and free from God. Paradoxically, then, the Christian attempt to safeguard God's transcendence laid the groundwork for the emergence of modern rationalism and secularism. In order to protect God's immutability and transcendence, nominalism posited an absolutely inscrutable God and, as a corollary, an absolutely inscrutable creation. It was thus left up to the human subject alone to construct meaning through the use of one's reason, conceived as disembodied and abstract.

Neo-scholastic theologians like Thomas Cajetan began to read Thomas Aquinas through a modern, dualistic lens. Their theology "detach[ed] the realms of nature and faith from each other."[14] The birth of *modern* Christianity is thus characterized by the splitting, or dichotomizing of reality: as God is severed from creation, the natural and spiritual realms are separated, and, in the end, the human person—now as an autonomous "individual"—is severed from both God and nature: "modern culture . . . detached person-hood from the other two constituents of the original ontological synthesis."[15] If, eventually, secular humanists would preach a world without God, it was only because Christians had already been preaching a God without a world. David Bentley Hart notes this connection between nominalist theologies and secularist philosophies:

> [When] the nominalists, or those of the *factio occamista* who followed them, succeeded in shattering the unity of faith and reason, and so the compact between theology and philosophy (or as, in an Occamist moment, Luther phrased it, "that whore"), both were rendered blind. In the curious agonies of modernity, once being's beauty, its poetic coherency, no longer enjoyed proper welcome, it became for some (both Catholic and Protestant) more or less axiomatic that faith, to be faith, must be blind; but then reason, to be reason, must be as well. . . .[The] incarnation of the Logos, the infinite *ratio* of all that is, reconciles us not only to God, but to the world, by giving us back a knowledge of creation's goodness, allowing us to see again its essential transparency—even to the point, in Christ, of identity—before God. . ."Now will I close my eyes," writes Descartes, "I will stop up my ears, I will avert my senses from their objects, I will even erase from my consciousness all images of things corporeal; or, at least . . . I will consider them to be empty and false."[16]

The breakdown of what Dupré calls the "medieval synthesis" also had important consequences for the Christian understanding of symbol. Medieval Christians had looked upon creation as intrinsically symbolic, making present its Creator in our midst. In the wake of nominalism and neo-scholasticism, however, the ultimate meaning of creation could no longer be encountered *in* creation, which could exist independently of its Creator; now meaning would have to be imputed to creation, or *imposed* on it from without. From without, the rational *mind* would impose a meaningful order on a world that itself lacked intrinsic meaning. Physical existence no longer "revealed" a God who lived in its very midst; now, physical existence "*pointed to*" a God who related to the world extrinsically. Creation-as-symbol became simply "an extrinsic intermediary, something really outside the reality [i.e., God] transmitted through it, so that strictly speaking the thing [i.e., God] could be attained even without the symbol."[17] The symbol and the symbolized were no longer *really* united; they would now have to be "mentally" united (to use Karl Rahner's phrase). If there was a relationship between God and creation, it would have to be one forged and explained by the human intellect. Previously the locus of the human encounter with the Sacred, the symbol became "just" a symbol. The medieval Christian world had been pregnant with symbolic meaning, for the world was recognized as the locus of God's self-revelation. From sometime in the sixteenth century on, the world-as-symbol could only point *away* from itself to a God who remained impassible and aloof. Creation would no longer be a privileged place of encounter with the Sacred but a mere sign pointing elsewhere, to the immaterial, "spiritual" realm where God dwelled.

Nevertheless, even as post-Tridentine Catholic theologians were making God evermore distant, the popular faith continued to reflect a stubborn insistence on God's abiding, concrete nearness in every aspect of life. That nearness was embodied above all in the elaborate religious symbols and, especially, the explicitly dramatic character of communal religious life that flowered during the Baroque period. Thomas O'Meara describes Baroque Catholicism as follows:

> There was a universality in which Catholicism experienced God in a vastness, freedom, and goodness flowing through a world of diversity, movement, and order. Christ appeared in a more human way, filled with a personal love, redemptive and empowering. . . . The Baroque world was also a theater . . . Liturgies, operas, frescos, or palatial receptions were theatrical, and Baroque Christianity was filled with visions and ecstasies, with martyrs, missionaries, and stigmatics. . . . The theater of the Christian life and the kingdom of God moved from the medieval cosmos and the arena of society to the interior of the Baroque church and the life of the soul. In the Baroque, light pours down through clear windows into the church and states that God is not distant nor utterly different from creatures. God is actively present in the church and in the Christian.[18]

Neither the Christian medieval synthesis nor the dramatic faith of the Baroque has, in fact, been completely destroyed—at least not yet. Their enduring influence can still be witnessed in, among other places, the lived faith of the Latin American and U.S. Latino/a Catholic communities.

The same deep faith in God's nearness reappears in Latin popular Catholicism, where dramatic reenactments like the *Via Crucis*, the *Posadas*, or the *Pastorela* serve as constant expressions of God's solidarity. It reappears in the polyphonic ambience of our churches, where angels and demons, saints and penitents, celestial stars and spring flowers are fully incorporated into our lives. Having been brought to Latin America by the Spanish, and having interacted with indigenous religions that often embodied similar beliefs in the nearness of the divine in creation, Latino/a popular Catholicism is the embodied memory of the integral worldview, with Jesus Christ at its center, that is at the very heart of the Catholic tradition and that evolved in the Iberian Catholicism of the Middle Ages and the Baroque.

The Liberating Nearness of God

The God of Latino/a Catholics is one who is encountered in the very warp and weft of everyday life, in what Hispanic theologians have called "*lo cotidiano*" (the everyday). For Latino/a Catholics, our faith is ultimately made credible by our everyday relationship with a God whom we can touch and embrace, a God with whom we can weep or laugh, a God who infuriates us and whom we infuriate, a God whose anguished countenance we can caress and whose pierced feet we can kiss. This, as Salvadoran Jesuit theologian Jon Sobrino avers, is no vague God but a very particular, incarnate God, the God of Jesus Christ:

> A vague, undifferentiated faith in God is not enough to generate hope. Not even the admission that God is mighty, or that God has made promises, will do this. Something else besides the generic or abstract attributes of the divinity is necessary in order to generate hope. This distinct element—which, furthermore, is the fundamental characteristic of the Christian God—is something the poor have discovered viscerally, and in reality itself: the nearness of God. God instills hope because God is credible, and God is credible because God is close to the poor. . . . Therefore when the poor hear and understand that God delivers up the Son, and that God is crucified—something that to the mind of the nonpoor will always be either a scandal or a pure anthropomorphism—then, paradoxically, their hope becomes real. The poor have no problems with God. The classic question of theodicy—the "problem of God", the atheism of protest—so reasonably posed by the nonpoor, is no problem at all for the poor (who in good logic ought of course to be the ones to pose it).[19]

Because Jesus Christ walks with us, we know he is real; because we experience his nearness, his presence in our everyday life, we know he is the way, the truth, and the life. "Be the problems of the 'truth' of Christ what they may," writes Sobrino, "his credibility is assured as far as the poor are concerned, for he maintained his nearness to them to the end. In this sense the cross of Jesus is seen as the paramount symbol of Jesus' approach to the poor, and hence the guarantee of his indisputable credibility."[20] It is not our Christian belief that makes God's nearness credible; rather, it is God's nearness that makes Christian belief, especially the paschal mystery, credible. And that nearness is experienced through the symbolic mediation of our world, which reveals God's presence at every turn.

Latino and Latina Catholics encounter Christ through his wounded, bleeding, holy countenance, the *Divino Rostro* (Holy Countenance) seen on the walls of millions of Latino/a homes. We encounter him through his body, beaten and broken as it hangs lifeless from the cross. We come to know him, above all, as he accompanies us on the Way of the Cross, the innocent victim who continues to cry out to God even at the moment of deepest anguish. The greatest threat to true faith is not that of mistaking a wooden statue for the real Christ (as if the real Christ were utterly immaterial and unrelated to material reality). Rather, the greatest threat to true faith is the relegation of God to an otherworldly, immaterial "heaven." The greatest threat to faith is precisely that represented by a rationalist or "spiritual" Christianity that preaches a God without a world, a Christ without a face, without a body, without wounds, a cross without a corpus. An immaterial God eventually becomes irrelevant.

Ours is not a "watchmaker" God who creates the world, winds it up, and then withdraws into some separate spiritual abode, leaving us to fend for ourselves. This, of course, is the modern understanding of freedom: to be left alone to do as one wishes. A liberating God would then be a God who leaves us alone. Yet this is neither the Latino/a understanding of God nor the Latino/a understanding of freedom. The Christ of Latino/a popular Catholicism liberates us precisely by *refusing* to leave us alone, by refusing to withdraw from *any* aspect of our lives, even the most insignificant or banal. The wounds, blood, and tears that cover his face and body are what make him present and, hence, real, for these are the source of our hope for ourselves, our community, our Church, and our world. This Christ accompanies us in our struggles and, in so doing, empowers us to go on; he empowers us to *live*—to continue to defend and struggle for *life*—in the face of social forces that would destroy us. Insofar as he accompanies us in our own crucifixion, Christ empowers us to hope against hope and witnesses to the ultimate invincibility of life, the ultimate indestructibility of God's love in the face of death. By accompanying us in our own crucifixion, Jesus witnesses to the truth of his resurrection as the source of life, for suffering shared is already suffering in retreat.

That resurrection is thus a resurrection *into* community, into materiality and embodiment, without which there can be no true life. Latino/a Catholicism presupposes the fundamental reality of community as the source of life. Even when life is but an ongoing crucifixion, in the compassion of a friend, in the compassion of Christ, we get a glimpse of the resurrection. For we know that what ultimately destroys the person is not physical death but abandonment—to be left alone is a fate worse than death itself. If the medieval Christian worldview posited an intrinsically symbolic cosmos, which makes present "God for us," then that worldview posited an intrinsically *relational* and intrinsically *symbolic* cosmos. The same can be said about the worldview expressed in Latino/a popular Catholicism. If our lives have meaning, it is not because we ourselves have constructed that meaning and imposed it on creation, but because we have been empowered to cultivate a meaning that we first *received* from others, ultimately from God, but that we help shape through our creative response to that gift—a meaning whose origins are outside ourselves, in God's creation and, especially, in those persons who have incarnated, or made present for us the concrete reality of God's abundant love. The meaning of life is not something we construct for ourselves but something that we *receive* from others, ultimately from God. And we encounter this meaning in "*lo cotidiano*," in the everyday experiences through which we discover God's presence in the world around us, whether in our families, friendships, struggles in the workplace, or in nature itself. All of these are the assurances of God's love for us; they are all real symbols of God, real mediators of God's presence. We need not, indeed we dare not, leave material existence and physical relationships in order to find God.

In Latino/a popular Catholicism, one of the most powerful expressions of God's unwavering solidarity with us is Our Lady of Guadalupe. After all, the story of Our Lady of Guadalupe is not just about her; it is also a story about Juan Diego, the indigenous man to whom she appears. The story of Our Lady of Guadalupe does not so much recount the apparition *of* someone *to* someone else; it recounts an encounter *between* two persons. In that encounter, as he comes to know and trusts in Guadalupe's profound love for him (in a world that dehumanized him), Juan Diego comes to know and trusts in his own dignity as a beloved child of God. The reality of Guadalupe's love, embodied in her desire to stay with him and accompany him, frees Juan Diego from the self-deprecation with which he first approached *la Morenita* at the beginning of the story. Juan Diego thus comes to know the truth of the Christian message because that truth has, quite literally, set him free—not in spite of but because of his bond with Guadalupe.

The intensity of the Mexican people's identification with Guadalupe and Juan Diego was manifested some years ago in Mexico City. The event that took place at that time also illustrated how different understandings of symbol can have serious pastoral consequences. In July, 1996, Abbot Guillermo Schulemburg of the Basilica of Our Lady of Guadalupe in Mexico City resigned from his position. A few days earlier, the Mexican media had quoted him as suggesting that Juan Diego, the indigenous man to whom *La Morenita* had appeared on December 9, 1531, was "only a symbol, not a reality." The national uprising that ensued had forced the Abbot's resignation. The abbot's statement reflected well the modern (and in this case post-Tridentine Roman, if not Anglo) notion of symbol as something that is "not real" but only "points to" the real: and the Mexican people's vehement reaction to the statement reflected their belief that the symbol, in this case Juan Diego, is indeed the manifestation of the real in our midst. For the Mexican people, I think it safe to say, Juan Diego is indeed *a reality* precisely *because* he is a symbol.

And it is the Mexican people, I would argue, who therefore exhibit the more traditional, pre-modern Catholic understanding of the symbol. They assume that if the Sacred is not expressed symbolically, if it does not make itself *visible, audible, and tangible*, then the Sacred simply disappears, it is no longer present. (Consequently, a modern secularist is simply someone who has dared to call the modern Christian's bluff, who has dared to cry out that, like the proverbial emperor, much of modern Western Christianity has no clothes.) For U.S. Hispanic Catholics, the Crucified Christ, Our Lady of Guadalupe, Juan Diego, the saints, and all creation are the assurance that God is indeed here—not up in heaven or in some ethereal realm, but *here* in our very midst; they are the assurance that God is indeed real.

Commentary: The Paradoxical Character of Symbols, Popular Religion, and Church: Questions for U.S. Latino/a Theology

James B. Nickoloff

For well over a decade now, theologian Roberto S. Goizueta and his Latino and Latina colleagues have been calling attention to Hispanic popular Catholicism not only as a source of new life for the larger church in the United States (and around the world) but also as a force for change in both church and society.[1] At the heart of his argument stand two convictions. First, he claims that the typical Hispanic way of being, thinking, and acting is profoundly relational and thus fundamentally at odds with the radical individualism of the dominant culture of the United States. Second, he asserts that Hispanics' ordinary experience of the divine (manifested in grassroots, or "popular," religious practices) is liberating for a group, which is at best marginalized and in some respects harshly oppressed in the U.S. Such assertions have prompted relatively little response, pro or con, outside Hispanic circles, a fact that illustrates the continued marginalization of Latino/a theologians within church and academy despite their groundbreaking and prolific scholarship and the striking growth of the Hispanic population in the United States.

In his contribution to the present volume, Goizueta locates the liberating power of popular Catholicism in the particular way symbols function for Hispanics. For them, he asserts, "because [something] is a symbol, it is real" (p. 178). As symbols, Juan Diego, Our Lady of Guadalupe, and Jesus Christ, for example, "re-present God," that is, they "make God present in time and space, here and now" (p. 178). Joining others, Goizueta traces the Latin American and U.S. Latino/a organic understanding of symbol to the pre-modern (but post-Tridentine) form of Baroque Catholicism prevailing on the Iberian peninsula at the time of Spain's conquest of the Americas. Iberian Catholicism must be distinguished from the modern, rationalist (and also post-Tridentine) form which flourished in northern Europe, and which arrived in the Western Hemisphere long after its Iberian counterpart, and shaped today's Euro-American Catholic view that something which is "merely" a symbol is somewhat less than "real." With this clarification Goizueta allows us to further refine our grasp of Christianity in the United States: not only are Christians divided by denomination and theology (both between and within denominations); we are also separated by our ways of responding to, and interpreting, symbolic realities. Goizueta makes a persuasive case that Euro-American Catholics have much to learn from Latino/a Catholics about creation as "*graced* from the beginning" (p. 177) and about God's nearness and participation in our daily lives ("*lo cotidiano*"). Lived experience more than formal study will, of course, foster such learning.

Goizueta's claims about symbols and, more specifically, about the liberating power of popular Hispanic religious symbols seem to this reader to invite further reflection on three distinct but closely related matters. I am referring to (1) the nature of symbols, (2) the political efficacy of popular religion, and (3) the consequences for ecclesiology of the first two considerations.

To begin with symbols: as we have learned from Paul Ricoeur and others, especially in recent years from feminists who build upon their work, symbols not only *reveal* what they symbolize but also—and, at the same time— *conceal* that reality. That is, a symbol "re-presents" what it symbolizes, but it never does so perfectly. Thus, according to Sandra Schneiders for example, God both *is and is not* like a (human) father. To ignore the negation of the copula in this statement is to turn a particular symbol—God as father—into an idol and thereby deprive the symbol of real meaning. Following the New Testament's own procedure, Schneiders proposes the use of multiple symbols in order to avoid fixating on any one representation of the God who, in the final analysis, is mystery. Thus a measure of self-correction is built into theological hermeneutics.[2] Such a view of symbol seems to require, in turn, that we make explicit the criteria by which we evaluate religious symbols. Which critical principles, then, do U.S. Latino/a theologians employ in their analysis of the symbolic life of Hispanic communities? More specifically still, in what ways does the faith life of Hispanic Catholic communities *conceal* as well as *reveal* the presence of God among us?[3]

Related to the problem of embracing the complex and even opposed meanings found in any particular symbol and in every symbol system is the difficulty of evaluating the liberating potential and the real-life socio-political effects of popular religion. The initial skepticism of Latin American liberation theologians vis-à-vis popular religion and its role in society did, it is true, reflect a careful reading of Karl Marx and his intellectual heirs. At the same time, pastoral work with the poor, personal participation in popular movements (of urban workers, rural *campesinos*, and poor women in cities and countryside), and, in some cases, an insider's knowledge of popular religion itself raised even more questions for theologians about the political efficacy of grassroots religious faith.[4] If symbols both disclose and hide the face of God, it follows that popular religion itself may be both a "source of empowerment," as Goizueta argues, and at the same time an "ideological diversion" (p. 169). Although Juan Diego's liberation from self-deprecation took place in his encounter with Guadalupe, what can we say about those whom Juan Diego's descendents sometimes deprecate while maintaining their devotion to the Virgin? (see note 3). How do religious symbols function in places where Latino gangs fight each other to death? What role does religion play in the construction of machismo generally and, more concretely, in the development of attitudes which allow people to ignore, or even justify, violence against Latinas? In Peru, for example, I have heard men assert their right to "discipline" their wives in one breath while in the next express their desire to carry the statue of the patron saint in the parish procession. And what can we say about the apparently deep-seated fear of homosexuality (especially in men) among Hispanics who in this regard appear to be no different from those whose attitudes are formed in a highly individualistic and rationalistic culture? Can we legitimately say that a deep sense of interpersonal relatedness prevents adherents of popular religion from ever being oppressive? I hope these questions reflect more than the merely "modern," individualistic mentality of an uncritical Euro-American observer.

The political efficacy of religious faith and practice is today a much-debated issue in the United States. Should faith guide political decision-making and political praxis? If so, in what manner and to what end? Roberto Goizueta sees U.S. Hispanic popular Catholicism as "a source of empowerment that exercises a subversive, countercultural role in the lives of U.S. Hispanics" (p. 169). What is not clear in this statement, however, is *what*, precisely, popular Catholicism tends to subvert, and *for whom*. Does God's solidarity with Hispanics free *them* in significant ways from the effects of the oppression to which they are subjected in the larger society? Or does God's nearness in the person of Jesus free them for the work of transforming the *whole of U.S. society*? "Freedom from," as Latin American theologians have reminded us, is also always "freedom for." Can any faith community legitimately excuse itself on Christian grounds from accepting some measure of responsibility for the liberation of the whole of the society in which it finds itself? An instructive and well-known example here is the African American church, a portion of which has taken up the legacy of Martin Luther King, Jr. by dedicating itself to the eradication of racism in the larger society. In King's view the United States is infected with a strain of racism which, if left untreated, could prove to be a "sickness unto death," inexorably destroying all of society, black and white.[5]

If the love of Jesus Christ "makes survival possible" (p. 169) for marginalized and oppressed Hispanics, can we avoid asking what is *done* with the gift of survival? I am aware that such a question seems to fall into the very trap of utilitarianism Goizueta is at pains to avoid. Yet contemplation, play, and love-making—humane ends in themselves and not means to an end—are activities which only people who have "survived" undertake. The question of political efficacy concerns the scope of a (surviving) community's perceived responsibility. Is it not appropriate to examine the perception of political responsibility found in those who place their faith in *Jesus*—and who do so in a world where injustice robs countless millions of their chance for survival and thus for contemplation, play, and love-making? Does Latino/a Catholicism, then, function "as a source of identity, resistance, and empowerment" (p. 172) for the Hispanic community alone, or does it promote the liberation of the larger society in the United States?[6]

Finally, taken together, Roberto Goizueta's reflections on the Hispanic sensitivity to symbol and on the liberating effect of popular Catholicism in the Hispanic community lead to a consideration of a third matter, one which presents us with a topical, yet permanent, theological problem. If symbols are simultaneously transparent *and* opaque media of the divine, and if popular religion is concurrently liberating *and* oppressive, theologians today, as I suggested above, face the task of developing criteria for distinguishing symbolic revelation from concealment and, likewise, true liberation from oppression. Yet a third reality in addition to symbol and popular Catholicism calls for careful analysis and a similar clarification of evaluative criteria: I am referring to the church itself.[7] Today, perhaps more than ever, we must come to grips with the complex lived experience of many of the faithful which has taught them that the church functions in history as *both* a vessel of grace *and* an instrument of sin. Pastoral and theoretical (that is, theological) demands converge here: the development of a theoretical framework capable of making sense of an apparent paradox could help ordinary Catholics avoid the simplistic and ultimately self-defeating attitudes born in the midst of crisis (e.g., "the church is always right" or, conversely, "the church is hopelessly corrupt"). Such outlooks may arise when Catholics—including Hispanic Catholics—find themselves caught between an inherited ecclesiology which describes the church as a "*societas perfecta*" and the irrefutable knowledge that the church qua church bears responsibility for enormous suffering and destruction in the course of human history. This painful dilemma is being experienced today in a particularly acute form in the United States in the face of the widespread abuse of clerical authority, but the pastoral and theological problem is felt around the world.

It is true that Catholic ecclesiological discourse has evolved in recent years: pre-Vatican II affirmations of a "sinless church" have given way to the postconciliar acknowledgement that we are a "church of sinners."[8] But is this development sufficient? Whether consciously or not, most Catholics probably know in their bones that the church is capable both of courageously witnessing to the Word of God and of fearfully running from it. The lives of Spaniard Bartolomé de las Casas in the sixteenth century, Peruvian Túpac Amaru in the eighteenth century, and Salvadoran Oscar Romero in the twentieth century and their rebuff by high church authorities remind us that individual sanctity and ecclesial sinfulness (as well as the reverse) have coexisted throughout the history of the church in Latin America. Many Catholics today—including Hispanic Catholics—may well be looking for a way both to affirm the church *and* to acknowledge its errors. To suggest that the faith of Hispanic Americans—or any other segment of the church in the United States—would be harmed ("scandalized") by openly confronting the "both/and" character of the church would merely prolong the history of paternalistic religion. Facing the paradoxes of symbolic representation, popular religion, and church may instead offer a way for Christians to verify the promise of Jesus Christ that "the truth shall make [us] free" (John 8:32).

PART V

Contemporary Mass Media as a Domain for Catholic Ritual Practice

Susan Rodgers

INTRODUCTION

This section includes three chapters that may surprise some readers, in terms of these essays' inclusion in a book on Catholic ritual practice. After all, readers might logically expect the focus to remain on the "obviously Catholic": the Mass worldwide, the official sacraments, and popular Catholicism in all of its fiesta-like effusiveness. But, this section of the book is comprised of essays on the use of cell phones in Manila, the Philippines, and on the imagery of a holy mystic girl, so to speak, from Worcester, Massachusetts, as she has been portrayed in television broadcasts and in video productions sponsored by her family and her large circle of devout followers (the girl is Worcester's well-known "Little Audrey," now 19 year old Audrey Santo, the focus of healing devotionalism and huge annual commemorative Masses held to celebrate her supposedly miraculous nature). Here we are suggesting that Catholic ritual has today spilled over into international media spaces such as television, text-messaging on cell phones, and the World Wide Web. Witness, for instance, the many websites devoted to Audrey Santo's status as a victim soul, a suffering person whose sanctified body can take on the pain of her faithful and offer it up to Christ. If the authors of these essays are correct, then research into Catholic ritual practice 20 or 30 years from now may well extend far into media studies, especially as that field intersects with feminist theory and comparative studies of modernities.

Historian and communications theorist Vicente Rafael suggests in "The Cell Phone and the Crowd: Messianic Politics in Recent Philippine History" that the Catholic Mass took on new, transformed social shape in street demonstrations of several years ago that succeeded in overthrowing a president. All religions, like all politics, Rafael contends, are fundamentally about time, and about hope. Many observers of Southeast Asian historical thought have commented on its "forwardlooking-ness," to quote Wang Gung-Wu; here, Rafael asserts that this thrust toward a coming future has taken on a specifically Catholic form in popular Filipino thought. And, where once that messianic vision was most forcefully concretized in the formal Catholic Mass and the stories about Christ's death and resurrection, today hope-in-the-future plays out in nationalist politics, in the imagination of a Philippine nation. Young street demonstrators were in effect "doing ritual" by sending each other heated text-messages via cell phones, in mass crowd scenes in Manila, in their efforts to unseat President Joseph Estrada in January, 2001. By sharing this community of texting, they were constituting a Church: a body of the faithful, gathered together to bring a new world into existence (that is, to topple Estrada and bring the nation back to its intended destiny). Rafael's work is thought-provoking in the extreme, in terms of stretching the boundaries of the Mass, sharing the Eucharist, and participating in Christian mythic stories.

Chapter 13 is my own, on Little Audrey as a media phenomenon, and on media viewing as a form of contemporary faith practice which allows some publics to witness the miraculous. As a toddler, Audrey Santo accidentally fell into the family swimming pool and nearly died. She has never regained consciousness, say the doctors; her family and devotees, however, hold that she has a sort of holy consciousness and presence in the world, in her near-comatose body (another definitional locus of controversy). She does not speak, nor can she feed herself or breathe on her own. Sick people sometimes come up into Audrey's presence to ask for miraculous healing. Until recently, her inert body was displayed on a frilly bed, in the family garage (turned into a kind of altar and pilgrimage site). My essay on Audrey's life as a paradoxically *active* media presence is paired here with a (again) surprising photo essay by Mathew Schmalz and his sister Julia Schmalz, a professional photographer who works for the newspaper *USA Today*. Mathew Schmalz is currently doing fieldwork on the whole "Audrey phenomenon" in New England (and in wider Catholic theology). With permission from the Santo family Schmalz and Schmalz took a series of black and white photographs of Audrey on her "public bed of viewing," so to speak (present readers will soon learn the details, which involve recent decisions by the Worcester Diocese to discourage the family from putting their daughter on public display). This photo essay's subject matter intersects exactly with the time frame treated in my own article, and the illustrations are offered here to drive home the point that ritual practice of the sorts at issue here must be experienced *visually*, in order for distant readers to grasp some small measure of the faith work at play here.

The Rafael and Rodgers articles are drawn together in useful ways by a Commentary by sociologist of American Catholicism John Schmalzbauer, a student of the media rhetorics used by American Catholics and American Protestant Evangelicals, to claim public culture space and legitimacy for themselves.

CHAPTER 12

The Cell Phone and the Crowd: Messianic Politics in Recent Philippine History*

Vicente L. Rafael

This essay follows in the wake of recent philosophical writings, principally by Jacques Derrida, on the ineradicable relationship between faith and knowledge, a relationship which comes to us by way of the history of Christianity. At bottom, what links the two is the act of promising; and what makes promising possible are the workings of the technological. Promises arguably lie at the basis of the political and the social. The possibility of making and breaking pledges, of bearing or renouncing obligations, of exchanging vows and taking oaths forges a sense of futurity and chance, allowing an opening to otherness. It is this possibility of promising that engenders the sense of something to come, of events yet to arrive, hence of a messianism underlying both historical time and political engagement. Without promises, neither covenants nor consensus nor conflicts could arise, and neither would the sense of contingency these invariably foster. These matters of hope in a messianic future and the technologies through which they are conveyed link the study of the Catholic Mass to studies of more subtle, less obvious, but Mass-like cultural scenes of the sort I consider here.

Promises can only be made and broken if they can be witnessed and sanctioned, confirmed and reaffirmed. They must, in other words, be repeatable and citable, capable of being performed again and again. Repetition underlies the making of promises, and thereby the practices of politics. We can gloss this iterative necessity as the workings of the technical and the mechanical that inheres in every act of promising. Technology as the elaboration of the technical, including the technics of writing and speech, is then not merely an instrument for engaging in politics. It is that without which the political and the futures it claims to bring forth would simply never emerge along with the very notion of emergence itself.

The promissory nature of technology and the technological articulation of promising are the key preoccupations of this essay. In what follows, I seek to situate these notions in relation to a set of telecommunicative fantasies among the middle classes in the contemporary Philippines within the context of a recent historical occurrence: the civilian backed coup that overthrew President Joseph Estrada in January of 2001. It does so with reference to two distinct media, the cell phone and the crowd. Various accounts of what has come to be known as "People Power II" (as distinguished from the populist coup that unseated Ferdinand and Imelda Marcos in 1986) reveal certain pervasive beliefs on the part of the middle classes. They believed, for example, in the power of communication technologies to transmit messages at a distance and in their ability to possess that power. In the same vein, they had faith in their ability to master their relationship to the masses of people with whom they regularly shared Manila's crowded streets, utilizing the power of crowds to speak to the state. They thus conceived of themselves capable of communicating beyond the crowd, but also with it, transcending the sheer physical density of the latter by technological means while at the same time ordering its movements and using its energy to transmit middle class demands. At its most utopian, the fetish of communication suggested the possibility of dissolving, however provisionally, existing class divisions. Communication from this perspective held the messianic promise of refashioning the heterogenous crowd into a people addressing and addressed by the promise of justice. But as we shall see, such telecommunicative notions were predicated on the putative "voicelessness" of the masses. For once heard, the masses called attention to the fragility of bourgeois claims to shape the sending and reception of messages about the proper practice of politics in the nation-state. Media politics (understood in both senses of that phrase as the politics of media systems but also politics as the inescapable event of mediation) in this context reveals the unstable workings of Filipino middle class sentiments. Unsettled in its relationship to social hierarchy, such sentiments at times redrew class divisions, at other moments anticipated their abolition, and still at others called for their reinstatement and consolidation.[1]

CALLING

Telephones were introduced in the Philippines as early as 1885, during the last decade and a half of Spanish colonial rule.[2] Like telegraphy before it, telephony provoked fantasies of direct communication among the colonial bourgeoisie. They imagined that these new technologies would afford them access to those on top, enabling them to hear and be heard directly by the colonial state. We can see this telecommunicative notion, for example, in a satirical piece written by the Filipino national hero Jose Rizal in 1889. Entitled "Por Telefono," it situates the narrator as an eavesdropper. He listens intently to the sounds and voices that travel between the Spanish friars in Manila—regarded as the real power in the colony—and their superiors in Madrid.[3] The nationalist writer wire-taps his way, as it were, into the walls of the clerical residences, exposing their hypocrisy and excesses. In this sense, the telephone shares in the capacity of that other telecommunicative technology, print, to reveal what was once hidden, to repeat what was meant to be secret, and to pass on messages that were not meant for those outside of a particular circle.[4]

It is this history of tapping into and forwarding messages, often in the form of ironic commentaries, jokes, and rumors that figured recently in the civilian-led coup in the Philippines known as "People Power II". From the evening of January 16 to January 20, 2001, over a million people massed at one of Metro Manila's major highways, Epifanio de los Santos Avenue, commonly called Edsa, site of the first People Power revolt in 1986 that overthrew the Marcos regime. A large cross section of Philippine society gathered to demand the resignation of President Joseph "Erap" Estrada after his impeachment trial was suddenly aborted by the eleven senators widely believed to be under his influence. These senators had refused to include key evidence that would have shown the wealth Estrada had amassed from illegal numbers game while in office. The impeachment proceedings had been watched avidly on national TV and listened to on radio. Most viewers and listeners were keenly aware of the evidence of theft and corruption on the part of Estrada and his family.[5] Once the pro-Estrada senators put an abrupt end to the hearing, however, hundreds of thousands of viewers and listeners were moved to protest in the streets. Television and radio had fixed them in their homes and offices attending to the court proceedings. But at a critical moment, these media also drew them away from their seats. Giving up their position as spectators, they now became part of a crowd that had formed around a common wish: the resignation of the president.

Aside from TV and radio, another communication medium was given credit for spurring the coup: the cell phone. Nearly all accounts of People Power II available to us come from middle class writers or by way of middle class controlled media with strong nationalist sentiments. And nearly all point to the crucial importance of the cell phone in the rapid mobilization of people. "The phone is our weapon now," one unemployed construction worker is quoted in a newspaper article. "The power of our cell phones and computers were among the things that lit the fuse which set off the second uprising, or People Power Revolution II," according to a college student in Manila. And a newspaper columnist relayed this advice to "would-be foot-soldiers in any future revolution: As long as you[r cell phone] is not low on battery, you are in the groove, in a fighting mood."[6] A technological thing was thus idealized as an agent of change, invested with the power to bring forth new forms of sociality.

Introduced in the latter half of the 1990s, cell phones in the Philippines had become remarkably popular by around 1999.[7] There are a number of reasons for their ubiquity. To begin with, there is the perennial difficulty and expense of acquiring land line phones in the Philippines along with the erratic service provided by the Philippine Long Distance Company (PLDT) and the more recent, smaller Bayan Tel. Cell phones seemed to promise to fill this pent-up need for connectivity. Additionally, cell phones cost far less than personal computers, of which less than one percent of the population own, though a larger proportion has access through internet cafes. By contrast, there are over eight million cell phone users in a population of about seventy seven million. The great majority of them buy pre-paid phone cards which, combined with the relatively low cost of the phone (as low as US $50 in the open market and half this amount in secondary markets) makes this form of wireless communication more accessible and affordable than regular telephones or computers.

Even more significant, cell phones allow users to reach beyond traffic-clogged streets and serve as a quicker alternative to slow, unreliable, and expensive postal services. Like many third-world countries recently opened to more liberal trade policies, the Philippines shares in the paradox of being awash in the latest technologies of communication such as the cell phone while mired in deteriorating infrastructures such as roads, postal services, rail-roads, power generators, and land lines. With the cell phone, one seems able to pass beyond these obstacles. And inasmuch as such infrastructures are state run so that their break down and inefficiencies are a direct function of governmental ineptitude, passing beyond them also feels like overcoming the state, which to begin with has long been overcome by corruption.[8] It is small wonder then that cell phones could prove literally handy in spreading rumors, jokes, and information that steadily eroded whatever legitimacy President Estrada still had amid his impeachment hearings, along with those of his congressional supporters. By-passing the complex of broadcasting media, cell phone users themselves became broadcasters, receiving and trans-mitting both news and gossip and often confounding the two. Indeed, one could imagine each user becoming a broadcasting station unto oneself, a node in a wider network of communication that the state could not possibly even begin to monitor much less control.[9] Hence, once the call was made for people to mass at Edsa, cell phone users readily forwarded messages they received even as they followed what was asked of them.

Cell phones then were invested not only with the power to surpass crowded conditions and congested surroundings brought about by the state's inability to order everyday life. They were also seen to bring a new kind of crowd about, one that was thoroughly conscious of itself as a movement headed toward a common goal. While telecommunication allows one to escape the crowd, it also opens up the possibility of finding oneself moving in concert with it, filled with its desire and consumed by its energy. In the first case, cell phone users define themselves against a mass of anonymous others. In the second, they become those others, assuming anonymity as a condition of possibility for sociality. To understand how the first is transformed into the second, it helps to note the specific form in which the vast majority of cell phone messages are transmitted in the Philippines—as text messages.

TEXTING

Text messages are e-mails sent over mobile phones and transferable to the internet. Recently, a verb, "texting," has emerged to designate the act of sending such messages indicating its popularity in such places as England, Japan, and Finland. In the Philippines, texting became the preferred mode of cell-phone use once the two major networks, Globe and Smart introduced free, and then later on, low cost–text messaging as part of their regular service in 1999. Unlike voice messages, text messages take up less bandwidth and require far less time to convert into digitized packets available for transmission. It thus makes economic sense for service providers to encourage the use of text messaging in order to reserve greater bandwidth space for the more expensive—and profitable—voice messages. From an economic standpoint then, texting offers one of those rare points of convergence between the interests of users and providers.[10] But there is obviously more than costs that makes text messaging popular among Filipino users. In an essay sent over the internet signed "An Anonymous Filipino," the use of cell phones in Manila is described as a form of "mania." Using Taglish, the urban lingua franca that combines Tagalog, English and Spanish, this writer, a Filipino "balikbayan" (that is, one who resides or works elsewhere and periodically returns to visit the motherland) remarks:

> HI! WNA B MY TXT PAL? [sic] They're everywhere! In the malls, the office, school, the MRT (Manila Railroad Transit), what-have-you, the cellphone [sic] mania's on the loose! Why, even Manang Fishball [i.e., Mrs. Fishball, a reference to older working class women vendors who sell fishballs, a popular roadside snack], is texting! I even asked my sisters how important they think they are that they should have cells? Even my nephew in highschool has a cell phone. My mom in fact told me that even in his sleep, my brother's got his cell, and even when they have a PLDT [i.e., land line] phone in the house, they still use the cell phone.[11]

"Mania" according to the *Oxford English Dictionary* is a kind of madness characterized "by great excitement, extravagant delusions and hallucinations and its acute stage, great violence." The insistence of having cell phones near by, the fact that they always seem to be on hand, indicates an attachment to them that surpasses the rational and the utilitarian, as the remarks above indicate. It lends to its holder a sense of being someone, even if he or she is only a street vendor or a high school student. Someone, in this case, who can reach and be reached and is thus always in touch. The "manic" relationship to cell phones is thus this ready willingness to identify with it, or more precisely with what the machine is thought capable of doing. One not only has access to it; by virtue of its omnipresence and proximity, one becomes like it. That is to say, one becomes an apparatus for sending and receiving messages at all times of the day and night. An American journalist writing in the *New York Times* observes as much in an article on Manila society:

> "Texting?" Yes, texting—as in exchanging short typed messages over a cell phone. All over the Phillipines, a verb has been born, and Filipinos use it whether they are speaking English or Tagalog. . . . The difference [between sending e-mail by computers and texting] is that while chat-room denizens sit

in contemplative isolation, glued to computer screens, in the Philippines, 'texters' are right out in the throng. Malls are infested with shoppers who appear to be navigating by cellular compass. Groups of diners sit ignoring one another, staring down at their phones as if fumbling with rosaries. Commuters, jaywalkers, even mourners—everyone in the Philippines seems to be texting over the phone. . . . Faye Siytangco, a 23 year-old airline sales representative, was not surprised when at the wake for a friend's father she saw people bowing their heads and gazing toward folded hands. But when their hands started beeping and their thumbs began to move, she realized to her astonishment that they were not in fact praying. "People were actually sitting there and texting," Siytangco said. "Filipinos don't see it as rude anymore."[12]

Unlike those on computers, cell phone users are mobile, immersed in the crowd, yet communicating beyond it. Texting provides them a way out of the very surroundings they find themselves in. Thanks to the cell phone, they need not be present to others around them. Even when they are part of a socially defined group—say, commuters or mourners—they are always someone and somewhere else, receiving and transmitting messages from beyond their physical location. It is in this sense that they become other than their socially delineated identity: not only cell phone users but cell phone "maniacs." Because it rarely leaves them, the phone becomes part of the hand, the digits an extension of their fingers. In certain cases, the hand takes the place of the mouth, the fingers that of the tongue. Writing about his Filipino relative, one Filipino-American contributor to Plaridel, an on-line discussion group dealing with Philippine politics, referred to the former's cell phone as "almost a new limb."[13] It is not surprising then that the consciousness of users assumes the mobility and alertness of their gadgets. We can see how this process of taking on of the qualities of the cell phone comes across in the practice of sending and receiving messages:

The craze for sending text message by phone started [in 1999] when Globe introduced prepaid cards that enabled students, soldiers [and others] too poor for a long-term subscription to start using cellular phones. . . . People quickly figured out how to express themselves on the phone's alphanumeric keypad. . . . "Generation Txt," as the media dubbed it, was born. Sending text messages does not require making a call. People merely type in a message and the recipient's phone number, hit the phone's send key and off it goes to the operator's message center, which forwards it to the recipient. Because messages are exchanged over the frequency the network uses to identify phones rather than the frequencies their owners talk on, messages can be sent and received the instant a phone is turned on—and can even be received when a phone call is in progress.

Sending text messages by phone is an irritating skill to master, largely because 26 letters plus punctuation have to be created with only 10 buttons. Typing the letter C, for example, requires pressing the No. 2 button three times; an E is the No. 3 button pressed twice; and so on. After the message is composed it can be sent immediately to the phone number of the recipient, who can respond immediately by the same process. People using phones for text messages have developed a shorthand. "Where are you?" becomes "WRU." And "See you tonight" becomes "CU 2NYT." People have different styles of keying in their messages. Some use their index fingers, some one thumb, others both . . . [Others] tap away with one hand without even looking at [their] phone.[14]

As is frequently the case with e-mail, conventions of grammar, spelling, and punctuation are evaded and rearticulated with texting. The constraints of an alphanumeric key pad means that one goes through numbers to get to letters. As a result, counting and writing become closely associated. Digital communication require the use of digits, both one's own and that of the machine, as one taps away. But it is a tapping that is done not to the rhythm of one's speech and in tempo with one's thoughts, but in coordination with the numbers through which one reaches a letter: three taps on 2 to get C, for example, or two taps on 3 to get to E. It is almost as if texting reduces all speech to writing, and all writing to a kind of mechanical percussiveness, a drumming that responds to an external constraint rather than one that emerges from and expresses an internal source. In addition, as it were, there are no prescribed styles for texting: one or two fingers will do, or one can use a thumb and look at the screen, while those adept enough can text while looking elsewhere as in the case of skilled typists. Neither standardized body postures are required with texting: one can sit or walk or drive while sending messages. Where hand writing in the conventional sense requires learning proper penmanship and body postures under the supervision of teachers within the confines of desk and classroom, texting frees the body, or so it seems, from these old constraints.

Mimicking the mobility of their phones, texters move about, unmoored to anything except the technological forms and limits of the medium. The messages they receive and send are condensed versions of whatever language—English or Tagalog and more frequently, Taglish—they are using and so belong to neither. The hybrid form of this language comes from the demands of the medium itself rather than reflecting the idiosyncrasies of their users. The introduction of a limit on the number of free text messages one can send and the assessment of a fee per character of text has meant the further shortening of words and messages. Instant messaging along with the mechanical storage and recall of prior messages require only the most drastically abbreviated narrative constructions with little semantic deferral or delay. Using the cell phone, one begins to incorporate its logic and technics to the extent of becoming identified with what appears to be a novel social category: "Generation Txt" (sic).

An obvious pun on Generation X, "Generation Txt" first began as an advertising gimmick among cell phone providers in order to attract young users to their products. Defined by their attachment to and skill with the cell phone, Generation Txt also troubled the older generation uneasy about the rise of texting. An anthropologist from the University of the Philippines, for example, writes about the dangers of texting in terms that have appeared in other countries where the practice has become popular, especially among youth: its propensity to stifle literacy by "[wreaking] havoc" on spelling and grammar, and, "working in tandem with mindless computer games and Internet chat rooms, are eroding young people's ability to communicate in the real world in real time."[15] Rather than promote communication, texting in this view actually obstructs it, cultivating instead a kind of stupidity. Such can be seen in young people's gullibility and willingness to surrender to the marketing ploys of cell phone providers so that they end up spending more, not less, in sending messages of little or no consequence. Furthermore, cell phones actually lead to "anti-social" behavior, as users "retreat to their own cocoons," while parents who give their children cell phones in effect evade the responsibility of "interacting" with them in any meaningful way.[16] Other writers report the occasional use of texting by students to cheat on exams, or the use of cell phones to spread rumors and gossip that may ruin someone's reputation.[17] As one Filipino online writer put it, cell phones are like "loaded weapons" and its avid use needs to be tempered with some caution. Another writes that "if the text [I received] felt like a rumor masquerading as news, I didn't forward it." An office worker from Manila writes, "Sometimes whenever you receive serious msgs (*sic*), sometimes you have to think twice if it is true or if perhaps someone is fooling you since there is so much joking [that goes on] in txt (*sic*)."[18]

Part of the anxiety surrounding texting arises from its perceived tendency to disrupt protocols of recognition and accountability. Parents are disconnected from their children while children are able to defy parental authority. Cheating is symptomatic of the inability of teachers to monitor the communication of students via cell phone. And the spread of rumors and gossip, along with irreverent jokes, means that the senders of messages readily give in to the compulsion to forward messages without, as the writer's just mentioned advice, weighing their consequences or veracity. Indeed, it's this capacity to forward messages almost instantaneously that proves to be the most dangerous feature of this "weapon." The urge to forward messages one receives seems difficult to resist. And under certain conditions, this urge becomes irrepressible as the events leading to People Power II proved. We can see this happening, for example, in a posting by theater actor and writer, Bart Guingona to the Plaridel Listserv. As part of a group that planned to stage demonstrations at Edsa on January 18, he initially expressed doubts about the effectiveness of texting for popular mobilization.

> I was certain it would not be taken seriously unless it was backed up by some kind of authority figure to give it some sort of legitimacy. A priest who was with us suggested that [the Church-owned broadcasting station] Radio Veritas should get involved in disseminating the particulars. . . . We [then] formulated a test message . . . and sent it out that night and I turned off my phone. . . . By the time I turned it on in the morning, the message had come back to me three times. . . . I am now a firm believer in the power of the text![19]

The writer is initially hesitant to resort to texting, thinking that messages sent in this way would be no different from rumors. They would lack authority by themselves. Anonymously passed on from phone to phone, texts seemed unanchored to any particular author that could be held accountable for their contents. Only when the Church-owned radio station offered to disseminate the same information did he agree to sending a text. Waking up the next day, he sees the effect of this transmission. Not only does his message reach others at a distance; they return to him threefold. From a doubter, he is converted into a "believer" in the "power of the text." Such a power has to do with the capacity to elicit numerous replies.

There are two things worth noting, however, in this notion of the power of texting: first, that it requires, at least in the eyes of this writer and those he sends messages to, another power to legitimate the text's meaning; and second, that such a power is felt precisely in the multiple transmissions of the same text. The power of texting here has less to do with the capacity to open interpretation and stir public debate as it does with compelling others to keep the message in circulation. Receiving a message, one responds by repeating it. One forwards it to others who, it is expected, will do the same. Repeatedly forwarding messages, one gets back one's exact message, mechanically augmented but semantically unaltered. They crowd one's phone mailbox just as those who read and believe in the truth of the call they've received end up crowding the streets of Metro Manila. In this view, the formation of crowds is a direct response to the repeated call of texts now deemed to have legitimacy by virtue of being grounded in an authority outside the text messages themselves: the electronic voice of the Catholic Church. Such a voice in effect domesticates the dangers associated with texting. Users can then forward texts and feel themselves similarly forwarded by the expectations they give rise to. Finding themselves called by the message and its constant repetition, they become "believers," part of Generation Txt.

Generation Txt thus does not so much name a new social identity as it designates a desire for seeing in messages a meaning guaranteed by an unimpeachable source residing outside the text. Most of those who gathered at Edsa and marched toward Mendiola, the road leading to the Presidential Palace, were united in their anger at the corrupt regime of President Estrada and their wish to replace him with a more honest leader. Doing so, however, did not mean changing the nature of the state or doing away with class divisions. Indeed, everything I have read about these events is at pains to stress the legality and constitutionality of these transitions, looking toward the Supreme Court and the Catholic church (rather than either the army or left-wing groups) for institutional legitimacy. In the end, Estrada was replaced not by a new leader, but by one who was part of the same old leadership: his vice-president, and daughter of a former Philippine president, Gloria Macapagal-Arroyo. It would appear then that Generation Txt comes out of what its "believers" claim to be a "technological revolution" that sets the question of social revolution aside.

Texting is thus "revolutionary" in a reformist sense. If it can be said to have a politics, it includes seeking the cleaning up and consolidation of authority, both that of the state and the source of messages. The interest of Generation Txt lies not in challenging the structures of authority but in making sure they function to serve the country's needs. This reformist impetus is spelled out in terms of their demand for accountability and their intention of holding leaders under scrutiny. Through their gadgets, they hold on to this holding, keeping watch over leaders rather than taking their place or putting forth other notions of leadership. Thus does Generation Txt conceptualize its historical agency: as transmitters of calls that come from elsewhere and which have the effect of calling out those in their homes, schools, dormitories, factories, churches to flood the streets in protest. Rather than originate such calls, they are able to trace them to their destination which, in this case, is the nation of middle-class citizens as it seeks to renovate and keep watch over the state. Like the first generation of bourgeois nationalists in the nineteenth century I cited earlier, Generation Txt discovers yet again the fetish of technology as that which endows one with the capacity to seek access to and recognition from authority.[20]

CROWDING

From the perspective of Generation Txt, a certain kind of crowd comes about in response to texting. It is one that bears, in both senses of that word, the hegemony of middle-class intentions. Texting in its apolitical mode, sought to evade the crowd. But in its reformist mode, it is credited with converting the crowd into the concerted movement of an aggrieved people. In the latter case, the middle class invests the crowd with a power analogous to their cell phones: that of transmitting their wish for a moral community, whereby the act of transmission itself amounts to the realization of such a community. Such a notion assumes the possibility of endowing the crowd with an identity continuous with that of middle class texters. However, this assumption had another aspect. Not only did it lead to the fantasy of ordering of the masses under bourgeois direction. As I demonstrate below, the middle-class interest in ordering the crowd also tended to give way to a different development. At certain moments, we also see the materialization of another kind of desire this time for the dissolution of class hierarchy altogether. How so?

To understand the contradictory nature of middle-class ideas about crowds, it helps to look at the streets of Manila at the turn of the twenty-first century. The city has a population of over ten million, a large number of whom are rural migrants in search of jobs, education, and other opportunities unavailable in the provinces. Congested conditions—packed commuter trains, traffic-clogged roads, crowded sidewalks, teeming shopping malls—characterize everyday life in the city making travel from one place to another slow and tedious throughout the day and late into the night. Such conditions affect all social classes. And because there is no way of definitively escaping them, they constitute the most common and widely shared experience of city life.

Just as the roads are clogged with vehicles, so the sidewalks seem unable to contain the unending tide of pedestrians who spill out onto the highways, weaving in and out of vehicular traffic. Indeed, urban space in Manila often seems haphazardly planned. It is as if no central design had been put in place and no rationalizing authority at work to organize and coordinate the movement of people and things.[21] Instead, such movement occurs seemingly on its own accord. Pedestrians habitually jaywalk and jump over street barriers. Cars and busses belch smoke, criss-crossing dividing medians, if these exist at all, inching their way to their destinations. Drivers and passengers find it difficult to see beyond a few feet of their vehicles. The windshields and windows of jeepneys, tricycles, and cabs are usually filled with decals, curtains, detachable sun shades, and other ornaments that make it difficult to get a view of the road, in effect obstructing one's vision and further heightening the sensation of congestion. Indeed, given Manila's topographical flatness, it is impossible to get a panoramic view of the city except on the commuter trains and from on top of tall buildings. In the West, the "view" is understood as the site for evacuating a sense of internal unease and a resource for relieving oneself of pressure, both social and psychic. Such a notion of a view is not possible in Manila's streets. Caught in traffic, one looks out to see the view of more stalled traffic so that the inside and the outside of vehicles seem to mirror one another.

Adding to the sense of congestion is the presence of garbage. The disposal of garbage has long been a problem in Manila owing to, among other reasons, the difficulty in finding adequate landfills. As a result, trash seems to be everywhere, as if it were dumped indiscriminately on street corners or around telephone poles, some of which have signs that explicitly ask people not to urinate or dump garbage there. What appears are thus scenes of near ruin and rubble. While certainly not exclusive to Manila, such scenes bespeak of a city giving in to the pressures of a swelling population. Rather than regulate contact and channel the efficient movement of people and things, the city's design, such as it is, seems to be under constant construction from the ground up and from so many different directions. No singular and overarching authority seems to be in charge. To walk or ride around in Manila then is to be impressed by the power of crowds. Their hold on urban space appears to elude any attempt at centralizing control. It is perhaps for this reason that the largest private spaces open to the public in Manila, shopping malls, play what to an outsider might seem to be extremely loud background music. A shopping mall manager once told me that turning the volume up was a way of reminding the crowd in malls that unlike the streets, someone was in charge and therefore watching their actions.[22]

The anonymity characteristic of crowds makes it difficult, if not impossible, to differentiate individuals into precise social categories. Clothes are at times clues to the social origins of people, but with the exception of beggars, it is difficult to tell on the basis of looks alone. The sense that one gets from moving in and through crowds is of a relentless and indeterminable mixing of social groups. This pervasive sense of social mixing contrasts sharply with the class and linguistic hierarchies that govern political structures and social relations in middle-class homes, schools, churches and other urban spaces.[23] One becomes part of the crowd by becoming other than one's social self. Estranged, one becomes like everyone else. Social hierarchy certainly does not disappear on the streets. But like the police who are barely visible, appearing mostly to collect pay-offs (*tong* or *lagay*) from jeepney drivers and sidewalk vendors, hierarchy feels more arbitrary, its hold loosened by the anonymous sway of the crowd.

The power of the crowd thus comes across in its capacity to overwhelm the physical constraints of urban planning and to blur social distinctions by provoking a sense of estrangement. Its authority rests on its ability to promote restlessness and movement, thereby undermining the pressure from state technocrats, church authorities, and corporate interests to regulate and contain such movements. In this sense, the crowd is a sort of medium if by that word one refers to the means for gathering and transforming elements, objects, people and things. As a medium, the crowd is also the site for the generation of expectations and the circulation of messages. It is in this sense that we might also think of the crowd not merely as an effect of technological devices, but as a kind of technology itself. It calls incessantly and we find ourselves compelled to respond to it. The crowd as a kind of technology refers then not merely to its potential as instruments of production or as an exploitable surplus for the formation of social order. It also constitutes the context of and the content for a technic of engaging the world. The insistent and recurring proximity of anonymous others creates a current of expectation, of something that might arrive, of events that might happen. As a site of potential happenings, it is a kind of place for the generation of the unknown and the unexpected. Centralized urban planning and technologies of policing seek to routinize the sense of contingency generated in crowding. But at moments and in areas where such planning chronically fails, routine can at times give way to the epochal. At such moments, the crowd as I hope to show below takes on a kind of telecommunicative power, serving up channels for sending messages at a distance while bringing distances up close. Enmeshed in a crowd, one feels the potential for reaching out across social space and temporal divides.[24]

As we saw, middle-class discourses on the cell phone tend to set texting in opposition to the crowd precisely as that which overcomes the latter during normal times. But in more politically charged moments such as People Power II, cell phones were credited along with radio, TV, and the internet for calling forth the crowd and organizing the flow of its desire, turning it into a resource for the reformation of social order. Other accounts, however, indicate the crowd's potential for bringing about something else, transmitting messages which at times converged with, but at other times submerged those emanating from cell phones. For at times, the crowd made possible a different kind of experience for the middle class. Such had to do less with representing the masses as becoming one with them. In so doing, the crowd becomes a media for the recurrence of another fantasy which emanates from the utopic side of bourgeois nationalist wishfulness: the abolition of social hierarchy.[25] We can see the recurrence of this fantasy and the desire to do away with hierarchy in one of the more lucid accounts of the crowd's power from a posting by "Flor C." on the internet discussion group, Plaridel.[26] The text originally in Taglish is worth following at some length.

"I just want to share my own way of rallying at the Edsa Shrine," (*Gusto ko lang ibahagi ang sarili kong siste sa pagrali sa Edsa Shrine*), Flor C. begins. She invites others do the same, adding, "I am also eager to see the personal stories of the 'veterans' of Mendiola," (*Sabik din akong makita ang mga personal na kuwento ng mga beteranong Mendiola*). Here, the urge to relate her experiences at the protests comes with the desire to hear others tell their own stories. What she transmits is a text specific to her life, not one that comes from somewhere else and which merely passes through her. Yet, by signing herself as "Flor C.," it is difficult to tell who this story pertains to outside of that signature. Neither is it possible to tell who authorizes its telling. In this way, she remains anonymous to her readers, the vast majority of whom similarly remain unknown to her.[27] What is the relationship between anonymity and the eagerness to tell and hear about experiences, one's own as well as that of others'?

Flor C. recalls the practice of protest marchers from the 1970s and 1980s of having what is called a "buddy-system" (*sic*) for guarding against infiltration from fifth columnists and harassment by the military and police. But because "my feet were too itchy so that I could not stay in the place that we agreed to meet," (*masyadong makati ang talampakan ko imbes na tumigil sa puwesto namin*), she ends up without a "buddy" at Edsa. Instead, she finds herself swimming in the "undulating river, without let-up from Edsa and Ortigas Avenue that formed the sea at the Shrine," (*ilog na dumadaloy, walang patid, mula sa Edsa sa Ortigas Avenue at bumubuo ng dagat sa Shrine*). She can't keep still. She feels compelled to keep moving, allowing heerself to be carried away from those who recognize her. At Edsa, she knows no one and no one knows her. Yet the absence of recognition is cause neither for dismay nor longing for some sort of identity. Instead, she relishes the loss of place brought about by her absorption into the movement of the crowd. She finds herself in a community outside of any community. It fills her with excitement (*sabik*). But rather than reach for a cell phone, she does something else: she takes out her camera.

And so I was eager to witness (*kaya nga sabik akong masaksihan*) everything that was happening and took photographs. Walking, aiming the camera here and there, inserted into the thick waves of people who also kept moving and changing places, walked all day until mid-night the interiors of the Galleria [shopping mall], around the stage and the whole length of the Edsa-Ortigas flyover. Sometimes stopping to listen for a while to the program on stage, shouting "Erap resign!," and taking close-ups of the angry, cussing placards, T-shirts, and posters and other scenes; "Good Samaritans" giving away mineral water and candy bars, a poor family where the mother and child were laying on a mat while the father watched over, a group of rich folks on their

Harley Davidsons, Honda 500's, and Sym scooters that sparkled. . . . And many other different scenes that were vibrant in their similarities but also in their differences.

Immersed in the crowd, Flor C. begins to take photographs. The camera replaces the cell phone as the medium for registering experience. In the passage just mentioned, she initially refers to herself as "*ako*," or "I," the first person pronoun singular in Tagalog. But once she starts to take photographs, the "I" disappears. The sentences that follow do not contain any pronouns at all. It is as if there is no person performing the acts of walking, moving, listening, and looking. While we can certainly read these sentences to imply a person carrying out these activities, we could just as easily infer the agency of some other thing at work: an "it" rather than an "I." That "it" of course is the camera that Flor C. takes out and begins to aim (*tinutok*). Led by her desire to be among the crowd, she begins to act and see like her camera. She stops to listen, then moves on, taking close-ups of "scenes" (*eksenas*) made up of the juxtaposition of various social classes. She is thus drawn to the appearance of sharp "contrasts" (*pagkaiba*) that are thrown together, existing side by side without one seeming to dominate the other. The juxtaposition of contrasts, the proximity of social distances, the desire to come up close to all manner of expressions and signs, to bring these within a common visual field, but one whose boundaries and focus keep shifting: such becomes the vocation of Flor C.'s camera. These are also the very features associated with the crowd. The crowd drives Flor C. to take out her camera; and the camera in registering the mixing of differences reiterates the workings of the crowd. Becoming the camera that brings distances up close and holds differences in sharp juxtaposition, Flor C. begins to take on the telecommunicative power of the crowd. Yet, unlike the cell phone whose political usefulness requires the legitimation of messages by an outside authority, the crowd in Flor C.'s account seems to draw its power from itself. It does not look outside of itself, at least in this instance, precisely insofar as the crowd tends to erode the border between inside and outside. We can see further this blurring of boundaries in Flor C.'s account of entering the Galleria shopping mall next to the center stage of the Edsa protest:

> During one of my trips there, I was shocked and thrilled (*kinilabutan ako*) when I heard "Erap resign!" resonating from the food center, cresting upwards the escalator, aisles and stores. The mall became black from the "advance" of middle-class rallyists wearing the uniform symbolic of the death of justice. But the whole place was happy (*masaya*). Even the security guards at the entrance simply smiled since they could not individually inspect the bags that came before them

She is thrilled and shocked (*kinilabutan ako*) by a sonic wave making its way from the bottom up of the shopping mall. Middle-class "rallyists" dressed in black surged through the aisles, protesting rather than shopping. Like all modern retail spaces, the shopping mall is designed to manufacture novelty and surprise only to contain them within the limits of surveillance and commodity consumption. But during these days, it is converted into a site for the wholly unexpected and unforseen. Ordinarily, the mall is meant to keep the streets at bay. Now it suddenly merges with them, creating a kind of uncanny enjoyment that even the security guards cannot resist. Formerly anonymous shoppers, middle-class protestors now come across en masse. As shoppers, they had consumed the products of others' labor. But as demonstrators, they now shed what made them distinct. They set aside their identity as consumers. They are instead consumed and transformed by the crowd. While still recognizably middle class, they nonetheless appear otherwise, advancing in their black shirts and chanting their slogans. To Flor C., their unfamiliar familiarity produces powerful effects. In the mall, Flor C. finds herself to be somewhere else. And as with the scenes in the streets, the intensification of this sense of displacement becomes the basis for the sensation of a fleeting and pleasurable connection with the crowd.

It is worth noting, however, that displacement as the source of pleasure can also, at certain moments, become the occasion for anxiety and fear. What is remarkable about Flor C.'s narrative is the way in which she takes on rather than evades this fear. The result, as we will see in the concluding section of her story, is neither the mastery nor overcoming of the crowd's disorienting pull. Rather, it is the realization of what she conceives to be the saving power of the crowd. Back on the streets, she wanders onto a flyover, or an on-ramp at the Edsa highway.

> When I first went to the flyover, I was caught in the thick waves of people far from the center of the rally. I could barely breath from the weight of the bodies pressing on my back and sides. I started to regret going to this place that was [so packed] that not even a needle could have gone through the spaces between the bodies. After what seemed like an eternity of extremely small movements, slowly, slowly, there appeared a clearing before me (*lumuwag bigla sa harap ko*). I was grateful not because I survived but because I experienced the discipline and respect of one for the other of the people—there was no pushing, no insulting, everyone even helped each other, and a collective patience and giving way ruled (*kolektibong pasensiya at pagbibigayan ang umiral*).
>
> The night deepened. Hungry again. Legs and feet hurting. I bought squid balls and sat on the edge of the sidewalk. . . . While resting on the sidewalk, I felt such immense pleasure, safe from danger, free, happy in the middle of thousands and thousands of anonymous buddies.

Finding herself in the midst of a particularly dense gathering of bodies, Flor C. momentarily fears for her life. She can barely breathe, overwhelmed by the weight of bodies pressed up against her. Rather than a medium for movement, the crowd in this instance becomes a kind of trap, fixing her in place. But ever so slowly, the crowd moves as if on its own accord. No one says anything, no directives are issued, no leader appears to reposition bodies. Instead a kind of "collective patience and giving way ruled" (*kolektibong pasyensya at pagbibgayan ang umiral*). The crowd gives and takes, taking while giving, giving while taking and so suffers the presence of all those that comprise it. It is for this reason "patient," which is to say, forbearing and forgiving while forgetting the identities of those it holds and who hold on to it. Forbearance, forgiveness, and forgetting are always slow, so slow in coming. They thus share in, if not constitute, the rhythm of the work of mourning which in turn always entails the sharing of work.

After what seemed like an eternity of waiting and very little moving, Flor C. suddenly arrives at a clearing. "*Lumuwag bigla sa harap ko*," "it suddenly cleared in front of me," she says, which can also be glossed as "the clearing came before me." Who or what came before whom or what remains tantalizingly uncertain. Earlier, she had started to regret being trapped in the crowd. But thrown into a sudden clearing by a force which came from within that which was radically outside of her yet which she had become an ineluctable part of, Flor C. is grateful. She survives, but that is not the most important thing for her. Rather, what matters is that she was given the chance to experience the "discipline and respect" of the crowd where no one was pushed or pushing, no one was insulted or insulting, and everyone seemed to help one another, a condition that in Tagalog is referred to as *damayan*, or cooperation, the very same word used to connote the work of mourning.[28] It is a strange sort of discipline that she undergoes. It is one that does not form subjects through systematic subjugation en route to establishing hierarchies of recognition. Instead, it is a kind of discipline borne of mutual restraint and deference which, inasmuch as it does not consolidate identity, sets aside social distinctions.

Crowding gives rise to an experience of forbearance and a general economy of deference. At the same time it does not result in the conservation of social identity. Rather, it gives way to a kind of saving which Flor C. refers to as the experience of "freedom" (*kalayaan*). Far from being a mob, the crowd here is a principle of freedom and incalculable pleasure. It is where a different sense of collectivity resides, one that does away momentarily with hierarchy and the need for recognition. Constraint gives way to an unexpected clearing, to a giving way that opens the way for the other to be free, the other which now includes the self caught in the crowd. And because it is unexpected, this freeing cannot last just as it cannot be the last experience of freedom. Emancipation, however brief—and perhaps because it is felt to be so—depends here not on submission to a higher authority that guarantees the veracity of messages. Rather, it relies on the dense gathering of bodies held in patient anticipation of a clearing and release.

Accounts of People Power II indicate that over a million people gathered in the course of four days at Edsa. These included not only the middle classes. As Flor C.'s earlier remarks show, many from the ranks of the working classes as well as the urban and rural poor who opposed Estrada were also there. A heterogenous crowd formed not simply in response to texting, for obviously not everyone had cell phones. It emerged primarily, we might imagine, in response to a call for and the call of justice. Put another way, the crowd at Edsa was held together by the promise of justice's arrival. Here, justice is understood not simply in terms of a re-distributive force acting to avenge past wrongs, one that in its use of violence is productive of more injustice. The non-violent nature of People Power II suggests instead that the crowd formed not to exact revenge but to await justice. To do so is to dwell in a promise which, qua promise, is always yet to be realized. Like freedom and no doubt inseparable from it, justice is thus always poised to arrive from the future. And it is the unceasing uncertainty of its arrival that constitutes the present waiting of the crowd. The crowd in this case is a gathering which greets that whose arrival is never fully completed, forbearing this coming that is always deferred. Yet, it is precisely because justice comes by not fully coming, and coming in ways unexpected that it comes across as that which is free from any particular socio-technical determination. It is this promise of justice that is conveyed by Flor C.'s experience of the crowd. The promissary nature of justice means that it is an event whose eventfulness occurs in advance of and beyond any given political and social order. Evading reification and exceeding institutional consolidation, such an event entails a telecommunication of sorts. It is what Jacques Derrida might call the messianic without a messiah. It would be "the opening up to the future or to the coming of the other as the advent of justice. . . . It follows no determinable revelation. . . . This messianicity stripped of everything, this faith without dogma."[29] In the midst of messianic transmissions, Flor C. along with others around her imagine the dissolution of class differences and feel, at least momentarily, as if it were possible to overcome social inequities. She sees in crowding therefore a power that levels the power of the social as such. Past midnight, Flor C. finds herself no longer simply herself. Her body hurting, bearing the traces of the crowd's saving power, she sits on the sidewalk, eating squid balls, happy and safe, free in the midst of countless and anonymous "buddies."

The Sacramental Body of Audrey Santo: A Holy Mystic Girl in Ritual and Media Spaces in Worcester, Massachusetts, and Beyond

Susan Rodgers

This exploratory anthropological essay concerns the paradoxically performative, ritually active body of 21-year old Audrey Santo, a Worcester, Massachusetts girl who has been largely paralyzed, bedridden, and unconscious since falling into her family's backyard swimming pool in 1987 as a three-year old. The toddler was rushed to a city hospital and soon thereafter to a major medical center. There, doctors and nurses managed to revive her, but brain damage was apparently extensive. That was the health situation to biomedical perception, at least: the exact nature of the girl's consciousness and intellect has become a point of contestation between the Worcester medical establishment and the family, which favors faith-based interpretations. The hospital staff soon urged the Santos to institutionalize Audrey, asking the mother Linda Santo in what she reports to have been unfeeling tones, "Where will you be placing her?" As Linda remembers (and as one of the family's several spiritual advisor priest associates has often recounted in special Masses) the mother replied forcefully that she would be placing her daughter not in an institution, but, "In my arms and home." The child was indeed soon brought back to the Santo house in a middle-class neighborhood of westside Worcester. In the ensuing years, the family and a circle of supporters have provided round the clock care for the girl, who is on a respirator and has received a diagnosis of akinetic mutism. This is a generic medical categorization indicating simply that Audrey cannot move independently and does not speak.

The deeply Catholic Santo family are of partly Portuguese background and participate in dual levels of American Catholic practice: they have sometimes attended their relatively liberal westside parish church, but they have also taken their daughter on a pilgrimage to the Medjugorje, Yugoslavia, shrine. This occurred a year after the swimming pool accident. This Worcester parish has other Medjugorje advocates and accommodates a variety of worship styles.[1] The Santo family themselves reportedly see their daughter's survival as a miracle, as a direct sign of grace from God, and as living demonstration that such institutional powers of "this world" as Worcester's elite hospitals pale in comparison to Christ's ongoing salvific work. The family and their spiritual advisors praise Audrey as having a special Christian mission in the world, despite her seeming lack of agency. She is here, they claim, to provide hope for medical incurables, and to demonstrate God's love of all children, however overtly "worthless" some may seem within "corrupt" modern worldviews (the family's apologia for their daughter's faith work does indeed intersect with certain American "pro-life" rhetorics).

Audrey is also said to be alive in order to intercede with Christ on behalf of the sick. In this regard her plight embodies sinlessness and purity, and her prone body works (some followers aver) as a conduit of Christ's blessings. More specifically and as many residents of Worcester well know, since the mid 1990s Audrey Santo has emerged in public imaginaries as "Little Audrey": a "victim soul" who takes on the sufferings of others and offers them up to Jesus. In this guise she has attracted wide publics. As Little Audrey, the girl has become the focus of intense devotional interest by followers throughout New England. The Santo family and a group devoted to the girl's care, the Apostolate of the Silent Soul, once arranged visits by supplicants and the sick seeking cures (by appointment) to the child's bedside in the family's home. The former bishop of Worcester, the Rev. Daniel Reilly, closed down parts of the family's apostolate after years of controversy regarding the public display of the paralyzed[2] child. Typically for the family's public relations dealings with the diocese hierarchy, Audrey's mother Linda portrays their relationship to the chancellery as cooperative and meek. For instance, in 1998 she commented to a reporter, "If the bishop came down tonight and said, 'Look Steve and Linda, this is wonderful, and, you know what? I personally believe in this, but I'm going to shut you down,' we'd shut down."[3]

Particularly in the years before Bishop Reilly put brakes on the Apostolate of the Silent Soul's public presence,[4] Little Audrey qua sinless holy body and victim soul was also celebrated in a series of large-scale, yearly, anniversary Masses on the date of the near-drowning. These events sometimes involved scores of priests, traffic jams, and over 5,000 attendees. In fact, one media estimate of the number of pilgrims to Worcester for the 1998 version of the event was 20,000.[5] The annual Mass involved Audrey's physical presence in her family's otherwise sedate westside parish church. Then, when crowds grew too large for that venue to accommodate the yearly special Mass (busloads of devotees were coming in from distant points of New England), Bishop Reilly asked the College of the Holy Cross for a one-time use of their football field for the event.[6] A Mass centered around Audrey's prone body was held there on August 9, 1998. This resulted in an odd juxtaposition of a liberal, Jesuit campus (one not caught up in the city's Audrey enthusiasms) with a flagrantly traditionalist, victim soul-centered Mass, led by otherwise rather marginalized and conservative priests. After the football field Mass more public controversy ensued, and the Holy Cross locale has not been used a second time. After this 1998 Mass, in fact, the Apostolate of the Silent Soul and the family's presentation of their daughter as a holy curative body have tended to be more restrained. Bishop Reilly in effect negotiated an informal agreement with the Santos to cease major public displays of the girl. The chancellery also banned the use of "A Prayer to Audrey," which had highlighted her intercessionary role with Christ.[7]

As Worcester residents know, Little Audrey, her Masses, and particularly certain purportedly miraculous events occurring in her bedroom have engendered extensive local, national, and indeed international media coverage. This is surely no surprise, as the bodily and gender symbolism of circa late 1990s Little Audrey devotionalism did have its sensationalist angles, despite the Santo family's protestations that their daughter's life is a matter entirely of faith.

Until the recent redrawing of the power dynamic between the Bishop's office and the family, Audrey's still body was displayed periodically to visitors seeking solace. At the height of the New England regional devotional interest in Little Audrey's victim soulhood, the girl would be arrayed in a frilly nightgown atop lacy pillows in a hospital bed, in the converted garage off to the side of her home. This garage, outfitted as a sort of hospital room, had been her bedroom since the near-drowning. The feminine, resolutely youthful-looking room was outfitted with numerous holy pictures and paintings of devotional scenes, crucifixes, and statuettes, all familiar from American Catholic popular devotionalism. Some of Audrey's devotees claim that a painting of Our Lady of Guadelupe hung on the wall has bled; further, that holy oil has sometimes coursed down the walls; and, that chalices fill up with holy oil at points of the Catholic calendar. For example, a chalice goes dry during Lent and refills after Easter. The girl is said by some of her faithful to be a stigmatic whose hands bleed from the wounds of Christ. Perhaps equally controversially, consecrated Hosts used in bedside Masses performed by some of her family's spiritual advisor priests have reportedly bled during these ceremonies. These home Masses themselves were remarkable: they necessitated special permission from Bishop Reilly's predecessor, former bishop Timothy Harrington.

The consecrated wafers from the home Masses have themselves become centerpieces of some of the anniversary Masses, whose sermons and spatial arrangements focus to a remarkable degree on Audrey's bedridden body (moved in some of these Masses from the home to these events). In the case of the large-scale Mass at Holy Cross's sports stadium, Audrey came across town in a hired ambulance.

So, given this penumbra of holy events surrounding the girl's body (and especially given the markedly traditionalist character of these "miracles") it was no surprise that Little Audrey became something of a media sensation in the mid to late 1990s. Audrey's public persona as a holy girl, dressed in angelic garb, poignantly paralyzed, caught in toddlerhood yet now well into physical adolescence, "modest" yet the center of attention for huge crowds, has had the effect of locating her at the intersection of several currents of popular American Catholic devotionalism. Beyond this, though, certain aspects of her embodied, even sensual symbolic life of faith have also placed her at the confluence of several, sometimes rather morbid and voyeuristic streams of American media curiosity and interest in "things Catholic."

Some media portrayals of the girl's faith life have been analytical and skeptical, but other media imageries have been near-voyeuristic. And, the Santo family's own specially commissioned videos have been hagiographic. A 1996 television documentary shown on EWTN, a Christian network, detailed Little Audrey's biography and sacredness and greatly increased national awareness of the exceptional events supposedly occurring in Worcester.[8] This documentary, still for sale, was John Clote's "*Audrey's Life: Voice of a Silent Soul*," financed by the Mercy Foundation.[9] Media cultural production along these conflicting planes of interpretation became intense in the late 1990s, just before the Bishop's office deftly turned down the public spotlights on the Little Audrey phenomenon.

In the late 1990s, Little Audrey's "cult-like" presence in an otherwise unexceptional neighborhood in west end Worcester attracted news stories and television coverage, for instance, from the *Worcester Telegram and Gazette*, the *Worcester Magazine*, the *Boston Globe*, the *New York Times*, the *Tablet* in the U.K., all three major Boston television stations, ABC's "20/20," CBS's "48 Hours,"[10] and The Learning Channel, in a special production entitled "Stigmata: Divine Blood." Audrey, and Linda Santo, were stars there in that latter, sensationalistic January 4, 2002 broadcast, which spotlighted Little Audrey's possible ties to medieval stigmatics. Audrey's life of miracles also appeared in the past on an unofficial website (www.cesnur.org/AUDREY_Santo.htm) and fragments of her public life are scattered throughout the Internet. Audrey's life as a precious child victim in special favor with Christ has also been the subject of print literature and devotional videos vetted by the Apostolate of the Silent Soul.

Historian of religion Mathew Schmalz has recently written an illuminating, fieldwork-based interpretive account of this Worcester girl's status as a sort of lightening rod of theological and popular devotional debate within American Catholicism. In "The Silent Body of Audrey Santo"[11] Schmalz asserts that this girl's very silence has elicited a marked amount of "talk" among American Catholics about what is sound and what is spurious in Catholic sacramentalism. Put differently, Little Audrey has been theologically generative, in part because of her puzzling holy muteness. Schmalz also notes that the Audrey phenomenon has also generated much talk about such matters as curative suffering by larger sectors of the culture as well, although his main focus concerns American Catholicism's internal debates over the girl. To devotees and skeptics alike, Schmalz writes, silent Audrey "speaks" eloquently, insistently of ritual purity, within a doubting, secularist, largely non-Catholic American mainstream culture. She also speaks for traditionalist Catholics, within a Catholic landscape that has lost some of its wellspring connections to miracles.

Here, I would like to push beyond Schmalz's excellent analysis to see how Audrey Santo, as victim soul, has not only been a silent body that elicits floods of Catholic spoken and written commentary about holiness but who has also been an immobile, unconscious girl who *performs, in ritual,* quite actively. Issues of agency within faith worlds located in complex social hierarchies are present here, making the phenomenon of Audrey Santo's public representations of interest to anthropologists.

This child, or perhaps better, this denied-woman, has accrued her ritually alive, performative, almost choreographic presence in several ways. Her bedroom itself has become a strikingly active place: an architectural space where holy things like consecrated oil and Eucharistic blood are seen by some to come out of their normal containers and fill the chamber with sanctity. The yearly public Masses at Audrey's neighborhood Catholic church, Christ the King, have been other centers for the girl's "actions." Audrey Santo's performativity (more precisely, Little Audrey's performativity) has been evident in even more spectacular fashion in the controversial Mass held around Audrey's body at Holy Cross's football field on August 9, 1998. In this Mass, the girl's admittedly quite still, largely unconscious, bedridden body was moved through space in a number of vigorous ways. In the Fitton Field event, for instance, after Audrey was driven from her westside home across town to the Holy Cross campus by private ambulance, she was dramatically removed from the vehicle at a precise point of the Mass going on in the field. She was then slid reverentially into a small, white, trailer-like unit. This had a glass picture window all across its side. Behind this the girl lay on a bed, in her usual, recognizable, signature, angelic posture known to onlookers from previous, less grand Masses, and from home displays.

As Audrey was rolled onto the field, a curtain covered the glass partition of the trailer. At a theatrical moment during this unusually elaborate Mass, however, the curtain was drawn back to reveal the girl's prone body, with its breathing apparatus. Schmalz has alluded briefly to this event, noting that this Mass went further than any previous family-led ceremony in constructing Audrey as a paschal victim, in forthrightly Christ-like terms.[12] Here I would like to delve even more deeply into some of the ways that Audrey Santo has moved through Catholic public spaces as an imagined holy mystic girl who does not *do* anything in a literal sense—but who has paradoxically been made to act in lively, evocatively sacramentalized ways. These carry considerable symbolic force.

I shall examine two American spaces through which Audrey has moved, comatose but mobile. First, I shall examine Audrey's performative body in the Fitton Field Mass itself, which I attended as an observor in the stands. Second, and now in American media space beyond observational ritual per se, I shall explore the Apostolate of the Silent Soul's devotional but also promotional 50 minute video about the Fitton Field event ("*Audrey Marie*

Santo: 11th Anniversary Mass, Holy Cross Stadium, Worcester, MA, August 9, 1998"). Audrey's performative agency varies considerably from the first of these venues to the second. This situation allows us to examine popular American Catholic ritualism in relation to its media translations, and to ask about a larger possibility: that electronic media renditions of Catholic sacramentality are themselves important ritual scenes in American public culture.[13]

I shall also, more briefly, trace out one of Little Audrey's later media appearances, again as she was visible in this same Fitton Field Mass as that event was reported in the ABC television news magazine program "20/20" from May 31, 1999. In this show, unexpected events occur, qua media representations of Catholic sacramentalism. Paradoxically, on "20/20," Little Audrey emerges as a more ritually powerful being than she does in the Santo family's own commissioned video. Taking these diverse appearances of the girl from overt ritual but also from mass media as ritual, I use this case study to explore new ways of looking at American Catholic popular devotionalism anthropologically. I contend that shows like the "20/20" segment may act as more than reportorial venues: they may work as performative religious sites on their own account.

AUDREY SANTO AS VICTIM SOUL: WORCESTER SETTINGS, MEDIA SETTINGS

Audrey Marie Santo was born on Dec. 19, 1983, in Worcester and experienced her near-drowning on August 9, 1987—a date significant to some of her followers, since it is the anniversary of the World War II nuclear bombing of Nagasaki, Japan. Her public life as a "victim soul" (one who suffers in the stead of countless others) has been constructed through such linkages, which have typically been proposed not by Worcester's Catholic hierarchy (far from it) but from the ground up. That is, either by family members, associates in the Apostolate of the Silent Soul, or the Santo family's spiritual advisor priests.

Audrey in repose has been, at once, paschal lamb whose normal childhood life has been sacrificed for the welfare of others; child-redeemer, of the sick but also of "forgotten children" such as other handicapped youth; sinless mediator with Christ for her devotees; and (though the family denies this) symbolic replica of the sacrificed and redemptive Christ Himself. Discussing "Audrey devotionalism" within the larger American and Continental victim soul tradition, historian Paula Kane points to the anomaly of a paralyzed, mute, unconscious girl within this type of popular Catholicism.[14] Kane notes that other victim souls were typically conscious and often acutely aware of their bodily pain. With God, they had a hand in choosing and embracing their suffering. In fact, their exemplary nature was thought to derive from this stance of choice. But Audrey is apparently oblivious to her public regard, as a holy victim. Kane finds this problematic, but I do not: the salient fact in my frame of analysis is that Audrey has the public persona of a victim soul.

Another central arena for 'imagining Audrey' has been Worcester's print media and a few sample stories can provide background detail on the girl's life and public impact, before we go on to the Fitton Field Mass and its various video and television transformations. The newsprint coverage of Audrey's life as a holy girl instantiates many of the conflicts swirling around her, since the print sources at issue range from the secularist national press such as the news pages of the *New York Times*, to the Boston papers (perennially enmeshed in jousting with that city's episcopate), to the Worcester daily paper, the *Telegram and Gazette*, to alternative papers such as the *Worcester Magazine*, to the Worcester diocese's weekly *Catholic Free Press.*

By the 1990s the Santo household had become a magnet for pilgrims who hoped that Audrey's holy victimhood and continued miraculous existence would facilitate their own cure, often in the face of overwhelmingly negative odds as these had been delivered by the secular medical establishment. One such visitor to the home was quoted in an August, 1998, *Worcester Magazine* article about "Victim Soul: The Enigma of Little Audrey" (Aug. 5, 1998, pg. 14):

> In addition to all the surreal happenings surrounding Audrey, many people believe she's also a healer.
>
> Father Meade [of Our Lady of Mt. Carmel in Metheun, and a skeptic turned family spiritual advisor] says he's seen it firsthand: people in wheelchairs walking out of the Santo house or Audrey absorbing the cancer from a sick person and then having God absorb it from her.[15]

Reporter Doug Hanchett goes on to note, "Whether Audrey actually helps people heal or serves simply as a human placebo is, of course, a matter open to debate." He later comments, "And according to believers, those who don't magically walk out of the Santo home 100 percent healthy will experience another kind of healing: the spiritual kind."[16]

This sort of focus on Audrey as a good storyline, due to her "cult-like" qualities, was often melded with caveats of this sort. Not surprisingly, the robust growth of the family's sacred healing reputation by the late 1990s (a curative ministry blossoming just a few short blocks away from the parish church, Christ the King) led to oversight by the Worcester Diocese. This also occasioned print coverage.

Former Worcester bishop Timothy Harrington at first allowed the Santos to receive Communion in their home, soon after the girl began to attract public attention. An altar was also consecrated there. Both situations were firsts for the Diocese. The Santo family built up its circle of spiritual advisors; the yearly Masses at Christ the King started and by 1997 some 5,000 people attended. By that same year, however, diocesan officials started to investigate the curing and miracles claims. That same issue of the *Worcester Magazine* quotes diocese spokesman Ray Delisle as saying, "It's really more a matter of should we be wary of something that's been said or done . . . Is there something contradictory [to Catholic teachings]?" Hanchett goes on, in the *Worcester Magazine*'s typically breezy style,

> Delisle wouldn't comment on how the investigation is going, but even if the diocese finds only good things emanating from Audrey's notoriety, it won't be nominating here for canonization anytime soon.
>
> "If it's something that can be helpful to an individual's faith, that's great," says Delisle. "But it's not something the [Catholic] Church turns around and professes that everyone has to believe in."
>
> In fact, official Catholic acknowledgement of miracles and the like is a rare occurrence. In 200 years, the Vatican has recognized only 14 such incidents. Even the famous Catholic pilgrimage site at Medjugorje remains a question mark.
>
> The Santos express confidence that the diocese investigation will bear out their belief that Audrey is carrying out God's will.
>
> "It could be the Evil One," says Linda, when asked how she knows there isn't another explanation for the phenomena. "But I think the answer there is where the fruits are. If the fruits are good, the tree is good."[17]

Delisle's wariness about the truth claims of the bedroom miracles has continued to characterize the Worcester diocese's handlings of the Santo family. Linda Santo for her part has also kept to her careful dance with church officialdom, asserting her fidelity to church authority. And, the print media of the city has maintained its mixed tabloidization/"serious investigative journalism" stance seen above. Electronic media venues have left more room for Little Audrey herself to proclaim sanctity.

THE MASS AT FITTON FIELD: AUDREY AS HOST

In observable, felt ritual action in Catholic Worcester of the late 1990s, Audrey Santo moved beyond a life emblematic for some of victim soulhood (a relatively minor sideline in Catholicism, whatever the case) toward a more resonant life as a Christ-like figure. Her family and especially her mother, as noted, have been careful to disavow such interpretations, saying that Audrey modestly just leads people to Jesus. While they have protested in this way, however, the family has also participated in lavish, specially staged Masses with Audrey's prone body as the centerpiece. A focus in this series of large-scale, family-sanctioned Masses has been the consecrated Host, which the Apostolate of the Silent Soul and several of the family's spiritual advisor priests have claimed bled in Audrey's presence. At the unusually traditionalist eleventh anniversary Mass held at Holy Cross's football stadium in August, 1998, four such extraordinary Hosts were prominently displayed on the wooden dais serving as the altar. Counterposed to this dais with its four ornate gold tabernacles was the small mobile home into which Audrey's unconscious body had been placed. This was the mobile home outfitted with a picture window in front, behind which Audrey was visible to the congregants by about halfway through the Mass. Off to one side of this white trailer was a statue of the Virgin Mary, in a small wagon. This statue had been crowned with flowers by a young Santo relative earlier in the ceremony. This stark juxtaposition of the Eucharistic Jesus in the Hosts and the mute, implicitly suffering and simultaneously merciful pure and sinless girl set up a tableau that operated at two levels: as the presentation of Audrey as a conduit of hopes and prayers to Christ, but also as an offering of Audrey as a replica Christ. The movement of Audrey's body through Worcester town spaces toward and within the field was replayed, and re-envoked, by the long processions of the consecrated wafers in their shining golden holders, at that point in the Mass in which these purportedly bleeding Hosts were walked out around the field in procession by some of the Mass's 25 or so priests. Congregants received Communion.

This juxtaposition of adolescent girl and Christ (and the symbolic claim here that one could be the other) struck me as a puzzle when I first saw it, that August day when I attended this Mass. I had been working on an article with medievalist art historian Joanna Ziegler about another holy girl, Elisabeth of Spalbeek, a thirteenth-century ecstatic trance dancer who threw herself into transports and communion with Christ by beating herself rhythmically on the chest with a wooden triptych.[18] Elisabeth was a Beguine nun, from near Liege in what now is Belgium. Inside her round chapel, to audiences of rapt Cistercian priests, Elisabeth performed 'Christ dances' of her own design. She tranced, and in ecstasy she danced her way around her chapel through all the Stations of the Cross, embodied in her choreography. She climaxed her highly dramatic and unbidden journey (performed numerous times throughout the year) by standing at the altar with arms outstretched: the crucified Christ on the Cross.

Elisabeth was young, female agency within a male dominated, official church personified—a girl at the margins of power, more attuned to artistic imagery than to doctrinal literacy, claiming a greater holiness than the official priesthood. She seems to have been a girl who used bodily abandon (crafted into artistic dance routines) to upend the conventional authority structures of the church, all the while claiming to be a pious young Beguine. She claimed not only direct, ecstatic and clearly highly sexualized union with Christ: Elisabeth also seems to have implicitly embodied Christ's journey to the Cross and even his Crucifixion. Elisabeth was a very active, performative girl indeed. But, I thought to myself in 1998 when I attended the Fitton Field Mass, Worcester's Audrey Santo cannot dance, cannot in fact move her legs or arms in any coordinated way—cannot, at base, even breathe for long periods on her own. She cannot speak or control her gaze. In all these ways she seemed the diametric opposite of Elisabeth and other forceful, inventively seditious mystic girls of the late Middle Ages. Yet, seeing that August Mass cum spectacle on Fitton Field, it occurred to me that Audrey or at least Audrey's implied holy presence in Worcester and Catholic New England did have an active, performative agency of its own—an agency in which a female, diminuative, even frilly Audrey slid symbolically into the outlines of a masculine, traditionalized Eucharistic Jesus. Media representations of the Fitton

Field event reconfigured the symbols still further. This sort of suspicion of agency and the electronic media's role therein allows us to get beyond a level of analysis lodged simply at attempting evaluations of Audrey's family's status as "Audrey handlers" into more interesting anthropological territory.

A FAMILY VIDEO CELEBRATING THE MASS AT FITTON FIELD

The Santo family and the Apostolate of the Silent Soul soon produced a laudatory 50 minute, full color video about this event, a film called "*Audrey Marie Santo: 11th Anniversary Mass, Holy Cross Stadium, Worcester, MA, August 9, 1998*." Footage begins with a note that the video is available for a payment of US$20.00 plus US$3.00 shipping and handling. Viewers also learn that the Apostolate's newsletter may be obtained for an additional US$15.00 a year. The video's voice over, its numerous flattering interviews with close family members of the girl, its songs, and its excerpts from the Mass's main homilies all shower praise on Audrey, as a sinless child who has given the public a great gift of drawing them closer to God, through her sacrificial suffering. Here, I shall review some of the concrete details of this folk art-like film (a video often saccharine in its earnestness). I shall make the central point that Audrey's status as a sacramental body as this was displayed with much power in the actual August 9 Mass loses part of its luster by being filmed and promoted for sale in this way. But, as we shall later see, paradoxically enough when Little Audrey re-emerges on wider American public culture stages, such as in network television news magazines, she gains dramatic force once again.

Briefly, the Apostolate of the Silent Soul's video footage goes as follows. After the titles and monetary information, an announcer proclaims, "This is Audrey's home," in westside Worcester, and viewers see that modest bungalow. Next they glimpse a crowded scene inside Audrey's garage/bedroom: a large cluster of priests gather around the prone girl on the early morning of August 9, "praying with Audrey," the voice over says, and giving her their blessing. Her face is turned to the side and her long, flowing, wavy, luxuriant black hair spills over her lacy pillows in the other direction. The tension between the sensuality of her glowing, bouncy dark locks and the way her family has posed her on the bed, as an innocent child (a toddler, even) is evident to social scientific observers, though apparently unremarked by her family and following. On the video, a small stuffed animal rests by Audrey's shoulder; a crucifix can be seen in the window.

Next viewers learn from the narrator that the couple who now appear on screen, in interview format at Fitton Field, are Linda and Steve Santo, the girl's parents. A producer from the ABC show "20/20" is there, starting to prepare a documentary on the family and this Mass, for airing later on in the television season. The parents review their daughter's history and comment that this day's annual Mass is not at its normal spot, the neighborhood church. As to why the Mass is being held at Holy Cross, Linda comments,

"This [the move this time to the college] was recommended [by the bishop] because it's a Catholic college." Her husband chimes in to say, "It's consecrated ground." Moments before Linda had said, "It seems that our Lord is beginning to bring Audrey out into the world," that is, to progressively more and more distant celebration spots beyond her home.

Linda and Steve then speak of the trauma of the near-drowning and the confused scene at the two hospitals to which Audrey was rushed. A more upbeat scene ensues in somewhat choppy fashion (segments of the video are sometimes separated by runs of black film). Steve is pictured in the driver's seat of a small truck, pulling the specially designed, glass-fronted mobile home away from the westside toward Holy Cross. The narrator notes that this vehicle was designed by the son of the person who made the Popemobile, for John Paul II. We see the truck pulling up onto Fitton Field, "placing Audrey [that is, when she is eventually inserted into the vehicle] beside the altar." It is a sunny, hot day.

Next come testimonials from audience members. One older woman proclaims that "last year [at the Mass at Christ the King] I got to kiss the Host. . . . it changed my life." A group of women visitors from the Philippines are also shown, saying how much they value the chance to attend this Mass. Tiffany McLaughlin then speaks: she is a 17-year old Worcester high schooler who relates how her recurrent rough skin rash totally cleared up, after attending one of the yearly Masses for Audrey. "I was completely overwhelmed by the Mass," she reports, as her mother stands by approvingly. We next see young mothers with babies in strollers, and a large group of children with their grandmothers: all have come from long distances by bus to participate in the event. The video celebrates large families and the maternal virtues at numerous points. Audrey, it seems, is a magnet for the morally good and traditional. Her own family is consistently portrayed in this video as close and loving, although Worcester's print media had reported by this time that Audrey's father Steve was once so overwhelmed by the accident and the ensuing health care demands that he temporarily took to drink and left the family home.

A middle-aged man then gives a heartfelt testimonial about the specialness of these annual Masses: only here, it seems, can one experience so many bleeding Eucharists (four, he exclaims) in one spot. A woman singer goes on to practice at a mike, an elderly nun recites the Lord's Prayer up on the high dais with its white skirting, and audience members finger rosary beads in detailed close-up shots. After the singing of Ave Maria, distinguished guests can be seen filing onto the field: the girl's extended family The song "Little Audrey" rings out at length, as it does at several points throughout the video.

A procession of teens and children with candles enters the field and then the video switches over to a statue of the Virgin Mary, being wheeled onto the field in a cart by teenage boys. Our Lady is placed over next to the mobile home, which has been stationed off to the side of the dais. Men enter the field carrying banners; one carries a tabernacle. Then approximately 25 priests dressed mostly in white process onto the field. Father Charles McCarthy is shown prominently here. He is a locally well-known married priest of the Eastern church, the father of 13 children. Parenthetically (though this point is not mentioned in the video), one of his daughters has garnered media and church attention in her own right: she nearly died of a medicine overdose, and the family prayed for her cure to Edith Stein, the famous World War II-era Carmelite nun and converted Jew. The girl did recover and this reported miracle was successfully used as part of the case to the Vatican for Edith Stein's beatification as a saint.

In the video again, Linda now appears at the dais, reading a dedication to Audrey by her "beloved grandmother." The Virgin off to the side of the dais is then crowned with flowers by one of Audrey's girl cousins. The Santo family and their spiritual advisor consultants have crafted a highly domesticated Mass accented at recurrent points with references to this one family's poignant biography.

Audrey herself is still en route, in the ambulance. Next Fr. George Joyce enters and mounts the dais. A major spiritual director for the family, he delivers a sermon, beginning, "So let me go along and narrate what has happened to this child." In redolent tones he repeats some of the formulaic characterizations of Audrey: before the accident she was "vivacious," "loquacious," "entertaining," "the life of the party." She was very mature for a three year old, always respectful in church—in fact, "people talking in church before the Blessed Sacrament disturbed her." Directly before the swimming-pool event she was "quiet and meditative," Fr. Joyce goes on to report. She fell in; her brother retrieved her after some minutes underwater; Audrey was taken swiftly by the caring family to the hospital. There she was given "an overdose of Phenobarbitol" by the doctors. And, "in therapy, they broke a number of her bones." The medical personnel asked Linda, 'So, where will you be institutionalizing her?' " 'In my arms and home,' " Fr. Joyce tells the assembly. He continues on: In the family home she has received round the clock care by the family. Professional nurses eventually came on the scene as well. Audrey received a diagnosis of akinetic mutism, Joyce goes on, "But her intellect was intact and clear . . . She knows as we know." Further, to confirm that she was suffering with Christ, oil dripped down from a painting of Our Lady of Guadelupe, in her bedroom. Fifty holy items in the chamber joined in: some dripped holy oil, others bled. Fr. Joyce goes on to say that a chalice spontaneously filled with oil. During Lent it dries up, to fill again after Easter. The oil has been tested by scientists; "the blood is human blood."

Fr. Joyce's rapid-paced narrative spins out: On June 15, 1995, a Host consecrated at Mass in Audrey's room and placed in the tabernacle bled. And, "Subsequently two other hosts bled from Masses we priests offered in the garage . . . These were also placed in the tabernacle and then bled." "On June 5, 1996, [the narrative continues] while I was concelebrating a Mass with Fr. McCarthy, the Host bled at consecration." Forty people were present, "while we priests were overwhelmed with emotion." Then, "You all will be blessed by these four, after Mass today."

Then Fr. Joyce goes on to lament the fact that the "times are so corrupt" that "He choses another innocent lamb" in sacrifice, as "He did send his precious Son to die for us." Fr. Joyce reiterates the idea that suffering of this sort is uniquely valued, saying (apparently speaking in the stead of Audrey, but perhaps for God) "Don't moan and groan . . . I will give you grace . . . to save the dear ones in your family." He concludes: "God is crying out through this little girl, to his children who have wandered away. He is calling them back, lest they die of wretchedness and hunger. My Son awaits you, to implore you once again to let him feed you with his Precious Body and Blood."

Another priest then takes Fr. Joyce's place at the microphone and a call and response segment of the standard Mass ensues. The female singer, also a guitarist, performs a number off to the side. Linda and Steve walk to the mike and they and their family members offer readings from the Old Testament. The guitarist and a young man at an electric piano keyboard again perform. The camera lingers over a nun in traditional habit, sitting in a wheelchair down in the space of honor on the field in front of the dias. In fact, the assembly has several handicapped people, along with elderly nuns in habit. The Bible readings continue and then Linda and family members walk to the mobile home. The priests stand up from their chairs (a scene captured by several wide-angled views of this impressively big assembly).

A younger priest follows with a lengthy homily. He dwells on several themes: "God is good . . . God loves us; we are a people of God longing for reunion with Him; we are a people of faith . . . a pilgrim people." And, "the things of this world are passing away" and Audrey's state of being "free of sin" shows believers this. Then he asserts that "We're not here [in this special Mass] for Audrey, we're here for our Lord God." Some might say (the priest goes on), 'What good could she be?' He answers, She is a powerful instrument of God. The homily ends and Audrey's sister Gigi then stands at the microphone to lead a series of prayers. She is followed by four other girls. The narrator then declares, "Audrey is now arriving at Holy Cross stadium and will be transferred to her [spot] by the altar." And, the ambulance pulls up, and Audrey strapped on her stretcher is slid out. She is wheeled over toward Our Lady for a moment, then moved back toward the side entrance to the white mobile home. The door to the trailer is opened wide and Audrey is slipped in. The white, partitioned curtain is drawn back. The "Little Audrey" song by a full-throated male singer is belted out on the soundtrack.

A standard sequence from the Mass ensues, presided over by the younger priest. The Host is consecrated; the guitarist and piano player contribute another number. A shot shows Linda and Steve Santo coming out of the trailer. Father McCarthy, the Eastern rite priest, distributes communion. He is introduced and begins an extraordinary sermon. This is made even more memorable by his appearance: with flowing gray locks and a large beard he resembles an Old Testament prophet. He tells the assembly the following, in mellifluous phrases: What happens when "we receive Communion is that that little Host contains the most powerful reality in the world." The "Eucharistic

Jesus" is the key reality for believers to fasten upon; that Jesus is the very same one "who walked the highways and byways" back in New Testament times, curing people in His ministry. Then, "53 years ago today, a tiny atom was pulled apart"—to create the first atom bomb. In nine seconds, he goes on, the world saw the destruction of 40,000 people in Nagasaki, Japan's oldest Catholic community. Eventually a full 200,000 people died of the bomb's after effects. "That little atom that we can't see did all the damage." Now, the very first medical notation about Audrey after the near-drowning in the hospital charts was recorded at 11:03 a.m., "precisely the time the bomb detonated." He goes on, "the vast majority of people who were killed were children." Moreover, 80 percent of the people who die every day worldwide of hunger "are children." Child labor is a major problem everywhere. Children seemingly have no power. But just imagine (McCarthy goes on to say), if the care given so long to Audrey were also to be given to every child, "the world would then be transformed." This is the mystery of the Holy Eucharist, he proclaims, also asking the assembly to also pray for him, on this, the anniversary of his ordination.

The sermon ends and the group of priests distribute Communion. The gold tabernacles are walked through the crowd, around the field. One is taken over to Audrey's trailer. In the background a song reminiscent of sentimental pop music of the crooner sort plays: "I give you Jesus . . . He passes all understanding." The refrain here is a frequently reiterated "You need someone," executed in syrupy pop love song fashion.

Audrey is rolled out of the trailer ("I give you Je—sus," in the song overlay), trundled along the ground on the wheeled stretcher, and slid back into the ambulance (which is marked "Patriot Ambulance" company on the side). This vehicle pulls slowly off the field. Viewers get a last close up shot of Our Lady. The "I give you Je—-sus" song resounds, in plummy tones, as the video ends.

Obviously made as a promotional as well as a testimonial video, this film celebrates the Santo family's self-sacrifice as much as it does Audrey's intercessory role as a suffering, ill virgin whose sacrifice offers up the pain of the faithful to Christ. As sheer ritual, the Fitton Field Mass had verve and drama, with its unusually dense clustering of images of Christ, Mary, consecrated Hosts in glistening tabernacles, and the half-dead/half-alive sinless girl, with her toddler-like mein in a teenager's body. The Mass had movement, and considerable drama above and beyond the basic ritual storyline of the universal Catholic Mass. Here was saintly, mysterious, suffering Audrey coming toward the scene; here she suddenly was, in her death-like prone pose of great sweetness. The faithful's visual field was filled with activity: tabernacles coursing across the field, the long dais, the crowned Virgin Mary, the standard motions of the Mass, the curtain sharply pulled back to reveal Audrey as sacrificial Host counterposed to the Eucharist wafers. But, once this complex Mass was put onto video, with this production's stress on lachrymose songs, family sentimentality, and these lengthy sermons with their non-standard historical claims, the Audrey phenomenon lost some of its impact. Ironically, by being made so self-consciously into theatre in this way, the anniversary Mass had some of Catholicism's basic dramatic power drained away from it. The Mass fell into media spaces of near self-parody.

The repetitive invocation of the sugary "I give you Jesus" song shows this larger process in fine. The inherent dignity of the standard Mass was consistently undercut by the musical interference here with teenage love song styles. Similar to this was the filmmakers' repeated tendency to highlight the sentimental and cliched: a saintly old nun in habit sitting in a wheelchair, fingering rosary beads; a sweet little child carrying a candle in procession; a pious-looking priest processing onto the field, eyes upraised—with all of these images captured in languorous close ups. The video's slippage between American 1950s style popular film romance sentimentality and high Catholic ritual was constant, in a way that was not present in the Mass itself.

The filmmaker also devoted much footage to the sermons of the two favored priests, Fr. Joyce and Fr. McCarthy. Shown in flattering close up, they were clearly meant to be stars of the production, alongside the Santo family. In the Mass itself both priests were featured speakers, indeed, but there they did not constitute such a large part of the action as they do in the video. What with this emphasis on family favorites and cliché, the Mass's Audrey, and Audrey's tense pictorial juxtaposition there to the consecrated Hosts, gets swamped in the video within a plethora of more minor, human dramas.

Other media reiterations of the Little Audrey phenomenon furthered this process of miniaturizing the girl's performative agency, by exoticizing it as part of what might almost be called the American Catholic macabre. However, a mainstream television news magazine show, ABC's "20/20," moved in the other direction, paradoxically enough. One might think that network television news productions, like much elite newspaper coverage, would be sharply secularist and skeptical in portraying Little Audrey and her surrounding swirl of miracles. But, a May 31, 1999, broadcast of this show entitled "Miracle of Audrey" showed just the opposite tendency. The program represented the girl's affectingly still body as quite possibly a source of 'real miracles' in contemporary Worcester. The "20/20" segment's admiring documentation of the girl's healing ministry, abetted by a flattering rendition of the Fitton Field Mass, seemed designed to re-enchant small sectors of the American landscape.

ABC's "20/20" Presents the Mass at Fitton Field

The May, 31, 1999, "20/20 Sunday" broadcast was a surprisingly disingenuous one, a program that eschewed any serious social scientific, historical, or investigative journalism approach to the phenomenon of Audrey's bedridden body and her mother Linda's claims that healing miracles had accrued to the teenager's relationship with her public. The producers spotlighted one central question: Could it be, on-air reporters ask repeatedly, that there actually *are* miracles? The Fitton Field Mass is a main scene for the program;

correspondent Lynn Sherr's interviews with Linda and Steve Santo are another. A third focus at several points of this sizeable Sunday night broadcast is Audrey's bedroom, filled to overflowing with holy pictures, saints' statues, and chalices. A core image for the scenes in that chamber is holy oil, which viewers see dripping copiously into small containers affixed to various of the devotional pictures and other objects on the walls. The ABC production does report that the oil, when tested, proved to be 75 per cent olive oil and the rest some unknown substance. But, the program recurrently suggests that aspects of the oil-dripping remain mysterious, even possibly—miraculous. In pursuing such a storyline (one more associated with grocery store check-out line tabloids than with mainstream, nighttime, news magazine programs) this segment of "20/20" opened up small media spaces for forthright Little Audrey devotionalism.

How this occurs can be glimpsed from a summary of the program's action. The show begins with anchors Barbara Walters and Diane Sawyer announcing and discussing the evening's topic. They go on to promise that viewers will hear of "magic, mystery," and for some, "spiritual experience." Do you believe in miracles? the anchors pose as their key question. In framing the material on Little Audrey they opine, "What you will see defies logic." Could God really be at work here? another of their queries goes. Sawyer ends the introductory segment by citing an Indian sect that subscribes to "the doctrine of maybe." TV viewers are implicitly asked to open themselves to the possibility that miracles have actually occurred in the vicinity of the mysterious (and let me note, telegenic) Audrey.

Correspondent Lynn Sherr takes over the account at this point. She is to prove a consistently respectful, even credulous interrogator of the Santo family. Viewers soon see Fitton Field with the August 9, 1998, attendees members filing in. The crowd is international and ethnically mixed. A scene inside a bus ensues: a woman seated there declared, "So, we are truly blessed" to be about to enter into the actual presence of Audrey Santo. TV viewers then witness Audrey herself loosely wrapped in blankets, being taken up in someone's arms from her bed for the day's activities and for the trip across town to the football field. Her ambulance pulls up to Fitton Field. Her father busses her on the cheek as she is wheeled out on her stretcher. Throngs crowd the field.

Then we see some flashbacks to more general aspects of the girl's holy life: pilgrims (mostly women) file through the family home; a picture of the Virgin on the wall appears (this is the portrait of the Virgin of Guadeloupe that first famously dripped oil in the Santo house). Linda is shown in the house, tending to her inert daughter. Holy statues, pictures, and crosses festoon the girl's bedroom. In fact, much of the entire surface of the walls and shelves are so outfitted. Audrey lies on her bed, in tones of light pink and white. Her wavy, lush hair flows out, combed down upon the linens.

Linda is interviewed in a series of softball questions. She avers, it is "God who does the healing," not Audrey herself. Sherr herself never frontally questions the veracity of the healing claims; she always leaves open the possibility that "something is actually going on here," in the mystery department.

Linda is then shown relating Audrey's early toddlerhood, before the pool accident. "She was perfect," her mother reports—a "really verbal" child. Audrey's sister Gigi and her mother then relate the familiar tale of the fall into the pool, the rush to the hospital, the medical personnel's prediction that "she'd be a vegetable." Linda recounts that this period was "probably the most hopeless place I've ever been in." Steve Santo chimes in to admit that he walked out on his family early on, for he was "burying my grief in a bottle of beer." Sherr summarizes the situation: "Your husband's walked out on you, you've got a three year old" in dire health straits—"*What* was in your head" at this tragic juncture? "God is good," Linda firmly answers. Indeed, the entire interview format provides her with repeated opportunities to proclaim her piety in the face of family and medical adversity and to emerge for TV viewers as an icon of Catholic motherhood.

Her maternal sacrifice narrative continues, again not critiqued or contextualized by Sherr. Linda prayed all the time during this difficult period, she recalls. She set up the garage with medical equipment. She took her daughter to Medjugorje, believing that the girl would be cured and would walk away from the shrine (Linda recalls that she brought along a pair of sandals). Audrey suffered a dangerous setback during the pilgrimage and had to be airlifted back to the United States. Linda had to re-mortgage the home in order to pay the air ambulance bills. Father Charles McCarthy is shown on screen at this point, asserting that "sane people shouldn't have done this," that is, devote so much time and money to caring for their ill daughter in such a loving way. He applaudes Linda's self-sacrifice.

Years go by, Linda relates. Steve contributed not so much as a phone call to family life during this time, viewers learn. Then, Linda discovers that she has breast cancer. But, she relates, she cut short her chemotherapy treatments, so as to be able to furnish uninterrupted high-quality care for her daughter. TV viewers are left with a fulsome portrait of maternal virtue, self-abnegation, and self-sacrifice, but surprisingly they are given no critical framing of this rhetoric by Sherr or the anchors. Linda and Father McCarthy jointly narrate the next stage of the saga: the family's ascent from this slough of despond after God sends a sign of favor to the household. That is, the sudden flow of holy oil from the portrait of the Virgin of Guadeloupe in the living room. The oil is soon "just dripping everywhere" around the house, Linda recalls. Father McCarthy relates that he made a visit to the home at this time in 1993 and found that the material coursing down from the pictures and statuettes was indeed oil. Lynn Sherr comes in to report that on her own trips to the house she too saw the oil ("I saw it for myself"). The family's oil miracle was "about to circle the globe," the family recalls.

This segment of the program is closed by Diane Sawyer noting that once prayers were said *for* Audrey, but that after the oil started to course down, prayers began to be said *to* her. After an advertisement, Lynn Sherr returns and the camera pans Audrey's bedroom, densely packed as it is with the holy objects of traditional Catholic piety. Oil is shown actively dripping into small receptacles. A group of pilgrims is in view, seated on chairs, getting a lecture on Audrey's biography from a member of the Apostolate of the Silent Soul. Another group of visitors appear, moving through the house toward the garage, snapping photos when they arrive. A little boy with brain damage lies in his mother's arms; he has been brought to the home so that his suffering can be taken on by Audrey and offered up to Christ. TV viewers learn that Audrey is often read the letters from her faithful, describing their ills. Linda is shown, reading her daughter a letter from a woman who writes that her husband is abusive ("The verbal abuse is awful"). Correspondents want only a "Chance to pray in front of Audrey," Linda says.

Suppliants do this through a glass window, which generally separates the visitors to the garage from the reclining Audrey herself. The faithful can peer into the bedroom through the portal, to its occupant on the bed and its clusters of statuettes, its crosses, and holy pictures. Lynn Sherr next enjoys special access to the room: she enters it directly and witnesses Audrey without the usual window arrangement. She holds the girl's hand as Linda hovers; the correspondent says that Audrey squeezed her fingers lightly (a first time, if not a second). Viewers hear a tale of a once-paralyzed motorcycle accident victim who was healed after Audrey's intercession for him. In this case, the voice over does note that the boy's physician had given him a 75 percent chance of getting better anyway. Apostolate staffers are shown stuffing oil-soaked cotton balls into small plastic containers, for shipment to suppliants who cannot come to the home in person.

The program then turns to the mystery of this oil and its supposedly near-constant exudation from the holy things in the house. Lynn Sherr questions Linda and Steve: You're not faking this in some way? Steve relates how he too was puzzled about the oil, when he first came back to the family. He came to believe; he won Linda's forgiveness.

The family now treats Audrey, Steve relates, just like all the rest of their children, including her in friendly workaday conversations ("Come on, let's go, Aud—let's go get an ice cream"). TV viewers gain more details about the girl's care, and learn how she once suddenly broke out in an all-over, rough red rash. This was just the sort of rash a cancer patient taking chemotherapy would get, Linda says. Audrey had taken on the sufferings of the cancer patients who had recently appealed to her for intercession with Christ. Lynn Sherr does not interrogate or frame this claim. The segment is rounded out with a comment from family spiritual advisor Father Joyce: the girl is either a flagrant fake or a genuine victim soul. His sentiments are clear on the issue. He then relates the story about the consecrated Hosts that bled, during a bedside Mass in the home.

Next viewers see the 1998 Mass at "a nearby football stadium." The photography here is striking: first, a glimpse of the entire scene, then a close up of the white trailer with Audrey inside and the curtain drawn back, then a song, then a shot of a large church cross seen dramatically from below, then a view of an impressive, huge stone church, also seen from below. Statues are inset into the gray church exterior. The trailer scene has been cleverly dovetailed within mainstream Catholic architecture.

Back at the anchor desk Barbara Walters introduces the next major topic of the broadcast: the Worcester diocese's formal investigation of the Santo family's miracle claims (and implicitly, the family's public treatment of their daughter). Walters asks her viewers to ponder, How does "the Church investigate such a mystery?" The focus here is on church policy and procedures, not on miracle beliefs as possibly springing from some larger historical or social context. Walters notes that the country is one "the brink of a new century" and is thus experiencing a wave of strange spiritual events, such as weeping statues. "How does the Catholic Church handle this?" she inquires. TV viewers next encounter four somber-looking middle-aged white men seated for an interview. They comprise the Worcester diocese's official commission to look into Little Audrey matters. Sherr reports that among them are physicians, psychologists, and clergymen. One member of the commission, Dr. John Madonna, says that when the group visited the westside home "we found nothing, no source of the oil" (that is, no concrete evidence of fakery). The group further acknowledges that an icon that they themselves had brought along "oozed oil that night," when the group spent the night in the home. The final verdict? That there was something "unexplainable" here.

Lynn Sherr comes back on to query Father McCarthy, who says that there has been no evidence of fraud vis-à-vis the flowing oil. He states that if the oil events were to be shown to be staged, that would surely "be a spiritual disaster." Sherr reports that outside auditors have determined that the oil is 75 percent olive oil and the rest, "unidentifiable." In other words, she tells viewers: "nothing conclusive" has been found. She ends the segment by suggesting that those in search of verifiable miracles need search no further than Linda Santo herself: an overwhelmingly devout mother to a needy daughter. Father McCarthy declares that the exuding statues point not to Audrey but to Linda herself, in her role as a mother. Viewers are shown Linda and Audrey in close up, cheek to cheek, with the mother whispering gently to the girl. Sherr asks Linda, if you could have one wish for Audrey for her future, what would it be? "For her to just get up and talk." The program ends back at the anchor desk with Diane Sawyer noting that the public should expect nothing definitive about the miracle claims from the official church. Barbara Walters adds that the local diocese may eventually issue a warning to the faithful, if it finds anything awry with the claims of wonders.

Many elements of Little Audrey devotionalism are familiar from older healing shrines within world Catholicism[19]: the central role played by women devouts in these curative places and practices; the presence of male spiritual advisors linked in intense ways to these prominent women; massive pilgrimages; and parades of the handicapped who come into the presence of a sainted child or young person, desperate for cures after official medicine has failed. Also common across much of this perennially creative range of Catholic healing shrine phenomena are motifs of embodied suffering, holy illnesses, and protestations that the focal body at the shrine is not usurping Christ's preeminence at all but is merely leading believers into prayerful regard for Him. Undergirding the shrine events, always, is the conviction that intercession with God works, and is not manipulative or self-directed on the part of the women and priests 'running' the shrine but is rather self-sacrificing and full of faith. What sets the 1990s Little Audrey healing devotions off from this much wider set of Lourdes-like practices, however, is the degree to which the Worcester events gained public currency not just in real time but in the electronic media. In this, Catholic body and spirit seem to have claimed new ritual territory, within mass media itself.

This "20/20" broadcast illustrates some of the rhetorical strategies through which this happened. The dense arrays of holy objects in Audrey's bedroom are shown repeatedly, in camera angles that highlight their rich profusion (recalling, in fact, the sacramental density of such scenes as Haitian popular Catholicism prayer altars). The camera shots of the reclining Audrey are also used redundantly, building up a memory bank of such portraits for the TV viewer. As noted, the white trailer scene is effectively allied in this broadcast, as well, to larger, more mainstream Catholic architectural repertoires of key symbols. While Audrey is being offered to TV viewers as a lovely child-in-amber, her mother is being constructed by the "20/20" program's photography and commentary as an exemplary mother—as Mary-like. One image of this sort succeeds another, until the program as a whole begins to work as an intense palimpsest of traditional Catholic iconography. The anchorwomen and the female correspondent serve as soft-toned guides to Audrey's life as a girl of miracles, more than they do as sharp-edged interrogators. Traditional femininity is recurrently highlighted.

In sum, the "20/20" program as a whole came to resemble the glass window to Audrey's bedroom: a portal through which at least some viewers could glimpse the sacred.

Commentary: Catholic Sacramentalism as Media Event: A View from the Sociology of Religion and Media Sociology

John Schmalzbauer

What is Catholic? What are "the media"? These are the sorts of questions raised by anthropologists Susan Rodgers and Vicente Rafael in two fascinating explorations of unconventional "ritual and media spaces." While Rodgers looks at media constructions of the "sacramental body" of a paralyzed young girl, Rafael analyzes the messianic significance of cell phones in the Philipino political protest. Both case studies push the boundaries of the words "Catholic" and "media," forcing us to rethink the meanings of both terms in theoretically suggestive ways. At first glance, neither a comatose mystic nor a Philipino cell phone user would seem to fit into the conventional territory of academic Catholic studies. In different ways, Rodgers and Rafael examine religious or quasi-religious phenomena that are on the margins of official Catholicism.

In Rodgers's Chapter we read about a paralyzed Massachusetts girl who has been presented as a kind of female Eucharistic host. In a prayer card distributed at her memorial Mass, devotees were instructed to pray *to* and not only *for* Audrey (a practice later forbidden by the Worcester Diocese). The extension of Audrey devotion into media spaces has raised more questions about the nature of religious ritual. Does Catholic ritual require that participants be physically present? What does a televised religious ritual do for believers? How do secular media represent Catholic practices and symbols? By focusing on such issues, Rodgers explores the same territory discussed by Ronald Grimes in his piece, "Ritual in the Media." Describing situations where a religious ritual is "extended by media," Grimes argues that it is possible for viewers to "participate" in such events, "even though we do so at a distance. In such cases, the event is not just described but made present. The rite reaches toward and includes viewers. No longer mere viewers, we are ritualists, participants of sorts."[1]

Still it is an open question how successful televised Catholic masses (including the Mass for Audrey) are at drawing viewers into the ritual. In

"The Electronic Golden Calf," Gregor Goethals contends that television "has limited use . . . in churches where the eucharist is central to worship," adding that watching the "movements of the participants in liturgical spaces, including the shots of those taking communion, may have little personal significance to a television observer."[2] In short, when it comes to the Catholic Mass, you had to be there.

But does one have to be there to participate in devotion to Audrey? In the case of the televised mass of Little Audrey, the consumption of bread and wine are secondary to the spectacle surrounding the "sacramental body" of Audrey herself. Like the pre-Vatican II devotion of Benediction of the Blessed Sacrament (a ritual where worshippers gaze at but do not consume the host), the point of devotion to Little Audrey is to *look* not to partake.[3] To the extent that one can gaze at Audrey Santo on a television screen, devotion to Audrey is possible in a football stadium, in a church, or in the comfort of one's own home.

At the same time, not all media extensions of religious ritual are created equal. In her comparison of the family-sanctioned Audrey video with the ABC News 20/20 special, Rodgers argues that the latter was far more successful in capturing the ritual power of the Audrey phenomenon. While the homemade video contained long sermons by priests close to the Santo family, the ABC 20/20 production lingered on the body of Audrey Santo and the material objects of devotional Catholicism. By downplaying the verbal in favor of the visual feast of holy pictures, saints, and Audrey close-ups, ABC was more in tune with what sociologist Andrew Greeley has called the Catholic imagination.[4] Though produced by a presumably secular crew at ABC News, the 20/20 documentary effectively conveyed a Catholic sense of the sacramentality of the material world (including Audrey's suffering body).

The ABC special told the story of Little Audrey in a way that a large American television audience could understand. Like a modern day hagiography, it focused on the saintly lives of Little Audrey and her self-sacrificing mother, emplotting their stories within stock narratives recognizable to both Catholic and non-Catholic viewers. According to media theorist Jack Lule, the myths of "The Victim" and "The Good Mother" are often employed by American journalists.[5] By portraying Linda Santo as a "Mary-like" mother to a Christ-like child, Rodgers notes, the 20/20 documentary "begins to work as an intense palimpsest of traditional Catholic iconography (p. 222).

To truly gauge the effectiveness of the two Audrey video productions, one would need to carefully observe the way viewers react to them. Lynn Schofield Clark's innovative study of teenage reception of media religion[6] provides one model for assessing viewer responses to the Audrey videos. Vicente Rafael's essay on "The Cell Phone and the Crowd" provides yet another. Through an analysis of participant accounts, he shows how the cell phone was appropriated by the crowd and how the crowd itself became a kind of medium. The strength of Rafael's analysis is his ability to convey the importance of both technology and the human beings who use it. In the case of Rafael's cell phone users, the lines between senders and receivers, media and audience, authors and readers, technology and people, are blurred, as both the cell phones and those who wield them become tools for political protest.

By provocatively describing political demonstrations in religious terms, Rafael also blurs the boundaries between the sacred and the secular. Likening the People Power II protests to Jacques Derrida's discussion of "the messianic without a messiah," he writes of the "promise of justice that is conveyed" by experiencing the crowd. Though Rafael does not develop this theme extensively, his use of Derrida's notion of "faith without dogma" raises all sorts of interesting issues (p. 201).

For starters, what is an essay on cell phones and political protest doing in an edited volume on Catholicism? A partial answer might be gleaned by considering the religious roots of mass communications. In a seminal piece in media studies, James Carey contrasts two dominant conceptions of the media in America, the "transmission" and the "ritual" approaches. While the transmission view emphasizes the sending and receiving of information, the ritual view focuses on shared meanings expressed in media messages. According to Carey, "[b]oth definitions derive, as with much in secular culture, from religious origins."[7]

On one level, the cell phone "texting" in Manila is a perfect illustration of the transmission view of the media. Rooted in American efforts to disseminate the Christian Gospel across the North American continent, a transmission approach helps make sense of the media behavior described in Rafael's chapter. Like the Word-centered Protestants who used Samuel Morse's telegraph for the "purposes of spreading the Christian message farther and faster" (ultimately, Carey argues, to control territory and the people who occupy it), the cell phone users in Manila worked to retake their country through electronically transmitted text.[8]

Upon further example, Carey's ritual view of communication makes even better sense of Rafael's crowds and cell phones. "Under a ritual view," writes Carey, media are "not information but drama."[9] They do not transmit facts but instead imagine an "arena of dramatic forces and action," inviting "our participation on the basis of our assuming, often vicariously, social roles within it." More than transmitters of data, Rafael shows how the cell phones in Manila "held the messianic promise of refashioning the heterogeneous crowd into a people addressing and addressed by the promise of justice." Caught up in the "mania" of texting, the cell phone users were able to imagine themselves as participants in a grand drama of social transformation (p.186).

If the transmission approach to media has its origins in Protestant America, a ritual view more closely reflects a Catholic conception of communication. In Rafael's account, the throng of demonstrators "brings to mind the experience of crowding in certain religious gatherings, notably the all male processions of the image of Black Nazarene that mark the high point of the fiesta of Quiapo, a district of Manila, on the ninth of January." In the rituals of political protest, the cell phone user finds herself "moving in concert"

with the crowd, "filled with its desire and consumed by its energy," an experience of secular communion (p. 188).

The fact that such communion does not take place within the walls of a
church should not exclude it from the purview of Catholic Studies. As this
interdisciplinary field matures it will have to look for both literal and
metaphoric connections between Catholicism and its cultural contexts. Both
Rodgers's discussion of Little Audrey media and Rafael's exploration of cell
phones and political protest fit within a big tent definition of Catholic
Studies.[10] Though one would have a hard time connecting what they
describe to the official Catholicism outlined in *The Catechism of the Catholic
Church*, both enrich our understanding of the rituals and practices of the
Catholic tradition.

CHAPTER 14

Performing the Miraculous in Central Massachusetts

Mathew N. Schmalz

MIRACLES

"Hey, Mister, where's the little girl?" I was asked by one young man as he walked down the residential street that led to the Santo home in Worcester, Massachusetts. "She's in the house over there, but you won't be seeing her until the prayer service tomorrow," I said. "What happened to her, Mister?" another young man asked. I briefly explained how Audrey Marie Santo fell into a swimming pool sixteen years ago when she was nearly four years of age and has remained in a coma ever since. "You mean there's a swimming pool at the house over there, Mister?" "No," I said, "that was in the other house." "Hey, Mister," another young man asked, "are we going to be on T.V.?" "Well, Univision's here, and 20/20 is too," I responded. "Really, what's 20/20 and when is it on?

The young men I spoke with were among some one hundred and fifty pilgrims who had come from Perth Amboy, New Jersey to Worcester, Massachusetts on August 9, 2003. These pilgrims had come to honor Audrey Santo on the sixteenth anniversary of her accident. The commemoration of the accident was to be more subdued than the spectacle at the College of the Holy Cross in 1998. This time, the pilgrims would have a mass at the Santo home and venerate one of the blood stained hosts. On the next day, there would be an anointing service for children, after which Audrey Santo would be displayed. The media was there, although not in much force as in previous years. Still they too were drawn by claims of the miraculous. Univision had come to tape the events as part of a larger report centering upon the claim of a man from Lynn, Massachusetts, whose relative in Columbia was purportedly healed of mouth cancer through the application of oil taken from one of the "weeping statues" in Audrey Santo's home. A producer from the ABC Network arrived as well, along with a cameraman and sound technician. The

ABC report would appear on a special edition of the television newsmagazine 20/20 that would update the original 1995 story on Audrey Santo. When I asked the producer what the appeal of the Audrey Event would be, she said simply, "Everyone likes a good miracle story."

When the young man from Perth Amboy asked me about the media, he was expressing not only the hope that he and his friends might be on television, but also curiosity about how the media were conducting themselves at the Santo home. Within the broad parameters of what is often called "ritual studies," a crucial theme remains ritual's performative nature. Stanley Tambiah[1] and Victor Turner, among many others, have argued that ritual is primarily communicative in that it embodies, or "performs," central values and socio-cultural meanings. While crews from 20/20 and Univision attended the Audrey Event to report on the miraculous, they too "performed" and thus became part of the very phenomenon they were examining.

HIERARCHY

When the ABC cameraman and sound technician were unloading equipment from their van, the pilgrims from Perth Amboy, New Jersey were making their way down the street. Some of the pilgrims had plastic rosary beads around their necks, and others wore T-shirts emblazoned with images of Padre Pio or the Virgin Mary (figure 14.1). Many were carrying food—casseroles, rice and fried plantains. The 20/20 cameraman and sound technician calibrated their equipment by briefly focusing them on the pilgrims. They then joined the producer who was talking with Mrs. Santo about the upcoming events (figure 14.2).

The pilgrims were directed to a tent that had been erected between the Santo home and the neighboring building that housed the offices of the Apostolate of a Silent Soul. While the ABC crew continued to converse with Mrs. Santo, the cameraman and correspondent from Univision began their work by engaging the pilgrims who had begun their lunch. The cameraman trained his viewfinder on the rather sumptuous dishes brought by the pilgrims. Univision also focused on the preparations for a Spanish mass that would be held after the communal meal. The camera lingered on a singer singing, "*Yo te amo Jesù*" as some pilgrims swayed to the lyrics with their arms outstretched (figure 14.3). Univision spent most of its time interviewing pilgrims, and the group of young boys I met followed them at a polite distance (figure 14.4). Pilgrims talked about their conversions to Christ and prophecies made by Mary at Medjugorje. Most of all, the pilgrims spoke of Audrey Santo and of the miraculous oil from the statutes at the Santo home, oil that they had distributed to relatives far beyond the confines of Worcester.

While Univision focused on what could be called "sacramental consumption," 20/20 was concerned with consumption of an apparently different kind. The ABC team did not interview pilgrims, much less eat with them. Instead, they filmed the purchase of plastic rosary beads and other materials

Figure 14.1   Pilgrims arrive at the Santo home

that had been placed near Audrey Santo as she lay in her bedroom. A number of close ups of the items for sale on a table draped by a Vatican flag (figure 14.5) were taken by 20/20. But more often than not, the cameraman climbed to the second floor of the Apostolate's offices, to get a panoramic or God's eye view of the buying and selling taking place below.

For 20/20, the primary story was Audrey Santo and the purported miracles surrounding her. The ABC cameraman took close-ups of the statutes in the chapel at the Santo home, although none were exuding oil that day (figure 14.6 and 14.7). But the key point of the photo shoot was Audrey Santo herself. When invited into the Santo home, the camera crews had to stop in the family living room and go through what is best described as a purification ritual by standing in front of an air conditioner. While this was presented as a sensible precaution to make sure no one carried allergens on their clothing, members of the Apostolate who had also been outside were not asked to cleanse themselves in a similar fashion.

Audrey Santo lies in her room as the focal point of what could best be called a Eucharistic tableau. Two tabernacles face her bed and the tabernacle motif extends throughout the room. The slipcover at the foot of Audrey

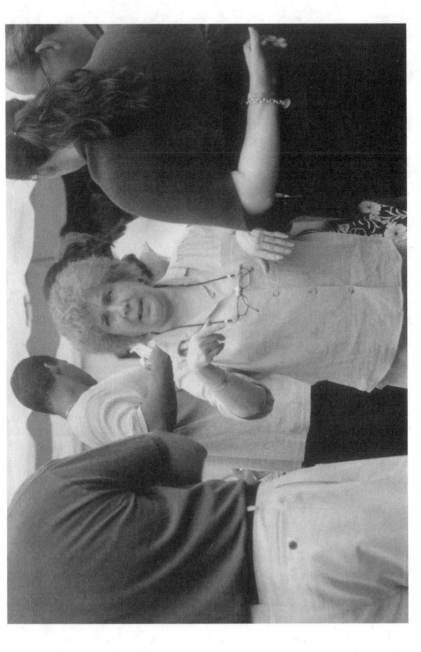

Figure 14.2 The 20/20 production crew meets with Linda Santo

Figure 14.3 Pilgrims before the mass at the Santo home

Figure 14.4 Univision interviews pilgrims

Figure 14.5 The cameraman from 20/20 focuses on relics connected with Audrey

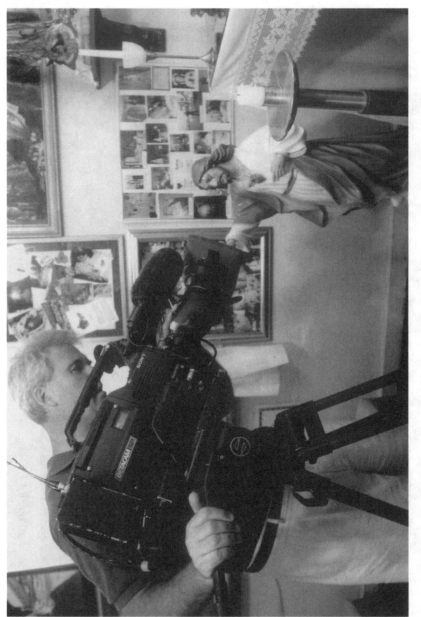

Figure 14.6 The cameraman from 20/20 moves to a close-up of a statue in the Santo chapel

Figure 14.7 A statue from the Santo chapel with plastic cup to collect exuding oil

236

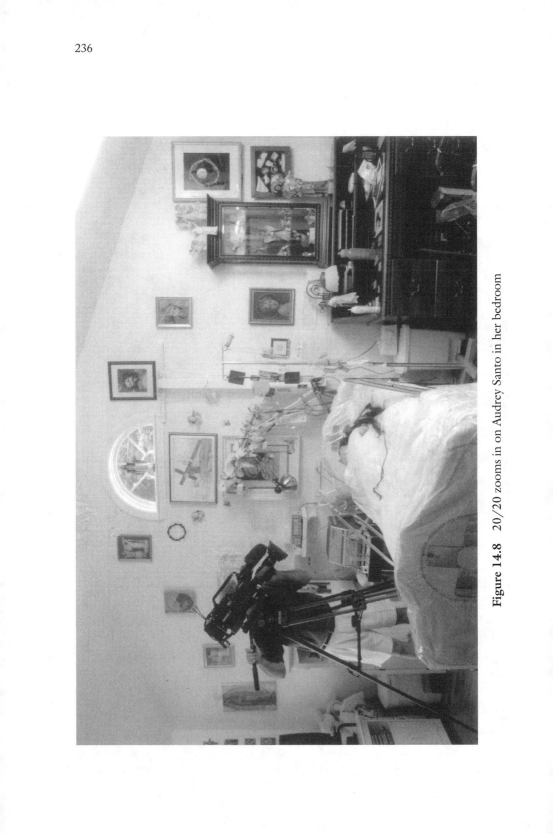

Figure 14.8 20/20 zooms in on Audrey Santo in her bedroom

Santo's bed displays an image of a Eucharistic host and its circular shape is echoed in the framing of Audrey herself, with successive halos of religious images over the headboard giving the impression of a penumbra of sanctity and divine protection. To Audrey Santo's left are relics of saints given to her by pilgrims and devotees, and between the relics and the bed is a frame that holds the cap she wore after she was born, as well as handkerchiefs stained by the blood from her stigmatic wounds. When 20/20 arrived in Audrey's bedroom, they did not pause to attend to the devotional cues that had been so carefully arranged. Instead, the cameraman penetrated the space surrounding Audrey Santo by setting his tripod so that the camera would bear down upon her from above (figure 14.8).

The day at the Santo home was about hierarchy. There was the hierarchy of the Apostolate of a Silent Soul, to which the media, in varying degrees, adapted. The Apostolate of a Silent Soul also assumed a hierarchy of audiences for the event, with the ABC Network and 20/20's audience considered to have a higher status than Univision and its audience. Ironically, Univision had the higher status for the audience that was actually present for the event. The media coverage itself also reflected various hierarchical judgments. This was most clearly the case with the ABC cameraman and sound technician who essentially ignored the pilgrims except as rather objects to be gazed down upon—as indeed was Audrey herself. The media performance thus inscribed hierarchy just as it reflected it.

SPECTACLE

Early on August 11, pilgrims began to stand in front of Christ the King Church on Pleasant Street in Worcester. In times past, pilgrims would line the street with loudspeakers broadcasting the sermons for the "Audrey Event," as the annual prayer service had come to be called. Since the bishop and the Santo family had mutually decided not to allow pilgrims into Audrey's bedroom, this was the only day that Audrey could be seen by the public. Because the Apostolate of a Silent Soul expected a large number of pilgrims, access to the service was tightly controlled. Only young children and accompanying adults would be allowed into the church for the service—the rest would be allowed to view Audrey later in the afternoon. The pilgrims waited patiently until Audrey Santo arrived by ambulance. There was then a rush to catch a glimpse of her as she was brought into the church. When Audrey was pushed through the church on her hospital bed, the congregation stood in reverence.

The first part of the service was the formal healing liturgy. The parish priest, Father Tom Foley, gave the sermon. He did not mention Audrey Santo by name. He did not refer to her case or the phenomena associated with her. Instead, Father Foley challenged those who "had come in search of a miracle." After the sermon, there was an anointing of those in need of healing. Father Foley then left the altar. The second part of the service did not have priests in conspicuous attendance. The second part of the service was led by Marty Rotella, a popular Catholic singer, wearing a Padre Pio t-shirt under his sport's jacket. His songs were accompanied by vigorous clapping from the audience. A group of children then came to the front of the church and sang, without irony, the Protestant standard "The B-I-B-L-E, that's the book for me." The singer then motioned to the ushers to distribute pink plastic rosary beads to all those in attendance. These rosary beads had been placed in Audrey's bedroom. As the beads were distributed, Marty Rotella declared, "Now all of you are in union with this wonderful person, Audrey Santo."

After the distribution of the rosary beads, pilgrims lined up to see Audrey Santo. Audrey had been placed in a room next to a tabernacle on the right side of the altar. There was a transparent plastic sheet, resembling a large shower curtain that separated Audrey from the pilgrims. Audrey was lying on her bed, with her nurse gently stroking her hair, and Linda Santo at the foot of the bed, her arms outstretched. Pilgrims would then file by, some taking the time to kneel before Audrey and to touch crucifixes to the transparent plastic boundary that remained between them and Audrey (figure 14.9). The static positioning of Audrey, flanked by her nurse and mother, was akin to a tableau vivant, a mother and daughter pietà. The plastic sheet was thus not unlike glass lunette of a monstrance or the screen of a television.

The carefully arranged display of Audrey Santo was often punctuated by the rather rambunctious play of children on and around her bed. Indeed, apart from Audrey herself, the welfare of children was the focal point of the entire service. Throughout the church that day were collages of pictures of children, often with accompanying letters that expressed sympathy for Audrey and her family. Upon closer inspection, it was clear that many of these children pictured were no longer alive, for many of them had written Audrey while they themselves were suffering from terminal illnesses. The whole structure of the service seemed to suggest, as passive and innocent victims, children are the ones who have the agency to mediate between heaven and earth.

With the distribution of the rosary beads, the intent of the service was not just to create a kind of confraternity of sufferers, but a veritable family of sufferers. Clifford Geertz has argued that ritual functions to integrate the social and cultural world of participants[2] or, in Catherine Bell's observation in her discussion of Geertz, "to fuse their sense of order with their affective dispositions."[3] The very real *pathos* of suffering children and their families was, to be sure, the "affective disposition" that united participants in the "Audrey Event." This affective disposition was, in turn, focalized upon the Audrey Santo "pietà vivant," a spectacle testifying to the silent agency of the victim soul.[4] In order to fulfill this role, the now nineteen-year-old Audrey Santo thus remains in an eternal childhood, a childhood emphasized by the artifacts of childhood which are always placed around her (figure 14.10). During the "Audrey Event," pilgrims would first walk in front of the altar and then the tabernacle before coming before Audrey herself. The sacrifice of the altar then is not the end or the focus of the service. Instead Audrey herself becomes the culmination a pilgrimage that passes by, but does not remain with, Christ as the clerically consecrated Eucharistic host.

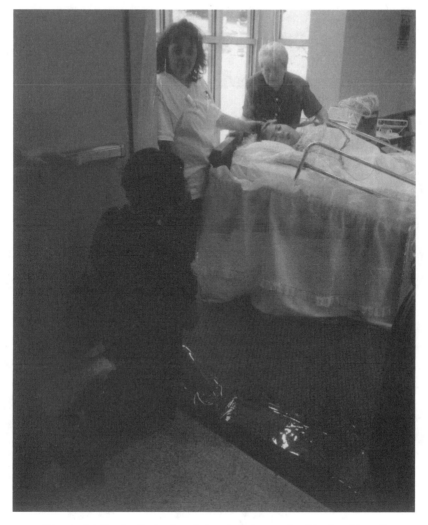

Figure 14.9   A pilgrim kneels in adoration at the "Audrey Event"

PERFORMANCES

As the late Valerio Valeri argued, ritual is also about programmed learning and "the apperception of codes."[5] What was perhaps most striking about the activities surrounding "The Audrey Event" was how much they demonstrated the media's successful "apperception" of the religious and social codes specific to the ritualized context. Univision and 20/20 were themselves performing as part of their coverage of the Audrey Santo phenomenon. Not only did their approaches reflect the sensibilities of their respective audiences, the camera crews and correspondents performed for the members of the Apostolate of a Silent Soul whose authority controlled access to Audrey

The image on the door sign reads:

Audrey

"NOBLE AND STRONG"

Trust in the Lord forever, for the Lord God is an everlasting rock.
—Isaiah 26:4

Figure 14.10 Audrey Santo's bedroom door

Santo herself. The media presence thus confirmed and even augmented this central Massachusetts performance of the miraculous.

The television media were not the only ones performing in relation to the Apostolate of a Silent Soul. My sister, Julia Schmalz, took the photographs for this article. Even though we both had our professional titles, with Julia the assistant director of photography for *USA Today* and me a professor, we were always referred to as "the brother and sister team" by the other media. Since that was the title given to us, that was the role we assumed, and thus apparently mirrored the Apostolate's valorization of the family. But while one of the subtexts of the performance of "The Audrey Event" was the unifying power of suffering, the performance also elided or obscured very real questions that could have been raised about a performance that so celebrated human suffering. Julia, who is responsible for the front-page layout of *USA Today* and edits pictures of everything from bombings in Baghdad to NASCAR races, was drawn to the humanity of Audrey Santo, and the first pictures she took of Audrey were of her face without the various devotional relics and images framing her. I, however, was particularly concerned with the religious paraphernalia that provided the clues to how Audrey Santo should be "read" by those who come to view her. Unlike the cameraman for 20/20, my sister and I were reluctant to move close to Audrey and instead we took shelter behind a long range telephoto lens, except for a moment when I approached Audrey's bed-side. Of course, one of the most pressing and difficult issues in any ethnographic project is the extent to which the research becomes shaped by relations of power often beyond the fieldworker's control.[6] For different reasons, Julia and I were both quite ambivalent of the nature of our "performance" that day.

After the photo shoot in the chapel and Audrey's bedroom, Julia and I returned home. As we were driving home, I asked her, "Do you smell it?" Julia immediately replied, "You mean the incense? Spooky!" When Julia and I went into the Apostolate's chapel for the initial photo shoot, it was filled with incense from the adoration of one of the blood stained hosts. Throughout the day, Julia and I both remarked to each other about the persistence of the smell of incense, evidence perhaps of the power of the olfactory and visual symbols in the Santo chapel. For the media, as well as for some scholars, the Audrey Event and other Catholic phenomena evoke a variety of exotic and nostalgic fragrances. In a context that seems so pervaded by incense, it is a temptation indeed to lose sight of the actors whose performances evoke such resonances of the miraculous.

PART VI

Conclusion: Between Theory and Practice

Joanna E. Ziegler

INTRODUCTION

In this final section of *Practicing Catholic*, the authors return to the themes of performance, practice, and ritual. Performance lies at the heart of ritual, where the body-in-action, the senses, and the mind are all marshaled in a visual, often impressive, and sometimes spectacular display of faith. A number of the essays appearing earlier in this volume approached this material as an arena for scholarly research: Fred Paxton's essay on the history of affective and therapeutic song, music, and architecture in early medieval religious women's lives; Joanne Pierce's study of the churching of women; Bruce Morrill's liturgical theology; and Therese Schroeder-Sheker's reflections on music thanotology and her performance of harp and song to those in *transitus*. All of these people, interestingly, are scholars *and* musicians or performers, and thus they embody the present challenge of fostering the primacy of performance, while also insisting on its centrality to a comprehensive scholarship on ritual.

In this section, we offer insight into how these perspectives function on a more theoretical level. The study of ritual demands that the distinctly artistic protocols involved in ritual be acknowledged and engaged. Yet a paradox lies at the heart of our project because, if we are concerned with the artistic aspects of ritual performance, then we must also be concerned with what is sensuous, intangible, and ephemeral—concerned, that is, with precisely those aspects of ritual that are most perplexing to, if not inconsistent with, scholarly research. The point to keep in mind is that the stage and the page have quite different sorts of expectations and expressions. This has to do with the role of evidence. Where lies the evidence for sensory and ephemeral experience? In other words, the core issue of ritual, its apparently intangible and momentary nature, eludes the assumptions—indeed the objectives and foundations—of modern scholarship.

It is hardly surprising, then, that researchers have steered clear of addressing these sorts of core issues of ritual, lest they be dismissed for engaging in less than scholarly inquiry. There are, however, other possibilities. By recalling ways in which the ancient Greeks thought about religious spectacle, participation, and art (or craft), Christopher Dustin furnishes a model of how to think theoretically about embodied ritual. He returns to ancient sources for help in doing this, not out of nostalgia but rather because, for the ancient Greek philosophers, there was no dichotomy between theory and practice. In fact, if anything, artistic practice and participation in religious ritual were believed to be *thinking*—to be "theory." Dustin goes on to examine the sort of knowledge, as conceived by the ancients, that craft (*techne*) such as shipbuilding or weaving (no less than ritual dance or theatrical performance) conveys—knowledge that is not only a means to an end or a product, but an end unto itself.

In his commentary on Dustin's essay, William Stempsey explores Dustin's model as a way of rethinking medicine as science *and* art. He suggests that physicians and patients might benefit from considering their roles in a new way, more sensitive to 'theory' and ritual. And then he raises questions "Medicine," Stempsey contends, "is an endeavor that wonderfully demonstrates the intimate relationship" between *theoria* and *techne*. He looks at the potential for this unique relationship to "open up a new and deeper vision of the meaning of suffering and healing."

While the other authors in Part VI take on the theoretical premises (and promises) of this sort of knowing, I approach the matter in the essay that follows by asking how performance can be seen as part of scholarship and, inversely, how scholarship may inherently constitute a performance. And here, of course, by scholarship I mean the body of learning and especially of research available in a particular field. Ritual's embodied or sensuous nature, its physical immediacy, if you will is not in question. Rather, my question is what style of writing can bring to life such physical and sensory phenomena— embedded in history's archaic past, no less than in the ephemeral moments of the present action of ritual—thereby preserving the true nature of performance. Johan's Huizinga's controversial notion of "historical sensation" as a valid (and promising) form of historical inquiry furnishes the case study from which to examine further these questions.

Finally, included are Katherine M. McElaney's reflections on the "Practicing Catholic" conference, delivered at Evening Prayer (Vespers), on the final day. This event embodied the 'theory' at work, with song and organ music, prayer, and a reflective atmosphere created by these artistic and spiritual forms. Ms. McElaney, Director of Campus Ministry at Holy Cross College, reminded the scholars present—in her meditative, poetic words—of the immediate and affective dimension of believed prayer and ritual—the object of our scholarly inquiry. At that special time of Vespers, observers and ritual process merged as living affirmation of precisely the sort of knowledge we seek to understand further in this volume. We researchers became, for a very brief while, *participants* (even when not believers) in the artistic, sensory, and ephemeral forms of the ritual. As participants—as more than mere detached observers, which we were by virtue either of belief or research practice at that time—we were informed and affected by the ritual with a sort of knowledge whose nature and import inform the questions upon which the *Practicing Catholic* conference and this book are founded.

There finally remains as well, and at least as importantly, the issue of how ritual performance itself—distinct from a description and analysis of the ritual activity—can play a legitimate role in scholarship, that is to say, ritual performance itself as an aspect of scholarship versus the study of ritual as scholarship.

It would seem obvious that participation in ritual performance by a scholar seeking understanding and enlightenment of and about the ritual in question and its role in the fabric of human experience would advance that understanding in a manner and to a degree not attainable in any other way. Thus, the ritual itself must assume a more serious and rightful place in the study in a deeply significant manner. The ritual itself, and opportunity to experience it directly—through actual attendance—must inform and become an indispensable part of the scholarship surrounding the subject in question.

Scholarship and/as Performance: The Case of Johan Huizinga and His Concept of "Historical Sensation"

Joanna E. Ziegler

In the pages that follow, we will explore a celebrated example of one scholar who strove, with ambiguous success, to put aesthetics—the "artistic"—into serious collaboration with scholarship. I refer to the Dutch historian, Johan Huizinga (1872–1945), the recurring subject of robust debate over matters of art and scholarship. The question following Huizinga's writings have centered on whether or not he is a "real" historian. Huizinga's *Herfsttij der Middeleeuwen: Studie over levens- en gedachtenvormen der veertiende en vijftiende eeuw in Frankrijk en de Nederlanden*.[1] *The Waning of the Middle Ages*, as hereafter it is referred to, has been read by great numbers of undergraduates for generations. Historians ask, however: is it history? Is it useful for anything other than displaying the dazzling stylistic and intellectual idiosyncrasies—and brilliance, some would contend—of the author? Indeed, conceived in total, Huizinga's work—with the possible exception of his influential study of civilization and "play," *Homo Ludens* (1938)—epitomizes the most lamentable reception a scholar can face: to be exceptionally popular but academically questionable.

Huizinga's reception has been well covered, in particular by Bryce D. Lyon[2] and Edward Peters and Walter P. Simons,[3] and the main aspects of that revealing history provide the groundwork for what follows in this chapter. Generally speaking, *The Waning of the Middle Ages* has seemed to elude traditional categories of scholarship. Much like Henry Adams' equally popular and widely read *Mont-Saint-Michel and Chartres*, Huizinga's *Waning of the Middle Ages* covers so many academic disciplines as to be nearly impossible to categorize: history, art history, poetry, literature, theology, history of devotion, and autobiography, to cite but a few of the possible catalogue headings. One is reminded in this of a more recent example; many of Gore Vidal's books have inspired readers to grapple with knotty historical matters—and yet no card-carrying historian would characterize these works as true scholarship. The reasons why "public intellectuals" such as Vidal are so often dismissed by academics lie well beyond the scope of this essay; there is relevance to the questions at hand. We focus on Huizinga's work in order to address one such question: how this contest, commonly cast as being between fact and fiction, "science" and intuition, or reason and emotion impacts, in particular, our comprehensive understanding of the performance of ritual.

The image Huizinga ultimately invokes is one of the outsider.[4] This is no simple matter, for outsiders to academic disciplines often are viewed (by insiders) as personally prone to—perhaps even provoking—alienation. It is true that Huizinga saw himself as an outsider to his discipline, but this had to do with intellectual matters. Huizinga sought an historical truth that was fundamentally different from his peers: the sensuous aspects of history—its aural and visual stimuli—fascinated him.[5] Where historians of his time were concerned with social and economic phenomena that could be documented in the official record, Huizinga wandered about the medieval town in search of sights, smells, and sounds, of people living, dancing, praying, and dying— in search of *forms*, that is to say, the outer, the artful and artistic, expressions and manifestations of life.

These pursuits brought Huizinga straight into conflict with his peer practitioners of history. How historians later decipher this conflict is enlightening, for they tend to view the 'problem' in Huizinga's personality, rather than the nature and demands of his historical interests. In other words, Huizinga's psychological makeup (his personal tendency to isolation) has been seen to account for his alternative and unconventional vision of history—not, it should be emphasized, that the history he believed in necessitated a different methodology of pursuit.

As the present book brings to the foreground, the nature of performance— of the forms of living ritual—does indeed challenge researchers with problems that are anything but uncomplicated or trouble free. Researchers, as we have read often in this study, must push beyond the boundaries that define the academic disciplines and that render the pursuits within them as both recognizable and acceptable. Huizinga is a classic example, which in his case meant that he was one voice confronting "the many." And what "the many" heard was critique, rebuke, warning, even a "professed distaste for 'scientific,' or positivist history. . . . He was not, he once said, a proper historical researcher."[6] Seeing this from Huizinga's perspective, the problem was rather that contemporary historical methodology was not of much help to him. In fact, Huizinga found it something of a hindrance.[7] Official records, he believed from early on in his career, could not reveal the sensuousness of the past. Hence his turn for help—and an immensely creative turn it was!— to everything his experience and knowledge could muster, whether or not it was identifiable by, or acceptable to, the dominant praxis of historical scholarship. Indian culture, Indo-European linguistics, the history of art, the activity in contemporary Modern art circles with modes of synesthesia (the association of one sense with another), anthropology, and psychology all come into play. In this regard, *Practicing Catholic*, by its interdisciplinary and inclusive nature, more than 85 years later validates both Huizinga's vision and his methodology.

Reevaluating Huizinga's interdisciplinarity yields a clearer picture of his contribution, as well as his value, to the present study. Keep in mind that the *official* history of Huizinga has been written by *official* historians. This is something like the history of the medieval church having been written by the clergy. To call a discipline to task, as Huizinga did, for what it cannot perform will naturally meet resistance, if not outright hostility, by those at whom one points. Yet, since previous critics for the most part thus far have been the ones to relate (and generally decry) Huizinga's accomplishments, it seems, then, that a more balanced history remains to be fleshed out by scholars who themselves strive to pursue similar paths to historical truth.[8] My appraisal of Huizinga's case here, as instructive for the methodological quest entailed in the *Practicing Catholic* project, also may serve as one contribution to that balanced view.

Literary and art historians, as opposed to historians per se; have taken to Huizinga's methods, which makes sense given his emphases on the artistic manifestations of late medieval life. This, however, is double-edged: it demonstrates the utility and adaptability, even importance of his approach, but to practitioners who are *not* themselves historians. Huizinga's own artistry, marshaled in hopes of grasping the historical forms of art, is the source of *The Waning of the Middle Ages* extraordinary accomplishment *and* its most questionable utility as history. Perhaps, for the comfort of documentary historians, Huizinga had been too susceptible to the world beyond the study walls. His innate and keen historical sensitivity to *what art really was* derived, paradoxically, from his empathic responsiveness to currents in his own culture. Experience, rooted in his very world, was what interested him and he mobilized various means to help him discover it in the past. Unfortunately, both for Huizinga and his methodology, the discipline of history has not quite managed to accommodate or endorse those discoveries with much enthusiasm.

For the study of ritual—with its living forms and embodied experience in history and in the present—Huizinga's example needs to be held strong and firm before our eyes. What sorts of things interested him, helped him, and struck him about the experience of contemporary life and its resonance with artistic form? It will be worth quoting Huizinga at length to gain a good sense of what's at stake, what interests him, and how he goes about communicating it:

> The contrast between silence and sound, darkness and light, like that between summer and winter, was more strongly marked than it is in our lives. The modern town hardly knows silence or darkness in their purity, nor the effect of a solitary light or a single distant cry.
>
> All things presenting themselves to the mind in violent contrasts and impressive forms, lent a tone of excitement and of passion to everyday life and tended to produce that perpetual oscillation between despair and distracted joy, between cruelty and pious tenderness which characterize life in the Middle Ages.

> One sound rose ceaselessly above the noises of busy life and lifted all things unto a sphere of order and serenity: the sound of bells. The bells were in daily life like good spirits, which by their familiar voices, now called upon the citizens to mourn and now to rejoice, now warned them of danger, now exhorted them to piety. They were known by their names: big Jacqueline, or the bell Roland. Every one knew the difference in meaning of the various ways of ringing. However continuous the ringing of the bells, people would seem not to have become blunted to the effect of their sound.[9]

How visceral, how evocative, keying our senses up to the intense emotional level of the content itself.

Of course it makes perfect sense in retrospect that someone of Huizinga's ready and passionate nature would be conscious of living in a world undergoing its own redefinition, being set in motion by manmade changes in light and darkness. This consciousness is at work in his broad, synthesizing, and inclusive grasp of Medieval culture, a culture that he sees shaped by the form of everyday life—a form that results from, among other things, the character of light and sound. Surprisingly, studies of light and sound as integral to the formation of cultural identity have emerged only recently as worthy of study, some 86 years after *The Waning of the Middle Ages* (the original Dutch appeared in 1919). Certain art historians are seriously researching Modern culture conditioned by the radical change in light and darkness—the change to a world potentially, if artificially, always light.[10] Though medieval culture did not witness a transformation to electricity, life was no less conditioned by light and sound, darkness and silence than Modernity was—and perhaps it was even more responsive to the nuance of day and night than Modern culture was. Yet, light and darkness in the Middle Ages is not a topic of serious intellectual inquiry—except, that is, in the case of Huizinga.[11]

Given our present concern in *Practicing Catholic* with how to understand and interpret sensory experience in Catholic ritual, let us take a moment to return to Huizinga's discussion of sound. "One sound rose ceaselessly," he writes, "above the noises of busy life and lifted all things unto a sphere of order and serenity: the sound of the bells." Would we really wish to contest that sound is important to culture? Does it not frame movement and interactions socially as well as personally? It is remarkable sociologically, for instance, that our present-day lives accommodate—are even framed by—a barrage of incessant and oftentimes offensive sounds: cars, motorcycles, hard rock, and rap music, TV ads and pop-ups, computer dinging, public cursing, cellphone 'texting' and talking on the streets and in public places, the ceaseless mindless babble of our age. Some of this, as Vicente Rafael has shown in his essay on "texting" in chapter 12, is responsible for fundamental shifts in the practice of Christianity.

Central to Modernity, too, were the tremendous changes in terms of sound, then brought on by the advent of the steam engine—particularly the steam locomotive, an explosive, raging, and thundering sound evoked so powerfully in the film, *Doctor Zhivago*. Modernity had its own "documentation" of this change in Claude Monet's painting of *Gare Saint-Lazare* (Musee d'Orsay, 1877), exhibited as *Le Chemin de fer* (the railway).[12] Any distinctiveness to the motifs (train, station, travelers) has been obscured by the steam, a dense vapor, which Monet's brush converts from haze to impervious substance. Monet's form not only materializes the sight of steam, but also strongly evokes (synesthesia) its sound, as well. No wonder that the picture became a sort of icon of modern life. I raise this example because it sheds light on Huizinga's perspicacity and imagination. He was deeply insightful about the sorts of elements of lived experience—the "real" elements of being alive—that scholars and artists of Modern life have assiduously observed.

Huizinga brought this same sort of sensory and artistic sensitivity to his thinking about the later Middle Ages. Yet why, one has to wonder, is it not also seen as capturing the phenomenal nature of historical truth? If one could "hear" the sounds of the past, how much more discerning and precise would our history be—how much more palpable would the essence of life in the past be? This was what Huizinga called "historical sensation,"[13] which brings us to the issue of writing *about* art historically versus historical writing *as* art.

From his friends and contemporaries in the art world, Huizinga learned as much about how to communicate and preserve this "historical sensation" as he did from written chronicle and narrative. Clearly, the sources for such a history of the senses and of the ephemeral will have to be eccentric, that is, non-traditional or non-official. Huizinga himself noted

> A scientific historian of the Middle Ages, relying first and foremost on official documents, which rarely refer to the passions, except violence and cupidity, occasionally runs the risk of neglecting the difference of tone between the life of the expiring Middle Ages and that of our own days. Such documents would sometimes make us forget the vehement pathos of medieval life, of which the chroniclers, however defective as to material facts, always keep us in mind.[14]

This search for pertinent evidence—as well as Huizinga's assessment of evidence—is one of his unique capacities.

Well-crafted writing, visual and visceral, is central to Huizinga's project. Arguably, it is the fundamental component of his method. Passionate, vehement, energized, a faithful and exacting description of sights and sounds, Huizinga's style triggers in the reader sensations that are analogous to the ones he is describing. It is a work of art itself and, in that, prompts the reader to participate in the artistic historical content, to be absorbed by the sensory imagination as it wraps itself around the verbal depictions.

Huizinga's ability to engage us this way is not surprising, given his interest in synesthesia—where the experience of one sense triggers that of another. Huizinga's contemporaries in art and music were wildly interested in synesthesia, which possibly received its most public and influential expression in the epic operas of Richard Wagner, embodying the *Gesamtkunstwerk*, or total work of art. Wagnerism spread rapidly across the European continent and into many of the *avante garde* art circles by the turn of the century, from

Monet to Kandinsky, Scriabin to Whistler.[15] Ultimately, synesthesia was far more than simply "fashionable." It gave rise to non-representational and abstract art—painting, music, poetry. Abstraction—the hallmark of Modernity's radical transformation in sight and sound—was hardly an idiosyncratic or passing fancy. Many academics, however, were less receptive than artists to this constituent of Modernism, something made readily clear by the following anecdote: When Huizinga proposed to study Indo-European linguistics by employing synesthesia, "His thesis advisor rejected the project as 'unscientific'."[6]

This lifelong interest in synesthesia—correspondence among the senses—accompanied Huizinga in the writing of *The Waning of the Middle Ages*. What is important to the readers of *Practicing Catholic* is that Huizinga used synesthesia as a writing device—a methodological tool that would trigger sensory and emotional response in the reader. Huizinga's writing, it seems, intentionally set about to evoke correspondences in us, as the instrument for making the sensory material present and alive, a living force in history, much the way our exploration of ritual strives to do in this study.

Peters and Simons find history currently taking a "narrative turn" that may sensitize the discipline to Huizinga's methodology.[17] I concur. Work of the sort happening in this book must be done before artistic methods—Huizinga's writing style, for instance—are at parity with currently accepted scholarship. Receptive and sensitive as they are to Huizinga's talent, Peters and Simons nonetheless corroborate the present disposition of the field of history when they describe Huizinga's work as "simply *too well written* to be real history."[18]

Huizinga is not the only scholar to "suffer" an excess of literary talent. Most academic specialists look skeptically on exceptional or idiosyncratic writing styles. A gifted writer still is somewhat suspect in the academic community. To craft elegant and refined prose can be something of a bane, because—in that view—it calls into question one's clear-headedness and sound rational inquiry. Wilhelm Voege also comes to mind, whose brilliant and foundational analyses of gothic sculpture were eclipsed by his fervent, impassioned, highly personal style of writing.[19] Not surprisingly, Huizinga had no interest in Voege's friend and opposite number, the empiricist Karl Lamprecht. Lyon attributes this to Huizinga's dislike of social science, "especially sociology of the American variety . . .,"[20] the discipline very much at the heart of the discussions in this book. Lyon submits the problem this way: "[Huizinga's] path to historical truth and understanding is one that only he or a few can tread."[21] In other words, great writing obstructs one of the cardinal characteristics and goals of scholarship: its potential to initiate a school and attract a following, a community of practitioners.[22]

Thus we come closer to the heart of the matter for *Practicing Catholic* and for the methodological challenges we face. Consider the words commonly used by historians to characterize—indeed to situate academically—*The Waning of the Middle Ages*: poetic, intuitive, aesthetic, evocative, and emotional. These concepts are perceived by most academics as being directly at odds with the highest aims of scholarly methods: to be rational, scientific, objective (detached), analytical, and empirical. To persist in using such terminology, however, is to keep the two approaches eternally opposed, with the one—the scientific—ultimately dominating the course of the other. No wonder that performance—which can scarcely be defined except on Huizinga's terms—has long been kept in the wings of academic relevance, as entertainment, or accessory to academic thinking. This long-standing arrangement is a good candidate for refashioning.

As we proceed to think about this situation anew, keep in mind the position of the official practitioners of the objectivist sort of history regarding the Huizinga-style historical writing. Essentially, that it is too poetic, too well written. Huizinga's writing *is* poetic, and his ability to picture the past stems from his keen awareness of artistic phenomena. As Lyon puts it so frankly and precisely: "Historians and scholars in related disciplines have shied away from him. Why? Because to use him one would have to develop or acquire his unusual mental, spiritual, and emotional gifts, obviously a difficult or impossible task."[23] Well said. Poetry and art in any form do demand our full participation—something that absolutely negates the mind-body dichotomy that is implicit in the art versus science opposition. This intentionally engaging "style," as we soon will read, not only *is* but should be a methodology in historical writing—not "mere" poetry, but the one that we believe harbors great promise for the study of Catholic ritual.

In Part I the editors of this volume proposed thinking about performance as a form of understanding, where we equated it with an "experientialist" apprehension of knowledge—one that originates and is consummated in the "right now," the presence and presentness of the physical and sensory immediacy of the performance, *for the performers as well as the authors* who study them.[24] In the present study, the concern is with performed actions, not only as the symbols or constructed realities they become in studies that take place afterward. Huizinga's prose illustrates the point: in its supreme artistry, Huizinga's writing offers an occasion for readers to be present at a performance of sorts. Writing, as the performance of "historical sensation," is the source of a kind of sensory information that is most fruitfully experienced as an end in itself, and not only as the conveyance of "useful" historical data.

In chapter 16, Dustin considers performance and participation in precisely these terms. He returns to ancient thinkers for whom there was no such dichotomy between theory and practice. If anything, artistic practice *was* thinking—it was "theory." This becomes extremely helpful for a reassessment of a methodology of participation and artistry, like Huizinga's. It puts the "aesthetic approach" in its proper place as having the potential to be "theoretical," in the way the ancients understood theory. Dustin insists that originally there had been no dichotomy between doing and knowing, between participation and theory, between contemplation and action. Therefore, his own theory has the potential to unravel and refashion one of the knottiest problems for students of ritual: to discern the connection between thought and action.

Huizinga is a striking example of a scholar who has worked through some important facets of what we in this volume seek in the way of methodology. He explored practice and performance of ritual in history: first, by looking at the *texts* with great powers of observation, as acute as an art connoisseur with a magnifying glass before an image; and, second, by his narrative style. Huizinga was interested in unearthing not only the patterns or sequences of ritual, or the identification and social status of the ritual actors or participants and players. More, he wanted to penetrate *the form*—the visual appearance—of persons and bodies, as well as the spaces they occupied. He "saw" the past—and we may think of that verb in its most literal terms—as one would "see" a painting. The past for him was a "presence," acting upon the senses and demanding the participation of the historian (or the reader) as sentient spectator. Huizinga narrated this history with artistic means by which the reader's experience would coincide, as it were, with the phenomenal content. To follow Huizinga's example and adopt his method for retrieving and conveying the physical forms of the ritual past, scholars have the potential to become participant and researcher, observer and beholder—unities that preserve the authenticity of the "presentness" that is central to the ritual experience.[25]

My quest at the outset was to identify a style of writing that can bring to life the physical and sensory phenomena—to be found in history's archaic past, no less than in the ephemeral moments of the present action of ritual—and thereby to preserve the true nature of performance. Therese Schroeder-Sheker in chapter 6 offers a rare instance—indeed a model—of this style. This method holds out the promise of disclosing the affinities of art and science, intuition and reason, making and thinking, performing and theory. If scholars embrace or at least entertain the potential for sensory data to be experienced via writing, they will be better equipped to deal with "living" data in specific ways that can yield insight into this issue of "participative knowledge."[26] This knowledge is, after all, the heart of the theological worldview. Keep in mind that Catholic ritual ultimately comes down to divine and hence transformative worship. With Catholics ritual, we are talking about "the religious."

The matter of religion may be the very thing that confounds historians and prevents them from accepting Huizinga's methodology and ideas. And here we recall Lyon's observation that to adopt Huizinga's approach "one would have to develop or acquire his unusual mental, spiritual, and emotional gifts, obviously a difficult or impossible task." Huizinga was a "deeply religious man, convinced of the fundamentality of spiritual values, [who] practiced what he preached."

> After a marvelously clairvoyant explanation of the Dutch golden age in the seventeenth century, he concluded that it was born by accident, that it was not a reflection of western civilization but was an exception and deviation that he described as a gift of God.[27]

Was it, then, simply a matter of Huizinga's idiosyncratic style, or his deep religiosity that for many has thrown into question his credentials as an historian?

Huizinga probed the matter of God directly and without embarrassment. This patent embrace of religious and ethical values accounts, more than anything else, I believe, for Huizinga's alienation from the academic specialists in his profession. Few things cause scholars—other than theologians—as much unease as talk about God. Yet, for studying the history and practice of Catholic ritual in any comprehensive or meaningful way, scholars cannot turn away from what is most deeply at stake in that practice—the matter of God and "the religious."

Huizinga maintained a commitment to the manifestation of divine order, or virtue, which for him, and the ancients to whom we presently turn, cannot be partitioned or dismembered according to intellectual (rational) versus personal (emotional or intuitive) lines. Lyon was correct in his assertion about the need to comprehend Huizinga's unusual gifts. We should indeed aspire to an engagement with Huizinga's mental, spiritual, and emotional landscape, however challenging the task. But we must do so, not in order to participate in what some consider Huizinga's "bizarre eccentricity," but because the failure to recognize and accommodate such gifts can only result in continued lost insight into the nature of knowledge in all its fullness and the range of authentic human experience.

CHAPTER 16

The Liturgy of Theory

Christopher A. Dustin

THEORY AND PRACTICE

Theories of liturgy abound.[1] What could it mean to talk about the liturgy of theory? *Leitourgia* originally meant "public service" or, more literally, public work (*leitos-ergon*) of a sort that was customarily associated with religious festivals. "Liturgy" today refers almost exclusively to the concrete practices of divine worship. To "theorize" about these practices is to observe and reflect upon them. Liturgy is practical, something one does (or that many do). Theory is, as we say, theoretical. It, too, is something one does. But if we see it as involving its own forms of activity, that is because we also see it as essentially removed from the practices it is reflecting upon. To theorize about religious practice is not itself a form of divine worship.

Or so we assume. My aim, in talking about the liturgy of theory, is to dislodge the conceptualizations on which this assumption is based. Since these conceptualizations are characteristically modern, any effort to dislodge them will have to draw, recollectively, on pre-modern (indeed, pre-Christian) sources. The primary motivation behind this effort is to gain a deeper understanding of what it could mean to talk about something we seem to have little trouble talking about. If the liturgy of theory is difficult for us to conceptualize, "contemplative practice" should be just as difficult. A great deal has been said about the sense in which contemplation is itself an activity, something one "does." But there is still room to wonder about what it could mean to talk about contemplation as being practical. There is, I believe, a pressing need to wonder about what it could still mean to say, with Josef Pieper, that

> Whenever in reflective and receptive contemplation we touch, even remotely, the core of all things, the hidden, ultimate reason of the living universe, the divine foundation of all that Is . . . whenever and wherever we thus behold the very essence of reality—there is an activity that is meaningful in itself taking place. Such reaching out in contemplation to the root and foundation of all that is, to the archetypes of all things, this activity . . . can happen in countless actual forms.[2]

The same conceptual gap that separates liturgy from theory, doing from thinking, service (or work) from speculation, has left contemplation—Pieper's "attitude of receptive observation"—stranded on the shores of the theoretical. This is most obvious where contemplation takes the form of philosophical reflection, which, for Aristotle, was not only the study of divine things but was itself a divine activity or way of life.[3] The idea that, in philosophizing, one is "just thinking"—its so-called impracticality—has led to its perceived irrelevance for life. Philosophy has now drifted almost entirely from its religious (and even its contemplative) origins. But forms of contemplative activity that are still more closely associated with religious practice are also viewed in this way. "To contemplate," Pieper says, "means first of all *to see*."[4] In response to the question, "what is your purpose in living?", the Greek philosopher Anaxagoras was supposed to have said: "*to behold* the sun, the moon, and the heavens."[5] How are we to understand, let alone embrace, such an "impractical" answer to such a vital question? How could we make practical sense of Teilhard de Chardin's claim that "all life is contained in the act of seeing"?[6]

We confront the same obstacles to understanding and to practical acceptance when it comes to the elements of Benedictine monasticism that Therese Schroeder-Sheker draws upon in her work. In her remarkable account of the Chalice of Repose project, she notes the centrality, to Cluniac spirituality, of the contemplation of the beautiful.

> The human being needed exposure to beauty in order to become inwardly beautiful, and in becoming inwardly radiant and beautiful, one integrated beauty back into the world. . . . [The monastic] community lived within a spiritual milieu wherein adoration was expressed, in addition to prayer and liturgy, through the maintenance, cultivation, and refinement of beauty. At the mystical level, one was encouraged to experience the countenance of God in the experience of beauty.[7]

In this context, beauty was not just an abstract idea. It was embodied in architecture, music, and "countless actual forms." Within the Cluniac community, beauty *mattered*—in the sense both of its spiritual importance and of its physical maintenance and perception—as something to be experienced concretely or "seen" in Pieper's sense.

Schroeder-Sheker is right in observing that beauty no longer matters, in this sense, for us, and that this is problematic. The problem is not simply one of secularization. It stems from the difficulty we have conceptualizing the centrality of contemplation to the practice of religious faith. It stems, at the same time, from the difficulty we have conceptualizing the centrality of practice to contemplation itself. It is to this aspect of the problem that I would like to devote some attention, in part because it has received less attention than the other, but also because I (along with Joanna Ziegler) take it to be more fundamental. It offers a way into our problem that might point to a way out.

One might object that this can only be a way *back*, and in a certain sense this is true. Pieper and Schroeder-Sheker are both appealing to historically remote practices and ideas. Schroeder-Sheker is explicit in her acknowledgment of the role history (both the historical past and the theoretical discipline) plays in her work. Her own effort to transform contemporary attitudes and practices raises a question that is crucial for any philosophical attempt to counter modern forms of understanding with ancient ones: what does it mean to "return" to Benedictine monasticism as it is documented in the manuscript tradition, to return (as I shall do here) to the "original" meanings of words, or to forms of experience and understanding as they are expressed in ancient writings? What does it mean to acknowledge historical sources, and in what sense might they still be "acknowledged" as "sources"? Can it mean anything more than their being "known" in the (modern) theoretical sense, or can they still be drawn upon in a way that allows for a sense of indebtedness? If the hermeneutic revisitation of the older meanings of words we still use is basic to what Schroeder-Sheker calls "contemplative scholarship," this practice would have to involve more than just a cognitive (or nostalgic) looking back. That ancient sources can be "recalled" in a vital and not just a narrowly documentary way cannot be ruled out in advance. It depends on how we conceive of our own situation. There is a difference between not knowing what something once meant and having forgotten what it originally means.

THEORIA

What could it mean to say that one's purpose in living is "to behold"? The phrase Anaxagoras used was *eis theorian*. Our word "theory" comes from the Greek *theoria*, of which the Latin *contemplatio* was a translation. It seems appropriate, then, that contemplation be understood as "theoretical." But what does this originally mean? Must it be the opposite of "practical"?

As Indra McEwen has pointed out, modern interpretations of *theoria* tend to emphasize its nonparticipatory, speculative aspect.[8] Such interpretations read backwards from the modern sense of theory as detached (scientific) observation or analysis. They find support in the derivation of *theoria* from *thea* (outward appearance or show, as in "theatre") and *horao* (to look at or examine something, closely and attentively). With a view to its primary meaning, *theoria* is perhaps best translated as "spectating" and *theoros* (theorist) as "spectator." But care must be taken in understanding the spectatorial attitude of the *theoros*. A *theoros* is someone who sees, but this seeing does not necessarily imply detachment in the way that a theoretical stance is supposed to be detached. *Theoroi* were, most commonly, ambassadors to sacred festivals who departed (and were in that sense separated) from their native cities. The goal of these emissaries was to learn from what they saw. They were looking for knowledge, or understanding. But while the assumption has been that these "theorists" observed without participating, according to McEwen, the ancient sources "show that many *theoroi* did in fact participate" in these public spectacles "by offering sacrifices, and by taking part in the dances and games" that formed an integral part of the practice of divine worship.[9]

To recall the original meaning of "theory" is to recall the original meaning of the human activity of theorizing, grounded as it is in the experience of *theoria*—not a matter of detached observation or purely cognitive analysis, but a performative spectacle in which one takes part with one's body as well as one's mind, with one's senses and emotions as well as what we narrowly conceive of as thoughts. "Theoretical" seeing was active and experientially engaged. The *theoros* did not just examine, but was literally and figuratively moved by what he saw.

It should be emphasized that these spectacles were not just visual. Music and dance (along with theatrical performances) were essential components. And while theoretical spectacles were usually, as a matter of historical fact, centered around religious festivals, *theoria* was understood as religious in a profounder sense. As we know, the Greek *theá* (with the accent on the second syllable) also means goddess. The *theá* of "theatre" could also be read as the *theá* of "theology." Ancient etymologists tended to assume that this was in fact the root of *theoria*, and that a *theoros* was someone who performed a service to, attended, or cared for (*ora*) a god.[10] Modern linguists tend to reject these ancient readings, together with the implications that philosophers like Martin Heidegger draw from them. But if we bear in mind that accents were not introduced into the Greek language until the third century BC, and that their introduction may not so much reflect as effect a differentiation between elements of meaning that were experienced as belonging together, we do better if we attempt to understand the root of *theoria* as being both divine and spectacular, and understand "theory" as originating in a seeing that was itself a form of worship. Heidegger's readings of *theorein* (*thean horan*) as "to look attentively on the outward appearance wherein what presences become visible and, through such . . . seeing, to linger with it," and of *theoria* as "the reverent paying heed to the unconcealment of what presences" are invitations to do just that.[11]

The ability not just to examine or explain but to gaze attentively upon— to dwell with—the outward appearances in which "the core of all things, the hidden . . . foundation of all that is" is made visible, is what Pieper means by contemplative activity. By harboring mystery, such spectacles move us to wonder.[12] In Homer, the verb *theaomai* means "to gaze upon with wonder" or to see with wondering eyes. Both the verb *thaumazein* (to wonder, or marvel), and the noun *thauma* (a wonder, or marvel) are closely related to *theaomai*, and thus to *theoria*. If it is the mind that thinks, McEwen notes, in Homer it is the eyes that wonder. Wonder wants a spectacle. This is the origin of theory. And while we are used to thinking that this pre-Socratic understanding has given way to another in Plato, we might recall how Plato's *Republic* begins: Socrates leaves the city proper and goes down to the Pireaus to attend a religious festival. He wanted to say a prayer to the goddess as well to behold the spectacle. The word Plato uses, to describe what Socrates set out to do, is *theasasthai*. Socrates is a *theoros*, one who goes to see and to pray. The opening scene of the *Republic* preserves the unity of these moments. To see, in the ancient sense of *theoria*, *is* to pray. While the "theoretical" discussion that follows—and that Socrates is compelled to engage in—appears to move away from this participatory (and prayerful) vision, and toward a way of seeing that is less experientially engaged (and more purely intellectual, or "Platonic"), it is only an interpretive prejudice that fails to see the connection between its point of origin and its ultimate goal. *Eidos*—the word that is used for what we call a Platonic Form or Idea—is rooted in the Greek words for (and concrete experience of) seeing and being seen. This is a link that our association of ideas with "concepts" has severed. *Eidos* still draws its meaning from its original source in Socrates' characterization of a philosopher as a *philotheamonas*—one who loves the "spectacle" (the "sights and sounds") of truth.[13] If we ourselves were better able to read Plato's text with wondering eyes—attentive to and moved by the particularities of the spectacle he paints in words—we might better understand what he has to say about the practice of philosophy.[14]

Techne

Theoria is, or was, contemplative seeing. While we can begin to understand this as a participatory activity (where one participates in what one sees), the sense in which contemplation is or involves "practice" remains to be understood. It might help to recall that, in Homer, one "sees with wondering eyes" when a spectacle reveals a divine presence or, as McEwen notes, "when the sight beheld is of something particularly well made."[15] A phrase that appears often in the *Iliad* and the *Odyssey* is *thauma idesthai*, "a wonder to behold." As McEwen points out, on every occasion this phrase is used, it describes a beautifully or divinely crafted piece of work.

Just as theory is conceptually opposed to practice, we also tend to distinguish it from mere craft or skill—in the way that botany, say, is distinguished from horticulture. The same is true of contemplation, especially when the contemplative state of the mystic is understood as an utterly passive or purely spontaneous one. Here the difference between contemplative "seeing" and the kind of practice that is associated with the acquisition or application of a craft or skill is even more pronounced. The Greek word for craft (skill or art) is *techne*. Here again, the recollection of origins enables us to see *techne* and *theoria* as more intimately related than we would otherwise take them to be. If *theoria* takes root in the "reverent" seeing of, and wondering at, a beautifully made thing that is in some way an intimation of the divine, *techne* was, as McEwen puts it, "the very revelation of the divine in experience."[16] While the technological has come to be understood in purely instrumental terms, as (in Heidegger's words) "a man-made means to an end established by man"— as a "bringing about" or a "making happen"—ancient sources suggest that *techne* was understood more fundamentally as a making *visible*.[17] The craftsman's activity, according to this ancient understanding, does not involve the imposition of form on matter, or the merely practical application of a body of knowledge (something already known, like an idea in the craftsman's head). What the craftsman "does" is let *kosmos*—order, form, arrangement—*appear* through the making of the artifact. Craft is the revelation of *kosmos*, which is simultaneously discovered (known or seen) and made to appear through the craftsman's activity.[18]

This "making visible" was not a matter of objective representation, but a "realization"—a recognition that is at the same time an actualization, or making real. It is not a product or outcome (the end result of the craftsman's work), but coincides with the actual practice of a particular craft. As McEwen writes,

> The discovery of a pattern seems—to be an inherent feature of the human experience of making. Whether he or she thinks about it or not . . . a person who makes something implicitly assumes the existence of an order or standard of rightness that transcends all recipes and rules of composition. . . . This pattern can be thought of as a single, immutable template to be traced or copied . . . or it can be thought of as a mutable rhythm governing a pattern of movement, like the figure of a dance: a rhythm or order (*kosmos*) that is rediscovered with each new tracing of the figure.[19]

As we know, *kosmos* could also mean adornment or ornament—as in "cosmetic," which for us has assumed the connotation of mere superficiality. In Homeric Greek, *chros* (meaning color or skin) was used to refer to the living body (as opposed to *soma*, for the nonliving body). As such, the living body was understood and experienced as "a surface and bearer of visibility," not in the sense in which we regard skin as mere surface, but in the sense in which visibility radiates being.[20] For the Greeks, *epiphaneia* meant both "surface" and "appearance," but did not carry the meaning that "epiphenomenal" carries for us (where the appearance is distinguished from the reality). What lay—or rather, showed—on the surface was not unreal, nor did it necessarily cover up. As McEwen observes, "when a woman *kosmese* (adorned) herself, she wrapped her *chros* in a second skin or body, in order to bring the living surface-body so clothed to light; to make it appear." When, in Homer, female divinities adorn or literally wrap themselves in *kosmos*, in order to go dancing, the *kosmos* of the dance is seen as a reflection of their own *kosmos*, and *vice versa*.[21] This order, or *kosmos*—which can refer not only to an objective order or arrangement but to an active "ordering" or arranging—is not one that is imposed on brute matter, but one that emerges reciprocally, as the dancer traces the patterns of the dance.

Dance is a craft. So is weaving. In Homeric usage, something that is well crafted, put together or assembled (carefully wrought) was called *daidalon*. In the *Odyssey*, this word is applied frequently to textiles. Textiles are *daidala* when they are tightly woven or well fitted, and display an especially luminous quality—when they "shimmer with dancing light and seem to have a life of their own."[22] Scholars have argued that the iridescent patterns that made a woven cloth *daidalon* were not embroidered on or applied to a material surface that was simply there, like formless matter. They were woven into the surface itself, in such a way that, as the weaver practiced her weaving, "the pattern (*kosmos*) would have appeared *with* the surface of the cloth, whose making would have been an activity that entailed great skill and a highly complex pattern of movement of shuttle over loom."²³ This physical movement would incorporate its own *kosmos*, whose display was not experienced as a merely human production, but as the revelation of an order that was not entirely subject to the human will. If anything, it was the order (rather than the surface of the cloth) that was experienced as "already there," unseen and waiting to be discovered. The word for weaving, or the actual practice of plying the loom, is, in fact, *hyphainein*, which literally means "bring to light." *Hyphainein* is related to *epiphaneia*. Weaving was an epiphany, or unveiling.

The order that *techne* makes visible is not, as we like to say, "merely aesthetic." *Areros* is a very old Greek word meaning well adjusted or perfectly fitted together. It is, McEwen suggests, both the etymological and experiential root of *harmonia*, which in Homer is often applied to the craft of shipbuilding.²⁴ In ship-building, *harmonia* "works," not just insofar as the proper fit or attunement of the joints allows the ship to stay afloat and to trace an orderly course through the water, but also in the way that it makes an otherwise unseen harmony visible. A well-made ship is in visual and functional harmony both with itself and with its surrounding element, whose own *kosmos* or patterns are revealed in its wake. These elemental patterns are made visible in and by the ship's form even when it is not afloat or literally functioning. One might say that, just as the shipbuilder's activity involves working *with*, rather than simply working on, his material (responding creatively to its grain), the artifact itself stands in a similar relationship to its natural environment. It serves, not only as an instrument of conveyance, but as an occasion for revelation and discovery.²⁵

In Homer, the spectacles that are described as *thauma idesthai* (wonders to behold) are all *daidala*—beautifully wrought artifacts. What makes them so "wonderful" is the unseen order they bring to light. This order could be understood (and experienced) as the source or ground, not only of the creative process, but of life itself. Things that are *thauma idesthai* are often so described because they seem to have a life of their own. This is not a life that the craftsman alone bestows. Art or craft is related to giving birth (as *techne* is related to *tiktein*) but is, as Heidegger suggests, an occasion or inducement, rather than a cause. The craftsman is not himself the source of the order that lives in the artifact, but rather, "lets it come forth into presencing."²⁶ The pre-Socratic philosopher Anaximander was a theorist. But he did not just think, or observe from an attitude of contemplative detachment. He was also a craftsman, and is credited with making (if not inventing) a map, a globe, and a sundial. McEwen suggests that Anaximander's "theorizing" be understood to encompass both his cosmological speculations and his practical inventions, that the latter not be understood as mere applications of the former. If, in fashioning a sundial, the craftsman succeeds in making a temporal order visible, he owes his success to something he does not make—the light of the sun, which is made to tell the time only by being interrupted, blocked or concealed. What the craftsman does is to provide the occasion for the sun to cast the shadow that allows *kosmos*—the periodic cycle of hours of the day and seasons of the year- to appear. What the craftsman makes, in fashioning the sundial, is not all of what is made visible. He gives form (*kosmos*) to the artifact, patterning it in a certain way. This is not an arbitrary choice, though it is a creative one. The craftsman can only "create" order by acknowledging, both theoretically and practically, its ultimate source. The *kosmos* that he makes visible, through his work, is one that is not of any human being's making. The "bringing forth into appearance" of *techne*, and the "reverent paying heed" of *theoria*—the beautiful and the divine—are thus joined.

"Practice" and the Liturgy of Theory

If *theoria* involves an attentive seeing, with wondering eyes, of a divine or beautifully made thing, *techne* involves the making visible of something that is seen as divinely made even if it is man-made. The skilled craftsman was himself a *theoros*. His making is grounded in and provides an occasion for contemplative seeing.

The convergence of these sources can help us to understand the deeper sense in which contemplation is or involves practice. *Theoria* is rooted in wonder, and we are unaccustomed to thinking about wonder as something that is "practiced"—either as an activity that is performed regularly or as one that requires preparation (as in practicing a musical instrument). A craft, or skill, is practical in both of these senses, in addition to being "useful." It is routinely practiced, and it takes practice. If we fail to understand the practicality of contemplative seeing, it is because we fail to understand how it is originally related to craft—not in the way that it produces a useful result, but in the way that *techne* itself was originally understood as both a revelation and a realization of the divine.

Just as the *theoros* beholds a spectacle but is not a detached spectator, the artist or craftsman (the "technician" in the original sense of *techne*) is not a mere doer. The Greek word that was used to designate a craftsman's function was *ergon* (task, work, deed). *Ergon* does not refer merely to the particular actions performed by the individual who builds a ship, weaves cloth, dances, or makes music. Nor does it refer to the finished product. The musician's *ergon* consists neither in the movement of fingers across strings, nor in the production of tones. It consists in the activity of making music. Like *kosmon* (which can mean not only order or arrangement but ordering or arranging), *ergon* comprises both the "working" and "the work"—the means and the end—and holds them together in the way that the English word still does, when we use it to refer to an artist's work. *Ergon* refers to an activity from which process and product cannot be separated out.[27] It recalls us to the sense in which *techne* might be what Pieper calls "an activity that is meaningful in itself."

In allowing *kosmos* to appear, the craftsman's work involves both an ordering and a revelation of order. Order is not simply "brought about" by the craftsman. It is what his making brings to appearance or makes visible.

A dance, or a musical performance, is both a technical making and a theoretical spectacle. The order that is revealed is not simply "produced" by the musician's playing or the dancer's dancing. Order and ordering are reciprocal, which we can see if we remind ourselves that the craftsman's activity—the ordering—is itself ordered. The bodily movements of the weaver at the loom, or the harpist at the harp, can be as beautiful to see as the music is to hear or the cloth is to look at and touch. They are—they have to be—as ordered, as carefully arranged, or intricately patterned (as "harmonious") as the finished product. They are not *ordered by* the craftsman or artist, but by the "work." They, too, are an epiphany of *kosmos*. If we take seriously the dual sense of *kosmon* as both order and ordering, and of *ergon* as both process and product, we do better to say, not just that music is a revelation of *kosmos*, but (following Heidegger) that the making of music *is kosmos* "presencing."

This is why it takes practice, both in the sense of regular engagement or participation—doing it over and over, as the shuttle moves over the loom—and in the sense of preparation—the repeated performance, or rehearsal, through which certain capacities or skills are developed or actualized.[28] If the craftsman's activity (*ergon*) is not a mere means, nor is the preparation it requires. Rather than aiming at a separate goal, it only draws one more deeply into that for which one is preparing oneself. One becomes a musician by, as Aristotle would say, performing musical actions—by playing repeatedly. The goal of this "practice" is to make oneself musical, so that one not only produces notes but plays musically (which is what the "making" of music truly involves).[29] What Aristotle said about philosophical contemplation could also be said about craft—that it is a form of human work that connects us, both as spectators and as practicing participants, with God's work.[30] If the "end" of *techne* is the realization of *kosmos*, then the practice for and of such work is practice for and of a kind of seeing that is at once contemplative and productive (to play musically, one must hear musically). The requirement that its performance be regular and repetitive is not just a matter of efficiency. The regularity of the practice of both *techne* and *theoria* is the regularity of ritual. *Techne* involves the formation, not only of an object or artifact, but of the participant or performer.[31] Just as the patterns that the weaver weaves emerge along with the surface of the cloth, there is an emergence of order in the craftsman, as motions are repeated, become habitual, or come together "harmoniously" (like the threads of the woven cloth). The formation that brings order to light in the craftsman is not merely physical. It can be seen as having the same divine source as the patterns the weaver brings to light in the cloth. The *kosmos* (adornment) in which dancers wrapped themselves—an "ordered second skin"—was seen both as reflecting, and as reflected by, the order of their dance. As *kosmos* clothes the body to bring it to appearance, the *kosmos* of the dance was itself seen to clothe the ground so as to make it appear.[32] The dancer's movements function, then, in the way that Anaximander's sundial functioned. They bring the ultimate source of their own order to light.

If the ancient craftsman was himself a *theoros* (a seer, or spectator), then we can begin to understand the sense in which *theoria* might itself be a *techne*—the sense in which 'contemplative seeing' could originally have been understood as an art or skill. Just as *techne* involves more than mere productive labor, *theoria* involves more than mere cognition or detached observation. Both involve (what I have called) a "realization"—a making visible that allows for active participation in the emergence of *kosmos*. Both are rooted in the seeing (with wondering eyes) of an order that transcends human making. The "making" that joins craft and contemplation is, fundamentally, the presencing (not just the making present) of the divine.

It is in this sense that the "work" both of craft and of contemplation is meaningful in itself. It is in this sense, too, that *theoria* is fundamentally liturgical. *Leitourgia* means "public service" or "work" in the sense not of production but of presencing. *Leitourgia* is public *ergon*. Its public nature consists in its providing a spectacle (*thea*) in which both performers and spectators, artists and audience, participate.[33] Its "work" is not a means to an end, or a separate product, but the performance itself. Liturgy is (or was) a "making visible" that provides for a realization of the divine. Those who "serve" do so in the way that the craftsman realizes his or her own function—not simply by producing artifacts that might or might not produce some useful result. What Schroeder-Sheker refers to as "the presence of being"—the seemingly paradoxical notion of being invisibly present in one's work so that something else can become visible—has its source in this understanding of liturgical work. *Ergon* is productive, not of future results, but of present actualities. The activity of making music lets *kosmos* appear, not as an objective representation, or a symbol (in the modern sense), but as what Heidegger calls a "self bringing-forth"—the *epiphaneia*, or appearance, that radiates being. By making something that is a wonder to behold, the musician's work furnishes an occasion for the kind of seeing that connects one, in a vital way, to God's work. This is its inherently liturgical function.

PRACTICAL IMPLICATIONS

Since the aim of these reflections has been to arrive at a deeper understanding of the role of practice in *theoria* and hence in contemplation, it might be expected that some practical considerations should issue from them. The inherently liturgical function of *techne* recalls us to the inherently liturgical function of *theoria*—to the original unity of thinking, seeing, wonder, and worship. It also recalls us to the sense in which *theoria* might itself be understood as a *techne*—as a skillful seeing. A superficial understanding of the usefulness of craft makes it difficult to understand the fruitfulness of contemplative seeing. Contemplation "serves," not in the production of future results, but in the original sense of *leitourgia*—through active participation in a spectacle that is itself the realization of a divine order.

While anyone but a classicist or a philosopher could be forgiven for having forgotten what *theoria* once meant, more is at stake in our having forgotten what it originally means. After all, we ourselves (most of us) are "theorists" as well as educators. Within the academy, attention is once again being paid to a very old question—the question of whether and how virtue can be taught. We see this as an urgent question because of its practical relevance. Perhaps now we might begin to acknowledge the practical importance of a question we have forgotten to ask. If it is possible to conceive of "theory" as itself a form of divine worship, what would it mean to teach *that*? If to see is to pray, how does one learn to see?

I am deeply interested in these questions. But there is another set of implications to which I would like to call attention. The idea of *theoria* as a form of worship (as liturgical) prompts further reflection on the idea of a worship service as a theoretical spectacle. The same unease that greets the association of theory and (artistic) performance is often elicited by the idea of performance in public worship. While we expect theory to be nonparticipatory, we want worship to be as participatory as possible. In the same way that theory is opposed to practice, "participation" is understood as the opposite of detachment. To participate is not to be a mere spectator. It is to take part. To ensure participation, we assume, liturgy cannot become a spectacle.

The *theoros* was a spectator—*and* a participant. If "theoretical" observation was originally participatory, there must also be a sense in which participation can be observational—*a sense in which "seeing" can itself be a form of participation*. The convergence of *theoria* and *techne* recalls us to the crucial difference between passive looking or listening and participatory beholding. The latter is not "merely" spectatorial, though it does require a spectacle of a certain sort.[34] The craftsman's work presents a spectacle (*thea*) in which the divine (*thea*) is itself present. As an epiphany of *kosmos*, such spectacles allow the spectator to participate in this divine 'presencing,' just as the *theoros* was actively and experientially engaged in the realization or making visible of a divine order. A spectacle provides the occasion for this kind of participation when it is "seen with wondering eyes" (*theaomai*) or presents itself as "a wonder to behold" (*thauma idesthai*). That is, when it is beautifully wrought, or well made. The spectator may not possess the skill necessary to make such a thing—the skill necessary to create *harmonia*—but the possibility of his participating in anything more than an entertaining show depends on the craftsman's ability to do so. Think again about ship-building, or weaving. The order (*kosmos*) that is woven through these creative processes—the patterns that govern the practice of making—is the order that is brought to appearance or made visible in and by the finished product. It is by virtue of its "harmonious" composition that any work of art allows *kosmos* to appear and thereby serves as a revelation of the divine. As McEwen points out, *harmonia* ("close fitting") is a quality only of those textiles that are well or tightly woven. A cloth with a loose or irregular weave—one that is poorly woven or not attuned with itself—is not harmonious. "It does not, properly speaking, *appear at all*."[35] Nor will a ship that does not embody the right *rhythmos* (*eurythmia*, or symmetry and proportion among the assembled parts) be attuned to its surrounding element in a way that lets its *kosmos* appear.

There is, of course, an important sense in which the joining together of an assembled congregation in the actual making of music—as when a musician accompanies a hymn—is integral to its liturgical function. There is also an important sense in which music that is "performed"—as when an anthem is sung by a practiced choir—must be chosen and presented in a way that invites participatory engagement. Appeals are often made, in this context, to the notion of "accessibility," without much thought for what it is that such performances might or might not enable human beings to "access," or what the deepest form of participatory engagement in such spectacles might ultimately be. What could it mean to "take part"? As Schroeder-Sheker observes,

> [T]raditions that include the singing of prayers as part of their spiritual praxis hold this in common: if particular sacred music is sung by a *prepared* community of liturgical singers *in the most appropriate way*, at some level, heaven and earth are linked.[36]

Here, I take it, "appropriate" does not simply mean psychologically, culturally, or aesthetically "accessible." If the most appropriate way is taken to mean the most *artful* way (in the ancient sense), it is indeed possible to understand how heaven and earth might be practically linked through the liturgical function of music.

It is also possible for us to understand why, in Plato's *Republic*, music plays such an important role in the kind of education that leads to justice, and why, in order to achieve this goal, "we must seek out craftsmen who are by nature able to pursue what is fine and graceful in their work" (401c). It is because "rhythm and harmony permeate the inner part of the soul more than anything else . . . so that if someone is properly educated in music . . . it makes him graceful, but if not, then the opposite" (401d). For Plato, what is true of the craftsman's practice is also true of the spectators. Education "in" music is education *by* music. It is preparation for a kind of seeing. This is the further reason why such education is "most important":

> [B]ecause anyone who has been properly educated in music . . . will sense it acutely when something has been omitted from a thing and when it hasn't been finely crafted or finely made by nature. And since he has the right distastes, he'll praise fine things, be pleased by them, receive them into his soul, and, being nurtured by them, become fine and good (401e).

To "become fine and good," as Plato pictures it, is to participate in a vision of the ideal Form of the Good. It is to participate in a vision (*eidos*) of *kosmos*. The person who "looks at and studies things that are organized and always the same," Socrates says, will not simply cognize but "consort with" and "imitate" them. For how can one gaze with wonder and admiration at such a spectacle, without being moved to imitate what one sees? It is "by consorting with what is ordered and divine," Socrates says, that one "becomes as divine and ordered as a human being can" (500c). This takes work, in the way that *theoria* and *techne* both take work. It is not a useful result that is produced—a "practical" accomplishment in that sense—nor is it a purely "theoretical" accomplishment in the modern sense. The *ergon* of education, as Plato describes it, *is* the liturgy—the "spectacular work"—of theory.

This might also be the work of liturgy itself. For, as the Athenian Stranger notes in Plato's *Laws*, the effects of even the best education can wear off or be lost altogether, in the same way that the original meanings of words (and the forms of understanding and experience in which their meaning originated) can be lost. It is liturgy that reconnects us with these sources. "The Gods," the Stranger suggests, "took pity on the human race . . . and gave it relief in the form of religious festivals to serve as periods of rest from its labors. They gave us the Muses, with Apollo their leader, and Dionysus; by having these gods to share their holidays, human beings were to be made whole again, and thanks to them, we find refreshment in the celebration of these festivals" (653c–d). We are "made whole again," Plato suggests, through the recollection of an original source. This re-collecting is, literally, a gathering together again. Can we experience liturgical gatherings, and the practices that underlie them, in this way? The ascent from Plato's cave began with Socrates' going down to see and to pray. There may yet be a sense in which the Stranger's words offer us some hope of understanding as well.

Commentary: The Medicine of Philosophy

William E. Stempsey, S.J.

Bruce Morrill reminds us that "healing" is a "remarkably fluid term." He does, however, provide us with a good general definition of healing as "transforming people's perceptions of a critical or painful situation by means of making it somehow meaningful."[1] Liturgy provides a rich context of meaning in which to find healing. My training has been in both medicine and philosophy, and one might reasonably call me a practitioner of the philosophy of medicine. In light of the centrality of liturgy to healing, and in the spirit of Christopher Dustin's stimulating thoughts about the liturgy of theory,[2] I want to tip my usual theorizing on its head and present a few thoughts about the medicine of philosophy. It takes, perhaps, a new way of seeing (*theorein*) to appreciate the rituals of medical practice, apart from but intimately conjoined with the treatments themselves, as liturgical means to the end of healing. This new way of seeing is a philosophical stance, and it is a stance that is itself healing.

Classical thinkers saw medicine as a science, but a special kind of science. Plato recognized that the knowledge of health possessed by "most professors of medicine" does not by itself produce health. In order to heal, the practitioner must also know the art of medicine.[3] Both Plato and Aristotle used medicine as a prime example of an art (*techne*). In the *Philebus*, Plato distinguishes the exact arts (e.g., numbering and measuring) from the empirical arts (e.g., navigation, agriculture, military science, and medicine).[4] Aristotle often uses medicine as an example of *techne*. Unlike the purely theoretical sciences, which study that which necessarily is, medicine is an art associated with *poiesis*; medicine aims to produce health. Indeed, for Aristotle, the discipline of medicine is the formal cause of health.[5] Hence, one cannot understand health without reference to medical science and the art of the physician.

As Dustin reminds us, *techne* and *theoria* are more intimately related than we ordinarily take them to be. *Theoria* is rooted in "reverent" seeing of and wondering at beautiful things. *Theoria* begins with an attentive gaze upon the outward appearances of things, but in the true contemplation that is *theoria*, the inner nature of things is made visible.[6] This recalls Michel Foucault's analysis of the emergence of modern clinical medicine in the context of the rise of the academic hospital, in which the "gaze" of the physi-cian shifts from outward bodily symptoms to the inner pathology of the body's organs.[7] The inner gaze that is necessary for healing, however, must go even deeper than looking at the body's inner organs. Thinking about medicine too often focuses exclusively on curing. Better thinking about med-icine recognizes that caring is as necessary as curing, and is possible even when curing is not. Caring moves toward true healing, whether or not it is coupled with curing.

Theory and practice are today seen as antitheses. But if *theoria* begins with a wondering gaze, *techne* aims, in a way, to concretize what *theoria* has begun—not as the *telos* of *theoria*, to be sure, but nonetheless a concrete end that might well serve as a proper object of further wondering gaze. Practitioners of an art allow *kosmos* (order, form and arrangement) to be revealed and discovered through the activity that is the art.[8] The order that *techne* makes visible is *harmonia*. What the art finely done produces is not just something functional; it is something that reveals on its surface the inner beauty and form that the activity of the art has allowed to become manifest. The skilled practitioner of an art, then, is a sort of *theoros*. What the artisan produces provides an occasion for the contemplative gaze. As Dustin nicely puts it, "A well-made ship is in visual and functional harmony both with itself and with its surrounding element, whose own *kosmos* or patterns are revealed in its wake."[9]

Medicine as *techne* aims at producing health. Physicians use knowledge of both universals and particulars in order to help their patients. Each type of knowledge is crucial, for the suffering of individuals is always particular to the individual. Although modern science is predicated on finding regularities in nature, even the "hardest" of natural sciences does not come to what Aristotle considered scientific knowledge, or *epist_m_*—an account of things that could not be otherwise.[10] This is especially true of the biological sciences, upon which medicine is based. Medicine, however, is not just applied science; it has always been considered both science and art. The art of medicine is aptly understood in terms of our present discussion of *techne*. Physicians do not produce health in their patients in the way we commonly understand production. They do not produce health in the same way that the shipbuilder produces a ship. Rather, the *kosmos* of health is revealed through the practice of medicine—through the very activity of the interaction between doctor and patient. It is the healing of nature, or God, if one is a person of faith, that is revealed in the activity of the practitioner of medicine.

The art of medicine, like the art of liturgy, is ritual. Ritual necessarily involves repetition of particular acts. As Dustin observes, skills are actualized only with repetition—doing something "over and over, as the shuttle moves over the loom." Furthermore, the activity of *techne* forms the artisan as much as it forms the artifact.[11] The rituals of medicine form the physician just as listening, practice, and performance form the musician. Just as the minister of the sacraments is transformed by liturgy, so the physician is transformed by healing relationships with patients.

Contemporary physicians, however, may have lost the ability to see their practice as ritual despite the fact that they engage in it every day. Traditional healers and faith healers require patients to confess misdeeds, to wear special garments, and to perform certain tasks. The healer interprets physical signs and touches with stylized gestures.[12] Such rituals are an inherent part of medicine. Physicians require patients to reveal the history of their illnesses, to wear special garments that tie in the back and do not quite cover what ought to be covered, and to fill out forms. Physicians vest themselves in white coats, use esoteric language, draw blood, and they touch, although sometimes mediated by highly technical devices. They go on hospital rounds, a highly ritualized way of seeing patients. Pressed for time and under great stress, physicians may not stop to reflect long enough to realize the healing power of their everyday rituals. Yet the rituals *themselves* can be powerful forces for healing. The rituals of medicine can calm the apprehensions of patients and foster their own participation in their treatment. Rituals are manifestations of the *techne* that is medicine, but it takes a philosophical disposition, *theoria*, to recognize them. Thus, as the ancients realized, philosophy itself is *therapeia* and the medicine of philosophy is a fundamentally important part of helping those who suffer.

If this claim is correct, it sheds new light on the old adage that medicine is both a science and an art. The light, however, is still just a precondition for seeing in a new way. The real seeing comes from the act of philosophizing. This should challenge both theoreticians and practitioners of medicine to consider more deeply how their disciplines blend. It should also challenge patients to consider their illnesses in new ways.

Practitioners of medicine might consider the ways in which their practice is theory. This practice/theory should generate new and deeper questions for the physician. What are the rituals of medical practice that go unnoticed as rituals? How are these rituals windows for new ways of seeing the practice? How do the rituals enable the practitioner to envision the inner nature of the healing practice? What is the inner nature, the *harmonia*, that the inner gaze reveals? To ask such questions enlightens the practitioner about the ways in which medicine is philosophy.

Theorists of medicine might consider the ways in which their theory is practice. This theory/practice should evoke new questions for the theoretician. How can philosophy be healing? What is the healing role of the theoretician? How does the attempt to understand the *harmonia* of the practice of medicine shape the actual rituals that are employed? How does a healing relationship between physician and patient shape the patient? How does it shape the physician? To ask such questions enlightens the theoretician about the ways in which philosophy is medicine.

Patients might consider the ways that might enable them to see their illnesses in a new way. If healing is to come about, patients need to be philosophers too. The medicine of philosophy should evoke new questions for patients as well as for physicians. How do relationships with physicians transform the ways in which they suffer? How do the rituals of medicine, which are increasingly incorporating advanced technology, heal? How does suffering reveal a deeper meaning, a *harmonia*, in human life? This last question is, perhaps, the central one both for those who seek healing and for those who heal.

Liturgy offers ritual to help people find meaning in their suffering. The ritualistic practices of medicine offer many parallels to the ritualistic practices of religion. Medicine is a mission that wonderfully demonstrates the intimate relationship of *theoria* and *techne*. An appreciation of this relationship can open up new and deeper visions of the meaning of suffering and healing.

Epilogue: Reflections at Vespers

Katherine M. McElaney

Editors' note: Preached on October 20, 2002, during the Sunday Vespers of the Practicing Catholic conference at the College of the Holy Cross, after the following reading from the Second Letter of Saint Paul to the Corinthians:

> *Blessed be the God and Father of our Lord Jesus Christ, the Father of mercies and the God of all consolation, who consoles us in all our affliction, so that we may be able to console those who are in any affliction with the consolation with which we ourselves are consoled by God.*[1]

As with Morning Prayer, Evening Prayer (Vespers) does not typically have a reflection following the reading.

I have always understood something about the why of that.
I understand a great deal more after the experience of today's conferences papers and performances.

In this prayer form—which is one part of a larger service of prayer—the Liturgy of the Hours—we are called to be fully present to the stunning elements of light, incense, chant, song, psalmody, word, silence.

We pause to dwell with God who is present to us in space and body and beauty.

We behold,
we see with wondering eyes,
we practice wonder,
and in this way, our participative silence following the reading—may be more instructive, more transforming than a spoken reflection.

This weekend we have been privileged to have scholars, performers, believers, and thinkers come together to consider the remarkable practices of Catholics and ways in which those practices mediate Christ and the communion of saints and constitute Catholics as Church.

It's beautifully fitting that this last practice/performance piece while communicating something germane to the conference, more significantly constitutes something that is us—Church.

These two brief verses both sing praise to God and at once call us beyond this space—this time of prayer—perhaps beyond this conference. Even as St. Paul sings hymns of praise to God, he is simultaneously calling each of us to bear the light of consolation to the world that awaits it.

If we understand, through the eyes of faith, anything to do with the practice of Catholics, we understand that *faithful practice* transforms us, heals us, moves us out of comfort—to console the world.

Notes on Contributors

Christopher A. Dustin (Ph.D., Yale University), Associate Professor and Chair of Philosophy, College of the Holy Cross, is coauthor (with Joanna Ziegler) of *Practicing Mortality: Art, Philosophy, and Contemplative Seeing* (Palgrave).

Roberto S. Goizueta (Ph.D., Marquette University), Professor of Systematic Theology, Boston College, is author of *Caminemos con Jesus: Toward a Hispanic/Latino Theology of Accompaniment* (Orbis).

Daniel M. Goldstein (Ph.D., University of Arizona), Assistant Professor of Anthropology, Rutgers University, is author of *Spectacular City: Violence and Performance in Urban Bolivia* (Duke).

Gary Macy (Ph.D., Cambridge University), Professor of Religious Studies, University of San Diego, is author of *Treasures from the Storeroom: Essays on Medieval Religion and the Eucharist* (Liturgical/Pueblo).

Bruce T. Morrill, S.J. (Ph.D., Emory University), Associate Professor of Theology, Boston College, is author of *Anamnesis as Dangerous Memory: Political and Liturgical Theology in Dialogue* (Liturgical/Pueblo).

Frederick S. Paxton (Ph.D., University of California at Berkeley), Brigida Pacchiani Ardenghi Professor of History, Connecticut College, is author of *Christianizing Death: The Creation of a Ritual Process in Medieval Europe* (Cornell).

Joanne M. Pierce (Ph.D., University of Notre Dame), Associate Professor of Religious Studies, College of the Holy Cross, is contributing editor of *Source and Summit: Commemorating Joseph A. Jungmann, S.J.* (Liturgical).

Vicente L. Rafael (Ph.D., Cornell University), Professor of History, University of Washington, is author of *The Promise of the Foreign: Nationalism and the Technics of Translation in the Spanish Philippines* (Duke).

Susan Rodgers (Ph.D., University of Chicago), Professor of Anthropology, College of the Holy Cross, is author of *Telling Lives, Telling History: Autobiography and the Historical Imagination in Modern Indonesia* (California).

Mathew N. Schmalz (Ph.D., University of Chicago), Associate Professor of Religious Studies, College of the Holy Cross, has most recently published articles based on research among North Indian converts to Catholicism funded by a Fulbright Fellowship.

Therese Schroeder-Sheker is founder and national spokesperson for the Chalice of Repose Project, Mount Angel, Oregon, teaches pastoral theology and music at Duke University, has recorded numerous video- and audio-discs, and has published numerous scholarly articles in the fields of music and palliative medicine.

Irene Silverblatt (Ph.D., University of Michigan), Professor of Cultural Anthropology and History, Duke University, is author of *Moon, Sun, and Witches: Gender Ideology and Class in Inca and Colonial Peru* (Princeton).

Joanna E. Ziegler (Ph.D., Brown University), Professor of Visual Arts, College of the Holy Cross, is coauthor (with Christopher Dustin) of *Practicing Mortality: Art, Philosophy, and Contemplative Seeing* (Palgrave).

Notes on Commentators

Anthony Cashman (Ph.D., Duke University, 1999), Visiting Assistant Professor of History, Assumption College, publishes articles on ritual in the Italian Renaissance.

Jennifer Wright Knust (Ph.D., Columbia University), Assistant Professor of Religious Studies, College of the Holy Cross, publishes in the areas of Pauline Christianity, early Christian asceticism, and gender studies.

Judith Marie Kubicki, C.S.S.F. (Ph.D., Catholic University of America), Assistant Professor of Theology, Fordham University, is author of *Liturgical Music as Ritual Symbol* (Peeters).

Katherine M. McElaney (M.Div., Weston Jesuit School of Theology) is Director of the Chaplains Office, College of the Holy Cross.

James B. Nickoloff (Ph.D., Graduate Theological Union, Berkeley), Associate Professor of Religious Studies, College of the Holy Cross, is contributing editor of *Gustavo Gutiérrez: Essential Writings* (Orbis).

John Schmalzbauer (Ph.D., Princeton University), Associate Professor and Blanche Gorman Strong Chair of Protestant Studies, Southwest Missouri State University, is author of *People of Faith: Religious Conviction in American Journalism and Higher Education* (Cornell).

William E. Stempsey, S.J. (Ph.D., Georgetown University), Associate Professor of Philosophy, College of the Holy Cross, is author of *Disease and Diagnosis: Value-Dependent Realism* (Kluwer).

Edward H. Thompson (Ph.D., Case Western Reserve University), Professor of Sociology and Director of Gerontology Studies, College of the Holy Cross, is contributing editor to *Men as Caregivers* (Springer).

NOTES

PART I PERFORMANCE, LITURGY, AND RITUAL PRACTICE

INTRODUCTION

1. Kevin Irwin, "A Sacramental World: Sacramentality as the Primary Language for Sacraments," *Worship* 76: 197–211.
2. Johann Baptist Metz, *A Passion for God: The Mystical-Political Dimension of Christianity*, trans. J. Matthew Ashley (New York: Paulist Press, 1998), 30–53.
3. Louis-Marie Chauvet, *The Sacraments: The Word of God at the Mercy of the Body* (Collegeville MN: The Liturgical Press, 2001), 156.
4. Don E. Saliers, *Worship as Theology: Foretaste of Glory Divine* (Nashville TN: Abingdon Press, 1994), 21–38.
5. Gordon Lathrop, *Holy Things: A Liturgical Theology* (Minneapolis MN: Fortress Press, 1993), 10–11, 163–4.
6. I. H. Dalmais, "Theology of the Liturgical Celebration," in *Principles of the Liturgy*, ed. A. G. Martimort, trans. Matthew O'Connell (Collegeville MN: The Liturgical Press, 1987), 266.
7. Lawrence Hoffman, *Beyond the Text: A Holistic Approach to Liturgy* (Bloomington: Indiana University Press, 1987).
8. Kevin W. Irwin, *Context and Text: Method in Liturgical Theology* (Collegeville MN: The Liturgical Press, 1994).
9. Philippe Buc, *The Dangers of Ritual: Between Early Medieval Texts and Social Scientific Theory* (Princeton NJ: Princeton University Press, 2001).
10. Among his major works, see Victor Turner, *The Forest of Symbols: Aspects of Ndembu Ritual* (Ithaca NY: Cornell University Press, 1967), *Dramas, Fields, and Metaphors: Symbolic Action in Human Society* (Ithaca NY: Cornell University Press, 1975), *The Ritual Process: Structure and Anti-Structure* (Ithaca NY: Cornell University Press, 1977), and *From Ritual to Theater: The Human Seriousness of Play* (New York: Performing Arts Journal Publications, 1982); Victor Turner and Edward M. Bruner, *The Anthropology of Experience* (Urbana: University of Illinois Press, 1986); Victor Turner and Richard Schechner, eds., *The Anthropology of Performance* (New York: Performing Arts Journal Publications, 1988); and Richard Schechner and Victor Turner, *Between Theater and Anthropology* (Philadelphia: University of Pennsylvania Press, 1986).
11. Catherine Bell, *Ritual Theory, Ritual Practice* (New York: Oxford University Press, 1992) and *Ritual: Perspectives and Dimensions* (New York: Oxford University Press, 1999); and Mary Suydam, "Background: An Introduction

to Performance Studies," in *Performance and Transformation: New Approaches to Late Medieval Spirituality*, ed., Mary Suydam and Joanna Ziegler (New York: St. Martin's Press, 1999).

12. Suydam, "Background," 3.

13. Herman Pleij, *Het gilde van de Blauwe Schuit: Literatuur, volksfeest en burgermoraal in de late middeleeuwen* (Amsterdam: Meulenhoof Nederland bv, 1979); and *De sneeuwpoppen van 1511: Literatuur en stadscultuur tussen middeleeuwen en moderne tijd* (Amsterdam: Meulenhoff Nederland bv, 1988).

14. In addition to Bell, *Ritual Theory, Ritual Practice*, and Suydam and Ziegler, *Performance and Transformation*, see Peter Arnade, *Realms of Ritual: Burgundian Ceremony and Civic Life in Late Medieval Ghent* (New York: Cornell University Press, 1996); Jack Goody " 'Against Ritual': Loosely Structured Thoughts on a Loosely Defined Topic," in *Secular Ritual*, ed. Sally Falk Moore and Barbara Myerhoff (Amsterdam: Royal van Gorcum, 1977), 25–35.

15. Suydam, "Background," 1.

16. See, for instance, Richard Schechner, *Essays in Performance Theory* (New York: Routledge, 1988).

17. Caroline Walker Bynum, *Jesus as Mother: Studies in the Spirituality of the High Middle Ages* (Berkeley: University of California Press, 1984); *Holy Fast, Holy Feast: The Religious Significance of Food to Medieval Women* (Berkeley: University of California Press, 1988); *Fragmentation and Redemption: Essays on Gender and the Human Body in Medieval Religion* (New York: Zone Books, 1992); and *The Resurrection of the Body in Western Christianity, 200–1336* (New York: Columbia University Press, 1995).

18. With her *Metamorphosis and Identity* (New York: Zone Books, 2002), Bynum is moving away from gender.

19. Bell, *Ritual Theory, Ritual Practice*, 1.

20. In the past decade or so, the concept of practice has been quite present in the discourse on ritual. One of the foremost writers in this area, Catherine Bell, writes on the topic at some length in both her books on ritual. In no way do we exclude that discussion or minimize the importance of practice as she defines it, especially in terms of Marxist *praxis* or Pierre Bourdieu's notion of *habitus*. Practice means roughly a way of acting, that is, a "set of activities," in Bell's words, "that construct particular types of meanings and values in specific ways" (*Ritual*, 82). Practice theory, it seems from Bell, looks at ritual as more than "a matter of enacting cultural rules," but "practice theory claims to take seriously the ways in which human activities, as formal as a religious ritual or as casual as a midday stroll, are creative activities by which human beings continually reproduce and reshape their social and cultural environment" (*Ritual*, 76). Although practice theory, as an academic activity, can present the problem in obscure and impenetrable (or even obvious and generalized) ways, actually it has to do with one of the most straightforward senses in which we use the word practice: as execution, or acting in a manner consonant with rules, that is, a mode of acting or proceeding. On my own particular application of ritual and performance theory to issues of art and aesthetics, see Christopher Dustin and Joanne E. Ziegler, *Practicing Mortality: Art, Philosophy, and Contemplative Seeing* (New York: Palgrave-MacMillan, 2005).

21. Bell, *Ritual Theory, Ritual Practice*, 69–93.

22. Charlene Spretnak, *The Resurgence of the Real: Body, Nature, and Place in a Hypermodern World* (New York: Routledge, 1999).

23. Brian Stock has been exploring the tradition of the practice of "contemplative or meditative reading." This model holds great promise for extension to performance. See his *Augustine the Reader: Meditation, Self-Knowledge, and Ethics of Interpretation* (Cambridge, MA: Belknap Press, 1998) and *After Augustine: The Meditative Reader and the Text (Material Texts)* (Philadelphia: University of Pennsylvania Press, 2001).

24. Buc (*The Dangers of Ritual*) is correct in articulating the problem to be one of identifying the source as a source and not the event itself. In other words, he believes that ritual turned medievalists away from holding before their eyes the fact that they were working with texts and not events.

25. Emile Durkheim, *The Elementary Forms of the Religious Life*, rev. trans. Karen Fields (New York: Free Press, 1995 [1912]).

26. The cultural ecology school within anthropology contends that some ritual systems in subsistence-oriented village societies, such as those in highland Papua New Guinea, do have practical effects, as environmental and social-systems' regulatory devices. However, the ecologists see those regulatory mechanisms to take place totally outside any "truth" of the folk systems of ideas about spirits and deities and the divine. See Roy Rappaport, *Pigs for the Ancestors* (New Haven CT: Yale University Press, 1968); *Ecology, Meaning, and Religion* (New York: North Atlantic Books, 1984); and *Ritual and Religion in the Making of Humanity* (Cambridge: Cambridge University Press, 1999).

27. Clifford Geertz, "Religion as a Cultural System," in Clifford Geertz, *The Interpretation of Cultures* (New York: Basic Books, 1973 [1966]), 86–125.

28. Sherry Ortner, "On Key Symbols," *American Anthropologist* 75 (1973): 1338–46.

29. Jane M. Atkinson, "Religion in Dialogue: The Construction of an Indonesian Minority Religion," *American Ethnologist* 10 (1983): 684–96.

30. I. M. Lewis, *Ecstatic Religion: A Study of Shamanism and Spirit Possession* (London: Routledge, 1989).

31. Gananath Obeyesekere, *Medusa's Hair: An Essay on Personal Symbols and Religious Experience* (Chicago IL: University of Chicago Press, 1984).

32. Max Weber, *The Sociology of Religion* (Boston MA: Beacon Press, 1993 [1922]).

33. Stanley Brandes, "Like Wounded Stags: Male Sexual Ideology in an Andalusian Town," in *Sexual Meanings: The Cultural Construction of Gender and Sexuality*, ed. Sherry B. Ortner and Harriet Whitehead (Cambridge: Cambridge University Press, 1987 [1981]), 216–39.

34. Homi Bhabha, "Of Mimicry and Man: The Ambivalence of Colonial Discourse," in *Tensions of Empire: Colonial Cultures in a Bourgeois World*, ed. Frederick Cooper and Ann Laura Stoler (Berkeley: University of California Press, 1997), 152–62.

35. Irene Silverblatt, *Moon, Sun, and Witches: Gender Ideologies and Class in Inca and Colonial Peru* (Princeton NJ: Princeton University Press, 1987), 43.

36. See, for instance, Ramon Gutiérrez, *When Jesus Came the Corn Mothers Went Away: Marriage, Sexuality, and Power in New Mexico, 1500–1846* (Palo Alto CA: Stanford University Press, 1991); and especially Vicente Rafael, *Contracting Colonialism: Translation and Christian Conversion in*

Tagalog Society under Early Spanish Rule (Ithaca NY: Cornell University Press, 1988).

37. Christine Greenway, "Healing Soul Loss: The Negotiation of Identity in Peru," in *Medical Pluralism in the Andes*, ed. Joan Koss-Chioino and others (New York: Routledge 2002).

38. Thomas Csordas, *Language, Charisma, and Creativity: Ritual Life in the Catholic Charismatic Renewal* (Berkeley CA: University of Califronia Press, 1997).

39. New Haven CT: Yale University Press, 1985.

40. David D. Hall, ed., *Lived Religion: Toward a History of Practice* (Princeton NJ: Princeton University Press, 1997), 7.

41. Robert Orsi, *Thank You, St. Jude: Women's Devotions to the Patron Saint of Hopeless Causes* (New Haven CT: Yale University Press, 1996).

42. Nancy Scheper-Hughes, *Death Without Weeping: The Violence of Everyday Life in Brazil* (Berkeley CA: University of California Press, 1993).

PART II   CATHOLIC RITUAL: PRACTICE IN HISTORY

CHAPTER 2   THE FUTURE OF THE PAST: WHAT CAN THE HISTORY SAY ABOUT SYMBOL AND RITUAL?

1. W. Scott Jessee, *Robert the Burgundian and the Counts of Anjou, c. 1025–1098* (Washington DC: Catholic University of America Press, 2000), 19. Dr. Jessee has kindly provided me the reference to this act of Agnes, while countess of Poitou, "In hoc anno jam dicta nobilissima comitissa Agnes obsedit castrum Volventem et ut est sua consuetudo, cepit eum." *Recueil des chartes de l'abbaye de Cluny*, ed. Auguste Bernard and Alexandre Bruel, 6 vols., (Paris: Imprimerie nationale, 1876–1903), vol. 4, no. 2855.

2. Jessee, *Robert the Burgundian*, 11–12, 24, 26–27, 30, 37–38, 42–43, 55–56, 76, 123.

3. Jerry Lembcke, *The Spitting Image: Myth, Memory and the Legacy of Vietnam* (New York: New York University Press, 1998).

4. Joseph Gremillion and Jim Castelli, eds., *The Emerging Parish: The Notre Dame Study of Catholic Life Since Vatican II* (San Francisco CA: Harper and Row, 1987), 30–76 119–143; and Bryan T. Froehle and Mary L. Gautier, eds., *Catholicism USA: A Portrait of the Catholic Church in the United States* (Maryknoll NY: Orbis Books, 2000), 151–65.

5. "Si quis autem plenius et perfectius quid sit sacramentum diffinire voluerit, diffinire potest quod »sacramentum est corporale vel materiate elementum foris sensibiliter propositum ex similitudine repraesentans, et ex institutione significans, et ex sanctificatione continens aliquam invisibilem et spiritalem gratiam.« Haec diffinitio ita propria ac perfecta agnoscitur, ut omni sacramento solique convenire inveniatur." pars 9, c. 2 PL 176: 318B.

6. Pars 3, q. 73, article 6, translation by the Fathers of the English Dominican Province, vol. 2 (New York: Benziger Brothers, Inc, 1947), 2438.

7. Yves Congar, "Note sur une valeur des termes «ordinare, ordinatio,»" *Revue des sciences religieuses* 58 (1984): 7–14.

8. Charles DuCange, ed., *Glossarum mediae et infirmae latinitatis* (Graz: Abakdemische Druck-U. Verlagsanstalt, 1954 [reprint of the Paris, 1983–87

edition, vol. 6), 58–59, 60–62; and Franz Blatt and Yves Lefévre eds., *Novum glossarium mediae; Latinitas ab anno DCC usque ad annum MCC*, vol. O (Copenhagen: Ejnar Munksgaard, 1983), 696–708, 714–29, 731–72.

9. For an example from the late tenth century, see "siquidem utroque sexu fidelium tres ordines gradus, in sancta et universalis Ecclesia esse novimus; quorum licet nullus sine peccato sit, tamen primus est bonus, secundus melior, tertius est optimus. Et primus quidem ordo est in utroque sexu coniugatorum; secundum continentium vel viduarum, tertius virginum vel sanctimonialium. Virorum tantum similiter tres sunt gradus vel ordines, quorum primus est laicorum, secundus clericorum, tertius monarchorum." Abbo of Fleury, *Apologeticus ad Hugonem et Robertum reges Francorum, PL* 139, 463A-B. On Abbo, see Lawrence K. Shook, "Abbo of Fleury (Floriancensis)," *Dictionary of the Middle Ages*, 1: 12–13. Cf. Marie Ann Mayeski's, "Excluded by the Logic of Control: Women in Medieval Society and Scholastic Theology," *Equal at the Creation* (Toronto: University of Toronto Press, 1998), 74, "During the ninth century, the emphasis on the superiority of virginity diminished, while the Carolingian Church promoted the idea that married people constituted a true *order* within the Church, equal to that of the celibates." (Emphasis by author)

10. Pierre-Marie Gy, "Les anciennes prieres d'ordination," *La Maison-Dieu* 138 (1079): 93–122.

11. James Brundage, *Medieval Canon Law* (London and New York: Longman, 1995), p. 68.

12. DuCange, *Glossarum*, 58, 60.

13. Gerard Fransen, "La tradition des canonistes du moyen age," in *Études sur le sacrament de l'ordre* (Paris: Cerf, 1957), 259.

14. Timothy Fry, ed., *The Rule of St. Benedict in Latin and English with Notes* (Collegeville MN: The Liturgical Press, 1981), 522. I want to thank Dr. J. Frank Henderson for providing this reference.

15. Blatt and Lefévre, *Novum glossarium*, 722–28.

16. Congar, "Note sur une valeur," 8.

17. "Primam praeterea praecipuamque tibi tuisque successoribus potestatem contradimus Francorum regis consecrandi: ut sicut Beatus Remigius ad fidem Chlodoveo converso primum illi regno regem Christianum instituisse cognoscitur; ita tu quoque, tuique successores, qui ejusdem sancti Remigii vice in Remensi Ecclesia, Domino disponente, fugimini, ungendi regis et ordinandi sive reginae, prima potestate fungamini." *Epistola* 27, *PL* 151: 310B-C.

18. "Mox convocata non minori multitudine profectus est rex Vesontionum urbem Burgundiae, et illic accipiens, quam praediximus, sponsam, duxit eam Mogonciacum ibique consecrari eam reginam curavit, consummatisque diebus ordinationis in Ingilenheim fecit nuptias regio, ut decuit, apparatu." *Annales Altahenses*, W. de Giesebrecht and E. von Oefele eds., *Monumenta germaniae historiae, Scriptores rerum Germanicarum in usum scholarum ex Monumentis Germaniae historicis recusi*, 1 (Hannover: Bibliopolii Hahniani, 1891), 33–34.

19. Reinhard Elze, ed., *Die Ordines für die Weihe und Krönung des Kaisers und der Kaiseren*, monumeta Germaniae historica, Fontes juris Germanici antiqui in usum scholarum separatim editi, vol. 9 (Hannover: Hansche Buchhandlung, 1995 [1960]), 12.

20. Henry Chadwick, *The Early Church*, The Pelican History of the Church, vol. 1 (New York: Penguin Books, 1967).
21. Yves Congar, "My Path-findings in the Theology of Laity and Ministries," *The Jurist* 32 (1977): 180.
22. John R. Quinn, *The Reform of the Papacy* (New York: Crossroad Publishing, 1999).
23. Terrence W. Tilley, *Inventing Catholic Tradition* (Maryknoll NY: Orbis Books, 2000).

COMMENTARY: RITUAL EFFICACY: CAUTIONARY QUESTIONS, HISTORICAL AND SOCIAL ANTHROPOLOGICAL

1. For a brief but informative introduction to practice theory, see Catherine Bell, *Ritual: Perspectives and Dimensions* (New York and Oxford: Oxford University Press, 1997), 76–83.
2. Sherry B. Ortner, *High Religion: A Cultural and Political History of Sherpa Buddhism* (Princeton NJ: Princeton University Press,1989), 14.
3. Ibid., 59–61.
4. Clifford Geertz, "Thick Description: Toward an Interpretive Theory of Culture," in Clifford Geertz, *Interpretation of Cultures* (New York: Basic Books, 1973), 3–30.
5. Jack Goody, "Against 'Ritual': Loosely Structured Thoughts on a Loosely Defined Topic," in Sally Moore and Barbara Myerhoff, eds., *Secular Ritual* (Amsterdam: Van Gorcum, 1977), 30.
6. James D. Davidson, "Increasing Indifference to Church is Concern," *National Catholic Reporter Online*, viewed June 24, 2003, http//www.natcath.com/NCR_Online/archives/102999/1029991.htm/
7. "American Catholics Survey/Table 06," *National Catholic Reporter Online*, viewed June 24, 2003, http://www.natcath.com/NCR_Online/archives/102999/web/pages/Table%2006.htm/
8. "American Catholics Survey/Table 06," *National Catholic Reporter Online*, viewed June 24, 2003, http://www.natcath.com/NCR_Online/archives/102999/web/pages/Table%2009.htm/
9. See Michael Kammie, "Catholic Church To Drop Bilingual Service," *The Herald Sun*, Monday, Oct. 14, 1996, Final Edition, A1; see also Pluralism Project, Harvard University, "Immaculate Conception Catholic Church," http://www.fas.harvard.edu/~pluralsm/affiliates/ackland/immaculate_conception.html/

CHAPTER 3 PERFORMING DEATH AND DYING AT CLUNY IN THE HIGH MIDDLE AGES

1. Bernard of Cluny, "Ordo cluniacensis," in *Vetus disciplina monastica*, ed. Marquard Herrgott (Siegburg: Schmitt, 1999 [1726]), 133–364; and Ulrich of Cluny. [1723] 1882. "Antiquiores consuetudines Cluniacensis monasterii" in *Patrologiae cursus completus, series latina*, vol. 149, ed. J.-P. Migne (Paris: Garnier, 1882 [1732]), columns 643–778.

2. Frederick S. Paxton, *A Medieval Latin Death Ritual: The Monastic Customaries of Bernard and Ulrich of Cluny*, Studies in Music-Thanatology 1 (Missoula MO: St. Dunstan's Press, 1993).

3. Arnold van Gennep, *The Rites of Passage*, trans. Monika B. Vizedom and Gabrielle L. Caffee (Chicago IL: University of Chicago Press, 1960 [1908]).

4. Victor Turner, *The Ritual Process: Structure and Anti-Structure* (Chicago IL: University of Chicago Press, 1969); and *Dramas, Fields, and Metaphors: Symbolic Action in Human Society* (Ithaca NY: Cornell University Press, 1974).

5. Frederick S. Paxton, *Christianizing Death: The Creation of a Ritual Process in Early Medieval Europe* (Ithaca NY: Cornell University Press, 1990).

6. Frederick S. Paxton, *Liturgy and Anthropology: A Monastic Death Ritual of the Eleventh Century*, Studies in Music-Thanatology 2 (Missoula MO: St. Dunstan's Press, 1993).

7. Therese Schroeder-Sheker, *Transitus: A Blessed Death in the Modern World* (Missoula MO: St. Dunstan's Press, 2001).

8. My reactions to the first visit are reported in Frederick S. Paxton, "From Life to Death," *Connecticut College Magazine*, May/June (1994): 26–9. After graduating five classes from its two-year program, the school closed in the autumn of 2002.

9. Kenneth John Conant, *Cluny, Les églises et la maison du chef d'ordre*, Medieval Academy of America Publications 77 (Mâcon: Protat, 1968); and Frederick S. Paxton, "Death by Customary at Eleventh-Century Cluny," in *From dead of night to break of day*, ed. Susan Boynton and Isabelle Cochelin (Turnhout: Brepols, forthcoming).

10. Jacques Hourlier, "Saint Odilon Bâtisseur," *Revue Mabillon* 51 (1961): 303–24; and Neil Stratford, "Les bâtiments de l'abbaye de Cluny a l'époque médiévale, état des questions," *Bulletin monumental* 150 (1992): 383–41.

11. Bernard of Cluny, "Ordo cluniacensis," 195.

12. As far as I can tell, the area which has the best claim to preserving the main cemetery has not been excavated, in spite of the fact that it is not built over, like so many other areas of the site. See Anne Baud, "La place des morts dans l'abbaye de cluny, état de la question," *Archéologie Mediévale* 29 (2000): 99–114.

13. Paxton, *A Medieval Latin Death Ritual*, 13–14.

14. Dominique Iogna-Prat, *Ordonner et exclure: Cluny et la sociéte chrétienne face à l'hérésie, au judaïsme et à l'islam 1000–1150* (Paris: Aubier, 2000), 103–52.

15. Dietrich Poeck, "Laienbegräbnisse in Cluny," *Frühmittelalterliche Studien* 14 (1980): 68–179.

16. Jean-Denis Salvèque, "La destruction de l'abbaye de Cluny," *Dossiers d'Archéologie* 269 (2002): 28–9.

17. Manuel Pedro Ferreira, "Liturgie et musique à Cluny." *Dossiers d'Archéologie* 269 (2002): 45.

18. Conant, *Cluny*, figs. 120–41.

19. Ferreira mistakes *fingit* for *pingit* and so mistranslates it into French as: *la troisième met en avant et peint la résurrection du Christ*. See "Liturgie et muscique," 46.

20. Ibid., 43–4.

21. Bernard of Cluny, "Ordo cluniacensis," 193.

22. Ibid., 192. Quotations from Ulrich are from my English translation of the reconstructive ritual which is based on text of the customary. See Frederick S. Paxton,

The Cluniac Death Ritual in the High Middle Ages: A Reconstructive Edition. On-line publication (2002), http://camel2.conncoll.edu/academics/web_profiles/paxton.html/

23. Bernard of Cluny, "Ordo cluniacensis," 190.

24. Geoffrey Koziol, *Begging Pardon and Favor: Ritual and Political Order in Early Medieval France* (Ithaca NY: Cornell University Press, 1992), 183; Paxton, *The Cluniac Death Ritual*, n. 1 to the English translation.

25. The customaries do not specify that the priest is to pause during the anointings to sing each of the psalms, so it is possible that he went ahead with all seven anointings at once. My sense that the Cluniacs would not have been so casual about their ritual performance was confirmed when I discovered a text from a fourteenth-century ritual book, from the abbey of St-Ouen in Rouen, which is clearly derived from Ulrich's customary and explicitly links each of the anointings to one of the psalms. See Edmond Martène, *De Antiquis Ecclesiae ritibus libri iv*, 2d. ed. (Hildesheim: Georg Olms, 1969 [1738]), bk. 3, ch. 15, ordo 13; Paxton, *The Cluniac Death Ritual*, n. 3 to the Latin text.

26. Bernard of Cluny, "Ordo cluniacensis," 192; and Frederick S. Paxton, "*Signa mortifera*: Death and Prognostication in Early Medieval Monastic Medicine," *Bulletin of the History of Medicine* 67 (1993): 631–50.

27. See Paxton, "Death by Customary."

28. Damien Sicard, *La liturgie de la mort dans l'église latine des origines à la réforme carolingienne*. Liturgiewissenschaftlichen Quellen und Forschungen 63 (Münster: Aschendorff, 1978), 135, 215–20; and Paxton, *Christianizing Death*, 37–44.

29. Bernard of Cluny, "Ordo cluniacensis," 197.

30. On commemoration of the dead, see Joachim Wollasch, "Les moines et la mémoire des morts," in *Religion et culture autour de l'an mil: Royaume capétien et Lotharingie*, ed. Dominique Iogna-Prat and Jean-Charles (Paris: Picard, 1990), 47–54; Paxton, *A Medieval Latin Death Ritual*; and Frederick S. Paxton, "*Oblationes defunctorum*: The Poor and the Dead in Late Antiquity and the Early Medieval West," in *Proceedings of the Tenth International Congress of Medieval Canon Law*, ed. Kenneth Pennington and others, Monumenta Iuris Canonici, Series C: Subsidia 11 (Città del Vaticano: Biblioteca Apostolica Vaticana 2001): 245–67.

COMMENTARY: NO TIME FOR DYING

1. Kathy Charmaz, *The Social Reality of Death: Death in Contemporary America* (Reading MA: Addison-Wesley, 1980); Ivan Illich, *Medical Nemesis: The Exploration of Health* (New York: Pantheon Books, 1976); and Paul Starr, *The Social Transformation of American Medicine* (New York: Basic Books, 1982).

2. David E Stannard, *The Puritan Way of Death: A Study in Religion, Culture, and Social Change* (New York: Oxford University Press, 1977), 4–5.

3. Peter Freund, Meredith B. McGuire, and Linda S. Podhurst, *Health, Illness, and the Social Body: A Critical Sociology*, 4th ed. (Upper Saddle River NJ: Prentice Hall, 2003).

4. Philippe Aries, *Western Attitudes Towards Death: From the Middle Ages to the Present* (Baltimore MD: John Hopkins University Press, 1974).

5. Illich, *Medical Nemesis*, 177.
6. Guenter B. Risse, *Mending Bodies, Saving Souls: A History of Hospitals* (New York: Oxford University Press, 1999), 72–9.
7. Peter Conrad, "Medicalization and social control," *Annual Review of Sociology* 18 (1992): 209–32.
8. Andrew M. Greeley and Michael Hout, "Americans' Increasing Belief in Life After Death: Religious Competition and Acculturation," *American Sociological Review* 64 (1999): 813–35; and Harold G. Koenig, "Religion, Spirituality, and Medicine: How Are They Related and What Does It Mean?" *Mayo Clinic Proceedings* 76 (2001): 189–91.
9. Anselm Strauss, Shizuko Fagerhaugh, Barbara Suczek, and Carolyn Wiener, *Social Organization of Medical Work* (Chicago IL: University of Chicago Press, 1985); and David Sudnow, *Passing On: The Social Organization of Dying* (Englewood Cliffs NJ: Prentice-Hall, 1967).
10. Frederick S. Paxton, *Christianizing Death: The Creation of a Ritual Process in Early Medieval Europe* (Ithaca NY: Cornell University Press, 1991).
11. Barney G. Glaser and Anselm L. Strauss, *Time for Dying* (Chicago IL: Aldine, 1968).
12. Eviatar Zerubavel, *Hidden Rhythms: Schedules and Calendars in Social Life* (Chicago IL: University of Chicago Press, 1981).
13. Risse, *Mending Bodies, Saving Souls*, 105.
14. Ibid., 104.
15. Sam Keen, "Building Your Ship of Death for the Longest Journey Over Endless Seas," in *Men Coping with Grief*, ed. Dale Lund (Amityville NY: Baywood Publishing, 2001), 21.

Chapter 4   Marginal Bodies: Liturgical Structures of Pain and Deliverance in the Middle Ages

1. For medieval criticism of the trials by ordeal, see John W. Baldwin, "The Intellectual Preparation for the Canon of 1215 against Ordeals," *Speculum* 36 (1961): 613–36. For a more theoretical analysis, see Charles M. Radding, "Superstition to Science: Nature, Fortune, and the Passing of the Medieval Ordeal," *The American Historical Review* 84 (1979): 945–69.
2. Charles Casper cites the *Rituale Romanum* and, in the 1985 edition, an alternative churching blessing when the mother does not attend the baptism. See "Leviticus 12, Mary and Wax," in *Purity and Holiness: The Heritage of Leviticus*, ed. M.J.H.M. Poorthuis and J. Schwartz (Leiden, Boston, Köln: Brill, 2000), 305, n. 49. He does not include the Book of Blessings material. Caspers concludes his essay with the observation that "churching itself disappeared . . . simply because it was experienced as an indignity" (308). This statement clearly needs to be supported by scholarly investigation, at best by interviewing those women who had gone through the churching ritual before the Catholic liturgical reforms of Vatican II. In her article in the same volume, Anne-Marie Korte cites a few instances of this kind of investigation in "Reclaiming Ritual," in *Purity and Holiness*, 315, n. 5. I suggest that further studies, involving Catholic women in many geographical areas, would be of enormous benefit.

3. See Adolph Franz, *Das Rituale von St. Florian aus dem zwölften Jahrhundert*, CFl XI 467 (Freiburg im Breisgau: Herder, 1904), 3–14. Early medieval nomenclature for various ritual books was not as "standardized" as it would later become. Texts for various "rites," later collected in books for the use of a priest (e.g. the rite for the anointing of the sick, in the *Rituale*) or for a bishop (e.g. ordination rites, in the *Pontificale*), could have earlier been found in a number of different liturgical books with more "mixed" contents (e.g. Sacramentary-Rituals). See the discussions in Pierre-Marie Gy, 1960. "Collectaire, rituel, processional," *Revue des sciences philosophiques et théologiques* 44 (1960): 441–69; and Cyrille Vogel, *Medieval Liturgy: An Introduction to the Sources*, trans. and rev. William G. Storey and Niels K. Rasmussen (Washington DC: The Pastoral Press, 1986), 257–64.

4. See Joanne M. Pierce, " 'Green Women' and Blood Pollution: Some Medieval Rituals for the Churching of Women after Childbirth," *Studia Liturgica* 29 (1999): 191–215. A classic study of these rites remains in Adolph Franz, *Die kirchlichen Benediktionen im Mittelalter*. vol. 2 (Freiburg/Graz: Herder/ Akadeischer Druk U.-Verlaganstalt, 1960 [1909]), 213–40. See also Susan Roll, "The Churching of Women after Childbirth: An Old Rite Raising New Issues," *Questions liturgiques* 76 (1995): 206–29; Natalie Knödel, "Reconsidering an Obsolete Rite: The Churching of Women and Feminist Liturgical Theology." *Feminist Theology* 14 (1997): 106–25; and Daniel Van Sylke, "The Churching of Women: Its Introduction and Spread in the Latin West," *Ephemerides Liturgicae* 115 (2001): 208–38.

5. This has been an on-going project of mine over the past few years.

6. Jacob Milgrom, *Leviticus 1-16: A New Translation with Introduction and Commentary. The Anchor Bible*, vol. 3. (New York: Doubleday, 1991), 763–8; and Pierce, " 'Green Women' and Blood Pollution," 191.

7. Pierce, " 'Green Women' and Blood Pollution," 195.

8. Ibid., 195–96. Perhaps the most accessible text of the letter is found in Bede's *Historia ecclesiastica gentis anglorum* (731). English translations and commentaries include Bede, *A History of the English Church and People*, trans. Leo Sherley-Price (New York: Penguin Classics, 1983 [1968]); and J. M. Wallace-Hadrill, *Bede's Ecclesiastical History of the English People: A Historical Commentary* (Oxford: Clarendon Press, 1988). The text can also be found in critical editions of Gregory the Great's *Registrum Epistularum*. See, for example, *Registrum epistularum/s. Gregarious Magnus*, Instrumenta lexicologica latina, series A, fasc.9 (Turnhout: Brepols, 1982).

9. Franz, *Das Rituale von St. Florian*, 46–7.

10. *Codex Lambacensis membranaceus* LXXIII, *Rituale Lambacense (Ceremoniale)*. Saec. 12–13 [12th–13th century]. The original is held by the Stift Lambach, Austria; a microfilm copy can be consulted at the Hill Monastic Microfilm Library, St. John's University, Collegeville, MN. I would like to thank the staff at HMML for their assistance in my work on this manuscript.

11. Franz, *Das Rituale von St. Florian*, 28.

12. *Exaudiat te dominus in die tribulationis; Mittat tibi auxilium de sancto; Anima mea illi uiuet; Domine exaudi orationem meam.*

13. Pierce, " 'Green Women' and Blood Pollution," 193–7. An interesting recent short piece on blood and purification sacrifice stresses a kind of dualism implicit in the texts themselves; according to Christophe Lemardelé, "[it expresses] un dualisme structurel au religieux mais particulièrement bien

integer dans le yahwism . . ." Christophe Lemardelé, "Le sacrifice de purification: un sacrifice ambigu?" *Vetus Testamentum* 52 (2002): 284–9.

14. Franz, *Das Rituale von St. Florian*, 47. The rite is entitled: *Ad introducendam mulierem.*

15. The illustration from the contemporary Lambach ritual (f. 77v) in the Franz edition depicts just this scene. See Franz, *Das Rituale von St. Florian*, 28.

16. Psalm 120/121 (*Levavi oculos*) has an interesting history in the churching *ordines*, especially in its reference to protection from the sun and the moon in verse 6. See Pierce, " 'Green Women' and Blood Pollution," 199, n. 44; and Gail McMurray Gibson, "Blessing from Sun and Moon: Churching as Women's Theater" in *Bodies and Disciplines: Intersections of Literature and History in Fifteenth-Century England*, Medieval Cultures, vol. 9, ed. Barbara A. Hanawalt and David Wallace (Minneapolis/London: University of Minnesota Press, 1996), 139–54.

17. *Benedicat tibi dominus ex Syon; Et uideas filios filiorum; Dominus custodiat te ab omni malo; Dominus custodiat introitum tuum et exitum tuum; Domine exaudi orationem meam.*

18. In the singular (*mens*), "mind," "heart," or "attitude."

19. This interesting prayer is found not only in churching ordines, but also in early sacramentaries. An early textual history of this prayer can be found in Eugenio Moeller, Ioanne Maria Clément, and Bertrandus Coppieters 't Wallant, *Corpus Orationum*, Tomus I, Corpus Christianorum Series Latina, vol. 160 (Turnhout: Brepols, 1992), 173, no. 352a. See also Hartmann Grisar, S.J., *Die römische Kapelle Sancta Sanctorum und ihr Schatz* (Freiburg im Breisgau: Herdersche Verlagshandlung, 1908); and Bernard Capelle, "Ad Sancta Sanctorum introire," *Revue liturgique et monastique* 23 (1937–38), 259–70. This prayer plays an important role in the evoution of the early medieval *ordo missae*; for a summary and analysis. See Joanne M. Pierce, "The Evolution of the *ordo missae* in the Early Middle Ages," in *Medieval Liturgy: A Book of Essays*, Garland Medieval Casebooks, vol. 18., Garland Reference Library of the Humanities, vol. 1884, ed. Lizette Larson-Miller (New York and London: Garland Publishing, 1997), 10–12. The prayer eventually becomes a standard text at the beginning of the *ordo missae*. It also plays a role in the rites for the dedication of a church and in rogation day liturgies.

20. This English translation taken from the *Saint Joseph Daily Missal* (New York: Catholic Book Publishing, 1959), 649. The original reads: *Aufer a nobis, quesumus domine, iniquitates nostras, ut ad sancta sanctorum puris mentibus introire mereamur. Per dominum.* See Franz, *Das Rituale von St. Florian*, 47.

21. *Adiutorium nostrum in nomine domini.*

22. Lawrence A. Hoffman has identified four different types of areas of meaning "conveyed" by ritual: private, official, public, and normative or paradigmatic. See his "How Ritual Means: Ritual Circumcision in Rabbinic Culture and Today," *Studia Liturgica* 23 (1993): 80. As cited in Pierce, " 'Green Women' and Blood Pollution," 12: on the official level "the things the experts say a rite means" is distinct from the public level, "agreed-on meanings shared by a number of ritual participants, even though they are not officially preached by the experts."

23. A fundamental study is Hermann Nottarp, *Gottesurteilstudien*, Bamberger Abhandlungen und Forschungen, Band II (München: Köstel-Verlag Nottarp, 1956). Other more recent works include: Robert Bartlett, *Trial by Fire and*

Water: The Medieval Judicial Ordeal (Oxford: Clarendon Press, 1986), with detailed bibliography; John W. Baldwin, "The Crisis of the Ordeal: Literature, Law and Religion around 1200," *Journal of Medieval and Renaissance Studies* 24 (1994): 327–53; and Richard M. Fraher, "IV Lateran's Revolution in Criminal Procedure: The Birth of *Inquisitio*, the End of Ordeals, and Innocent III's Vision of Ecclesiastical Politics," in *Studia in Honorem Eminentissimi Cardinalis Alphonsi M. Stickler*, Studia et Textus Historiae Iuris Canonici, vol. 7 (Rome: LAS, 1992), 97–111. For a short introduction, see Radding, "Superstition to Science." The basic study of ordeal liturgy itself, however, remains Franz, *Die kirchlichen Benediktionen im Mittelalter*, 307–98. There are other studies of trials by ordeal in the Old Testament; see William McKane, "Poison, Trial by Ordeal and the Cup of Wrath," *Vetus Testamentum* 30 (1980): 474–92.

24. Paul R. Hyams, "Trial by Ordeal: The Key to Proof in the Early Common Law," in *On the Laws and Customs of England: Essays in Honor of Samuel E. Thorne*, ed. Morris S. Arnold and others (Chapel Hill: University of North Carolina Press, 1981), 110.
25. Ibid., 111.
26. Margaret Kerr, Richard Forsyth, and Michael Plyley, "Cold Water and Hot Iron: Trial by Ordeal in England," *The Journal of Interdisciplinary History* 22 (1992): 573–95. The authors' main thesis is that these trials by ordeal were in fact weighted in favor of acquitting the person accused on the basis of no substantial evidence: "The ordeal was an instrument of mercy" (574).
27. In fact, the Florian ritual contains four, in this order: hot iron; hot water or iron; cold water; and a trial/examination by bread and cheese.
28. The illustration in the Lambach manuscript (f. 72r) shows the accused, accompanied by a figure Franz suggests is his guardian angel, just about to take the heated iron in his hand; an assisting minister offers it to him on the end of what appears to be a stout stick. See Franz, *Das Rituale von St. Florian*, 28.
29. Bartlett, *Trial by Fire and Water*, 91.
30. According to Franz (*Die kirchlichen Benediktionene im Mittelalter*, 365, n. 4), at least one manuscript gives the option of placing the hot iron in the hand or set on the foot.
31. Radding, "Superstition to Science," 259.
32. *Iudicium [ferri igne] feruentis*, in Franz, *Das Rituale von St. Florian*, 119–22.
33. "*ferens in leua sanctum euuangelium cum crismario et patrociniis sanctorum calicemque cum patena.*"
34. This phrase does not just refer to the coming trial, but also communicates the hope that the accused will be "approved" or vindicated. The same phrase is used at the blessing of the water, see later.
35. The Lambach manuscript also contains a detailed illustration of this trial (f. 64v), seemingly as the accused, bound hand and foot, is about to be dropped over the side of a boat into a body of water; see also Franz, *Das Rituale von St. Florian*, 27–8.
36. The use of the masculine pronoun is deliberate; a study of English cold water trials between 1194 and 1208 reveals that women were never put to the trial of cold water. One explanation is that contemporary officials recognized that women were much more likely to float because of their higher proportion of body fat. For a detailed discussion of the physiological factors involved, see Kerr, Forsyth, and Plyley, "Cold Water and Hot Iron," 581–7.

37. Radding, "Superstition to Science," 259.
38. *Iudicium aque frigide*; Franz, *Das rituale von St. Florian*, 124–9.
39. One might note among them the more "local" Germanic or Benedictine/monastic saints: among the men, Gereon, Florianus, Kilianus, Lambertus, Ulricus, and Gallus and, among the women, Walburga and Afra.
40. *Dominus deus sancta spiritus*; note the rather unusual direct address to God the Holy Spirit, requesting that the Spirit fill the hearts of the gathered community and unify them, that nothing would turn them from the truth.
41. *hunc hominem uel uicarium eius*; see also Radding, "Superstition to Science," 260.
42. "[if guilty of this] make him float upon you . . . we admonish you in his name, that through his name you might obey us, he whom all creatures serve, whom the Cherubim and Seraphim praise, saying, Holy, Holy, holy."
43. For example, to "know" or "have seen" or "received at home" or "consented"; in other words, to have colluded in the crime in any way.

COMMENTARY: BODY-CRITICAL EMBODIMENT

1. Nancy Jay, "Sacrifice as Remedy for Having Been Born of Woman," in *Women, Gender, Religion: A Reader*, ed. Elizabeth A. Castelli with assistance from Rosamond C. Rodman (New York: Palgrave, 2001), 174-94.
2. Ibid., 181.
3. Catherine Bell, *Ritual Theory, Ritual Practice* (New York: Oxford University Press, 1992).
4. Peter Garnsey, *Social Status and Legal Privilege in the Roman Empire* (Oxford: Clarendon Press, 1970).
5. Judith Perkins, *The Suffering Self: Pain and Narrative Representation in the Early Christian Era* (New York: Routledge, 1995).

CHAPTER 5 RACE, RELIGION, AND THE EMERGING MODERN WORLD: INDIANS, INCAS, AND CONSPIRACY STORIES IN COLONIAL PERU

1. The Lima office of the Spanish Inquisition had jurisdiction over all of contemporary South America, minus present day Colombia. Neither Inquisitors nor their commissioners outside Lima had the kind of totalizing control that they are often projected as having (or that the tribunal wished it had). But, I think it fair to say that the institution's presence was felt over a much broader region than might be expected given the limited personnel at the tribunal's disposal.

There is an extensive literature on the Spanish Inquisition and a growing one on the Lima Office. Some of the works I have consulted include Henry Kamen, *The Spanish Inquisition: A Historical Revision* (New Haven: Yale University Press, 1998); Paulino Castañeda Delgado y Pilar Hernández Aparicio, *La inquisición de Lima* (Madrid: Demos, 1989), 3 vols.; Joaquin Perez y Villanueva and Bartolome Escandell Bonet, eds, *Historia de la Inquisicion en Espana y America*, 3 vols. (Madrid: Biblioteca de Autores Cristianos/Centro de Estudios Inquisitoriales, 1984); Rene Millar Carvacho, *Inquisición y sociedad en el virreinato peruano: estudios sobre el tribunal de la*

Inquisición de Lima (Lima: Instituto Riva-Agüero, Pontificia Universidad Católica del Perú, 1998); Teodoro Hampe-Martinez, "Recent Works on the Inquisition and Peruvian Colonial Society, 1570–1820," *Latin American Research Review* 31:2 (1996): 43–63; Teodoro Hampe Martínez, *Santo Oficio e historia colonial: aproximaciones al Tribunal de la Inquisición de Lima (1570–1820)* (Lima: Ediciones del Congreso del Perú, 1998); Maria Emma Mannarelli, *Hechiceras, beatas y expósitas: mujeres y poder inquisitorial en Lima* (Lima: Ediciones del Congreso del Perú, 1998); Nancy E. Van Deusen, *Between the Sacred and the Worldly: The Institutional and Cultural Practice of Recogimiento in Colonial Lima* (Stanford: Stanford University Press, 2001); Ricardo Palma, 1833–1919,*Anales de la Inquisición de Lima* (Madrid: Ediciones del Congreso de la República, 1997); Jose Toribio Medina, *Historia del tribunal del Santo oficio de la inquisición de Lima (1569–1820)*, 2 vols. (Santiago: Impr. Gutenberg, 1887); Joaquin Perez Villanueva, ed, *La Inquisición Espanola, nueva vision, nuevos horizontes* (Madrid: Siglo Veiniuno de Espana, 1980); Ana Sanchez, *Mentalidad popular frente a ideologia oficial: El Santo Oficio en Lima y los casos de hechiceria (siglo xvii)* (Lima: CBC); Boleslao Lewin, *El Santo Oficio en America y el mas grande proces inquisitorial en el Peru* (Buenos Aires: Sociedad Hebraica Argentina, 1950); Julio Caro Baroja, *Inquisición, brujería y criptojudaísmo* (Barcelona: Ediciones Ariel, 1972).

2. See *Archivo Historico Nacional* (Madrid, hereafter cited as AHN) Inquisition, Legajo 1647, no. 13.
3. Medina, *Historia del Tribunal*, vol. 2, 45–6.
4. See George Alexander Kohut, "The Trial of Francisco Maldonado de Silva," *American Jewish Historical Society* 11 (1903): 166–67.
5. Juan de Solorzano Pereira, *Politica Indiana* [1647] in *Biblioteca de Autores Espanoles*, vols. 252–56 (Madrid, 1972), Lib. I, tomo ii, 262.
6. AHN, Inq, Legajo 1647, no.013, f.53v.
7. AHN, Inq, Legajo 1647, no.13, f.266.
8. AHN, Inq, Legajo 1647, no.13, f.53–53v. The parenthetical definition is part of the original testimony.
9. Ibid., vol.2, 35–41; citation, 38.
10. Gustav Henningsen, *The Witches' Advocate: Basque Witchcraft and the Spanish Inquisition, 1609–1614* (Reno: University of Nevada, 1980); Brian Levack, *The Witch-Hunt in Early Modern Europe* (London and New York: Longman, 1987), 201–06.
   Studies of colonial women accused of practicing witchcraft in the New World constitute a relatively small but growing field. See Maria Manarelli, "Inquisicion y mujeres: las hechiceras en el Peru durante el siglo XVII," *Revista Andina* 3 (1985), 141–56, For an important first examination of women tried for witchcraft in colonial Peru, see Carol Karlsen, *The Devil in the Shape of a Women* (New York: Norton, 1987) for pioneering analysis of the gendered aspects of New England witchhunts of women of European descent. For important feminist analyses of witchcraft practices among Spaniards and Mestizos in eighteenth-century Mexico, see Ruth Bejar, "Sex and Sin, Witchcraft and the Devil in Late Colonial Mexico," *American Ethnologist* 14 (1987): 35–55; and "Sexual Witchcraft, Colonialism, and Women's Powers: Views from the Mexican Inquisition" in *Sexuality and Marriage in Colonial*

Latin America, ed. Asuncion Lavrin (Lincoln: University of Nebraska Press, 1989), 178–206. For an analysis of indigenous women accused of practicing witchcraft in colonial Peru, see Irene Silverblatt, *Moon, Sun, and Witches: Gender Ideologies and Class in Inca and Colonial Peru* (Princeton: Princeton University Press, 1987).

11. See, for example, AHN:Lib.1030, f.194v.

12. AHN:Lib.1028, f.512,514; also see AHN:Lib.1028, f.507–511.

13. AHN:Lib.1031, f.332v.

14. *Tercer Concilio Limense, 1582–1583*, ed. and intro. Enrique Bartra (Lima, 1982).

15. AHN:Lib.1029, f.502v, 504v. Luis Martin, *Daughters of the Conquistadores* (Dallas: Southern Methodist University Press, 1983), 280–309. This discussion on tapadas is indebted to Martin's work.

16. AHN:Lib.1031, f.374v–375.

17. Fernando de Avendano, *Sermones de los misterios de nuestra santa fe catolica, en lengua castellana y la general del inca* (Lima, 1648), 114–115.

18. AHN:Lib.1031, f.399v. Dona Luisa was a woman of great strength. One witness overheard her telling a *comadre* that the Inquisitors were going to have her tortured, and she responded that "she should have womanly valor . . ." (*"valor de muger"*) and "trying to hearten her comadre, she taught her a special charm against Inquisitors to give her strength to face the judges when called in front of the tribunal." See AHN:Lib.1031, f.385v–86.

19. AHN:Lib.1031, f.529v.

20. Martin de Murua, *Historia del origen y geneologia real de los Incas* [1590] (Madrid, 1946), 301. See AAL:Exp.1; Leg.XII. Also see Silverblatt, *Moon, Sun, and Witches* (Princeton: Princeton University Press, 1987), 159–81.

21. Father Pablo Jose de Arriaga, *The Extirpation of Idolatry in Peru* [1621], L. Clark Keating, trans. (Lexington: University of Kentveky Press, 1968), 6, 9; and Cyrus Adler, ed. and trans., "A Contemporary Memorial Relating to Damages to Spanish Interests in America Done by Jews of Holland [1634]," *American Jewish Historical Society* 17 (1909): 45–51.

PART III CONTEMPORARY RITUAL PRACTICES
OF HEALING

CHAPTER 6 THE *VOX FEMINAE*:
CHOOSING AND BEING AS CHRISTIAN FORM
AND PRAXIS

1. See http://www.chaliceofrepose.org/ for a comprehensive bibliography of over 75 citations, including books, recordings, scores, book chapters, videos, and scholarly articles on our work. See also Therese Schroeder-Sheker, *Transitus: A Blessed Death in the Modern World* (Missoula MO: St. Dunstan's Press, 2001), and the video *The Chalice of Repose Project: A Contemplative Musician's Approach to Death and Dying* (Boulder CO: Sounds True, 1997). See also my 1990 disc, *Rosa Mystica* (Celestial Harmonies).

2. See Schoeder-Sheker, *Transitus.*

3. Ibid.

CHAPTER 7 PRACTICING THE PASTORAL CARE OF THE SICK: THE SACRAMENTAL BODY IN LITURGICAL MOTION

1. *Sacrosanctum concilium*: Constitution on the Sacred Liturgy, Second Vatican Council (1963), no. 10.
2. See Margaret Mary Kelleher, "Hermeneutics in the Study of Liturgical Performance," *Worship* 67 (1993): 292–318.
3. Victor Turner, *The Anthropology of Performance* (New York: PAJ Publications, 1987), 139–55.
4. Susan Rodgers and Joanna Ziegler, "Elizabeth of Spalbeek's Trance Dance of Faith: A Performance Theory Interpretation from Anthropological and Art Historical Perspectives," in *Performance and Transformation: New Approaches to Late Medieval Spirituality*, ed. Mary Sudyam and Joanna Ziegler (New York: St. Martin's Press, 1999).
5. Ronald Gagne, Thomas Kane, and Robert VerEecke, *Introducing Dance in Christian Worship* (Portland OR: The Pastoral Press, 1999), 87–91, 151–6.
6. Pastoral Care of the Sick: Rites of Anointing and Viaticum (Washington DC: National Conference of Catholic Bishops, United States of America, 1983). Hereafter, PCS.
7. Charles Gusmer, *And You Visited Me: Sacramental Ministry to the Sick and the Dying*, rev. ed. (New York: Pueblo Publishing, 1989), 106–14.
8. PCS, nos. 8, 53.
9. Gagne, Kane, and VerEecke, *Introducing Dance in Christian Worship*, 99–102.
10. Granger Westsberg and Jill Westberg McNamara, *The Parish Nurse: Providing a Minister of Health for Your Congregation* (Minneapolis MN: Augsburg Fortress, 1990).
11. Rite of Christian Initiation of Adults (Washington DC: National Conference of Catholic Bishops, United States of America, 1988), nos. 84–89.
12. Marty Haughen, *Shepherd Me, O God and Gathering Rite* (Chicago IL: GIA Publications, 1986, 1996).
13. Andrew Witchger, *Rite of Anointing* (St. Louis MO: Morning Star Music, 1991).

CHAPTER 8 CHRIST THE HEALER: AN INVESTIGATION OF CONTEMPORARY LITURGICAL, PASTORAL, AND BIBLICAL APPROACHES

1. "Preface, Anointing Within Mass." *Pastoral Care of the Sick: Rites of Anointing and Viaticum* (International Commission on English in the Liturgy, 1983), no. 145. Hereafter, PCS.
2. Susan K. Wood, "The Paschal Mystery: The Intersection of Ecclesiology and Sacramental Theology in the Care of the Sick," in Genevieve Glen, ed., *Recovering the Riches of Anointing: A Study of the Sacrament of the Sick* (Collegeville MN: The Liturgical Press, 2002), 5–7.
3. PCS, no. 135.

4. Mark McDougall, "Day of Community Healing Brings Closure to Tragic 2001–02 Year," *Holy Cross Crusader*, 20 September 2002, 4.

5. Robert J. Levens, S.J., to the Society of Jesus of New England, Province Memorandum 2002/20, 16 September 2002.

6. PCS, no. 1.

7. Ibid., no. 3.

8. Ibid., nos. 9, 97, 108.

9. Ibid., no. 8.

10. Ibid., nos. 8, 13, 99, 108.

11. See Charles W. Gusmer, *And You Visited Me: Sacramental Ministry to the Sick and the Dying*, rev. ed. (New York: Pueblo Publishing, 1989), 87.

12. See George H. Tavard, "Tradition," in *The New Dictionary of Theology*, ed. Joseph Komonchak and others (Wilmington DE: Michael Glazier, 1989), 1037–41; and Sandra Schneiders, *The Revelatory Text: Interpreting the New Testament as Sacred Scripture* (San Francisco CA: Harper Collins, 1991), 67–86.

13. PCS, no. 1.

14. Translation is *New American Bible with Revised New Testament* (Washington, DC: Confraternity of Christian Doctrine and National Conference of Catholic Bishops, United States of America, 1986).

15. See Second Vatican Council, *Lumen Gentium*: Dogmatic Constitution on the Church (1964), nos. 18–21; and John Paul II, *Ordinatio Sacerdotalis*: Apostolic Letter on Reserving Priestly Ordination to Men Alone (1994), no. 2.

16. See Edward Schillebeeckx, *Christ the Sacrament of the Encounter with God*, trans. Paul Barrett (New York: Sheed & Ward, 1963); *Jesus: An Experiment in Christology*, trans. Hubert Hoskins (New York: Crossroad, 1979); and *Christ: The Experience of Jesus as Lord*, trans. John Bowden (New York: Crossroad, 1981).

17. See John J. Pilch, *Healing in the New Testament: Insights from Medical and Mediterranean Anthropology* (Minneapolis MN: Fortress Press, 2000), 1–54.

18. John Dominic Crossan, *The Birth of Christianity: Discovering what Happened in the Years Immediately After the Execution of Jesus* (San Francisco CA: Harper Collins, 1998), 295.

19. John Dominic Crossan, *The Historical Jesus: The Life of a Mediterranean Jewish Peasant* (San Francisco CA: Harper Collins, 1991), 317–318.

20. See Stevan L. Davies, *Jesus the Healer: Possession, Trance, and the Origins of Christianity* (New York: Continuum, 1995) 100, 198.

21. See Ibid., 147–50; Crossan, *The Historical Jesus*, 367–76; and Paula Fredriksen, *Jesus of Nazareth, King of the Jews* (New York: Knopf, 2000), 232–34.

22. Leander Keck, *Matthew-Mark*, The New Interpreter's Bible, vol. 8 (Nashville TN: Abingdon, 1994), 251.

23. See the series of N. T. Wright, *Christian Origins and the Question of God*, vols. 1, 2, 3 (Minneapolis MN: Fortress Press, 1992, 1996, 2003); and John P. Meier, *A Marginal Jew: Rethinking the Historical Jesus*, vols. 1, 2, 3 (New York: Doubleday, 1991, 1994, 2001).

24. Paul Minear, *To Heal and To Reveal: The Prophetic Vocation According to Luke* (New York: Seabury, 1976), 75.

25. Ibid., 24.

26. Ibid., 100.

COMMENTARY: EMBODIMENT, INTEGRATION, AND AUTHENTICITY: KEYS TO RESHAPING THE CATHOLIC SACRAMENTAL IMAGINATION

1. Judith Marie Kubicki, *Liturgical Music as Ritual Symbol: A Case Study of Jacques Berthier's Taizé Music* (Leuven: Peeters, 1999), 161, 179–80.

PART IV   CATHOLIC RITUAL AS POLITICAL PRACTICE

1. Vicente Rafael, *Contracting Colonialism: Translation and Christian Conversion in Tagalog Society under Early Spanish Rule* (Ithaca NY: Cornell University Press, 1988).
2. Nancy Scheper-Hughes, *Death without Weeping: The Violence of Everyday Life in Brazil* (Berkeley CA: University of California Press, 1992).

CHAPTER 9   THE DEATH OF COMRADE MOTI: PRACTICING CATHOLIC UNTOUCHABLE RAGE IN A NORTH INDIAN VILLAGE

Names of some people and places in this paper have been changed to protect anonymity. All translations from the Hindi are my own. This paper draws from research presented in my doctoral thesis, "A Space for Redemption: Catholic Tactics in Hindu North India," (Ph.D. diss., University of Chicago, 1998). Fieldwork was conducted between January 1995 and May 1996 and was supported by grants from the United States Doctoral Dissertation Research Abroad Program (Fulbright-Hays) and the American Institute of Indian Studies (AIIS). Additional research was conducted in December 2000, sponsored by a grant from the Wabash Center for Teaching and Learning in Theology and Religion. My thanks to Peter Gottschalk for introducing me to Mudrarakshasa and my special gratitude to Ujagir and Jude.

1. Jose Luiz, *Evangelization in Uttar Pradesh* (Bombay: Coordination Center, St. Xavier's College, 1974); and J. Prasad Pinto "The Cultural Contribution of the Capuchins in India," *Indian Missiological Review* 12 (July, 1990): 137–47.
2. See Mathew N. Schmalz, "*Ad Experimentum*: Theology, Anthropology and the Paradoxes of Indian Catholic Inculturation," in *Theology and the Social Sciences*, ed. Michael Barnes (Maryknoll NY: Orbis Books, 2001), 161–80.
3. See also Mathew N. Schmalz, "Dalit Catholic Tactics of Marginality at a North Indian Mission," *History of Religions* 44 (February, 2005): 216–51.
4. On Ujagir, see also Mathew N. Schmalz, "Dalit Christian Pentecostalism in a North Indian Village," *Dalit International Newsletter* 7 (October, 2002): 7–9.
5. Mudrarakshasa, *Dandavidhana* [The criminal Code] (Nahi Delhi: Radhakrishna Prakashan, 1986).
6. See Schmalz, "Dalit Catholic Tactics."
7. Gayendra Pandey, "In Defense of the Fragment: Writing about Hindu-Muslim Riots Today," *Representations* 37 (1992): 27–55.

8. Ibid., 27.
9. Ibid., 28.
10. Ibid., 34–5.
11. See Arun Shourie, *Harvesting Our Souls: Missionaries, Their Designs, Their Claims* (New Delhi: ASA Publications, 2000); and Ramsevak Srivastav "Kya Katholik Charch Sacmuch ek Taim Bam Hai?" [Is the Catholic Church Really a Time Bomb?], *Dinman* (February, 1986): 20–5.
12. Rabindra Ray, *The Naxalites and their Ideology* (New Delhi: Oxford University Press, 1992), 176.
13. Ibid., 213–19.
14. Prabhu Ghate, *Direct Attacks on Rural Poverty: Policy, Programmes and Implementation* (Delhi: Concept Publishing, 1986), 114–39.
15. Ibid., 438–70.
16. Ibid., 440.
17. Ibid., 441.
18. Ibid., 443.
19. Shahid Amin, *Event, Metaphor and Memory: Chauri Chaura 1922–1992* (Delhi: Oxford University Press, 1995).
20. Dipesh Chakrabarty, "Postcolonality and the Artifice of History: Who Speaks for the Indian Past?" *Representations* 37 (1992): 1–26.
21. Mudrarakshasa, *The Hunted*, trans. Robert A. Hueckstedt (New Delhi: Penguin Books, 1991), 235.
22. Mathew N. Schmalz, "Images of the Body in the Life and Death of a North Indian Catholic Catechist," *History of Religions* 39 (November, 1999): 184–7.
23. On inculturation, see Schmalz, *"Ad Experimentum."*
24. Jean E. Jackson, "I am a Fieldnote: Fieldnotes as a Symbol of Professional Identity," in *Fieldnotes: The Makings of Anthropology*, ed. Roger Sanjek (Ithaca NY: Cornell University Press, 1990), 13; see also Roger Sanjek, "Fire, Loss, and the Sorcerer's Apprentice," in *Fieldnotes: The Makings of Anthropology*, ed. Roger Sanjek (Ithaca NY: Cornell University Press, 1990), 34–46.

CHAPTER 10 THE CUSTOMS OF THE FAITHFUL: EVANGELICALS AND THE POLITICS OF CATHOLIC FIESTA IN BOLIVIA

A different version of this article was first published in 2003 in the *Journal of Latin American Lore*, 21(2): 179–200. Bruce Morrill and I wish to thank the Regents of the University of California and The UCLA Latin American Center's permission to reprint that copyrighted material. Research was funded by grants from the Wenner-Gren Foundation, the Inter-American Foundation, Fulbright IIE, the University of Arizona, and Sigma Xi. Additional work was funded by a Grant for Research and Writing from the John D. and Catherine T. MacArthur Foundation, a Richard Carley Hunt Post-doctoral Fellowship from the Wenner-Gren Foundation, and the College of the Holy Cross. My thanks to Bruce Morrill, David Nugent, Susan Rodgers, and John Schmalzbauer for their helpful comments on this essay.

1. The definition of "folklore" in a context of national state formation is discussed by David M. Guss, *The Festive State: Race, Ethnicity, and Nationalism as Cultural Performance* (Berkeley CA: University of California Press, 2000).

2. Alberto Guerra Gutierrez, *Folklore Boliviano* (La Paz-Cochabamba: Los Amigos del Libro, 1990).

3. Oruro's greatest international recognition came in 2001, when UNESCO named the Carnaval de Oruro to its "World Heritage List." See Peter J.M. Nas, "Masterpieces of Oral and Intangible Culture: Reflections on the Unesco World Heritage List," *Current Anthropology* 43:1 (2002), 139–43; and UNESCO, *Masterpieces of the Oral and Intangible Heritage of Humanity: Proclamation*, http://www.unesco.org/culture/heritage/intangible/masterp/html_eng/declar.shtml/, 2001.

4. Herbert S. Klein, *Bolivia: The Evolution of a Multi-Ethnic Society*, 2 ed. (New York: Oxford University Press, 1992).

5. David Stoll, *Is Latin America Turning Protestant? The Politics of Evangelical Growth* (Berkeley CA: University of California Press, 1990).

6. See Rebecca Tolen, " 'Receiving the Authorities' in Chimborazo, Ecuador: Ethnic Performance in an Evangelical Andean Community," *Journal of Latin American Anthropology* 3:2 (1999): 20–53.

7. Max Gluckman, *Order and Rebellion in Tribal Africa* (New York: Free Press of Glencoe, 1963); and Victor Turner, *The Ritual Process: Structure and Anti-Structure* (Ithaca NY: Cornell University Press, 1969).

8. Guss, *The Festive State*, 9.

9. Richard Bauman, "Performance and Honor in 13th-Century Iceland," *Journal of American Folklore* 99 (1986): 131–50; Abner Cohen, "Drama and Politics in the Development of a London Carnival," *Man* 15 (1980): 65–87, and *Masquerade Politics: Explorations in the Structure of Urban Cultural Movements* (Berkeley CA: University of California Press, 1993); Nestor Garcia Canclini, *Hybrid Cultures: Strategies for Entering and Leaving Modernity*, trans. C. L. Chiappari and S. L. Lopez (Minneapolis MN: University of Minnesota Press, 1995); and Milton Singer, *Traditional India: Structure and Change* (Philadelphia PA: American Folklore Society, 1959).

10. Zoila S. Mendoza, *Shaping Society through Dance: Mestizo Ritual Performance in the Peruvian Andes* (Chicago IL: University of Chicago Press, 2000).

11. Elsewhere (Goldstein 1998a, 1998b, 2004) I present more detailed discussions of Villa Pagador's history, and the role of the barrio fiesta in consolidating local identity. See Daniel M. Goldstein, "Dance on the Margins: Transforming Urban Marginality through Popular Performance," *City and Society* 4 (1998): 201–15; "Performing National Culture in a Bolivian Migrant Community," *Ethnology* 37 (1998): 117–32; and *The Spectacular City: Violence and Performance in Urban Bolivia* (Durham NC: Duke University Press, 2004).

12. Jorge Urquidi Zambrana, *La Urbanización de la Ciudad de Cochabamba: Sintesis del Estudio Antecedentes. Ptimera Parte* (Cochabamba: Editorial Universitaria, 1967).

13. Xavier Albó, Thomás Greaves, and Godofredo Sandoval, *Chukiyawu: La Cara Aymara de la Paz: El Paso a la Ciudad*, Cuaderno de Investigacion, vol. 1, no. 20 (La Paz: Centro de Investigatión y Promoción del Campesino, 1981).

14. Humberto Solares Serrano, *Historia, Espacio, y Sociedad: Cochabamba 1550–1950: Formación, Crisis y Desarrollo de su Proceso Urbano* (Cochabamba: CIDRE, 1990).

15. Rafael Mondragón, *De Indios y Cristianos en Guatemala* (México, DF: COPEC/CECOPE, 1983); and Maria Albán Estrada and Juan Pablo Muñoz, *La Invasión De Las Sectas al Ecuador* (Quito: Editorial Planeta, 1987).

16. Elizabeth E. Brusco, "Colombia: Past Persecution, Present Tension," in *Religious Freedom and Evangelization in Latin America*, ed. Paul E. Sigmund (Maryknoll NY: Orbis, 1999), 235–52.

17. David Martin, *Tongues of Fire: The Explosion of Protestantism in Latin America* (Oxford: Blackwell, 1993), 51.

18. Virginia Garrard-Burnett, *Living in the New Jerusalem: Protestantism in Guatemala* (Austin TX: University of Texas Press, 1998); Lesley Bill, " 'Like a Veil to Cover Them': Women and the Pentecostal Movement in La Paz," *American Ethnologist* 17:4 (1990) 708–21, and *Precarious Dependencies: Bender, Class, and Domestic Service in Bolivia* (New York: Columbia University Press, 1994); Karsten Paerregaard, "Conversion, Migration, and Social Identity: The Spread of Protestantism in the Peruvian Andes," *Ethnos* 59 (1994): 168–86; and Harald O.Skar, "Quest for a New Covenant: The Israelita Movement in Peru," in *Natives and Neighbors in South America: Anthropological Essays*, ed. Harald O. Skar and Frank Salamon (Gothenburg: The Ethnographical Museum, 1987), 233–66.

19. Brusco characterizes some Colombian women's involvement in evangelical Protestantism as a "strategic" form of collective action, by which women strengthen domestic relations and achieve a healthier and more equitable balance in the home with men. See Elizabeth E. Brusco, *The Reformation of Machismo: Evangelical Conversion and Gender in Colombia* (Austin TX: University of Texas Press, 1995).

20. For the ethnographer doing research among evangelicals, the ban on alcohol means that one is frequently required to drink enormous quantities of soda pop, to satisfy people's cultural obligation to extend hospitality in the form of a beverage offered the visitor.

21. This claim—that a religious wedding in the Catholic Church obliges one to host an elaborate party afterwards—is denied by Church representatives. The Catholic priest in Villa Pagador also told me that the Church does not encourage drinking, but views drunkenness as a social problem to work against. However, he acknowledged that "Andean custom" does require the routine consumption of alcohol in ritual functions like the Saint's Day celebration.

22. Emilio Willems, *Followers of the New Faith: Culture Change and the Rise of Protestantism in Brazil and Chile* (Nashville TN: Vanderbilt University Press, 1967; and David Stoll, "Introduction: Rethinking Protestantism in Latin America," in *Rethinking Protestantism in Latin America*, ed. Virginia Garrard-Burnett and David Stoll (Philadelphia PA: Temple University Press, 1993), 1–19.

23. Others go so far as to suggest that the evangelical church serves as a replacement for the lost patronage of the old *hacienda* system, with the pastor standing in for the *patrón*. See Christian Lalive d'Espinay, *Havens of the Masses: A Study of the Pentecostal Movement in Chile* (London: Lutterworth, 1969).

24. Stoll, "Introduction," 5.

25. Martin, *Tongues of Fire*, 234.

26. I have used pseudonyms throughout this chapter, to protect the identities of my consultants.

27. There are many denominations within the umbrella designation of "Pentecostal," but people in Pagador refer to their institution simply as "the Pentecostal church." I am unaware of its specific denominational attribution.
28. See Gill, *Precarious Dependencies*.
29. They were able to accomplish this because Nestor's cousin is a pastor of the church, and so was willing to tolerate this deviation from the rules. Thus, while many anthropologists in Latin America take on godparent obligations, I may be one of the few who is a *padrino* in the Baptist church.

Chapter 11   Making Christ Credible: U.S. Latino/a Popular Catholicism and the Liberating Nearness of God

1. William A. Christian, Jr., "Spain in Latino Religiosity" in *El Cuerpo de Cristo: The Hispanic Presence in the U.S. Catholic Church*, ed. Peter Casarella and Raúl Gómez. (New York: Crossroad, 1998), 326–7.
2. Ibid., 327.
3. Gary Macy, "Demythologizing 'the Church' in the Middle Ages," *Journal of Hispanic/Latino Theology* 3:1 (August, 1995): 27.
4. Orlando Espín, *Faith of the People: Theological Reflections on Popular Catholicism* (Maryknoll NY: Orbis Books, 1997), 117.
5. Ibid., 119.
6. Orlando Espín, "Pentecostalism and Popular Catholicism: The Poor and *Traditio*," *Journal of Hispanic/Latino Theology* 3:2 (November, 1995): 19.
7. Ibid.
8. Mark Francis, "Popular Piety and Liturgical Reform in a Hispanic Context," in *Dialogue Rejoined: Theology and Ministry in the United States Hispanic Reality*, ed. Ana María Pineda and Robert Schreiter (Collegeville MN: The Liturgical Press, 1995), 165–6.
9. Macy, "Demythologizing 'the Church' in the Middle Ages," 40.
10. Louis Dupré, *Passage to Modernity: An Essay in the Hermeneutics of Nature and Culture* (New Haven CT: Yale University Press, 1995), 94.
11. Caroline Bynum, "Why All the Fuss About the Body? A Medievalist's Perspective," in *Beyond the Cultural Turn: New Directions in the Study of Society and Culture*, ed. Victoria Bonnell and others (Berkeley CA: University of California Press, 1999), 251–2.
12. See ibid.
13. Dupré, *Passage to Modernity*, 3.
14. Ibid., 179.
15. Ibid., 163–4.
16. David Bentley Hart, *The Beauty of the Infinite: The Aesthetics of Christian Truth* (Grand Rapids MI: Eerdmans, 2003), 133–4.
17. Karl Rahner, "The Theology of the Symbol," in *Theological Investigations*, vol. 4, trans. Kevin Smyth (New York: Crossroad, 1982 [1966]), 244.
18. Thomas F. O'Meara, *Theology of Ministry* (New York: Paulist Press, 1999), 115–16.
19. Jon Sobrino, *Spirituality of Liberation: Toward Political Holiness* (Maryknoll NY: Orbis Books, 1988), 166–7.
20. Ibid., 171.

COMMENTARY: THE PARADOXICAL CHARACTER OF SYMBOLS, POPULAR RELIGION, AND CHURCH: QUESTIONS FOR U.S. LATINO/A THEOLOGY

1. The development of U.S. Latino/a theology may be traced in the pages of the *Journal of Hispanic/Latino Theology*, published by the Academy of Catholic Hispanic Theologians of the United States (ACHTUS) from 1993 to the present. Roberto Goizueta's own publications are numerous; his most complete treatment of Hispanic popular Catholicism is found in *Caminemos con Jesus: Towards a Hispanic/Latino Theology of Accompaniment* (Maryknoll NY: Orbis, 1995).
2. Professor of New Testament and Christian spirituality, Sandra M. Schneiders offers her most complete treatment of biblical hermeneutics in the second edition of *The Revelatory Text: Interpreting the New Testament as Sacred Scripture* (Collegeville MN: The Liturgical Press, 1999), especially 27–61. For a shorter treatment, see her *Women and the Word: The Gender of God in the New Testament and the Spirituality of Women* (New York: Paulist, 1986).
3. Like most of his Latino/a colleagues, Goizueta sees relationality as fundamental to Hispanic culture and thus takes it as a primary source for theological reflection on the doctrines of God, Jesus Christ, grace, and sin. As I have argued elsewhere, the description of relationality offered by Goizueta and others seems to overlook the marginalization of some groups within Hispanic communities and families by Hispanics themselves. Mistreatment of persons for reasons of race, class, gender, and/or sexual orientation, often justified on religious grounds, bespeaks a flawed relationality which, in turn, would mean that Hispanic communities as such not only reveal but also hide the face of God. See James B. Nickoloff, "Sexuality: A Queer Omission in the U.S. Latino/a Theology," *Journal of Hispanic/Latino Theology* 10:3 (2003): 31–51.
4. The work of pastoral agents in Latin America following the Latin American bishops' conference in Medellin (1968), especially the experiences of lay Catholics and foreign mission groups such as Maryknoll and the Columbans, who have been deeply committed to the liberation of the poor, remains a largely untold story. It thus constitutes an untapped resource for theological reflection, particularly on popular religion.
5. See Clayborne Carson, ed., *The Autobiography of Martin Luther King, Jr.* (New York: Warner, 1988).
6. See Donald Gelpi, *Grace as Transmuted Experience and Social Process, and Other Essays in North American Theology* (Lanhan MD: University Press of America, 1988), especially 97–139, in which he expands Bernard Lonergan's model of conversion by adding "affective" and "socio-political" conversions to intellectual, moral, and religious.
7. It is striking that U.S. Latino/a theologians have not, to date, spelled out in systematic fashion the consequences for ecclesiology of their analyses of popular Catholicism.
8. See Vatican II, *Lumen gentium* 8, which affirms that "the Church, embracing sinners in her bosom, is at the same time holy and always in need of being purified," and *Gaudium et spes* 43, which claims that although the church "has never ceased to be the sign of salvation on earth, still she is very well aware that among her members, both clerical and lay, some have been unfaithful to the Spirit of God during the course of many centuries."

PART V   CONTEMPORARY MASS MEDIA AS A DOMAIN
FOR CATHOLIC RITUAL PRACTICE

CHAPTER 12   THE CELL PHONE AND THE
CROWD: MESSIANIC POLITICS IN RECENT PHILIPPINE
HISTORY

Previously published as, Vicente L. Rafael, "The Cell Phone and the Crowd," in *Public Culture* 15: 399–425. Copyright, 2003, Duke University Press. All rights reserved. Used by permission of the publisher.

1. The link between telecommunication technologies and the politics of belief that I pursue here is indebted partly to the work of Jacques Derrida, especially in such writings as "Faith and Knowledge: The Two Sources of 'Religion' at the Limits of Reason Alone," in *Acts of Religion*, trans. Sam Weber, ed. Gil Anidjar (New York: Routledge, 2002), 42–101; "Signature Event Context," in *Margins of Philosophy*, trans. Alan Bass (Chicago IL: University of Chicago Press, 1982), 307–30; and *The Politics of Friendship*, trans. George Collins (London: Verso, 1977).

2. See the bundle entitled "Telefonos, 1885–1891" at the Philippine National Archives, Manila, for sketches of a plan to install a telephone system in the city as early as November, 1885. By December 1885, an office of Telephone Communication had been established (*Communicacion Telefonica*) and the first telephone station set up on the same date at Santa Lucia, Manila.

3. Jose Rizal, "Por Telefono," Barcelona, 1889. Reprinted in (Manila: R. Martinez and Sons, 1959) and in various other anthologies of Rizal's writings. For a more extended discussion of telegraphy and the formation of a wish for a lingua franca among the first generation of nationalists, see Vicente L. Rafael, "Translation and Revenge: Castilian and the Origins of Nationalism in the Philippines," in Doris Sommer, ed., *The Places of History: Regionalism Revisited in Latin America* (Durham NC: Duke University Press, 1999), 214–35.

4. For an elaboration of other modalities of these telecommunicative fantasies and their role in shaping nationalist consciousness, see Vicente L. Rafael, *White Love and Other Events in Philippines History* (Durham NC: Duke University Press, 2000), especially chapters 4 and 8 on rumor and gossip as populist modes of communication in Philippine history.

5. For a useful collection of documents and newspaper articles relating to the corruption case against Estrada, see Sheila Coronel, ed., *Investigating Estrada: Millions, Mansions and Mistresses* (Quezon City: Philippine Center for Investigative Journalism, 2000).

6. The quotations mentioned come respectively from Uli Schmetzer, "Cell Phones Spurred Filipinos," *Chicago Tribune*, January 24, 2001; Ederic Penaflor Eder, "Tinig Ng Genertion Txt", *Pinoy Times*, February 8, 2001; Malou Mangahas, "Text Messaging Comes of Age in the Philippines," *Reuters Technology News*, January 28, 2001.

7. Wayne Arnold, "Manila's Talk of the Town is Text Messaging," *New York Times*, July 5, 2000.

8. For a succinct historical analysis of the Philippine state, see Benedict Anderson, "Cacique Democracy in the Philippines," in *The Specter of Comparisons* (London: Verso 1998),192–226. See also John Sidel, *Capital,*

Coercion, and Crime: Bossism in the Philippines (Stanford CA: Stanford University Press, 1999); and Paul D. Hutchcroft, *Booty Capitalism: The Politics of Banking in the Philippines* (Ithaca NY: Cornell University Press, 1998).

9. The technology for monitoring cell phone use does exist and there is some indication that the Philippine government is beginning to acquire these. It is doubtful, however, that such technology had been available under Estrada. It is also not clear whether the current regime of Gloria Macapagal-Arroyo has begun monitoring or intends to monitor cell phone transmissions.

10. See Arnold, "Manila's Talk of the Town is Text Messaging"; Mangahas, "Text Messaging Comes of Age in the Phillipines"; and Schmetzer, "Cell Phones Spurred Filipinos." See also Leah Salterio, "Text Power in Edsa 2001," *Philippine Daily Inquirer* (hereafter PDI), January 22, 2001; Conrad de Quiros, "Undiscovered Country," *PDI*, February 6, 2001; Michael L. Lim, "Taming the Cell Phone," *PDI*, February 6, 2001. There are certain limits to this economic advantage, however. For example, it is expensive to call across networks, so that calling or texting from a Globe phone to a Smart phone is rarely ever done. Indeed, the Department of Transportation and Communication (DOTC) at one point had to intervene in late 1999 to get the two companies to improve inter-connectivity and service as well as lower their costs.

11. This article was being circulated around the listserves of various NGOs in the Philippines and bore the title "Pinoy Lifestyle." I have no knowledge as to the original source of this piece and so it exists in some ways like a forwarded text message. Thanks to Tina Cuyugan (tinacuyugan@mindanao.org) for forwarding this essay to me. All translations are mine unless otherwise indicated.

12. Arnold, "Manila's Talk of the Town is Text Messaging."

13. rnrsarreal@aol.com, in Plaridel, (plaridel_papers@egroups.com), January 25, 2001.

14. Arnold, "Manila's Talk of the Town is Text Messaging"; See also Richard Lloyd Parr, untitled article on People Power II and cell phone use in *The Independent*, London, January 23, 2001.

15. Michael Tan, "Taming the Cell Phone," *PDI*, February 6, 2001.

16. Ibid.; De Quiros, "Undiscovered Country," *PDI*, February 6, 2001.

17. Arnold, "Manila's Talk of the Town is Text Messaging."

18. These messages were forwarded by rnrsarreal@aol.com, to the Plaridel discussion group (plaridel_papers@yahoogroups.com), January 25, 2001.

19. Bart Guingona, Plaridel, (plaridel_papers@yahoogroups.com), January 26, 2001. Texting is widely credited with bringing about the rapid convergence of crowds at the Edsa shrine within approximately seventy-five minutes of the abrupt halt of the Estrada impeachment trial on the evening of January 16. Even prior to Cardinal Sin and former president Cory Aquino's appeal for people to converge at this hallowed site, it has been estimated that over twenty thousand people had already arrived there, perhaps lured by text messages they received. As Danny A. Gozo, an employee at Ayala Corporation, points out in his posting on Plaridel, of January 23, 2001 (plaridel_papers@yahoogroups.com), Globe Telecom reported an average of forty-two million outgoing messages and around an equal number of incoming ones as well, while Smart Telecom reported over seventy million outgoing and incoming messages texted through their system *per day* during the days of People Power II.

He observes enthusiastically that "the interconnectedness of people, both within the country and outside is a phenomenon unheard of before. It is changing the way that we live!"

20. I owe this term to James T. Siegel, *Fetish Recognition Revolution* (Princeton NJ: Princeton University Press, 1997), perhaps one the most important and incisive works on the relationship between nationalism and technology.

21. My remarks on Manila's streets were gleaned from the notes and observations I made in the 1990s. On Manila's urban forms, see the excellent essay by Neferti X. Tadiar, "Manila's New Metropolitan Forms," in Vicente L. Rafael, ed., *Discrepant Histories: Translocal Essays on Filipino Cultures* (Philadelphia PA: Temple University Press, 1995), 285–313. For a lucid portrait of Manila's fantastic street life, see the novel by James Hamilton-Paterson, *The Ghosts of Manila* (New York: Vintage, 1995). Contemporary Philippine cinema, which often traverses the divide between rich and poor and acutely explores the spaces of their habitation, are excellent primary source materials for the study of Manila's urban forms. For a recent collection of essays on Philippine cinema, see Roland Tolentino, ed., *Geopolitics of the Visible: Essays on Philippine Film Cultures* (Quezon City: Ateneo de Manila University Press, 2000).

22. I owe this information to Mr. David Rafael, former manager of the Glorietta shopping mall in the Ayala Center in Makati.

23. For a discussion of the historical link between linguistic and social hierarchies, see Vicente L. Rafael, "Taglish, or the Phantom Power of the Lingua Franca," in *White Love and Other Events in Filipino History* (Durham NC: Duke University Press, 2000), 162–89.

24. Here, I draw from Martin Heidegger, "The Question Concerning Technology," in *The Question Concerning Technology and other Essays*, trans. William Lovitt (New York: Harper and Row, 1977), 3–35. See also the illuminating commentary by Samuel Weber, "Upsetting the Setup: Remarks on Heidegger's 'Questing After Technics'," in *Mass Mediauras: Form Technics Media* (Stanford CA: Stanford University Press, 1996), 55–75. My remarks on the crowd are indebted to Walter Benjamin, *Charles Baudelaire: A Lyric Poet in the Era of High Capitalism* (London: Verso, 1977).

25. For a discussion of the history of this nationalist fantasy, see the introduction to Vicente L. Rafael, *White Love and Other Events in Filipino History*, 1–18. For a comparative approach to the radical potential of nationalist ideas, see Benedict Anderson, *Imagined Communities: Reflections on the Origins and Spread of Nationalism*, rev. ed. (London: Verso, 1991).

26. Flor C., Plaridel listserv (plaridel_papers@yahoogroups.com), January 24, 2001.

27. "Flor C.," I have subsequently learned, is Flor Caagusan. She was formerly editor of the editorial page of the *Manila Times* and at one point served as the managing editor of *Diliman Review*. I owe this information from the journalist Pete Lacaba. While she would be known to a small group of journalists who are part of the Plaridel discussion group, she would presumably be unknown to the majority of participants in this group. The matter of her anonymity thus remains crucial.

28. For an elaboration of the notion of *damayan*, see Reynaldo Ileto, *Pasyon and Revolution: Popular Uprisings in the Philippines, 1840–1910* (Quezon City: Ateneo de Manila University Press, 1979). See also the important work of

Fenella Cannell on Bikol province, south of Manila, *Power and Intimacy in the Christian Philippines* (Cambridge: Cambridge University Press, 1999).

29. Derrida, "Faith and Knowledge," 56–7.

CHAPTER 13 THE SACRAMENTAL BODY OF AUDREY SANTO

1. Two of my students, Meghan Cerretani and Andrew Reinhart, did two semesters of fieldwork in this parish in 1998–1999, and I draw gratefully on that material here. As noted below, I attended the August 9, 1998, Fitton Field Mass and lodge my analysis there, and in some of the video and television representations of that event. I have not done fieldwork with the Santo family; for a good discussion of the difficulties of fieldwork on Little Audrey devotionalism see Mathew Schmalz, "The Silent Body of Audrey Santo," *History of Religions* 42:2 (2002). My own main ethnographical fieldwork focuses on quite different issues, in fact, in Indonesia. See for instance Susan Rodgers, "Compromise and Contestation in Colonial Sumatra: An 1873 Mandailing Schoolbook on the 'Wonders of the West'," *Bijdragen tot de Taal-, Land- en Volkenkunde* 158:3 (2002): 479–512; Susan Rodgers, "Folklore with a Vengeance: A Sumatran Literature of Resistance in the Colonial Indies and New Order Indonesia," *Journal of American Folklore* 116:460 (2003): 129–58; and *Telling Lives, Telling History: Autobiograpy and Historical Imagination in Modern Indonesia* (Berkeley and Los Angeles: University of California Press, 1995), on matters of Indonesian state power and minority print literatures. See also Susan Rodgers, "Batak Tape Cassette Kinship: Constructing Kinship through the Indonesian National Mass Media," *American Ethnologist* 13:1 (1986): 23–42, on Indonesian mass media and Batak identities.

2. As noted, much of the medical world terminology about Audrey Santo's condition ("paralyzed," "unconscious," "comatose") is problematic, since some family members and caregivers such as nurses assert that she is often aware of her surroundings, hears much of what is said to her, and can make minor movements such as gentle hand squeezes. I use these words with those caveats in mind. Later in the paper I employ another conflicted term, holy oil, for the substance that purportedly drips from pictures and devotional statuettes in the home. The Worcester diocese does not consider this oil to be holy oil, as it has not at all been blessed by a Catholic priest. The Santo family, however, does apparently see the oil as special.

3. Doug Hanchett, "Victim Soul: the Enigma of Little Audrey," *Worcester Magazine* 22:46 (August 5–11, 1998): 14.

4. On January 31, 1999, the Most Rev. Daniel P. Reilly, Worcester's Roman Catholic bishop, issued a press release stating that miraculous events had not been demonstrated in the Santo home. Referring to the oil exudations, this statement noted, "one cannot presume that the inability to explain something automatically makes it miraculous." The commission convened by the bishop to investigate the miracle claims also expressed a degree of skepticism and caution about the Apostolate of the Silent Soul's invocation of the term "victim soul" in reference to Audrey Santo. The commission's preliminary findings were posted on the bishop's website, www.worcesterdiocese.org.

5. Martha Akstin, "Audrey-nomics," *Worcester Magazine* 22:46 (August 5–11, 1998): 10.

6. Ibid.

7. Mathew Schmalz, "The Silent Body of Audrey Santo," 129.

8. Paula M. Kane, " 'She Offered Herself Up': The Victim Soul and Victim Spirituality in Catholicism," *Church History* 71: 80 (March 2002): 80.

9. Other major hagiographic materials on Little Audrey include Thomas Petrisko, *In God's Hands: The Miraculous Story of Little Audrey Santo* (McKees Rocks, PA: St. Andrew's Productions, 1997); and the videotape, "*Audrey Santo: Mystic and Victim Soul*," produced by the Apostolate of the Silent Soul (Worcester, 1998). See also Antonia Felix's largely laudatory *Silent Soul: the Miracles and Mysteries of Audrey Santo* (New York: St. Martin's Press, 2000).

10. A small part of this profuse news coverage includes the following: Gene Weingarten, "Tears for Audrey," *Washington Post* (July 19, 1998); John Larabee, "Thousands Seek God at Girl's Sickbed," *USA Today* (August 7, 1998); Gustav Niebuhr, "Unconscious Girl Inspires Streams of Pilgrims," *New York Times* (August 30, 1998); and extensive coverage of the main anniversary Masses in the Worcester *Telegram and Gazette*. The Worcester Diocese's *The Catholic Free Press* also has extensive Little Audrey coverage. In television sources beyond the ABC program discussed in this paper see also "48 Hours," "Desperate Measures," June 24, 1999.

11. Schmalz, "The Silent Body of Audrey Santo," 116–42.

12. Ibid., 127–8.

13. Especially illuminating anthropological studies of Catholic and larger Christian ritual practice that I have drawn on here include Fenella Cannell's *Power and Intimacy in the Christian Philippines* (Cambridge: Cambridge University Press, 1999), and John Burdick's *Blessed Anastacia: Women, Race, and Popular Christianity in Brazil* (New York and London: Routledge, 1998). See also Michael Cuneo, *The Smoke of Satan: Conservative and Traditionalist Dissent in Contemporary American Catholicism* (New York and London: Oxford University Press, 1997). On music and ritual see Elizabeth McAlister's excellent *Rara: Vodou, Power, and Performance in Haiti and its Diaspora* (Berkeley and Los Angeles: University of California Press, 2002). Also suggestive here, from history, are Caroline Walker Bynum's *Holy Fast, Holy Feast: The Religious Significance of Food to Medieval Woman* (Berkeley and Los Angeles: University of California Press, 1987), Robert Orsi's *Thank You, St. Jude: Women's Devotion to the Patron Saint of Hopeless Causes* (New Haven CT: Yale University Press, 1996), and especially his " 'Mildred, Is It Fun To Be a Cripple?': The Culture of Suffering in Mid-Twentieth Century American Catholicism," in *Catholic Lives, Contemporary America*, ed. Thomas Ferraro (Durham NC: Duke University Press, 1997), 19–64.

14. Kane, "She Offered Herself Up."

15. Hanchett, "Victim Soul," 14.

16. Ibid.

17. Ibid.

18. Susan Rodgers and Joanna Ziegler, "Elisabeth of Spalbeek's Trance Dance of Faith: A Performance Theory Interpretation from Anthropological and Art Historical Perspectives," in *Performance and Transformation: New*

Approaches to Late Medieval Spirituality, ed. Mary Sudyam and Joanna Ziegler (New York: St. Martin's Press, 1999).

19. Ruth Harris, *Lourdes: Body and Spirit in the Secular Age* (New York: Penguin Compass, 1999).

COMMENTARY: CATHOLIC SACRAMENTALISM AS MEDIA EVENT: A VIEW FROM THE SOCIOLOGY OF RELIGION AND MEDIA SOCIOLOGY

1. Ronald L. Grimes, "Ritual and the Media," in *Practicing Religion in the Age of the Media*, ed., Stewart M. Hoover and Lynn Schofield Clark (New York: Columbia University Press, 2002), 220, 221.
2. Gregor Goethals, "The Electronic Golden Calf: Transforming Ritual and Icon," in *Religion and Popular Culture in America*, ed., Bruce David Forbes and Jeffrey H. Mahan (Berkeley CA: University of California Press, 2000), 140.
3. Patricia O'Connell Killen, "Benediction of the Blessed Sacrament," in *Religions of the United States in Practice*, vol 2., ed., Colleen McDannell (Princeton NJ: Princeton University Press, 2001), 44–52.
4. Andrew Greeley, *The Catholic Imagination* (Berkeley CA: University of California Press, 2000).
5. Jack Lule, *Daily News, Eternal Stories: The Mythological Role of Journalism* (New York: Guilford Press, 2001).
6. Lynn Schofield Clark, *From Angels to Aliens: Teenagers, the Media, and the Supernatural* (New York: Oxford University Press, 2003).
7. James Carey, "A Cultural Approach to Communication," in *Communication as Culture: Essays on Media and Society* (New York: Routledge, 1992): 14, 15.
8. Ibid., 17.
9. Ibid., 21.
10. Paul Crowley, "Finding 'The Catholic Thing': In Aquinas, Marx, and Billie Holiday," *Commonweal* (April 20, 2001): 16–19.

CHAPTER 14   PERFORMING THE MIRACULOUS IN CENTRAL MASSACHUSETTS

1. Stanley Tambiah, "A Performative Approach to Ritual," *Proceedings of the British Academy* 65 (1979): 113–69.
2. Clifford Geertz, *The Interpretation of Cultures* (New York: Basic Books, 1973), 142–92.
3. Catherine Bell, *Ritual Theory, Ritual Practice* (Oxford: Oxford University Press, 1995), 27.
4. See also Mathew N. Schmalz, "The Silent Body of Audrey Santo," *History of Religions* 42 (November 2002): 116–42.
5. Valerio Valeri, *Kingship and Sacrifice* (Chicago IL: The University of Chicago Press, 1985).
6. See Mathew N. Schmalz, "American Catholic, Indian Catholics: Reflections on Religious Identity, Ethnography and the History of Religions," *Method & Theory in the Study of Religion* 13 (January 2001): 91–7.

PART VI   CONCLUSION: BETWEEN THEORY AND
PRACTICE

CHAPTER 15   SCHOLARSHIP AND/AS PERFORMANCE: THE
CASE OF JOHAN HUIZINGA AND HIS CONCEPT OF
"HISTORICAL SENSATION"

1. The translation of the title is itself challenging, for *Waning* might also be translated as Autumn, Harvrest, Decline, or Evening. Then, the subtitle: *A Study of the Forms of Life and Thoughts in the Fourteenth and Fifteenth Centuries in France and the Netherlands,* could read for Netherlands the *Low Countries* or the *Burgundian Low Countries*. It helps the reader in English to be aware of these nuances.
2. Bruce Lyon, "Henri Pirenne and Johan Huizinga in Search of Historical Truth: Two Different Approaches," in *Papers of the Second Interdisciplinary Conference on Netherlandic Studies*, ed. William H. Fletcher (Lanham MD, New York: Leiden, 1987), 3–16.
3. Edward Peters and Walter P. Simons, "The New Huizinga and the Old Middle Ages," *Speculum* 74:3 (July 1999): 587–620.
4. Ibid., 601.
5. Lyon, "Henri Pirenne and Johan Huizinga."
6. Peters and Simons, "The New Huizinga," 601.
7. Ibid., 608.
8. Lionel Gossman, "*Kulturgeschichte, Kunstgeschichte, Genuss*: History and Art in Burckhardt," in *History and Limits of Interpretation: A Symposium* (Dallas TX: Rice University Press, 1996).
9. Johan Huizinga, *The Waning of the Middle Ages: Study of the Forms of Life, Thought, and Art in France and the Netherlands in the Dawn of the Renaissance.* (New York: Doubleday Anchor Books, [1919] 1956), 10.
10. Dietrich Neumann, ed., *Architecture of the Night: The Illuminated Building* (Munich, Berlin, London, and New York: Prestel Verlag, 2002).
11. While I was writing this essay, a study appeared by Jean Verdon, *Night in the Middle Ages*, trans. George Holoch (Notre Dame IN: University of Notre Dame, 2002). It was given low marks for its "disregard for the traditional scholarly apparatus." Cf. Albrecht Classen, review in *The Medieval Review* (September 2, 2003).
12. Juliet Wilson-Bareau, *Manet, Monet, and the Gare Saint-Lazare* (New Haven CT: Yale University Press, 1998).
13. Peters and Simons, "The New Huizinga," 610.
14. Huizinga, *The Waning of the Middle Ages*, 15.
15. Kermit Swiler Champa, "A Little Night Music: The Play of Color and Light," in *Architecture of the Night*, 20.
16. Peters and Simons, "The New Huizinga," 609.
17. Ibid., 620.
18. Ibid., 592. Italics mine.
19. Kathryn Brush, *The Shaping of Art History: Wilhelm Voege, Adolph Goldschmidt, and the Study of Medieval Art* (Cambridge and New York: The Cambridge University Press, 2002).
20. Lyon, "Henri Pirenne and Johan Huizinga," 12–13.
21. Ibid., 11.

22. Fairly recently, a new reading of this situation has been offered by Lionel Gossman at a Rice University conference, during which, citing Frank Ankersmit, he says: "Nevertheless, Ankersmit sees some relation between Huizinga's idea of historical sensation and the current vogue of highly qualitative forms of historiography: *Histoire des mentalites*, German *Alltagsgeschichte*, the micro-stories exemplified by the work of Carlo Ginzburg and Natalie Davis. Unlike traditional historicist and narrativist histories, these new forms do not seek synthesis and coherence; they focus on the small detail and reveal its strangeness." Gossman, "*Kulturgeschicte, Kunstgeschicte, Genuss.*" This deserves further exploration, although Huizinga's emphatic emphases on sensory data and form is not quite similar to an emphasis on detail.

23. Lyon, "Henri Pirenne and Johan Huizinga," 15–16.

24. Christopher A. Dustin and Joanne E. Ziegler, *Practicing Mortality: Art, Philosophy, and Contemplative Seeing* (New York: Palgrave Macmillan Press, 2005).

25. Bruce T. Morrill, "Practicing the Pastoral Care of the Sick: The Sacramental Body in Liturgical Motion," see above, pp. 99–114.

26. Ibid.

27. Lyon, "Henri Pirenne and Johan Huizinga," 15–16.

CHAPTER 16   THE LITURGY OF THEORY

1. A subsequent version of this paper became the Tangeman Lecture, which I was invited to deliver at the Yale Institute for Sacred Music and the Arts in May of 2003. See Christopher A. Dustin, "The Liturgy of Theory: Lessons on Beauty and Craft," *Colloqium: Music, Worship Arts* 1(2004): 11–20. The ideas that were first presented here have also been more fully developed in *Practicing Mortality: Art, Philosophy, and Contemplative Seeing*, which I co-authored with Joanna E. Ziegler. (New York: Palgrave Macmillan, 2005).

2. Josef Pieper, *Only the Lover Sings: Art and Contemplation*, trans. Lothar Krauth (San Francisco CA: Ignatius Press, 1990), 23.

3. See, for instance, Aristotle's *Metaphysics* I.2, 983a5.

4. Pieper, *Only the Lover Sings*, 72.

5. See Ibid., 72. The quotation from Anaxagoras (cited by Pieper) is from Diogenes Laertius, II. 10–12.

6. See Pieper, *Only the Lover Sings*, 73.

7. Therese Schroeder-Sheker, *Transitus: A Blessed Death in the Modern World* (Missoula MT: St. Dunstan's Press, 2001), 24–25.

8. McEwen, Indra Kagis, *Socrates' Ancestor: An Essay in Architectural Beginnings* (Cambridge MA: MIT Press, 1995), 20ff.

9. Ibid., 21.

10. Ibid.

11. See Martin Heidegger, "Science and Reflection" in *The Question Concerning Technology*, trans. Alfred Hofstadter (New York: Harper and Row, 1977): 163–4.

12. It is worth noting here that ancient sources often use *theoros* to refer to a person who travels to consult an oracle. (See McEwen, *Socrates' Answer*, 21). Oracular sayings are not simply informative. They are revelatory, but also notoriously obscure. The wonder to which they give rise is inseparable from the illumination they provide.

13. See Plato's *Republic*, 475e. All quotations from Plato's *Republic* and *Laws* are from *Plato: Complete Works*, ed. John Cooper (Indianapolis IN: Hackett Publishing). Specific textual references are indicated by Stephanus numbers included (in parentheses) in the main text.

14. See S. Sara Monoson's helpful study, *Plato's Democratic Entanglements: Athenian Politics and Practice of Philosophy* (Princeton NJ: Princeton University Press, 2000), esp. chapters 4 and 8, where she examines the use of "spectatorial" imagery in the *Republic* as well as the participatory character of spectating in the Ancient Greek theatre. See also Andrea Wilson Nightingale, *Spectacles of Truth in Classical Greek Philosophy: Theoria in its Cultural Context* (Cambridge: Cambridge University Press, 2004), which explores the meaning of *theoria* in Greek philosophy and culture.

15. McEwen, *Socrates' Answer*, 21.

16. Ibid., 27.

17. See Martin Heidegger, "The Question Concerning Technology," in *The Question Concerning Technology*, trans. Alfred Hofstadter (New York: Harper and Row, 1977): 5–14; and McEwen, *Socrates' Answer*, 41–7.

18. McEwen, *Socrates' Answer*, 47.

19. Ibid., 41–2.

20. See Ibid., 43–4.

21. Ibid., 45.

22. Ibid., 53.

23. Ibid., 54.

24. Ibid., 51.

25. Speaking of waves (which are ephemeral), McEwen suggests that the "deathless" (and therefore divine) nature of *daidala*, or well-made things, derived partly from the notion that they could always be remade. If they were "put together" or assembled (as the primary meaning of such *techne*-related terms as *daidalon*, *areros*, and *harmonia* connotes), they could always be put *back* together. "Like the gods," McEwen writes, "and unlike mortals, [the well-made thing] never entirely disappeared. It was because it was itself a deathless appearing that the well-made, cunningly crafted thing was able to reveal an unseen divine presence." *Socrates' Answer*, 56. This suggests another way of thinking about the essentially temporal or ephemeral quality of music. Because it is never simply "there," or statically present as an object, it is never simply "absent" in the way that an object might be experienced as being. In that way, its ephemerality is a reflection of its deathlessness and an intimation of immortality (it makes immortality as such "visible," or audible, as well as teaching us something about what immortality might mean).

26. Heidegger, "The Question Concerning Technology," 9.

27. McEwen, *Socrates' Answer*, 72.

28. In the *Nicomachean Ethics* (I.7, 1097b25–30), Aristotle speaks of *ergon* both as the actualization of a specific potentiality (referring directly to craft) and as the realization of one's nature (referring to human life). In neither case is this a separate result, product. Nor is it a mere means, or productive power. The way to realize one's humanity is by living a fully human life.

29. See *Nicomachean Ethics* 1103a30. Note that there is a real (and important) difference between playing correctly (producing the right notes) and playing musically.

30. Aristotle himself seems unwilling to make this point about craft. See *Metaphysics* I.1.
31. This is something Aristotle says about the acquisition of (ethical) virtue. It too could be said about craft, but was not said (explicitly) by Aristotle. In fact, we find passages where he draws an explicit contrast between craft and ethical virtue (see, for example, *Nicomachean Ethics* 1105a15–1105b5).
32. McEwen, *Socrates' Answer*, 83–4.
33. See Monoson, *Plato's Democratic Entanglements*, esp. chapter 4.
34. See Ibid., 220. Here Monoson notes that, in Plato's famous allegory of the cave, "Plato does not use the theatrical [or *theoria*-related] vocabulary to describe the prisoners viewing the shadows. They are watching a sequence of images, but they are not depicted as 'spectating' or 'theorizing.' Rather, they only see." It is the philosophers seeing that is active and participatory. The prisoners are looking passively at something that is a mere image, and not a true spectacle.
35. McEwen, *Socrates' Answer*, 83–4. Emphasis added.
36. Schroeder-Sheker, *Transitus*, 25.

Commentary: The Medicine of Philosophy

1. Bruce T. Morrill, "Christ the Healer: An Investigation of Contemporary Liturgical, Pastoral, and Biblical Approaches," see above, p. 116.
2. Christopher A. Dustin, "The Liturgy of Theory," see above, pp. 257–69.
3. Plato, *Timaeus*, in *The Collected Dialogues of Plato Including the Letters*, ed., Edith Hamilton and Huntington Cairns (Princeton NJ: Princeton University Press, 1985), 88a.
4. Plato, *Philebus*, in *The Collected Dialogues of Plato Including the Letters*, ed., Edith Hamilton and Huntington Cairns (Princeton NJ: Princeton University Press, 1985), 56a-c.
5. Aristotle, *Metaphysics*, in *The Collected Works of Aristotle: The Revised Oxford Translation*, ed., Jonathan Barnes (Princeton NJ: Princeton University Press, 1984), 1070a.
6. Josef Pieper, *Only the Lover Sings: Art and Contemplation* (San Francisco CA: Ignatius Press, 1990), 34.
7. Michel Foucault, *The Birth of the Clinic: An Archaeology of Medication Perception* (New York: Vintage Books, 1975), 135–6.
8. Indra Kagis McEwen, *Socrates' Ancestor: An Essay on Architectural Beginnings* (Cambridge MA: MIT Press, 1993), 41–7.
9. Dustin, "The Liturgy of Theory," see above, p. 263.
10. Aristotle, *Nicomachean Ethics*, in *The Collected Works of Aristotle: The Revised Oxford Translation*, ed., Jonathan Barnes (Princeton NJ: Princeton University Press, 1984), 1139b15–35.
11. Dustin, "The Liturgy of Theory," see above, p. 265.
12. M.L. Elks, "The Key Role of Ritual in Modern Medicine," *Chronicle of Higher Education* 44:13 (1997): B9.

Epilogue: Reflections at Vespers

1. 2 Corinthians 1:3–4 (New Revised Standard Version).

Name Index

Subject Index